9/11 Fiction, Empathy, and Otherness

9/11 Fiction, Empathy, and Otherness

Tim Gauthier

LEXINGTON BOOKS
Lanham • Boulder • New York • London

Published by Lexington Books
An imprint of The Rowman & Littlefield Publishing Group, Inc.
4501 Forbes Boulevard, Suite 200, Lanham, Maryland 20706
www.rowman.com

Unit A, Whitacre Mews, 26-34 Stannary Street, London SE11 4AB

Copyright © 2015 by Lexington Books

British Library Cataloguing in Publication Information Available

Library of Congress Cataloging-in-Publication Data

Gauthier, Tim S.
9/11 fiction, empathy, and otherness / Tim Gauthier.
p. cm.
Includes bibliographical references and index.
ISBN 978-0-7391-9345-7 (cloth : alk. paper) – ISBN 978-0-7391-9346-4 (ebook)
1. September 11 Terrorist Attacks, 2001, in literature. 2. Fiction–21st century–History and criticism. 3. Empathy in literature. 4. Other (Philosophy) in literature. I. Title.
PS374.S445G38 2015
813'.6093587393–dc23
2015000408

∞ ™ The paper used in this publication meets the minimum requirements of American National Standard for Information Sciences Permanence of Paper for Printed Library Materials, ANSI/NISO Z39.48-1992.

Printed in the United States of America

To Marta, always

Contents

Permissions		ix
Introduction		1
1	Empathetically Unsettled: The Falling People in Art and Fiction	47
2	Otherness as Counternarrative in the Graphic Novel: Spiegelman, Rehr, Torres	79
3	French Fiction and the Utopian Potential of 9/11	101
4	"Toward These Uncanny Young Men": Entering the Mind of the Terrorist	127
5	"Selective in Your Mercies": Privilege, Vulnerability, and the Limits of Empathy in Ian McEwan's *Saturday*	167
6	The Otherness of Islam in Amy Waldman's *The Submission*	191
7	Communal Trauma?: The Wounded City in Hunt and Lethem	217
Epilogue		251
Bibliography		257
Index		271
About the Author		275

Permissions

Reprinted with the permission of Scribner Publishing Group, a division of Simon & Schuster, Inc. from *Falling Man* by Don DeLillo. Copyright © 2007 by Don DeLillo. All rights reserved.
Laird Hunt, excerpts from *The Exquisite: A Novel*. Copyright © 2006 by Laird Hunt. Reprinted with permission of The Permissions Company, Inc., on behalf of Coffee House Press, www.coffeehousepress.org
Excerpts from THE SUBMISSION by Ann Waldman. Copyright ©2011 by Ann Waldman. Reprinted by permission of Farrar, Straus and Giroux, LLC
Excerpt from *The Submission* © 2011 by Amy Waldman. Published by HarperCollins Publishers Ltd. All rights reserved.
From *The Submission* by Amy Waldman. Published by William Heinemann. Reprinted by permission of The Random House Group Ltd.
Salim Bachi, *Tuez-les tous*. Reprinted with permission from ©Éditions GALLIMARD.
Reprinted by permission of HarperCollins Publishers Ltd © 2004 Frédéric Beigbeder.
From *Saturday* by Ian McEwan. Published by Jonathan Cape. Reprinted by permission of The Random House Group Ltd.
Excerpt(s) from *Saturday: A Novel* by Ian McEwan, copyright ©2005 by Ian McEwan. Used by permission of Nan A. Talese, an imprint of the Knopf Doubleday Publishing Group, a division of Random House LLC. All rights reserved.
Article initially published in *Studies in Twentieth and Twenty-First Century Literature*. "French Fiction, Empathy, and the Utopian Potential of 9/11." Vol. 37.1 Winter 2013. Reprinted with permission.
Article initially published in *College Literature*. "Selective in Your Mercies': Privilege, Vulnerability, and the Limits of Empathy in Ian McEwan's *Saturday*." Vol. 40.2 Spring 2013. Reprinted with permission.
Article initially published in *Journal of Postcolonial Writing*. "9/11, image control, and the graphic narrative: Spiegelman, Rehr, Torres." Vol. 46. 3–4. July 1, 2010. Reprinted by permission of the publisher (Taylor & Francis Ltd, http://www.tandfonline.com).
Excerpt(s) from *Chronic City: A Novel* by Jonathan Lethem, 2009 by Jonathan Lethem. Used by permission of Doubleday, an imprint of the Knopf Doubleday Publishing Group, a division of Random House LLC. All rights reserved.
Excerpt from *A Day at the Beach: A Novel* by Helen Schulman. Copyright ©2007 by Helen Schulman. Reprinted by permission of Houghton Mifflin Harcourt Publishing Company. All rights reserved.
"11 septembre, mon amour" by Luc Lang ©Editions Stock 2003.

Introduction

This study sets out to examine the extent to which "us" and "them" narratives proliferated after 9/11, and to what degree calls for greater empathy and a renewed emphasis on cosmopolitan values served to counterbalance an apparent movement towards increased polarization, encapsulated in the oft-mentioned "clash of civilizations." A principal objective of the book is thus to examine the ethical and political implications revealed in the exercising or withholding of empathy. Though empathy, in and of itself, may not be sufficient, it is nevertheless a vital component in the generation of actions one might identify as cosmopolitan. In other words, I examine the responses to 9/11 in order to uncover what their dramatic renderings might tell us about the possibility of a truly globalized community. And while the book focuses primarily on novels written in the past decade, attention is also devoted to the writings of theorists who call for the creation of counter-narratives to the dominant strains presented by the government and the media. In this construction, the government (with the support of the media) pushes for retaliation and demonstrations of military strength, solidifying narratives of division and difference, accentuating the gap between us and them. These proposals, on the other hand, use the language of sameness and commonality, emphasizing that a "global event" such as 9/11 should awaken us to our ever-increasing participation within a larger network of communities. From this vantage point, the only real solution to our current geopolitical crisis (or "the problem of otherness," as David Palumbo-Liu labels it) is an identification of those elements that link us with the other rather than those which set us apart. In other words, instead of seeing the divisive nature of the event, these writers focus on its capacity to unify.

This appeal to sameness and the notion of an increasingly global community bears a strong resemblance to the argument put forth by those who urge

1

for recognition of the cosmopolitanization of the world. In the light of various global crises (including terrorism), Ulrich Beck proposes a cosmopolitan outlook in which "the old differentiations between internal and external, national and international, us and them, lose their validity and a new cosmopolitan realism becomes essential to survival." And a number of writers argue that the boundaries separating us from them can best be circumvented through the evocation of "cosmopolitan sentiments," as James Brassett calls them: sympathy, compassion, and empathy. Of the three, however, a greater degree of emphasis has been placed on empathy, in part because it requires an active engagement on the part of the empathizer, but also because the intimations of inequality between observer and sufferer are far less strong.

The attainability of any cosmopolitan engagement is contingent upon our abilities to understand the other, knowing always that the otherness of the other remains beyond our grasp, and that the best we can do is imagine some version of it. It is primarily in this capacity that the novel has a role to play. Whether it is the challenge of connecting with the survivors of trauma and the inhabitants of a traumatized city, or with a hyperpower that has experienced its own vulnerability for the first time, or even with the terrorist who seeks to commit violent acts, these novels afford us the means of examining the complex dynamics involved in any exhibition of fellow-feeling for the other, and the ever-present potential failure of that engagement. So in what ways do these novels help to reveal the obstacles that prevent us from acting on our cosmopolitan impulses? Does a recognition of sameness necessarily guarantee that one will be moved to engage in more peaceful relations with the other? Many of these advocates seem to presume that such a scenario is the most likely outcome. But the idea of responding with humility and generosity to those with whom we share very little, to say nothing of those who seek the path of aggression, seems unlikely.

Through my readings of the novels, I question the degree to which an empathetic connection can be achieved and maintained, particularly in these limit-situations. For though I recognize the necessity of this sentiment, these texts make clear the many challenges lying along the path to such cosmopolitan engagement. As various writers have pointed out, one's ability to empathize is sorely tested when one is under duress. Empathizing with another when in mourning is no easy task. There are any number of challenges linked to what we might call "being in vulnerability." And, in just this way, terrorism poses its own particular set of obstacles to a cosmopolitan outlook; an appeal to sameness is not so easily met when one is confronted by a violent and menacing other. One might also question the extent to which individuals are willing to forego those components that constitute the greater parts of their identity—nation, religion, ethnicity, class—as a means of rapprochement, particularly when they feel they are living in a heightened state of assailability. My emphasis in this study is on a number of 9/11 novels and the ways in which they cast a light on the limitations of, but also the potential for, empathetic connection. At the same time, I read these novels in order to identify the obstructions standing in the way of any drive towards commonality and the dream of a global community. Intentionally or not, then, these novels reveal potential pathways to cosmopolitanization while simultaneously raising questions as to the attainability of any such endeavor.

Writing for the *Los Angeles Times* two days after the attacks, architectural critic Nicolai Ouroussoff argues that the country is now faced with a decision—to either close in upon itself or to embrace the moment as an opportunity to foster new relationships with the rest of the world. He emphasizes "the symbolic importance such buildings play in the collective conscience of a people" and suggests that by attacking these specific skyscrapers, symbols of the nation's immovable faith in progress, the terrorists undermined "a fundamental tenet of the American identity" (Ouroussoff). As such the essay stresses the symbolic impact of the event, for the nation, but also for a New York in which the World Trade Center was "the city's emotional anchor." While he may overstate his case, he does emphasize the symbolic impact of the event and the due consideration this should be given. At the same time, he expresses concern that the reaction to the attacks will emanate from a need to demonstrate power and self-confidence, the same impulses that led to the creation of the Twin Towers in the first place. Instead, he hopes the opportunity will be grasped to create "an urban landscape shaped by qualities of openness and empathy, not paranoia" implying, whether consciously or not, that the now-destroyed Towers had symbolized an insular, impenetrable, and suspicious nation. Indeed, Ouroussoff's conclusion suggests that the destruction of the Towers signaled the end of an era in which they had stood as the "symbols of the relentless urge of American capitalism, its triumphant self-confidence even in the face of economic distress." He hopes that whatever replaces the Twin Towers will come to symbolize a new national spirit, reflecting "the best principles of a democratic society." Perhaps most interesting, he suggests that this is the most viable response to lashing out and engaging in military reprisals.

Less than two weeks later, Homi Bhabha forcefully argues against seeing the attacks as expressions of "cultural or civilizational 'difference.'" Instead, he contends that we must conceptualize the use of terror as an "organized political action," which then allows for the creation of a common global front against it:

> To confront the politics of terror, out of a sense of democratic solidarity rather than retaliation, gives us some faint hope for the future. Hope, that we might be able to establish a vision of a global society, informed by civil liberties and human rights, that carries with it the shared obligations and responsibilities of common collaborative citizenship. (4)

The unifying tenor of Bhabha's missive is clear. Within the second sentence alone we find the words "global society," "shared," "common," and "collaborative," to say nothing of the assumed "we." Bhabha's emphasis on the communal will therefore not be lost on the reader. In the face of a potential "clash of civilizations," he pleads for global unity. I offer these two examples as expressions of hope that were echoed by a number of writers in the aftermath of the attacks, all using the language of sameness and commonality. This appeal to mutuality and the notion of a global community strongly resemble the arguments put forth by those advocating the cosmopolitanization of the world. The only real solution to our current geopolitical crisis, they contend, is an identification of that which links us with, rather than that which separates us from, others. Instead seeing the divisive and polarizing nature of the event, these writers stress its unifying potential.

One of the most ardent proponents of this approach is Judith Butler, who bemoans the path of violence chosen by an American administration, and who wonders, "whether the experiences of vulnerability and loss have to lead straightaway to military violence and retribution" (xii). Instead, Butler argues, we should seize the opportunity to recognize how mutual vulnerability and loss link us to the greater global community. The victims of 9/11 should make us aware of the "precarious life of the Other." From Butler's perspective, the attacks created conditions of similarity that might now enable Americans to sympathetically identify with the many suffering others previously beyond their scope of consideration. After all, one is more likely to empathize with someone with whom one shares similarities. Having suffered, one should now be more open to contemplating the suffering of others: "To be injured means that one has the chance to reflect upon injury, to find out the mechanisms of its distribution, to find out who else suffers from permeable borders, unexpected violence, dispossession, and fear, and in what ways" (xii). And, ideally, this awareness would extend to those others living beyond one's borders. Instead of causing one to focus on one's own vulnerability (and the fear and anxiety elicited by that knowledge), the attacks might serve to expand one's consciousness about the fragility of the lives of all others.

Such knowledge, she suggests, should lead to an ethics of non-violence; rather than seeking revenge and imposing our selfhood on others, we should strive to find that which links us to others who have suffered equally, or perhaps more. This cognizance can help us to achieve a "keener sense of the value of life, all life" (xviii). In essence, the attacks might, somewhat paradoxically, emphasize a shared communality instead of accentuating isolationist tendencies on the part of the United States. 9/11 not only tore away at the illusion of invulnerability, it also exposed the falsity of American self-sufficiency. As Butler observes, being injured causes one to consider an irrefutable array of others on whom one's well-being may depend: "This fundamental dependency on anonymous others is not a condition that I can will away. No security measure will foreclose this dependency; no violent act of sovereignty will rid the world of this fact" (xii). At the same time, Butler remains purposely vague as to whom those others might be. Are they individuals who can help us or are they those who mean us harm? Either way, she argues for recognition of those whose lives may impinge upon mine, but also on those on whose lives I may impinge.

In many ways, we might thus think of 9/11 as the (ultimate?) intrusion of an other demanding to be recognized and acknowledged. We must move, in other words, from a consideration of self to a contemplation of a wider web of interconnections within which everyone interacts. In this light, the terrorist attacks are a symptom of an expanding and inevitable contemporary "condition of togetherness" in which we live and from which there is no refuge. As Christian Moraru points out, we now exist in an "age of networks"—"one of unparalleled panopticity, of a hitherto peerless scopic presence of individuals, groups, and cultures to one another" (3). More so than ever, as Moraru emphasizes in *Cosmodernism*, one is obliged, willingly or not, to define oneself *vis-à-vis* the other. These evolving conditions undermine the viability of American exceptionalism. Rather than state that the world has changed, then, it may be more accurate to note the ways in which the narratives Americans have been telling themselves have begun to crumble under increased scrutiny.

The attacks elicited the question "Why do they hate us?" primarily aimed at understanding the other's motivations, and maintaining the "us-them" binary. Taken a step further, however, the question hints at self-reflection since it seeks to determine what it is about *us* that fostered such animosity. Asking the question and being open to the answer are two very different things, however. The question can serve as an exculpatory strategy. We have not given them reason to hate us, they are simply misguided and delusional. A less-guarded, and perhaps more truthful answer to the question, on the other hand, would require imagining an unfiltered voice that speaks unabashedly and unequivocally about all of our misdeeds (real, presumed, and/or imagined) offering no rationalization to abate the condemnation. Because, in all likelihood, the reply coming from the mouth of such an other would contain pronouncements with which we disagree, as well as ones we are simply unwilling to hear.

Butler thus argues that the "decentering" caused by the events of September 11 might have served as an instigation for questioning American unilateralism. Instead of being open to this reconfiguration, we maintain the first-person narrative, spoken by an unaltered "I," and struggle against adopting the other's perspective "as if to explain these events would accord them rationality, as if to explain these events would involve us in a sympathetic identification with the oppressor, as if to understand these events would involve building a justificatory framework for them" (8). Here, empathy is presented as undesirable, as something to avoid. Part of the discomfort in seeking to connect with a perspective different from one's own (particularly if it is one in stark "opposition" to one's own) is that one potentially runs the risk of discovering one is wrong, or at least not as blameless as one would like to believe. We also run the risk of discovering a level of sameness heretofore unimagined. Such recognition, of course, disables oppositional stances. As Butler notes, "Our fear of understanding a point of view belies a deeper fear that we shall be taken up by it, find it is contagious, become infected in a morally perilous way by the thinking of the presumed enemy" (8).

Common to many of these discussions is the idea of contagion, that one might somehow be "infected" through one's contact with the other, so that one is somehow compromised and/or tainted in the interaction. Butler's allusion to "sympathetic identification" raises questions about our "relationship" with the terrorist. But even if we are unwilling to consider such a radical possibility, our negation of said relationship is only the most extreme indication of a general reluctance to acknowledge our connection with the multifarious others who populate the planet. So despite these perceived "dangers," Butler maintains that Americans need to be open to constructing precisely these types of narratives. For although she never actually uses the word "empathy," there are key moments in the text when she highlights the necessity of placing oneself in the other's shoes. At one point, for instance, she notes that possessing the "ability to narrate ourselves not from the first person alone, but from, say, the position of the third, or to receive an account delivered in the second, can actually work to expand our understanding of the forms that global power has taken" (8). Imagining a narrative in which someone speaks of us, or even more forcefully, speaks for us, is liable to open one's eyes to one's own assumptions about the other and the manner in which one negotiates the presence of others in one's day-to-day existence. The shift from conceiving of oneself as the narrator to imagining oneself as the narratee is likely to cause a re-appraisal of one's standing in the world. Because, as Butler well knows, empathy is not simply thinking about how the other sees and feels the world, it also means accessing how he sees us as part of that world. Even if we may still be writing about ourselves, a shift in perspective, or the angle from which one views oneself, is bound to significantly reshape one's conception of one's relationship with the other. Of course, such an approach is central to the mission of the novelist, an idea to which I will return shortly.

Butler also contends that a breaking down of barriers can be occasioned through a thoughtful meditation on grief and mourning. These destabilizing experiences, she argues, have the capacity to make one "other" to oneself. In other words, such pain should raise questions as to one's assumed self and thus increase one's empathic abilities. Yet again, she posits the possibility of an opposed reaction. She points to the ways grieving and mourning might have been employed to awaken Americans to a range of interdependencies. Having now been victimized, Americans should find the means of reflecting, with their new-found humility, on what it means to victimize. However, she also recognizes the apparent American discomfort with grief. Rather than sitting with it, processing it, and coming to some deeper understanding of what it might mean to self and one's relations with others, rapid solutions are implemented to foreclose upon these "negative" feelings. Because such reflection is not the American way. And Butler points to President Bush's comments on the need to stop grieving, suggesting that this imperative reflected the dominant national impulse in the wake of the attacks. From that standpoint, grieving is perceived as emanating from a position of weakness, therefore making one vulnerable to further attack. As Butler notes, "When grieving is something to be feared, our fears can give rise to the impulse to resolve it quickly, to banish it in the name of an action invested with the power to restore the loss or return the world to a former order" (29–30). In the process, the nation foreclosed on the possibility of greater connection with other parts of the globe. Instead of using this moment to accentuate commonalities (which the overwhelming sympathy the US received seemed to indicate) the Bush administration used the attacks as an opportunity to reassert American dominance and strength. Rather than embracing its grief, the United States "seeks to reconstitute its imagined wholeness, but only at the price of denying its own vulnerability, its dependency, its exposure, where it exploits those very features in others, thereby making those features 'other to' itself" (41). Instead of identifying pain and vulnerability as shared traits, they are presented as only happening to others.

Recognition of the other, in Butler's conception, is thus contingent upon one's capacity to acknowledge mistakes, admit weakness, and relinquish previously held beliefs about one's power and superiority. Any one of these actions requires a true exercise of will, for all three to occur seems an impossibility. In many ways, she is more concerned with identifying the forces that can derail the cosmopolitan project rather than outlining its inherent limitations. So while she propounds the need for a greater global connection, her observations often reveal a certain degree of hopelessness. This feeling emanates from the work as a result, in part, of the author offering alternatives to what has already happened. 9/11 evoked a set of visceral responses that Butler wishes had been replaced by an entirely different one. She repeatedly states that things did not have to be this way, while events prove her wrong. As Angela McRobbie observes, "the multiplicity of forces that hinder the possibility of a truly cosmopolitan ethics and politics are at the heart of Butler's sorrowful reflections" (70). But there is also an "if only" quality to Butler's writing. At times, it appears as though she truly believes things could have gone either way—that violence or peace, for example, were equally likely outcomes. As such, *Precarious Life* ends up being, in many ways, an expression of wish-fulfillment. For although it is clear that Butler is aware of natural human propensities, it is not as clear that she believes her remedies to be any less achievable than the harsh solutions invoked by the Bush Administration. (I shall offer further critique of Butler's emphasis on vulnerability in my reading of Ian McEwan's *Saturday* in chapter 4.) McRobbie, for instance, suggests,

> The idea of making our dependency on others the basis for a new politics: of mobilizing our bodily vulnerability as a means of transcending the invoking of fear by government, so as to forge a connection with others who are daily exposed to such vulnerability: of responding with humility and generosity to those others with whom we have little or no shared understanding: and the posing of these ethical stances as priorities, is to bring into political discussion at this moment in time a radically distinct vocabulary which might be seen by many as profoundly unrealizable. (84)

While McRobbie does not necessarily place herself among the "many" she does, in essence, argue that Butler's "politics of humility" is a tall order, particularly in these times of growing fundamentalisms and estrangements between factions. Nevertheless, she applauds the effort. Proposing a means of counteracting natural impulses, of finding ways of moving closer to (not further from) strange, unfamiliar, or even violent others, are laudable objectives in helping one move towards an empathic and ethical relationship with the rest of humanity. They are not, however, without their considerable challenges—as Butler's work makes clear.

James Brasset begins his essay, "Cosmopolitan Sentiments After 9/11?" with a discussion of these very challenges. Like Butler, Brassett recognizes the dichotomous nature of the responses to the attacks, divided between those clamoring for revenge and those who "sought to 'use' 9/11 to reflect upon the meaning of vulnerability, and how it reaches into many more lives than were taken that day" (12). And like Butler, Brassett identifies vulnerability as the lynchpin through which a connection can be made with all others, even those (or perhaps primarily those) who do not share one's values, beliefs, or politics. He notes, however, that sympathy for the vulnerable other is an almost natural outcome of tragedy. While acknowledging the significance of these "initial cosmopolitan sentiments," however, he declares that he will endeavor "to engage with a critical questioning of how they play out—*and how they might play out differently*—in political processes of governance" (13, emphasis in text). In contrast to Butler, then, he is a little more cautious and uncertain as to how these sentiments will actually be enacted within what he terms the "politics of vulnerability" (13).

He expresses doubt, for instance, in the image of a unified community. He questions the assumption that trauma is a naturally unifying force, pointing out that "attitudes towards trauma can actually lead to divisive and alienating responses" and that there is "less agreement on our global togetherness" than is often taken for granted (19). As such, he concludes that "there is no 'natural kind' at work in trauma, it neither naturally divides nor unites, but is a subject of governance and, therefore, politics" (19). In essence, Brassett expresses dismay at the homogenization of trauma, where each victim is grouped in with all others, his or her own experiences categorized according to established guidelines. Consequently, he is also wary of the notion of "global vulnerability," noting how such a term washes over and fails to identify significant variations between groups and individuals. The appeal to cosmopolitan sentiments, however, is often grounded in the belief in global togetherness. But does a recognition of sameness necessarily guarantee that one will be moved to engage in more peaceful (less violent) relations with the other? Many advocates seem to presume that if such sentiments are honestly and genuinely engaged then such a scenario is the most likely outcome. However, the idea of responding with humility and generosity to those with whom we share very little, to say nothing of those who seek the path of aggression, seems unlikely if not improbable. Indeed, many others would deem these prospects profoundly unfeasible. Brassett expresses an idea similar to McRobbie's when he notes, "Despite the claims to openness and inclusion, there is a sense of irreconcilability about how to be both global and democratic when 'anti-global' or 'localising' sentiments might best describe the attitudes of many of those included" (18). The statement suggests that recognition of similarity, while an essential first step, is not in of itself sufficient. It also alludes to those circumstances when the other openly rejects one's efforts to connect, refuses to acknowledge similarity with his other, and/or expresses no desire to be enfolded within the community.

Brassett suggests that the mechanisms now in place, while aimed at aiding the suffering other, often serve to foreclose further inquiry. He questions the "normative framework of cosmopolitan democracy" whose implementation may lead to the suppression of "laudable cosmopolitan sentiments ... within a project of cosmopolitanism that closes down consideration of 'vulnerability'" (15). Returning to the concept of "the politics of vulnerability," he further cautions against the impulse to impose solutions on the problem of vulnerable others. He points to a power differential at work, with the empathizer controlling the action at the expense of the empathized. This may be carried out with the best of intentions, always thinking of the "good" of the empathized, but still suffer from shortsightedness, insensitivity, and presumption—of thinking one knows what is "best" for the other. In this regard, Suzanne Keen highlights the inequality inherent in "the directional quality of empathy" since "an empathizer feels with a subject who may or may not be empowered to speak for herself, to correct misconceptions about her feelings, and to refuse the pitying gaze" (162). Space thus must remain available for survivors to contest and question established parameters and notions of trauma that are likely to be imposed on them. As such, Brassett advocates for a "democracy of engagement, where people are included in the negotiation of meanings that affect their lives" (25).

He thus contends that we must seek to move beyond merely recognizing, or even assuming, a mutual vulnerability, to finding the means of enacting an interaction based on the incomplete knowledge we have gleaned in our gesture towards the other. As such, he highlights the necessity of transforming our sympathy into empathy, the latter requiring a degree of self-engagement not necessary in the former. In his concluding paragraph, Brassett postulates:

> Engaging the politics of vulnerability associated with trauma involves both grappling with the production of sympathy for suffering and the recognition that, in doing so, we also necessarily express empathy. The distinctiveness of empathy in the context of trauma is that it can only ever be based on the recognition of our inability to "know vulnerability." In this sense, I suggest, it may be helpful to think about the politics of vulnerability in terms of an ethico-political conversation where many of the words either do not exist or, rather, the speakers (and listeners) are engaged in the process of inventing them. (26)

The significance of empathy, as Brassett points out, is that it is a sentiment that moves in two directions. Unlike sympathy which is pointed strictly in the direction of the suffering other, empathy, in its conscious interaction with the other, has the capacity to reveal just as much (if not more) about the self. As Peter Rosan observes, empathy is only possible if we think of "the subject as an engaged participant, indeed an instrument, attuned to and thereby illuminating an interiority, the other's as well as his/her own, not otherwise accessible had the subject remained a dispassionate or neutral observer of the other" (116). If the empathizer is genuinely committed to knowing the empathized, then, she must strive to overcome the "directional quality" of the gesture and work to establish a sphere wherein each voice has an equal opportunity of being heard.

Perhaps most significantly, then, there is an expressed need for a new language or vocabulary with which to communicate about trauma: "Once we move from a technology of sympathy to open up empathy as an important (though problematic) question, we press the idea that we currently lack an ability to hear and understand the voices of the vulnerable" (23). Brassett's work is important in pointing out the need to think beyond the mere requirement of these sentiments to the ways in which they lead to knowledge about our "conditions of togetherness," and how one subsequently responds to the acquisition of such knowledge. By necessity, then, knowledge and understanding of the other's situation can only be demonstrated through its incorporation within a recognized form of expression. The discovery of a new language may not necessarily come from the victims themselves, but rather one who can assist by translating the trauma into a set of communicable feelings. At the same time, as we shall note, this requires the translation of the other's experience into a communicable form, primarily language, but also other forms appealing to the senses. Such activity, of course, is not without its risks. Something is always lost or transmuted in translation. The challenge is to not to infringe upon the truth of the experience, maintaining its essential qualities, while finding the means of communicating these to oneself and others. So what mechanisms are currently at our disposal that might increase one's capacity to empathize? What systems might "deliver" otherness in a manner that allows careful and moral consideration of self-other relations? As will become clear, I believe that literature can play a vital role in the contemplation of these questions. This is made clear in a number of full-length studies on the literary subgenre now known as post-9/11 fiction.

An analysis of these studies reveal some interesting commonalities, not least of which is the significant place accorded to otherness in much of the literature. A reading of these studies also highlights the changing concerns reflected in the literary output over the course of the last decade. Perhaps not surprisingly, then, the interests and preoccupations reflected in the studies themselves also tell us a good deal about the changing post-9/11 landscape and the contexts in which the events of September 11, 2001, are now understood. It is to these studies that I now turn.

9/11 FICTION: FOUR STUDIES

In the wake of the attacks, much was made of the scarcity of fictional responses. Fiction was replaced by non-fiction as the authoritative form of discourse for examining the post-9/11 world. But this, of course, has changed dramatically. Despite whatever debates surround the "quality" of this output, there are now more than a sufficient number of "serious" texts included within this field of study. It was almost as though there needed to be a period of silence before novelists could recover their voices. So it is somewhat surprising, considering the number of texts now making up this literary subgenre, that only a small number of full-length studies have been devoted to their analysis (though this may also change, of course). A good deal of the critical trepidation, as we shall see, stems either from definitional issues, questions as to what precisely constitutes "9/11 fiction" or, finally, debates as to whether the subgenre should even exist in the first place. For the sake of some expediency, I shall examine four of these studies at some length, rather than attempting blanket coverage of the criticism. These works speak directly to the major themes that have arisen in the fiction created in the last decade or so and, as such, help establish the parameters of the subgenre, thus contributing significantly to an understanding of texts that now make up its core.

Versluys: *Out of the Blue*

At the forefront of this movement is Kristiaan Versluys's *Out of the Blue*, published in 2009. As one of the earliest critics of the field of literary study that has now become known as "9/11 fiction," Versluys might be said to be responsible for laying some of the groundwork in the establishment of a 9/11 canon. *Out of the Blue* offers readings of four novels and one graphic narrative that have now become mainstays: any consideration of the fiction written in response to the attacks must at least allude to DeLillo's *Falling Man*, Safran Foer's *Extremely Loud and Incredibly Close*, Beigbeder's *Windows on the World*, Updike's *Terrorist*, and/or Spiegelman's *In the Shadow of No Towers*. A fuller canon would no doubt also include a number of other texts such as McEwan's *Saturday*, Messud's *The Emperor's Children*, Kalfus's *A Disorder Peculiar to the Country*, and O'Neill's *Netherland*. Nevertheless, the insightful and critical attention Versluys pays to these texts no doubt helped ensure their inclusion in the canon.

In *Out of the Blue*, Versluys is primarily concerned with contemplating September 11, 2001, as a traumatic event, its subsequent unrepresentability, and the challenges this poses to writers of fiction. In his eyes, 9/11 is primarily a "semiotic event, involving the total breakdown of all meaning-making systems" (2). In the face of such trauma, so the argument goes, language is utterly and thoroughly inadequate. As such, throughout his study, he pays close attention to questions of language, often focusing on the linguistic manipulations of authors (and sometimes their characters) as the means of making sense of the trauma. Versluys invests fiction with a certain meaning-making capability: "Novelists arrogate to themselves a certain power of explanation comprising not systematic knowledge but a kind of affective and empathic understanding" (12). Confronted with this unrepresentable tragedy, novelists have no choice but to represent. Perhaps more significantly, he looks to these texts to provide alternatives, or counternarratives, to the "revanchist rhetoric" that erupted in the aftermath: "these indirect treatments of 9/11 are also pervaded by an effort to see the terrorist attacks as an event that, rather than enforcing a logic of revenge, appeals for an ethics of responsibility" (16). This is a refrain found to varying degrees in each of the studies examined here: We have an obligation to think and work through what these events tell us about the others with whom we share the planet, but also, and perhaps more important, what they tell us about ourselves, no matter how uncomfortable or complicit such discoveries might make us feel. These works of fiction, Versluys and the others maintain, can help instigate and contribute to this vital and necessary process of (self)discovery. Throughout his chapters, each devoted to a single text, he constructs a trajectory within which each of these novels is framed as a negotiation with trauma, a "working through" of the traumatic experience. The chapters thus move from the narratives of personal recovery of varying degrees, described in DeLillo, Spiegelman, and Foer, to the more "international dimension" of Beigbeder's novel, to the anti-binary thinking and a confrontation with otherness in Updike's text. This attention to "working through"—an active and willful engagement with traumatic memory—frames his evaluation of the texts, so that they are ranked by the degree of energy expended by the protagonist in making sense of the trauma. So though he is cognizant of the dangers of putting too much emphasis on healing and closure, Versluys nevertheless privileges those texts wherein the traumatized protagonist establishes some kind of control or mastery over his traumatic experiences. As such the novel receiving the harshest criticism is DeLillo's *Falling Man*, which Versluys designates as "without a doubt, the darkest and starkest" of all 9/11 narratives (20). He faults the text for presenting "a trauma with no exit, a drift towards death with hardly a glimpse of redemption" and of offering the reader "pure melancholia without the possibility of mourning" (20). He bemoans the presentation of shocked and benumbed characters who exhibit no apparent desire to recover from their current conditions. In this novel, he contends, the attacks "in no way precipitate a cleansing or catharsis" (21). The implied critique is that it is the author's task to make them do so. He thus faults DeLillo's novel, finally, for its resolute stance, arguing that its treatment of the traumatized subject is too negatively inflected, too ensconced in the darkness of the experience, to offer the reader any solace: "Such a submersion in unrelieved gloom may well run counter not only to basic narrative schemata, which ask for a resolution and even a happy ending, but, more importantly, also to the basic human need to work through grief, to counter melancholia with mourning" (47).

The literary output he values is made clear, however, when he turns his critical attention in the next chapter to Art Spiegelman's graphic novel, *In the Shadow of No Towers*. Making an implicit comparison with DeLillo's novel, Versluys maintains that Spiegelman offers a narrative that "does not preclude agency and, in the presence of an all-absorbing fixation, does not succumb to unrelieved pessimism" (49). In contrast to *Falling Man*'s persistent and unrelieved melancholia, then, the graphic novel "balances collapse and resurgence" (49). Spiegelman's first-person narrative (he was present for the collapse of the towers) speaks to the necessity of bearing witness, of *not* remaining silent about the event. In his assessment of the work, Versluys demonstrates a strong belief in the therapeutic powers of this telling: "After the shock of a violent and unexpected event," he observes, "narration is instrumental in reconstituting the shattered self" (61). The text becomes the location within which the traumatized witness can work through his experiences while simultaneously commenting on the misrepresentations of the events presented by the media and the government. Versluys makes clear that he privileges those narratives wherein "the victim or witness succeeds in loosening the coils of the traumatic obsession, gets over the psychic wound, and resumes life as a responsible and participating citizen" (68). From this angle, the graphic novel becomes nothing less than Spiegelman's "victory" over trauma (68). In his thoughtful and thorough reading of Foer's *Extremely Loud and Incredibly Close*, he similarly lauds a narrative that refuses to acquiesce to the shock and destabilization caused by the events.

Versluys's inclusion of Beigbeder's *Windows on the World* in his study is thus somewhat perplexing—in no small part because he immediately identifies it as a "shallow book" where "the commonplace reigns. The cliché wins out" (121). At the same time, he recognizes that some of the author's narrative strategies (including hyperrealism) may in fact provide different ways of seeing 9/11. His reading thus remains torn between damning and praising the novel. This equivocation extends to his criticisms of the novel's two narrator-protagonists who "resemble each other to a fault" (136). At the same time, he identifies this "doubleness without difference" as indicative of a desire for rapprochement between the Americans and the French. The contemplation of the novel's two narrators thus touches upon issues of sameness that are often erased in the promotion of difference. The similarities between the French and American narrators make the book "an international novel . . . that reestablishes the category of the Transatlantic West" (137). The novel is thus recognized for seeing 9/11 as a global event, one that has the potential to unite individuals through a shared recognition of commonalities (this is, in part, the focus of my chapter on French fiction). In this way, the reading of Beigbeder's novel serves as a bridge between the two principal themes Versluys addresses in *Out of the Blue*: 9/11 as trauma and the question of otherness. Because the subject of the fifth chapter and the epilogue clearly signals a shift in focus. Moving away from the posttraumatic paradigm that guided the first four chapters, he turns his attention to issues of the other. Indeed, the epilogue seems to signal a conviction that examinations of "9/11 as trauma" may have now run their course and that more fruitful topics for discussion need to be explored: "almost eight years after the events, the immediate shock has worn off and that, as a result, the concerns expressed will be less directly related to the experience of trauma" (183). No more are the victims (both dead and alive) the sole focus of these fictions. A fuller understanding of 9/11 requires an expansion of the critical horizons to include a much more extensive range of participants, including the perpetrators.

Versluys therefore devotes his fifth chapter, "September 11 and the Other," to a theme discussed in the three other studies I will examine (as well as my own). He points out that in the aftermath of the attacks, there was an understandable urge to engage in "othering." As the recipient of a brutal and horrific act of violence, the citizens of the United States naturally sought to dehumanize and demonize the aggressor. Not surprisingly, Versluys contends that we have an ethical responsibility to question and react to such impulses, and that novelists can serve a guiding role in such actions. As individuals predisposed to acting empathetically (as part of their art), novelists are "supposed to have a special affinity with the Other" (150–51). At the same time, he observes that 9/11 posed challenges to the ethical imagination, particularly when seeking to come to terms with the viewpoint of the terrorist. And while he recognizes there are moments when there is no escaping this impasse, when "the Other insists on an otherness so complete that it refuses to be addressed and excludes all common ground" (155), he still highlights the ethical import of the work of those novelists who nevertheless seek "to triangulate the situation, to find a way to avoid a stark binary split or dichotomy between one side that is totally right and the other side that is totally wrong" (155). Counteracting one's dichotomizing impulses means willfully engaging in a genuine attempt to understand that which appears as opposite and antithetical to oneself—in this case the "ultimate other," as Versluys refers to the terrorist. He thus offers readings of three texts that present events from the terrorist's point of view: Martin Amis's "The Last Days of Muhammad Atta," Michael Cunningham's "The Children's Crusade," and John Updike's *Terrorist*, for which he reserves the highest praise. In contrast to a significant number of critics and reviewers, Versluys reserves his highest praise for Updike's *Terrorist* which he identifies as the "most elaborate attempt to understand the mind of a terrorist" (167). He sees these criticisms as misplaced arguing that the novel is not so much "the portrait of a terrorist," but rather "the portrait of a terrorist manqué" (172). More specifically, he praises the novelist for the degree of sympathy he demonstrates towards his subject. For instance, moments before he is supposed to blow himself up, along with the Lincoln Tunnel, Ahmad has a change of heart. Touched by visions of the humanity all around him, he is now unwilling to detonate the device. However, there are some who have issues with Ahmad's relenting, noting that the 9/11 hijackers did no such thing. Versluys, for his part, chooses to interpret this gesture as Ahmad's act "of respect for the Other," which is then further "reciprocated" by the novelist who remains true to his own sympathetic connection with the would-be terrorist (172). Versluys sees in Ahmad's internal struggle, between his disgust for America and a growing sense of some of its virtues, a strategy that serves to make him real for the reader. "Updike's attempt to represent the Other (the terrorist, the Muslim) results in the Other discovering the Other (Ahmad's discovery of his own fealty to mundane American reality). As a literary achievement, this is very different from rendering the Other as the same" (175). In other words,

Updike has engaged in some sleight of hand in which he has found some commonality with the terrorist, but has also put forth a vision of a terrorist who recognizes his commonality with us. In ending his study with an analysis of these terrorist narratives, Versluys points the way, as we shall see, to an area of study potentially more fruitful than the consideration of 9/11 as trauma.

Gray: *After the Fall*

As its title indicates, Richard Gray's *After the Fall* is less concerned with 9/11 literature and more properly preoccupied with works created in the aftermath of the event. For a time, of course, all fiction written during or after September 11, 2001, was, in some form or another, *post-9/11 fiction*. This was particularly true of American fiction. [1] Instead of focusing on trauma and the inadequacies of language to represent said trauma, however, Gray offers a reading that emphasizes the post-lapsarian qualities of the event—the fall of the towers embodying America's own "descent from innocence to experience" (2). In this way, he consciously seeks to distinguish his study from that of Versluys. Gray, like Georgiana Banita to whom I shall turn later, actively seeks to expand the boundaries of the 9/11 canon. His study thus includes readings of novels whose subject is 9/11, while others reflect the mood and ethos of living in a post-9/11 world. A third group, that Gray identifies as transnational, includes selections which (somewhat problematically) were in fact published prior to 2001. Thus we get a reading of Lynne Schwartz's *The Writing on the Wall* next to Cormac McCarthy's *The Road*, Reynold Price's *The Good Priest's Son* alongside Lan Cao's *Monkey Bridge*. At the same time, a principal concern lies in allotting varying degrees of success to the fictions he has selected, largely in terms of their capacity to accurately represent and embody the realities of this newly shaped world. Interestingly, Gray bemoans the existence of a great deal of literature which he accuses of utilizing a "strategy for disappearing crisis" (122). In other words, he criticizes much of the fiction of 9/11 for using devices that allow the incorporation of the events of September 11 into a soothing and redemptive narrative.

Gray provides examples of such novels in his second chapter entitled "Imagining Disaster." Somewhat confrontationally, he includes a number of texts now securely entrenched in the 9/11 canon: Claire Messud's *The Emperor's Children*, Jay McInerney's *The Good Life*, Don DeLillo's *Falling Man*, as well as Ken Kalfus's *A Disorder Peculiar to the Country*. Each of these texts (and the authors thereof) reflect an American propensity for seeking shelter in the known. In doing so, these novels fail to "dramatize the contradictions that conflict engenders" (18–19). Having been caught unawares, American writers fell into default mode, resorting to the tried and true.

They enact, in his words, little more than "a desperate retreat into the old sureties" (16). As such, Gray argues, these texts do nothing new; they "simply assimilate the unfamiliar into familiar structures. The crisis is, in every sense of the word, domesticated" (30). And in the process they fail to provide the reader with new means for contemplating the new world. Thus despite a multitude of declarations from these authors (among many) that everything had changed, Gray identifies a desire to assert precisely the opposite. In constructing their narratives, then, these writers rob the event of its significance. By speaking of it through the use of recognizable and conventional structures, they fail to capture a sense of the ongoing global transformation announced in the event's occurrence. The "domestication" of the crisis also suggests that no effort has been made to grapple, or come to terms, with that which disturbs or destabilizes—with those very things that made it a crisis in the first place. A successful rendering of the contemporary condition, Gray contends, depends upon a text's "enactment of difference." Doing justice to the events requires that fiction writers not only possess "the capacity to recognize that some kind of alteration of imaginative structures is required to register the contemporary crisis," but also, and more important, "the ability and willingness imaginatively to act on that recognition" (29–30).

In offering a reading of Cormac McCarthy's *The Road* in the second half of the chapter, Gray communicates a conviction that the events of 9/11 cannot be addressed directly. After all, he dismisses a quartet of novels whose subject is patently post-9/11 life, and privileges a novel that, while surely emerging from the shadow of 9/11, speaks of the event on the most metaphoric or, to use Däwes's typology, metonymic of levels. In contrast to the failed attempts that seek "to shepherd that sense of crisis into the realms of the familiar," McCarthy's approach is "not to domesticate but to defamiliarize. His way of telling a story that cannot but has to be told is to approach it by circuitous means, by indirection" (40). Gray suggests that through indeterminacy, *The Road* "takes the measure of that sense of crisis that has seemed to haunt the West, and the United Sates in particular" since the attacks (39). In this vein, Gray values novels that find "some means of saying the unsayable"—the standard he uses in measuring the "successes" he enumerates in his next chapter, entitled "Imagining Crisis." He thus seeks to elevate those texts that approach the crisis "by roundabout means, using indirection to find historical directions out" (55). Because part of this outmoded thinking is the instinctive creation of binaries as a means of representing the current crisis, Gray argues that a number of 9/11 fictions are guilty of dichotomous constructions that simply "locate crisis in terms of opposition—them and us, the personal and the political, the private and the public, the oppressor and the victim" (65). Works that manage to dodge such thinking, from Gray's perspective, include Deborah Eisenberg's *Twilight of the Superheroes*, Mohsin Hamid's *The Reluctant Fundamentalist*, and Joseph

O'Neill's *Netherland*. These texts succeed because they "pursue a different course: locating crisis in an interstitial space, where such oppositions are contested: a site where a discourse founded on either/or distinctions is interrogated and even subverted" (65). In seeking a form that may speak and not speak about the crisis, then, Gray highlights texts that accentuate the liminality of the contemporary condition. He places a good deal of emphasis on that which usurps and questions the dominant narrative: the hybrid, the interstitial, the transnational. Each of these constructions counteracts the prevailing propensity to fall into binary thinking. Citing Homi Bhabha, Gray suggests that the novels that "get it right" do so "thanks to a strategy of convergence, rooted in the conviction that the hybrid is the only space in which the locations of cultures and the bearing witness to trauma can really occur" (17). Gray thus advocates for the creation of such spaces where apparent opposites may exist in a state of interaction, rather than conflict, and where each may more effectively illuminate the other. Invoking Bhabha once more, he asserts that

> the narratives themselves become interstitial spaces—or, perhaps more accurately, a series of interstitial spaces: here, as it were in the spaces between the tale being told, the reader is required to intervene, to engage with a continuing production of meanings that are necessarily partial and provisional. Meaning, signification, along with identity, becomes performative. (66)

Successful texts thus invite the reader to participate in the working through of meaning and the repositioning of dominant (read American) narratives. Finally, he identifies transnational fiction for its very questioning of the notion of "nation"—an issue brought to the fore in the aftermath of the attacks. The novels to which Gray provides insightful readings present protagonists caught between two cultures (often their own and that of the United States), but who have also had experiences with the American war machine. The mutuality of experiences—exposure to violence and an increased sense of vulnerability—highlights the degree to which 9/11 was in fact unexceptional, and that Americans now share (whether they wish to or not) a great deal more with a variety of other cultures around the globe. Such global recognition—what Gray labels deterritorialization—underlines the need to interrogate national narratives and rhetoric generated in the wake of the attacks.

After the Fall thus privileges a literature of disequilibrium, deterritorilization, and defamiliarization. In other words, works that eschew sameness and embrace difference. Or to put this another way, that embrace both the difference and the sameness of the other. And although Gray rarely uses the word empathy, his invocation of interstitial space, of the in-between, suggests a zone wherein a commingling of the self and other might occur, where a mutuality is afforded, helping us to move beyond the traditional dichotomous constructions. The requisite "sense of convergence" to which Gray frequently refers certainly suggests a melding of sorts, a kind of Venn diagram where same and other meet and overlap. Successful novels are those that reflect a world in which otherness is ubiquitous and in which encounters with strangeness are foregrounded. He argues that September 11 is part and parcel of an inevitable American exposure to otherness brought about by globalization and the increased diversification of cultures and ethnicities living within the nation's own borders:

> Facing the other, in all its difference and danger, is surely one of the challenges now for writers: not just because of obscene acts of terrorism committed by a small group of people but because the United States has become, more than ever, a border territory in which different cultures collide and in some instances collude with each other. (32)

It is in the imaginative recreation of these collisions and collusions that the contemporary novel obliges the reader to rethink notions of self and other, of local and global. Any striving after consolation is nothing more than an act of evasion or, worse, a falsifying of the real meaning of September 11. Like Banita in some ways, Gray suggests that any lack of attention paid to difference (to the other, to being deterritorialized) is detrimental to a clear understanding of the post-9/11 world. Any good novel will seek to destabilize and unsettle. There can be no assuredness, no confidence, no belonging, if one is to paint a true portrait of the aftermath.

Däwes: *Ground Zero Fiction*

But what does one actually mean by the term "post-9/11 fiction"? Any discussion of this designation must address its increasingly amorphous and malleable quality. Is this literature that deals specifically with the events of September 11, 2001, and their repercussions? And when we say "repercussions," how far do these actually extend? Do novels such as *Saturday*, *Netherland*, or *Let the Great World Spin*, which deal only tangentially with the events, but are clearly concerned with living in a world altered and colored by them, still constitute "post-9/11 fiction"? A quick review of the literary criticism reveals that such is often thought to be the case. And if this is indeed so, then do novels that re-enact or represent the events themselves—*Falling Man*, *Between Two Rivers*, *Windows on the World*—consequently belong in a category of their own? Birgit Däwes's work, *Ground Zero Fiction*, is an attempt at answering some of these questions through the creation of a typology that seeks to categorize the plethora of novels that have emerged in the last decade or so (now at approximately 250 and growing, two thirds of which are written by American writers). Däwes's study is the most ambitious of the four examined here, if for no other reason than its breadth and scope. She offers readings of various lengths of no less than 107 American novels! Indeed, early on, she announces that her work will attempt a "systematic analysis of the 9/11 novel as a literary subgenre" (6). In naming this subgenre, Däwes opts for the label "Ground Zero Fiction" since it reflects the "geographical hierarchy" that places New York at the center of most of these works, and the ways in which the significance and meaning(s) of the site continue to alter over time. As such, Däwes argues, Ground Zero Fiction is "much more than a mere inventory of crisis . . . it provides the textual outlines for a multilateral cultural reorientation and thus makes a significant contribution to the transnational relocation of September 11, 2001" (13).

Däwes sets out to chart the ways in which fiction responds to the tragedy, but also how fiction is impacted, in both form and content, by the events. She argues that two questions emerge in an analysis of the scholarly responses to fiction written in the first decade after the attacks. The first regards the nature of fiction itself: "Has [it] changed after 9/11, and if so, in what ways?" (55–56). The second question, Däwes contends, "addresses the wider framework of fiction's role and functions, as well as its political, cultural, and ethical work in the global community" (56). In order to answer these questions, she suggests that one needs "to take into account the widest possible spectrum of novels" (56). Däwes's typology is created in an effort to do just that. In essence, she argues that reading these novels can help us understand how the event is incorporated into the narrative of American life. She contends that "a systematic inquiry into the literary responses to 9/11 benefits much more from a fundamental questioning of the boundary between fact (the unrepresentable original) and fiction (its narrative transformations) . . . than from the quest for symptoms of trauma or from questions of literary propriety" (60–61). Examining the variety of approaches exhibited in these novels "brings to light the specific (geographical, historical, cultural, religious, and aesthetic) hierarchies and exposes the complexities involved in their making" (77). In other words, Däwes turns to these texts to examine how they seek to make meaning out of 9/11 through a wide range of rhetorical and semantic approaches. While recognizing the permeability of her categories, she offers six designations within which to slot the literary output devoted to the terrorist attacks on the United States and their aftermath: metonymic, salvational, diagnostic, appropriative, symbolic, and writerly (8).

The first category of texts, those designated as *metonymic*, address the events indirectly, practicing what Däwes labels "the art of *not* writing about 9/11 in a Ground Zero novel" (99). By utilizing projection and indirection, these texts seek to evade the representational challenges of trauma. Citing Robyn Warhol's notion of "unnarration," she suggests that a number of these texts are notable for their "textual silence" or for the conspicuous absence of any mention of the events. The sparsity of referents makes their significance all the more pronounced when they do occur. Däwes argues that such an approach permitted writers to deal with the "creative paralysis" with which many were afflicted in the aftermath of the attacks. She points to novels such as Brett Easton Ellis's *Lunar Park* and Jonathan Lethem's *Chronic City* as exemplars of this category. Through the presentation of narrative gaps and ellipses, these texts return some of the mystery to the most mediated event in world history. This approach, Däwes concludes, "enables writers to keep a respectful distance while also engaging with the topic and exploring its reverberations" (133). In contrast, a second category of texts utilize the *salvational* approach, giving voice to "the widespread desire for healing, rescue, and closure" (139). Däwes notes that a significant number of these texts are self-published, or fall into the realm of popular literature, and thus have not received sufficient critical attention. Their "sheer number" alone, she contends, "make a significant contribution to the cultural memory of the September 11 attacks" (141). Few of these texts, with perhaps the exception of Karen Kingsbury's *One Tuesday Morning* and William Gibson's *Pattern Recognitions* (strange bedfellows in and of themselves), are likely to be recognizable to those familiar with the 9/11 canon. It is safe to conclude that with the passing of time, fewer texts will adopt this approach.

Däwes's next two categories, the *symbolic* and the *writerly*, are closely related. Symbolic approaches examine the events though "their cultural semes of fire, burning and collapsing buildings, twins, towers, terrorism, hijackings, falling people, dust, absence, death" in order to uncover their "larger symbolic potential" (285). Pointing to Jonathan Franzen's *Freedom* and Lynne Schwartz's *The Writing on the Wall*, Däwes contends that such novels offer complex and nuanced renderings of how individual lives were impacted by the events, but also the ways in which the events were subsequently incorporated into these lives. These texts seek to "uncover discursive layers that may not be as easily accessible as the mainstream narratives of innocence, heroism and retaliation" (289). Texts utilizing the *writerly* approach, for their part, engage directly with the "profound sense of aesthetic crisis" brought on by the attacks and respond by translating these "aesthetic challenges into formal and structural innovations" (343, 345). Rather than conceding the impossibility of such representation, the novels included here reveal "a notable self-reflexive dimension to Ground Zero Fiction—both in form and content" (344). Thus, novels such as Ward Just's *Forgetfulness*, Joseph O'Neill's *Netherland*, and, of course, Jonathan Safran Foer's *Extremely Loud and Incredibly Close* expose "the volatile intersection between the event's historicity and its fictional transformation" (345). Not surprisingly, the figure of the artist struggling to represent is a recurring trope, as he or she becomes the focal point for our own making sense of the event. Resorting to sometimes experimental, sometimes metafictional, strategies these writers seek alternative means for representing the meanings of 9/11. In the process, these texts creatively expand our relationship with the event by "filling the semiotic emptiness of the cipher '9/11' with words and thus meaning, recovering original imagery and formal innovation, leaning on indirectness and a metarepresentational stance of self-reflexive inquiry" (397). One can detect in this description the overlap that exists between Däwes's categories. Certainly, there is a bit of the metonymic and the symbolic to be found in these writerly approaches. One might suggest that we are still dealing with degrees of literary indirection, primarily as a means of tracing the web of endless connections and repercussions stretching out from the epicenter now known as Ground Zero.

Most relevant to this study are the two categories Däwes designates as *diagnostic* and *appropriative* respectively. Diagnostic novels, she suggests, are not concerned with representing the events of September 11, but rather in the aftermath and the larger contexts within which the attacks might be framed. Quoting Jess Walter, she contends that these texts might more aptly be named "9/12 novels." They provide a framework within which the events of September 11, 2001, might be understood by situating the attacks "on a larger map of temporal and geopolitical contexts" (203). As such, Däwes argues, these novels serve to subvert the narratives of American exceptionalism and innocence consequently take part in the "global positioning of the memory of 9/11" (203). These narratives counteract the sentiment expressed early on that any attempt at explanation was to be interpreted as a form of justification or exoneration. At the same time, this broadening of perspectives serves to historicize 9/11 while accentuating a greater interconnectedness between peoples of the earth: "This recognition of historical embeddedness ... simultaneously differentiates and universalizes; it develops, from its critical engagement with the local, a larger understanding of global human solidarity" (203). This (re)discovery of solidarity with others is also meant, of course, to lead to an acknowledgment of, and a consequent acting upon, one's ethical responsibility to those same others.

For their part, texts that utilize the *appropriative* approach adopt a far more direct and overt strategy in coming to terms with the other. These texts exhibit and perform a direct engagement with the radical other whose presence was announced on that Tuesday morning in September. As Däwes observes, these are "appropriations of the perpetrator's voice from the outside" (248). Through a representation of the inner workings of the terrorist mind, and most specifically by adopting/adapting his voice, these writers set out to construct narratives that will somehow make sense of what many termed an "irrational" and "senseless" act of violence. As Däwes observes, "Fictionalizing the hijackers' perspectives—by either empathy or abjection—these novels attempt to close the gaps of comprehension and diversify the dichotomous order" established after the attacks (21). However, in discussing some of the same texts as Versluys—Amis's "The Last Days of Muhammad Atta," Updike's *Terrorist*, DeLillo's *Falling Man* among others—she is cognizant to point out both the pitfalls and the benefits of appropriation. For while some texts are primarily concerned with condemning the acts and the terrorists themselves (see Amis), Däwes contends that these "aesthetic acts of appropriation testify less . . . to a return of the monstrous than to the immense human need for comprehension, logic and agency" (282). Aware of the hegemonic potential of empathy, Däwes nevertheless endorses the use of the appropriative approach because "this transgressive move also (however inadvertently) exposes the unstable nature of the identity that derives from it" (283). In other words, in asserting one's difference from the radical other one may be forced to concede a degree of sameness heretofore unrecognized. As Däwes notes, such direct engagement ultimately leads to the identification of "the Other as simultaneously outside and within" (248). Chapter 3 of this study returns to some of these appropriative texts, examining in greater detail the role that empathy may or may not play in our coming to terms and connecting with a radical other who, for all intents and purposes, seems to have shaken himself free from the earth.

These quick summaries do not do justice to the expansive and clearly painstaking work Däwes has undertaken in mapping out her typology. Her study contradicts and questions a number of much-posited theories about fiction and 9/11—first and foremost that the event is unrepresentable. Second, *Ground Zero Fiction* highlights the variety and scope of narrative strategies adopted in the pursuit of meaning and understanding, negating the sense of the subgenre as the purview of upper-class white male writers. Finally, she argues that a number of texts undermine the notion of American fiction as insular and self-concerned. As she observes, "The globally discernible shockwaves of secondary or vicarious trauma notwithstanding, there are economic and political consequences to claiming the event, which makes it impossible—especially ten years on—to memorialize 9/11 without a universal perspective" (403). She concludes by pointing to the role these novels play in illuminating the new dynamics of the world in which we now live: "especially through the various geopolitical and historical threads woven into its intricate tapestry, Ground Zero Fiction invites universal empathy, lays open transnational and transhistorical connections, and points to the necessity for global perspectives" (409). Däwes thus highlights the increased presence of otherness in the contemporary world and the role fiction can play in delivering interactions with that otherness. The broad compendium of novels analyzed in *Ground Zero Fiction* attest to the ongoing significance of the event, and to an ever-present narrative desire to incorporate it into a broader tapestry of meanings and connections. The themes of interconnectedness, relations between self and other, and the ethical responsibilities contained therein, are also fundamental components of the next full-length study—Georgiana Banita's *Plotting Justice*.

Banita: *Plotting Justice*

The title of Georgiana Banita's introduction—New Ethics, New Literatures, New Americas—asserts the idea that 9/11 announced or brought about profound moral, cultural, and demographic change. *Plotting Justice* is clearly concerned with the notions of responsibility and engagement, particularly in light of the attacks: "The formal features of these fictions and their employment of ethical thought, I argue, dovetail with an increased anxiety about what it means to assume or defy the responsibilities that emerged in the wake of the terrorist attacks" (1). In essence, she argues that through 9/11 and its aftermath we have had our awareness of the other heightened and that, subsequently, we are more conscious of our own responsibilities on local, national, and global levels. The principal question that emerged in the wake of the attacks—"Why do they hate us?"—certainly reveals just how inadequately that possibility had been contemplated up to that point. The formulation of the question would seem to suggest that its subject is *them*, but it can certainly be turned around so that its answer concerns *us*. Because while the question seeks to discover what they do not like about us, it can also aid us in uncovering what we have done to make them hate us (early on, the latter was often not considered in constructing a response). The question reveals the dynamics at work in much of the discourse following the terrorist attacks, shuttling back and forth between learning more about the other and gaining a clearer understanding of self. Banita's work examines the degree to which the event has brought the concepts of ethics and empathetic engagement to the fore. She admits, for instance, that "the idea that literature after 9/11 manifests unparalleled interest in the Other is unlikely to elicit tremendous surprise" (22). But she rightly notes that interest and awareness in and of themselves are insufficient. They must be complemented with some conscious attempt to connect with, and bear some responsibility towards, that other who had heretofore been more or less invisible to us. As Banita's study reveals, these dynamics are often elaborated and exposed in the fiction that emerges in the wake of the attacks. To demonstrate, she offers a "cursory overview" of eight novels (Walter, Ballard, Schwartz, Price, Nissenson, Just, Franzen, Auster) that "reveal the abiding concern of various post-9/11 fictions with the moral landscape of an era" (11). It is in the reading of these fictions, Banita argues, that we may gain a grasp the "new ethics" at work in this altered world. She asserts that by "attending to literary rhetoric and form, we espy a process of ethical narration that unravels types of knowledge, identification, and sentiment in ways that reaffirm traditional ethical mandates as newly pertinent in the light of September 11 and its continuing aftermath" (12).

She finds the closest parallel between new ethical theory and 9/11 fiction in their shared interest in otherness. The novel, as Nussbaum and others have pointed out, is a location where the reader is placed in close proximity, and sometimes intimate contact, with the other. The question, as Banita observes, is what the reader does with that contact. Banita relies on Dorothy Hale's seminal article, "Fiction as Restriction: Self-Binding in New Ethical Theories of the Novel," to formulate an answer to that question and to construct her own notion of ethical reading. The novel creates circumstances allowing the reader to approach the other more openly, without the defenses normally utilized in day-to-day situations. She quotes Hale who puts herself in the reader's shoes, "Will I submit to the alterity that the novel allows? An affirmative answer launches the novel reader into a transactional relation with another agent, an agent defined by Otherness from the reader" (Hale, quoted 21). At the same time, we must remain cognizant of the limitations of this activity, particularly when constructing similarities between fictional characters and the actions of real people. We are finally obliged, she contends, to accept the ultimate inaccessibility of the stranger; there must always be something about the other that remains *other*. As such, she suggests that a number of these fictions are more concerned with revealing the shortcomings, than the possibilities, of such engagements—"situations that fail to achieve their potential for sympathy . . . situations that evince a greater capacity for indifference—or even cruelty—than for empathetic response" (24–25). In other words, the reader is thus made aware of the possibility of empathetic connection, but also of its potential misapplications and pitfalls. Drawing on Hale's variation of Hillis Miller's notion of the reader's accountability, Banita argues that the text places us in a situation to "judge" the other, all the while making us accountable for our judgments:

> the aim of the post-9/11 novel is not to cease judging the Other but to show we are judging even when we think we are not, how we have judged wrongly and how to make amends for it, how simply ceasing to judge is not the solution to a political crisis where judgment continues on, no matter how loftily we may condemn it in the realm of literary study. (26)

These texts thus force us to confront the quality of our relations with the other, whether we wish to acknowledge it or not. One implication of Hale's work (as well as Nussbaum's and Butler's) is that reading will make us "better" people. In struggling to grasp the other, we also grasp an understanding of ourselves. For her part, Banita suggests the fictions she examines problematize this assumption. She contends that a sense of unease, of readerly disturbance, is key to a number of these texts: "Not only are we denied access to meaning, but a rather distasteful understanding of ourselves, of our willful solidarity in ignorance, becomes palpable" (27). In certain texts, then, the knowledge gained pertains far more to the self than it does to the other. The events of 9/11 led far too easily to American claims of victimization, which these novels seek to counteract: "Post-9/11 fiction divests the self of its innocence by recasting it as violent, condemnable, and abject through narratives that effectively block the path of self-exoneration and raise suspicions about the self's rhetorical reliability and coherence" (33). A growing uncertainty about the self, Banita suggests, should thus undermine any sureties we have held about our determinations of the other. In the process of reading novels that depict characters wrestling with these questions, we are led to tangle with questions of our own. Gazing upon the other—a passive, but also inevitable and unavoidable action—causes the initial unsettlement of the self. It is what one does with this unease that ultimately matters. As such, Banita proposes "an ethics of vision" that stresses "the responsibility of not merely seeing, but looking" (39). It is not enough to be aware of the other's presence, one must commit oneself to engaging with, and being responsible for, the other. This requires, she argues, "a self-committing system of looking and spectatorship rather than mere visual detection of Otherness" (39). The move away from passive recognition of the other to active engagement with alterity describes what I see as the fundamental difference between compassion and empathy. The latter demands a conscious working through of that which makes me both same and different from the other. It is through this negotiation that I may glimpse some understanding, become different from myself, and thus closer to the other. As writers on empathy note, empathetic engagement does not mean the sublimation of the one for the sake of the other. Rather, empathy, if fully exercised, blurs the lines between self and other.

Despite a number of allusions to "empathetic response" (6, 12, 24), however, Banita pays little direct critical attention to the notion of empathy (her index offeres but three mentions). But this does not accurately reflect her theory, since empathy is a fundamental component of Banita's ethical and moral equation. Early on, for instance, she recognizes that "events such as 9/11 may act as a catalyst to release waves of empathy that it is our responsibility to channel toward morally defensible goals" (20). This observation identifies empathy as the initiatory emotion that may lead to moral reasoning and action. And she returns to this notion in her concluding remarks when she observes, "An essential attribute of post-9/11 fiction resides in its concrete suggestions about how the experience of terror can be sublimated into an empathetic code of conduct" (295). The impact of the event is seen as producing change in individuals who reconsider and reconfigure the ways in which they interact with their fellow human beings. Banita warns, however, that the objective of these fictions "is not merely (and never directly) the promulgation of specific moral principles or the prescriptive delineation of how to interpret or respond to Otherness" (296). Instead, she argues that these novels "seek to train what may be called the reader's moral intuition. The process of empathetic connection they effect does not single out the producer of the recipient of compassion, but aims to prepare and decongest the channels of compassion itself" (296). In other words, the reading of these fictions may instigate empathetic feelings in the reader, leading to further ethical action. On this level, this study and Banita's work share a good deal. I would suggest that it is a question of emphasis, of degree not kind. This study will also demonstrate how fictions responding to the "Otherness Provocation" reveal both the possibilities and pitfalls of empathy. After all, if empathy is misdirected or misused, or simply fails to connect, then the possibility of "morally defensible goals" is seriously shortcircuited.

In *Plotting Justice*, Banita only briefly acknowledges earlier scholarship: one finds but a couple of passing references to Versluys and Gray, and no mention of Däwes. She dismisses these earlier forays into the literary subgenre, including Keniston and Quinn's collection, by highlighting the myopic narrowness of their approach and criticizing them for being "focused on fiction that portrays the terrorist attacks overtly at the expense of more oblique intimations of a post-9/11 world with its global risks and permutations" (2). Like Däwes, Banita bemoans the lack of critical consideration given to the broader historical context within which these events occurred and within which these fictions are produced. Interestingly, while Banita seeks to distinguish *Plotting Justice* from these earlier studies—"differentiating my stance from posttraumatic approaches to 9/11 literature" (56)—her text still shares a number of common concerns. Her emphasis on what she terms, "The Otherness Provocation" of contemporary literature does suggest some obvious similarities (21–29). It may well be that earlier studies were more preoccupied with trauma and its immediate aftermath, but to suggest that the texts examined by Versluys, Däwes and Gray (to say nothing of those included in Cilano's collection) are primarily concerned with the self, and not the other, is to give them short thrift. Both Versluys and Däwes devote entire chapters to the issue (as we have noted, the latter's categories of "diagnostic" and "appropriative" are concerned with the manner in which these fictions manage, respond to, or appropriate, the figure of the Other). For his part, Gray argues that it is only by turning our attention to otherness in all of its forms (local, transnational, etc.) that we will emerge from the writerly impasse that has plagued much of the early fiction produced in response to the attacks. The texts he examines in his chapter entitled "Imagining Crisis," the ones he believes succeed in capturing some of the "interstitial reality" of 9/11, would no doubt meet many of Banita's criteria as novels more concerned with other than with self.

Perhaps most significantly, all four of these texts make a number of allusions and references to types of empathetic actions or behaviors. As we have seen, Versluys argues for the importance of connecting with the "radical other" of terrorism. The possibility of such an empathetic connection is enabled through the work of novelists whose "creative imagination is usually associated with a certain power of explanation, a kind of affective or empathic understanding" (150). Readers' minds are opened to the possibility of sameness, while being made cognizant of the ineluctable difference always residing at the heart of any encounter with the other. Richard Gray, for his part, does not use the word "empathy," but continually alludes to interstitial and hybrid spaces within which self and other can connect. He maintains that novels offer spaces that blur any dichotomous constructions, demonstrating the existence of commonalities between apparently disparate groups and peoples. Similarly, Däwes notes that her Ground Zero Fiction "invites universal empathy," and points to its significance in bridging the gap between self and other, thus undermining the binary thinking. Finally, Banita makes occasional mention of the "empathetic response," particularly with respect to coming to terms with otherness, but never addresses the topic of empathy directly. The events of September 11, along with other occurrences, brought to the fore the realization that there was no longer avoiding or ignoring the presence of others. As I have noted, the attacks were perhaps, first and foremost, an assertion of otherness, an expression of an identity different from that of the American hegemon. And though the terrorists were certainly not thinking about rapprochement and how the two cultures might seek out a mutual meeting point, one of the results was an increased emphasis on understanding those others with whom one shares the planet. As such, I wish to extend the work of the previous studies by examining the ways in which works of post-9/11 fiction highlight the increased presence of others and the role empathy may play, or not, in negotiating these interactions. Our current global state of affairs requires a more focused recognition of the other and the existence of potential sites of difference, in order to find the means for living more peacefully and responsibly with one another.

THE ROLE OF EMPATHY

So how do we explain this renewed interest in empathy to which I alluded earlier? Perhaps the simplest explanation is the fact that otherness and interactions with others are ubiquitous components of contemporary life (an idea to which I will return). Successful interactions often depend on one's ability to empathize, to find points of sameness, with the various others with which one comes into contact. However, as Keen points out, we live in a world far more concerned with acknowledging and celebrating difference than in seeking out sameness: "Our contemporary celebration of our diversity and our differences may make the call to recognize our similarities more difficult to heed, though advocates of virtue ethics and ethics of care hope not" (Keen 165). In part this is due to the fact that a sameness imperative remains tainted by a colonial past that was intent on molding everyone to its image, and destroying all those who would not conform. A shift away from such homogenizing and domineering impulses was deeply necessary, but have we perhaps moved too far in the other direction? Has difference been accentuated to the point where one feels little or no connection with either near or distant others? Have we stretched the line so thin that feeling for these others has become a near-impossibility? Because focusing on otherness or difference has its share of potential drawbacks as well. Keen quotes Ihab Hassan who observes, "It can discourage mutual obligation, cripple empathy, defeat transcultural judgments, leaving only raw power to resolve human conflicts. It can lead to hostility, exclusiveness, less respect for others than solidarity with ourselves" (Keen 165). In other words, focusing on difference can lead to intransigency and the cutting off of fellow-feeling to all but those inhabiting one's "inner circle." Indeed, Hassan seems to suggest that it can produce conditions in which something like 9/11 happens. Maintaining one's national fortress and keeping others at bay is no longer a viable or practicable option. Exposure to otherness has become an irrefutable fact of the contemporary condition. Otherness, now more than ever, requires attention and acknowledgment.

Empathy can serve precisely this function, opening up channels of potential interaction and understanding between diverse others. Inherently requiring active and conscious engagement, empathy creates a self-aware, and self-critical, empathizer better disposed to assess and implement her ethical responsibilities to others with whom she shares the world. In *The Moral Dimensions of Empathy*, Julinna Oxley argues this very point, identifying empathy as "essential to the moral life" and "instrumental to developing a wide range of moral capabilities" (4). And though she warns that empathy "is not intrinsically moral and does not always lead to moral thought or action," (4), she nevertheless contends that the kind of knowledge acquired during the empathetic engagement offers the best possible avenue for the eradication of the dichotomizing discourses, to say nothing of actions, continuing to plague the contemporary world. Conceding that empathy is not in itself sufficient, she still maintains that it can provide access to the other in ways that other affective strategies may not:

> Most importantly, the knowledge gained through empathy is different from knowledge gained about others with theories or in a strictly rational way. Knowledge gained with empathy is framed in reference to oneself, and this is why it is important for moral deliberation: empathy can transform one's view

of others, one's view of what is valuable, and one's view of what matters, both to others and to oneself. (12)

In other words, empathy can allow us to think and feel as others do. Perhaps most significantly, it may provide us with a sense of how we are perceived by others, in the process opening up the possibility for self-reflection and a reassessment of how we think about, and act towards, these others. Karsten Stueber similarly flaunts these double-sided virtues: "Empathy not only allows me to solve the basic problem of other minds; that is, not only allows me to recognize another person as being minded. It also enables me to develop myself more fully as a reflective and self-critical individual, since it enables me to recognize the opinions of others about myself" (9). Engaging in empathy is a more reciprocal activity than other attempts at understanding the other, since it also requires self-diagnosis. I must seek to find that which makes me and the other same. This implies the bi-directionality of the empathic gesture, since empathy becomes more than simply a way of assessing and judging the other, but also the means through which the empathizer is exposed to different ways of thinking and feeling. Such exposure "can transform the empathizer and her view of others and the world by bringing her attention to features of another's situation that enable her to expand her range of beliefs and values" (37).

Of course, engaging in empathy is not without its dangers, such as misreading the other due to cultural and other differences, or imposing one's own view on the other simply by virtue of trying to empathize. Since empathy "can generate conjectures that cannot be verified, and the kind of knowledge generated by empathy is limited to the observer's understanding of the situation," Oxley warns that it must not be the only means by which we seek to know others (44). For her part, Megan Boler contends that we all too often fall victim to a "passive empathy" that "produces no action towards justice but situates the powerful Western eye/I as the judging subject, never called upon to cast her gaze at her own reflection" (259). Thus, Boler asserts that we should apply empathy with a critical eye and an awareness of our own motivations for engaging in the activity. Similarly, in *Empathic Vision*, Jill Bennett closely examines the various strategies and motivations that come into play in the interactions between empathizer and empathized. And her warnings about the mis-applications of empathy are even more forcefully stated. The sympathetic impulse that leads one to empathize with another (I realize I may be confusing terminology here) may serve to disguise the extent to which one is appropriating that other's experience as a means of achieving one's own personal relief or objectives. She points out, for instance, that "There is a certain hubris in colonizing [the traumatic] experience—and particularly . . . in art's claim to *salvage* damaged experience and thereby redeem life" (3). And perhaps there is no greater colonizing gesture than empathy—in the assumption (no matter how well-intended) that one has achieved the objective of standing in the other's shoes, that the other stands fully revealed and at one's ready disposal. Such actions, of course, risk being accused of appropriation. Suzanne Keen also pointedly critiques "the directional quality of empathy" which invests the empathizer with the authority to grasp the thoughts and feelings of the empathized "who may or may not be empowered to speak for herself, to correct misconceptions about her feelings, and to refuse the pitying gaze" (162). Most frequently, as we shall see, there is an underlying sense of inequality in the empathetic gesture, with the empathizer adopting or holding a dominant position. The empathizer feels for the other's misfortune, and seeks to understand how one might feel in dire circumstances. In this iteration, Keen notes, empathy "becomes yet another example of the Western imagination's imposition of its own values on cultures and peoples that it scarcely knows, but presumes to 'feel with,' in a cultural imperialism of the emotions" (148–49). Therefore Keen, among others, strongly prescribes humility and modesty on the part of the empathizer in any such engagement. Furthermore, she points to the ways that empathy can go wrong. She distinguishes between *failed empathy*—marked by the empathizer's inability to connect with the empathized—and *false empathy*: "the self-congratulatory delusions of those who incorrectly believe they have caught the feelings of suffering others from a different culture, gender, race, or class" (159). Each of these writers make the point of highlighting the importance of recognizing both the limits of empathy (that the other's experience cannot be translated into my own and that, indeed, might be said to openly resist such a translation) as well as the possible motivations for engaging in the empathic exercise (that personal emotions or desires may well contribute to my own urge to empathize). A true empathic connection, then, largely depends on the degree to which the empathizer is both self-aware and self-critical. I agree wholeheartedly with this assessment of empathy's limitations, and this study in no way suggests that it is the solution to the geopolitical impasses that stand in the way of planetary harmony. Rather, I wish to argue that empathy is a good starting-off point for generating further moments of direct connection with others, such as dialogue and genuine debate. Empathy effectively serves to bridge the gap, for instance, in circumstances where the margin of overlap between the two parties may appear minimal or virtually non-existent. As Oxley maintains: "we have a scarcity of resources for transcending our own perspectives, and this is why empathy is extremely valuable in providing an opportunity to learn something new" (55).

FICTION AND EMPATHY

I would like to extend this idea, arguing that the reading of fiction can aid in the "transcending" of one's situation, providing moments of stasis within which connections between self and other can be safely and logically considered. Fiction presents opportunities to witness empathy in action—in the text's very attempts to represent the inner lives of its diverse characters, in the empathetic gestures of the characters themselves to understand each other, and in the reader's recognition of her own empathetic efforts at connecting (or not) with the characters presented in the text. In this matter I concur with a number of writers who identify literature as offering one of the few imaginative spaces within which both self and other can be contemplated. For instance, Martha Nussbaum notes,

> Narrative art has the power to make us see the lives of the different with more than a casual tourist's interest—with involvement and sympathetic understanding, with anger at our society's refusals of visibility. We come to see how circumstances shape the lives of those who share with us some general goals and projects; and we see that circumstances shape not only people's possibilities for action, but also their aspirations and desires, hope and fears. (CH 88)

In a similar vein, Dorothy Hale contends that the reader, in giving herself over to the world of the novel ("self-binding"), willingly suppresses the self (or is in a situation where there is no real need for the self to express itself). Under these circumstances, the reader becomes more open to the other. As Hale explains, "This agent is the social Other that is produced by two related readerly acts: the act of self-subordination that enables the apprehension of alterity; and a prior act that makes self-subordination itself possible—the will to believe in the possibility of alterity" (189). In other words, one must be willing to subjugate the self in order to connect with the other, but one must first recognize the existence of an other, a being different from oneself. Novels, in Hale's Words thus provide "a training in the honoring of Otherness" (189).

It is here that the novel serves a function, allowing the reader to get beyond "egoistic moral reasoning" by presenting the moral deliberations of the implied narrator, as well as a host of other figures. Through this triangulation with the text and the empathized, the reader may become a more self-aware, and self-critical empathizer. Because the emotions elicited in the empathizer are not meant to replicate those of the empathized, but rather produce an unsettledness that compels the former to explore the experiential differences separating her from the latter. Bennett thus concludes that a certain kind of art "by virtue of its specific affective capacities" is capable of instigating

> forms of embodied perception in order to promote forms of critical inquiry. This conjunction of affect and critical awareness may be understood to constitute the basis of an empathy grounded not in affinity (*feeling for* another insofar as we can imagine *being* that other) but on a *feeling for* another that entails an encounter with something irreducible and different, often inaccessible. (10)

Bennett here highlights a common theme amongst writers on empathy: the irreducible otherness of the other. More significant, however, is the emphasis she places on these affective encounters as impetus for critical inquiry and ethical contemplation. To this end, she invokes the Deleuzian notion of the *encountered sign*, the term referring to "the sign that is felt, rather than recognized or perceived through cognition" (7). She quotes Deleuze who states, "More important than thought there is 'what leads to thought' . . . impressions which force us to look, encounters which force us to interpret, expressions which force us to think" (7). The repeated use of the word "force" suggests that art must instigate a process which the viewer might not willingly undertake otherwise. Bennett further argues, however, that we should not think of any of these works as simply acting as a "mechanistic trigger or stimulus" for the viewer's own emotions. Rather the work should be evaluated for its capacity to cause "a jolt that does not so much *reveal* truth as thrust us involuntarily into a mode of critical inquiry" (11). Bennett's reader may have difficulty in parsing her distinction between "trigger" and "jolt," but the use of the word "involuntarily" affirms the implication that the viewer is being manipulated to see things otherwise. Integral to the connection, then, is the making uneasy of the empathizer, causing her to shift and inhabit a space wherein the possibility of connection with the other is heightened. Again, it is not a case of the empathizer acquiring unfettered access to that other, so much as being troubled to a degree that contemplation of one's relation and responsibility to the other is engendered. The necessity for such discomfort is made apparent in her emphasis on what she terms the viewer's "squirm," signaling the stimulus as something from which one instinctively pulls back.

In the true spirit of empathy, Bennett envisages a reciprocal and mutual relationship between empathizer and empathized, in which the latter preserves her primary (though not necessarily desired) position, and the former fulfills an ethical function in wrestling with the truths revealed by the other's experience. It is only under such conditions, she contends, that the empathizer may confront his own involvement (complicity?) in the course of human events and assess the degree to which one has met one's responsibility towards all others. Art thus serves as the springboard for empathic vision, providing an "interstitial meeting place" wherein the "inside" of the other and the "outside" of the viewer may safely meet (131). In this transaction, one comes to comprehend how such things may happen to other human beings, and identify one's place in a range of human experience that often appears beyond one's grasp. This study shall consider the ways that the contemporary novel exists as a "meeting place" of its own, opening up the possibility of empathic connection for the reader.

In closing, I want to examine one further explanation for our preoccupation with otherness (and the attendant interest in empathy): the incontrovertible fact that we are now exposed to otherness on a far more frequent, and perhaps more meaningful, way than ever before in history. In this configuration, literature acts as a "space" from which to safely apprehend, contemplate, and perhaps prepare to responsibly engage with otherness. Indeed, the issue of our increased interconnectivity, and its impact on questions of sameness and difference, is a central concern in two recent studies of contemporary American fiction: David Palumbo-Liu's *The Deliverance of Others* and Christian Moraru's *Cosmodernism*. Palumbo-Liu argues that, in contrast to earlier times, we now live in a world overrun by otherness:

> Globalization has delivered to us far more distant spaces and peoples than ever before, with greater regularity and integration on multiple fronts—economic, political, social, cultural, ecological, epidemiological, and so on. "Otherness" is thus not only increasingly in contact with the "same," but the points of contact and contagion with otherness are far more numerous. (3)

Similarly, Moraru underlines the extensive otherness to which a good many of us are exposed on a regular basis. Early in his study, he observes that "others' presence in American life is becoming more substantial than ever. More than at any point in our past, being-in-relation, with an other, makes for the cornerstone of America and its self-perception" (2). *Cosmodernism* emphasizes the importance of the other in the construction of the self. This is not a new concept, of course, as the various epigraphs sprinkled throughout Moraru's text make abundantly clear. What is perhaps new is the degree of exposure to otherness and the challenges this may pose to self-identification: "having a being, being somebody—occurs, now more than ever, transnationally" (9). At the same time, Moraru repeatedly asserts that this otherness requires something from us; it makes us vividly aware of our obligations to those others with whom we share the world. Both writers, as we shall see, invest literature with a significant role in the negotiation of otherness.

In *The Deliverance of Others*, Palumbo-Liu proposes the existence of a number of "delivery systems" through which we are exposed to sameness and difference: the media, political doctrines, religious codes, rituals, and so on. Notably, he accords fiction a place of privilege (hence his focus on the contemporary novel) as not only a delivery system in its own right, but also as a "metasystem" positioned to reflect and comment on itself as well as other discursive systems. For though other forms of discourse are often slanted towards uncovering that which makes the reader same with the other, literature's role is to confront the reader with people and experiences beyond his or her current frame of knowledge:

> What we obtain through reading is a life not like our own and a life specifically beyond "our lot." Not only does it not seem like what we have experienced, it also comes from experiences that are not likely ever to be ours at all. And that is the point of great art—it stirs in us a sense of difference, and this difference, if delivered well, in turn prompts us to reach beyond the ordinary sphere and broader sort of empathy. And at that moment, we "become" something different, something inflected with otherness. (11)

In the process of this exposure, then, we not only recognize the difference of the other, but also become more like the other. We have now been touched by that which made the other different and have become a little more different ourselves. As with Bennett's formulation, Palumbo-Liu's language implies some kind of contamination, as though the reader has no choice but to be impacted by this contact. He concedes, however, that the identification of these essential human traits is not in itself sufficient to ensure a strong connection. Indeed, we might consider whether these areas merely serve as the foundation for relations between people to come into being. They provide the margin of overlap within which a conversation can be initiated.

At the same time, he outlines the challenges of living in a world constantly on the verge of being de-stabilized by an excess of otherness. He points to the existence of "too much otherness" as an "essential problem": "how much otherness is required? How much confounds us, rather than enriches us? How different can their 'lot' be from ours before it recedes into unintelligibility? We become caught in an oscillating movement, identifying and de-identifying, weighing what we can, and cannot, learn from" (12–13). I would add that this juxtaposition can have other, even greater, negative consequences. After all, *confounds* is not the antonym for *enriches*. At the opposite end of this spectrum should we not find a kind of otherness that depletes us, makes us worse off for having been exposed to it? As Palumbo-Liu observes, "The adjudication of how much otherness we need to encounter and grapple with in order to be better people and how much will prove to be our undoing is, again, both a logistical and a political problem" (13). Since there are far more opportunities to be overwhelmed by otherness, and fewer for its contemplation, he suggests that we must turn to literature as "a space for imagining our relation to others and thinking through why and how that relation exists, historically, politically, ideologically" (14). Contemporary fiction serves to illuminate the problematics of these relations and some of the assumptions birthed from our nearness to others.

Moraru, for his part, argues that these new circumstances require a greater degree of awareness and responsibility: "What, how, and where we are *obligates*. Next to 'them' more than we have ever been, 'we' are responsible to and for them, more specifically, to and for what makes them other to us rather than others like us" (53). But he also contends that we need to reconsider what we mean by otherness, and how we define our relations with others in the world. He points to the fact that these relations are often conceptualized in oppositional terms (us/them) that create barriers to recognition of one's real connections with others. Moraru argues instead that we need to think of the other not as supplementary to the self, but rather as complementary:

> The other's *appositionality* in our world represents, in summation, "the way the world is"—again, now more than at any previous stage—and also a way if not *the* way to make sense of this world; it is indeed a "fact" of life, a tool for understanding, and I have been arguing, an ethical injunction. For the other I am with is not just a cultural ontological "supplement" of which I need to be "tolerant," a newcomer, a newly-arrived, or a neighbor who has recently moved in. His or her juxtaposition to me is not additional but foundational. Because of that, it also explains, and obligates. (74)

According to Moraru, we have a greater responsibility no "make sense" of the other, because excessive otherness is now "the way the world is." In this regard, and most pertinent to this study, is the emphasis both Palumbo-Liu and Moraru place on literature's ability to capture and communicate these current conditions. Literature both dramatizes encounters with others and reflects upon its own struggles to make sense of the other. The paradox of literature, as Palumbo-Liu points out, is how it "can both present radical otherness and simultaneously be disarmed by it" (22). Novels concerned with depicting encounters with difference often represent this constant vacillation between two poles. This is not to say that the novel maintains control over otherness. Rather it grapples with the issue in two not entirely gratifying ways. In the first scenario, the narrative tames otherness, offering a pale domesticated version of the other. In the second, at the other end of the spectrum, the text contains so much otherness that the other is rendered incomprehensible to the reader. Literature creates a space permitting the reader to move between these two poles. As Moraru contends, "we must at least consider the notion of a *radically distinct cultural other* who need not be, and in practice often is not, hopelessly inaccessible to us and yet, at the end of our probing day, may still prove irreducible to our approaches, conceptual grids, and overall rationality" (23). Literature illuminates those moments of transient connection, but also alludes to that which lies beyond the veil, giving us a deeper appreciation for the complexity of the lives and minds of other. Finally, Moraru argues, the self is made richer through these literary interactions: "It is in this other-world [of the text] that the self comes about, in exchanges with others and their locutions, with their words and stories" (54). Palumbo-Liu makes a similarly strong pitch for the value of literature in its wrestling with the tensions between sameness and difference, as well as its self-conscious capacity to illuminate this very activity:

> Put concisely, there is no way to say in advance what the proper response to alterity should be or what would be the grounds on which to judge the proper or complete deciphering of meaning. Rather, it is important to turn our attention to the purchase we make in the names of sameness, otherness, commonality, radical incommensurability, and so on . . . And it is in a careful attention to a newly invented, contemporary literary form that such imaginings and meditations are made possible, as the literary text, in refusing or at least deferring meaning, gives us pause to see more precisely our relationship to others—what enables or disables certain modes of connection and meaning-making. (15)

As Palumbo-Liu makes clear, there is no prescription, no formula for assessing the proper measure of connection between self and other. We need to be cognizant, however, of our motivations for engaging in such activities, as well as our reasons for appointing degrees of sameness or otherness. As he observes, "The task is not only to measure the distance, but also to try to account for it" (15). Again, the text "gives us pause," allowing us to contemplate more fully our relationship with the other. Fiction permits an examination of these points of connectivity, those moments when the empathetic gesture succeeds or fails. For if one undertakes this exercise based on a foundation of sameness, how does one identify that which makes the other *other*? The metafictional and self-reflexive aspects of fiction allow us to step back and contemplate the manner in which we make sense of otherness:

> Literature, and more specifically *reading* literature, helps us fess up to our standards of measurement, our yardsticks, because the text takes us outside our usual habitations of meaning, sense-making, self-assurance. In this process, the way literature comes to be written in different, difficult ways shows its elastic powers, but also its breaking points. Sometimes the system is overwhelmed by the task of delivering too much otherness, of reconciling radically disparate actions that cannot be made into sense. We are then forced to ask why and how we set those limits. (15)

The reading of these novels, as encounters with otherness, show us how empathy and empathetic actions play out in the world, how they are received, but also how they are sometimes stalled, circumvented, opposed or, indeed, rejected altogether. In presenting lived situations ("a dramatization of world with-ness," as Moraru calls it), works of fiction afford the reader glimpses into that which divides or joins, the (sometimes self-inflicted) obstacles that prevent the connection of self and other or the bridges that momentarily afford mutual recognition.

THE CHAPTERS

Chapter 1 examines the presence of the falling people in a number of works of art and fiction, including DeLillo's *Falling Man*. Both the title of DeLillo's text and the inclusion of a performance artist named Falling Man reflect a preoccupation with the victims of September 11 who leaped to their deaths, and with the necessary justification of any aesthetic representation of those horrors. DeLillo is not alone in his preoccupation. The falling people are central to fictional works by Jonathan Safran Foer and Frédéric Beigbeder, are represented in a controversial works by Eric Fischl and Sharon Paz, and are the subject of a 2006 documentary. This chapter attempts to come to grips with this preoccupation, the apparent aesthetic desire to express it, and the outrage from others that often accompanies such expression. The artists who create works representing the falling people often frame them as acts of compassion and empathy. We have a responsibility to the dead, they claim, and these works provide the means for recognizing the essential sameness we share with them. In contrast, members of the public are often outraged, seeing these gestures as exploiting and disrespecting the dead. The chapter begins by examining the ways various works treating the subject of the falling people (including the now-famous photograph by Richard Drew) were subject to sometimes vitriolic criticism and varying degrees of censorship. The chapter thus considers whether there is any way of empathizing with the victimized other without arousing such emotions.

Invoking LaCapra's "empathic unsettlement," I consider whether empathy can be expressed for the dead through art and the ways this unsettlement must be maintained so that the victim remains sufficiently other. Emy Koopman's formulation of "under-distanced" and "over-distanced" reactions to trauma also proves useful as it highlights the necessity for the empathizer to remain cognizant of the ways he or she may simply colonize the other's experience to satisfy his or her own needs. To demonstrate the dangers inherent in "under-distancing," I offer a reading of Helen Schulman's *A Day at the Beach*. Schulman's novel offers a protagonist who unconditionally identifies with a falling person, often as the means of addressing her private pains and tribulations. Such a construction, I argue, diminishes the degree to which the text initiates empathy in the reader. In contrast, DeLillo uses a device that distances the reader from the actual event while still connecting the reader to the experiences of the victims. DeLillo's use of the Falling Man allows him to examine the aesthetic representations of this private/public trauma, but also to defuse the criticism leveled against representers of that trauma. To that end, the novel offers an alternative dynamic that may serve to instill empathy in the reader not only for the victims, but also for the people who were the traumatized witnesses that September morning. Through a character, Lianne, who observes and is herself unsettled by the actions of the performance artist, DeLillo provides the reader with a mirror to his own potential actions. Lianne's unsettlement causes her to empathize with the unsettlement of others and in the process come to a greater understanding of what precisely the falling people mean to the community in the aftermath of the tragedy.

In chapter 2, I analyze three first-person eye-witness accounts of the events of September 11, told in the form of graphic narratives. With its penchant for autobiography, the graphic narrative has demonstrated its capacity as a forum for the individual voice. With its amalgamation of text and image, the genre offered a vehicle for testimony in the wake of the events of 9/11. This chapter examines three graphic narratives—Art Spiegelman's *In the Shadow of No Towers*, Henrik Rehr's *Tribeca Sunset*, and Alissa Torres's *American Widow*—as individual responses to both the events of September 11, and more important, to the dominant reconstructions spawned in the days and months that followed. This chapter, along with the one on French fiction, actually seek to reverse Palumbo-Liu's formulation, so that they address "the problem of sameness." In other words, both chapters are concerned with the manner in which narratives are often imposed on others in the name of establishing sameness. Each graphic novelist reacts to his or her private experiences being incorporated into a national narrative.

9/11 was first and foremost a visual event. Indeed its literally "graphic" nature and scope was the inevitable result sought by the hijackers. The trauma visited upon the nation induced a repetition-compulsion played out in the viewing and reviewing of what have now become standard representations of the event. These graphic narratives highlight the ways in which images were manipulated to create a prevailing narrative (mostly of survival and resilience, but also revenge and retribution). In turn, they present images that offer alternative perspectives from those proliferated by the media and the government. In different ways and at varying levels of magnitude, each author seeks to wrest control away from the prevailing ideologies and insert degrees of nuance not to be found in the endless loop of over-televised images. An analysis of these texts also reveals the manner in which images constitute their own narrative strains that can proliferate with each use and juxtaposition. As autobiographical works these texts blur the line between public and private discourse. The depersonalization of the event that was inevitable in the (re)presentation of a limited set of images is countered by those presented in the graphic narrative. They present the complex dynamics involved in any empathetic connection with the survivor/witness in these limit-situations wherein individual needs are subjugated to those of the perceived communal good. As such, they can be read as full-blown expressions of otherness in the face of overwhelming sameness. The chapter thus analyzes each author's re-appropriation of sometimes iconic images to speak of their own experiences of 9/11 and its aftermath. Through this process, each author seeks to elicit empathy and understanding from the reader, not only for their specific challenges but for the tribulations of the many caught up in this catastrophic and globally mediated event.

In *From Solidarity to Schisms*, Cara Cilano conceptualizes September 11 as a moment "characterized by unfathomable vulnerability and the possibility of a better future" (13). She argues the event, while traumatic, might have served as an impetus to reconfigure American self-perceptions and thoughts about its place in the world. Instead, she contends, the United States squandered the "utopian potential" of this moment. Cilano remains optimistic, however, because she sees European fictional discourse on 9/11 as emblematic of a desire for a melding of divergent perspectives. Their critique aims to keep America's sense of itself unbalanced, thus providing fuel for self-reflection, analysis, and, most important, renewal. Taking the measure of current Franco-American relations, chapter 3 tests the validity of this contention by examining works of French fiction published in the five years after the attacks. Four of these texts—Christian Garcin's *La jubilation des hasards*, Didier Goupil's *Le jour de mon retour sur terre*, Luc Lang's *11 septembre, mon amour*, and Frédéric Beigbeder's *Windows on the World*—are the focus of this chapter. I argue that we can acquire some measure of the degree to which someone truly wishes to engage in this rapprochement, by reading literary output for signs of empathetic connection. Do these texts express empathy for the American situation? Are they imaginative attempts to genuinely feel the emotions of the Americans, to perceive the event from an American point of view? For the most part, as we shall see, 9/11 simply provides an opportunity for critiquing (and even insulting) a downed opponent. These writers, reacting to what they perceive as an increased Americanization of the world, interpret (or even conceptualize) the attacks as a form of overt geopolitical criticism. This chapter also attempts a reversal of sorts, examining the ways in which French writers depict the American "other" to their readership. We need to consider the ways in which the specific dynamics of Franco-American relations might handicap or limit the possibilities of empathy, on the part of the novelists, but also that of a French readership. The chapter contemplates the extent to which self-interest and questions of identity—personal, political, national—interfere with empathy, thus posing a considerable challenge to the utopian dream of a cosmopolitan world.

Because, as has been noted, a number of commentators have advocated the use of empathy as a way out of the impasse now existing in Western relations with Islam and, more specifically, Muslim extremism. Gayatri Spivak argues that all proposed solutions to the current crisis are contingent upon our capacity for empathy: "Unless we are trained into imagining the other, a necessary, impossible, and interminable task, nothing we do through politico-legal calculation will last" (83). As Spivak intimates, true empathy is not simply putting yourself in someone else's shoes, it is also recognizing how the other remains *other*. But what if the other remains *so* other that he is virtually unfathomable? This is a principal characteristic of the novels examined in chapter 4, as they tackle this question head-on by presenting the final moments in the life of a terrorist who took part in the attacks on September 11, from the perspective of that terrorist. By focusing on this limit-situation, the texts strive to capture the thoughts and motivations of an individual whose actions many find incomprehensible. These narratives exhibit a moving beyond the examination of the operations of terrorist groups and a striving towards an empathic understanding of the individual who chooses terrorism as an expression of his or her identity. As such, these writers seek to tackle Spivak's "necessary, impossible, and interminable task." These efforts thus raise a number of questions about narrative and its relationship with empathy: Is it possible to unconditionally inhabit the mind of the terrorist? Can common ground be established? In other words, can the writer find an accessible portal through which to connect with the thoughts and motivations of the terrorist? Or are texts about Islamic fundamentalists written in the West always going to be handicapped as outsider perspectives? Is literary skill enough to invoke the imaginations and motivations of the other who wishes one harm? And to what degree does the presence of threat (and consequent fear) incapacitate one's ability to empathize? One might suggest that terrorism is the most salient example of the "problem of otherness" and that these texts seek to achieve a balance that will invoke at least a modicum of empathy in the reader. This balance, as we shall see, is imperiled by an inevitable allegiance to the victims and a reluctance on the novel to entirely commit to the vision of the terrorist.

Set in an anxious and fearful post-9/11 setting, Ian McEwan's *Saturday* addresses how an endorsement of privilege and rationality similarly inhibit an understanding of a confrontational other, one who fails to appreciate the trappings within which one lives in "civilized society." The protagonist, already existing in a state of heightened alert, is assailed by an other in whom he recognizes anger and hatred, but also suffering. Arguably, these should prove optimal conditions for the exercising of empathy. Chapter 5 examines how the novel (perhaps not always consciously) demonstrates the problematics of just such an exercise. For while *Saturday* may declare the need for empathy and extol it as a cornerstone of Western, secularized society, the text simultaneously reveals how easily its application is constructed and perverted. The seemingly benign and benevolent actions of the novel's neurosurgeon emphasize the blindspots of privilege and the co-opting of empathy to assert a superior moral stance over that of the other. As such, the dialectics of the novel suggest that tha retrenchment of differences is a more probable response to violence, rather than a recognition of shared vulnerability. With its subtext of the war on terror, *Saturday* advocates for the superiority of a Western perspective, with its ability to adopt a pluralist perspective and in its capacity for forgiveness. Nevertheless, the privilege of the West, as well as its technological and economic dominance, weaken its capacity to connect with the less fortunate, but more desperate, other who seeks to redress past wrongs and equalize global footings. The novel stands, then, as an artifact of Western complacency and mystification, highlighting the extent to which Western society remains incredulous that others might wish for its destruction and perplexed about the reasons driving that wish.

Through a reading of Amy Waldman's *The Submission*, chapter 6 examines the debates surrounding the ultimate purpose(s) of the memorial, as well as those concerned with the treatment of Arab and Muslim-Americans after 9/11. Both issues make evident the cracks and fissures existing in the supposed national consensus presented by the Bush Administration and much of the media. Waldman's text depicts the siege mentality that permeates in the aftermath of the attacks, and the subsequent emphasis placed on the need for all citizens (perhaps all New Yorkers first, but eventually all Americans) to project a unified front. This was effected largely though the construction of an "us" in response to a perceived "them." In other words, high levels of vulnerability and fear led to an all-or-nothing philosophy that demanded that one assert one's belonging to one group or another. There was no room for nuance or contradiction. No consideration was given to those who might not so easily fit into these new designations. In this strained and shocked atmosphere, the site of the wound becomes both a rallying point and a source of discord. What might normally engender communal agreement soon instigates a series of heated debates within the supposedly unified community. In *The Submission*, the author imagines the fallout (political, emotional, social) from an anonymous selection process in which a Muslim architect is chosen to design the 9/11 memorial. One of the text's accomplishments is the manner in which it captures the competing impulses at work within the traumatized community, as well as the principles of inclusion and exclusion that were implemented in the aftermath of the attacks. Because the furor that erupts, and the outrage connected to the name of Mohammad Khan, at once makes clear how raw the wound still is, but also the extent to which Arab and Muslim-Americans are now viewed with nearly as much suspicion and anger as al-Qaeda operatives. Interestingly, the furor Waldman depicts in her novel was mirrored in many ways by the outrage that erupted in the summer of 2010 over a proposal to build an Islamic cultural center some blocks from Ground Zero (soon misnamed the Ground Zero mosque controversy). The vehemence with which this idea was opposed confirms many of the author's assumptions about the potential reaction to a Muslim designer, but also about how little relations with the Arab and Muslim community have improved. For many the construction of a memorial whose design is Muslim in origin is the equivalent of creating a "victory garden" for jihadists. Because it is of no consequence whether Mohammad Khan is a practicing Muslim or not (he is not), or whether he is an American citizen or not (he is). The population's lack of knowledge about Islam short-circuits their capacity to contemplate other scenarios. In their minds, all Arabs are Muslims, all Muslims are Islamists, and all Islamists seek the destruction of the Western world. Any commonalities Khan may share with his "fellow" American citizens are overshadowed by his Muslim background. It makes no difference whether these thoughts are rational or not—the existence of a link between the designer and the violent otherness that wreaked havoc on the city serves to seriously handicap the possibility of any empathetic connection.

In *The Rhetoric of Terror* Marc Redfield emphasizes the intensely mediated nature of the catastrophe that was 9/11. The sheer audacity of the attack served to highlight heretofore untapped feelings of vulnerability which were then hyper-magnified by the protracted treatment of the media. Redfield argues, however, that not all people were equally traumatized and, in fact, some people were not traumatized at all. Thus, he coins the term "virtual trauma" to designate the experience undergone by the majority, those not directly impacted by the events. The very mediated nature of the experience, however, guaranteed that the event did have a collective impact on a great number of people (as the terrorists fully intended). I contend that this dismissal of collective trauma is based on an emphasis on the more dramatic forms of trauma, ignoring its less powerful manifestations. And perhaps this type of trauma is more difficult to identify and/or address precisely because of its diffuse, but pervasive nature. In many ways, of course, the American people suffered a symbolic trauma, to which Redfield alludes. The panacea, it seems to me, may reside in discourses that are equally symbolic. Rebuilding and commemoration carry their own symbolism. Narratives, for their part, work on another level of symbolic signification. Thus, I examine various fictional discourses written in the aftermath of September 11 and their attempts to communicate the experience(s) of the collective. At the same time, I extrapolate on the connections a community may enact with its (imagined) landscape and the landmarks contained therein.

As such, the final chapter attempts a gambit of sorts, postulating the ways in which a city (and its buildings) might be thought of as an "other" with whom we can empathize, and the extent to which trauma suffered by that entity impacts the citizens with whom we share this particular space. The chapter is in some ways a foray into unexplored territory. Scrutinizing at the idea of a traumatized city, it also examines the ways that such violent upheaval and disruption may actually cause the citizenry of that city to feel "other" to themselves. To that end the chapter offers readings of Laird Hunt's *The*

Exquisite and Jonathan Lethem's *Chronic City*, analyzing how these narratives depict both the city's fall and its newfound, sometimes tenuous, equilibrium. They reflect the painful, uneven, and sometimes awkward incorporation of the traumatic event into an imagined sense of self and community, and the ways these are often inextricably entwined. As these novels make clear, the sheer absence of the Towers is compounded by a lingering sense of their continued "presence," in the imaginations and psyches of many Manhattanites. This feeling of doubleness—of simultaneously living in a past and present New York—is a theme explored in both texts. Novels may be particularly well-poised to communicate the communal/cultural effects of trauma, so I contend that examining fictional works depicting (and expressing feeling for) the wounded city enables a greater understanding of trauma in its secondary, but no less sinister, manifestations.

CONCLUSION

Reading these 9/11 novels, then, we should remain cognizant of how the text frames the other, how exactly the other is, or is not, delivered to us. If we accept Bennett's contention that 9/11 was a "global event" (and she is not alone in making this claim), then we might examine it as a symptom of the "problem of otherness" to which Palumbo-Liu alludes. Indeed, some have argued that the terrorist attacks were in part the result of poorer countries being repeatedly made aware of the sheer economic inequities through this new interconnectivity, their "otherness" now transmitted to them on a daily basis. Worth noting, as well, is the terrorists' use of elements of a globalized world (technology, visas, etc.) to perpetuate an act of violence. As such, we might say that the terrorists used elements of globalization as a means of undermining its supposed dominance. We might thus consider the attacks as a kind of reversal. Instead of overcoming otherness through the identification of sameness, the attacks can be framed as an assertion of otherness in the face of an onslaught increased homogeneity. It is in the light of these current conditions that I propose a reading of novels which identify the events of September 11, 2001, as their focal point, or at least whose plot construction is linked strongly to the notion of living "in the shadow of no towers." As noted, the event highlighted our "conditions of togetherness" at the same time that it put into relief the difficulty of negotiating issues of difference highlighted within these conditions.

If Butler puts forth a more theoretical prescription for the application of empathy, Bennett and Palumbo-Liu offer methods for identifying the ways in which art and literature respectively can open pathways to a greater understanding of the other and, perhaps more ambitiously, how these empathic impulses can lead to stronger communal and global interconnections. This study investigates the value of cosmopolitan sentiments, particularly empathy, in improving relations around the ever-shrinking globe. It also looks to literature written about 9/11, a global event, as the means of evoking empathy in the reader. I am interested in the ways that empathy is invoked and deployed and then, in turn, how it is responded to and received by various others. But to what degree, and in what ways, can empathy actually help address what Palumbo-Liu calls the "problem of otherness"? One of the principal challenges posed by the events of 9/11 is finding the middle ground between sameness and otherness. To adapt a phrase from Hartman, the reading of literature will not necessarily make us more empathic human beings, but it can teach us about the possibilities and the limitations of such engagement.

NOTE

1. Addressing this issue of categorization, Pöhlmann proposes the designation "9/11 fiction," removing the *post-* that has caused much confusion, as well as the inclusion of an overabundance of texts within the category.

Chapter One

Empathetically Unsettled

The Falling People in Art and Fiction

The sheer incomprehensibility of 9/11 is captured first in the images of jetliners sinking into skyscrapers, then in those of individuals leaping from immense structures into the blue September sky, and finally by the sight of those very structures imploding in upon themselves (to say nothing of the effect of the rapidity with which all of these events occurred). Of these now iconic images, the most heart-wrenching are the photographs of men and women plummeting to their horrific ends. As Elizabeth Anker observes, "Those deaths have so consumed the American cultural imaginary that almost any vulnerable form splayed against the backdrop of a skyscraper recalls them, raising the question of whether and why those images paradigmatically harness the affective texture of 9/11" (470–471). Anker's words are corroborated by the recent reaction (February 2012) to billboards placed around Manhattan, announcing the upcoming season of the television series *Mad Men*, including one on Seventh Avenue and 30th Street. The billboard depicts the figure of Don Draper, the protagonist of the series, in free fall tumbling headlong through open air. As some have noted, the image bears a startling similarity to the famous photograph taken by Richard Drew of a man falling to his death on September 11. This effect is further compounded by the placement of the billboard up against the windows of buildings, so that it appears as though the figure has leapt from one of the offices above. That such a seemingly innocuous gesture—the producers claimed to have been oblivious to thoughts of 9/11—could elicit such a response, more than a decade after the fact, attests to the continued emotional resonance of the falling people.

At the same time, this reaction to the billboard is typical of responses to representations of the falling people. The emotional upheaval and disruption caused by the viewing of these images meant that they often elicited a strong desire to censor and limit their presentation. Emblematic of the controversy surrounding the depiction of the falling people was the furor that erupted in the aftermath of the publication of the now-famous (or infamous, depending on one's perspective) photograph of a falling man taken by Richard Drew on September 11. The uproar aroused by the photograph, published in many of the nation's leading papers on September 12 but then removed from circulation, has been well-documented in an *Esquire* piece by Tom Junod, a documentary produced by the Canadian Broadcasting Corporation, and other works.[1] Those who decried the publication of the photograph argued that it was sensationalistic, exploitative, and morbid. It was a public appropriation of private suffering, an example of the worst kind of voyeurism. But the reactions to these images also make apparent the tension between knowledge and denial, between the realization that this can actually happen to a human being (including myself) and the refusal to believe that this can actually happen to a human being (especially myself). As Susan Lurie observes, "Images of these people compel identification because they are like us both in our everyday assumption of immunity from such attacks and in our new vulnerability to them. But for the same reasons, it is compelling to see the falling and the imagined dead in ways that assure us both of our difference from them and of safety restored" (45). As the victimized others of 9/11, they demand acknowledgment of the responsibility we owe them. We must thus resist the temptation to frame them as others, and empathically seek to understand how they are same. It is the objective of much of the art discussed in this chapter (including Drew's photograph) to (re)present the sameness of the falling people making empathic connection possible.

Drew's photograph also links us to the falling people by recalling an unwitting spectatorship. Many observers were shocked to discover that those were not birds or furniture, but actual people plummeting from the towers. Often the moment of recognition came in the final seconds, preventing any turning away. So a (secondary?) trauma was also inflicted on the viewer, the "traumatized spectatorship" of which Lurie speaks (51). In that way, the photograph recalls and freezes our own moment of shock and our roles as unsuspecting witnesses. The ambivalent relationship with the falling people thus raises questions as to the main purpose of the empathic urge. Because, complicatedly, our drive to empathize is also intertwined with our own reconceptualization of self and situation. As viewers, are we not, in some way, exploiting their vulnerability in order to assuage troubling intimations of our own? Might we not conceive that whatever we say about the dead is of little or no consequence to them? To what extent is this concern (fascination?)

more clearly directed towards the future dead (to which we all belong)? As Karen Engle observes,

> The call for decency and tastefulness in the documentation of this disaster is not innocent. *Show respect for the dead*, we are told. But the dead are not troubled by images of death and dying. It is the living who experience disruption, or rather, it is the memories of those lost, held onto desperately by the living, that are interrupted by the scenes of violence and death recorded on that day. Our task is to interrogate the narratives imposed on these images. (48, italics in text)

So we might consider whether objections to these representations emanate in part from an unwillingness to contemplate a situation in which one could well have been the figure of contemplation. In other words, the thoughts of sameness are so troubling that we seek after the differences that will help to sever this connection. A contemplation of these responses tells us a good deal more about the viewer than the viewed. In this vein, Andrea Fitzpatrick suggests that we should examine these images in order "to identify what one sees in them, how the perception of movement alters the subjectivity of those falling, and what the stakes are for the subjects involved, namely, those made visible and those who view them" (85). Both Engle and Fitzpatrick thus raise questions about the relationship between the living and the dead and, more precisely, what the former might owe the latter.

Writing two years after the event, Richard Drew tackles this very question. He admits to still being perplexed by the response to his photograph. As the author of another famous picture depicting a person *in extremis*—that of the dying Robert Kennedy moments after being shot in 1968—he attempts to make sense of the disparity in the popular responses to the two photographs. Drew concludes the picture of the falling man so troubles due to its capacity to elicit empathic identification; his photograph disturbs precisely because viewers do not perceive the falling man as other. In contrast, though somewhat counterintuitively, the photographs of Kennedy were deemed acceptable because, once more, the empathic connection was minimal or absent altogether. Regular readers did not share the senator's station in life, nor its celebrity, and therefore the connection was lost: "We felt we knew Bobby Kennedy, but we didn't identify with him" (Drew). In the case of the falling man, however, it is all about "personal identification." Drew suggests that "We look at [the photo] and we put ourselves in the jumper's place." The figure embodies our fear of random and meaningless death. The notion that one could make one's way to work on a beautiful September morning and less than two hours later be leaping to a horrific demise is both unbearable and inconceivable. Still, we are likely to admit, "That very well could have been me." Like the falling man, I make my way to work each day, giving little thought to the fact that it might be my last. In concluding, Drew points to the fruitless search to discover who this man was, but suggests the search was unnecessary since the anonymity of the individual dictates that "we already know the identity of the man in the picture." He ends his piece by declaring, "He is you and me" (Drew). The power of the photograph thus lies in its evocation of mutual vulnerability; in its telling the viewers more about themselves than they are willing to know. The photograph thus serves as delivery systems for communicating an essential sameness: human mortality and assailability. So we might consider whether it is not these very empathic impulses that viewers are seeking to repress or deny when they reject the photograph. One of the functions of art in this case is to reawaken our horror, to trouble whatever desensitization we may have embraced. After all, meaning is to be found in what we share with the victims, not what set us apart. A Drew photograph, a Skarbakka performance, a Fischl sculpture, or a DeLillo novel trouble because they force us to reassess, to rethink our own relationship with the occurrences of that day. In dealing with representations of trauma, however, the relationship between artist and viewer can sometimes be characterized as conflictual. As we shall see, viewers often object to the methods used to "trouble" them, often using accusing the artist of condescencion or of holding a superior attitude towards the audience and the subjects he depicts.

REPRESENTATION AND REACTION

In June 2005, in collaboration with Chicago's Museum of Contemporary Art, Kerry Skarbakka, a performance artist, executed a number of staged leaps from the roof of the museum. The captured images were intended to be included in a series entitled "The Struggle to Right Oneself." This type of performance was nothing new for Skarbakka, who had perfected the art of photographing himself in mid-fall, stumble, or plunge (with the use of wires, of course). In an interview given some time before his show, he told the *Chicago Sun-Times*, "Falling is such a metaphor for life in general. Mentally, physically, emotionally, from day to day, we fall." In its multiple iterations, Skarbakka's art seeks to illuminate our tenuous relationship with gravity, and grapples with this irrefutable existential fact. The difference this time was the response his performances elicited, particularly and not surprisingly, from citizens of New York City. In the wake of the 9/11 attacks, the images Skarbakka constructed were interpreted in only one way—as an intentional affront. "He just offended an entire city," said Chris Burke, a former employee of Cantor Fitzgerald whose brother was killed on September 11. Mayor Bloomberg himself called the project "nauseatingly offensive." In their outright condemnation, these objections assume a number of motives on the part of the artist: a heartlessness towards the victims of the tragedy his work recalls, an awareness of the pain he will cause and, most damningly, a willingness to stop at nothing to gain notoriety.

For his part, Skarbakka insists he was completely oblivious to the possibility that his works might be interpreted in this way. Even when he received hate mail and death threats, he claimed to be completely surprised by the reaction: "I did nothing wrong. I was doing a performance piece that had nothing to do with 9/11." In his defense, one notes that he had been creating such pieces long before the terrorist attacks. One nevertheless senses a degree of well-orchestrated disingenuousness on the artist's part. For whatever Skarbakka's intentions may have been, he should have anticipated the emotions these images would evoke. One might also suggest that he is guilty of over-identifying with the victims. First, this leaves him blind to the reactions of others. In seeking an empathic connection with the victims, he fails to empathize with the potential viewers, not considering how others might perceive his performance. Second, it leads him to authoritatively declare his ability to divine the motivations of the falling people. On that September morning, Skarbakka observes, the falling people "had released themselves completely. . . . They left the constructs of society, they left their family, they left their bills they had to pay. They left everything but the choice of what they were going to do in their final moments" (*Chicago Reader*). Here Skarbakka, like the relatives of some of the victims, invests the falling people with a degree of agency they may not have had. He implies that the victims had time to deliberate on their fates, and this small degree of choice, if this is what one wants to call it, brings some measure of affirmation. Skarbakka goes further, however, grasping this solitary action and transforming it into an individual's conscious statement on his or her own life. In Skarbakka's conceptualization, the falling people chose this moment to throw off the shackles of their mortal existence. These attributions, of course, serve to give his representations a positive spin. One should not interpret his performance as replicating the final moments of a life, a desperate plunge leading to a quicker, and hopefully less painful, death. In his version of things, he is depicting and celebrating an individual's existential comment on his or her entire life.

But the work created by Skarbakka was not alone in eliciting outrage and contention. In September 2002, Eric Fischl unveiled a bronze sculpture at the Rockefeller Center to commemorate the victims of 9/11. *Tumbling Woman* depicts a contorted naked female figure, the title signaling that spectators are meant to see her in free fall. The woman's head and upper back, however, come in contact with the ground, intimating to some viewers the dreadful moment of impact. Confronted with the exhibit, in this most public of spaces, observers were forcefully, and perhaps against their wills, reminded of the tragedy. Coming a year after the events, the sculpture ignited a firestorm of controversy, spread in no small part by a column in the *New York Post* by

Andrea Peyser entitled "Shameful Art Attack." Peyser calls the sculpture "violently disturbing" and criticizes the work for catching people unaware. She also accuses Fischl of second-hand witnessing since he was in the Hamptons, not Manhattan, at the time of the events. Finally, there is the suggestion that this type of art only serves to re-traumatize the onlookers. She quotes one individual who "felt as if he were being dragged against his will back to the terrible day" (Peyser). Due to this outcry, a spokeswoman for the Center apologized, and the sculpture was soon covered up, less than a week after its unveiling.

Words such as "attack" and "violently" are meant to suggest malice on the part of the artist who inflicts this experience on an unwary public and, in the process, evokes similar emotions to those felt on 9/11. Implicit within this accusation, and the language used, is the suggestion that artist and terrorist are involved in analogous activities. The critique of placing such a work in a public space, is also pivotal, since it depicts the artist as taking advantage of the unguardedness of individuals who chance upon the work. Just as many were shocked and dismayed to see people plunging to their deaths in the heart of a thriving metropolis, the argument infers, so too are residents caught unawares by this "violently disturbing" reminder. In this regard, an interviewer asks Fischl,

> In a place like Rockefeller Center, a sculpture assumes the character of a monument, rather than a work of art. Maybe there's a danger that if the work isn't seen as heroic or in some way celebratory, it seems inappropriate. Do you think you would have gotten the same response if *Tumbling Woman* had been exhibited in a less public forum, such as an art gallery? (Fishko)

The question infers a population not yet ready to address or deal with the darker sides of the tragedy. Instead, the interviewer suggests, they want art that will focus on "positive" aspects of that day, though these may be rare. In answering, Fischl recognizes that he did not correctly anticipate the reception of the sculpture. From his perspective, such art aids with the grieving process, helping individuals commune with their pain. He concedes, however, that he did not adequately gauge the rawness of the wound: "I misjudged that. I saw *Tumbling Woman* as a healing tool. One of the ways to heal is to make visible the things that hurt us, so they can be dealt with. I thought it would heal, but I was wrong" (Fishko). This raises questions about the role of the observer and the individual need to deal with trauma on one's own terms, one's own sense of preparedness. People expect to exercise a degree of agency in regards to re-visiting trauma; generally, they do not wish to have the trauma forced upon them by an artist who has deemed them ready, or believes they *should be* ready, to confront past horrors. As Schepen notes, "such a traumatic imprint of memory can . . . be too much for the perceiving subject to bear remembering. Its elicitation may cause them to experience the re-engaging with such memories through art as oppressive and confrontational" (136). Having judged himself ready, Fischl believed others to be as well. But instead of establishing a moment of connection with fellow survivors, and having his feelings about the tragedy corroborated, precisely the opposite occurs. He is guilty of presumption, and criticized for lacking empathy towards the victims as well as the survivors, since his attempts to share his feelings are deemed misplaced and potentially damaging.

Again, we might think about the ways in which creating art out of trauma, or about trauma, is an inherently presumptuous gesture. No matter the degree to which the artist claims to be merely exploring his or her own responses to the event, the work of art is still generally perceived as an attempt to master, to exert control over, that which troubles—if only because making sense of trauma means imposing some kind of meaning on the experiences of the victims. The very existence of the work of art would then seem to imply the artist's superior positioning in relation to his or her subject. Such inferences often lead viewers to draw conclusions as to the artist's "attitude" towards his or her subject. Indeed, Fischl suggests that the attribution of intent was key in the demand for the work's removal from the Rockefeller Center: "I was trying to say something about the way we all feel . . . but people thought I was trying to say something about the way they feel—that I was trying to take away something only they possessed. They thought I was trying to say something about the people they lost" (quoted in Junod, 4). But Fischl's seeking after empathy ("the way we all feel"), is interpreted as arrogance. Instead of identifying the work of art as an empathic gesture, viewers object not only to the artist presuming to know the experiences of the victims, but also believing he has some privileged access to their own experiences, and is thus at liberty to speak for them.

Much the same dynamic was present that same month when Sharon Paz presented her work, *Falling*, a series of cutouts of tumbling figures pasted onto the windows of the Jamaica Center for Arts and Learning in Queens. Public outcry erupted once more, with many labeling the work "insensitive," and it too was soon removed. In explaining her actions, Paz released the following press statement, choosing words quite similar to Skarbakka's:

> My interest was to explore the moment of falling to bring the psychological human side of the event, the moment between life and death. Falling is one of the basic fears of humans but in the same time we dream to fly. . . I found the images of people falling the most disturbing and wanted to deal with them, to overcome the fear, I felt the need to explore this moment, to bring out the reality within the memory that this event burns into our mind. (Paz)

Paz makes clear that the art is a means of "working through" her own experiences of the falling people. And like Fischl, she contends the best way to deal with one's fears and vulnerabilities is to address them directly, not evade or repress them. But we must also address the question of agency. It is not improbable that many artists possess temperaments that enable them to confront difficult and sometimes painful situations. Whether this actually occurs or not, in these instances the artist has clearly chosen to work on this piece at this moment. As such, he or she is positioned to address the issue on his or her terms, determining where and when such a confrontation will take place. This is often not the case for the unwitting observer who literally stumbles upon these works, so strategically placed in the public realm. We might thus consider the disparity existing between the artist and the observer in such situations, noting a certain power differential and its potential impact on reception of the work in question. In her defense, Paz argues that her art refocuses attention on aspects of the event obscured by its sheer magnitude, and, in large measure, by a self-imposed censorship that emerged in the wake of the attacks. Paz reacts to this latter impulse. For although she apologizes for causing any offense, she also affirms that the media and peoples' own discomfort have led to partial truth, repression, and denial: "I believe fear will not disappear if you will close your eyes" (Paz). Paz thus insists the artist bears a responsibility to unveil truths many would prefer left unseen.

But which truths does one expose, and when, and to whom? And who is best positioned to make such determinations? In such circumstances, the artist runs a very real risk of coming across as a self-appointed arbiter, as someone assuming a lofty position from which to dictate the proper course of action to others. For instance, Paz insists that her work provides access to a perspective not revealed in the news broadcasts: "I felt the media concentrated in using the building or nationalism for memory and left the human side out of the event. The work shows another perspective about the issue, the human side that makes people confront the hard reality" (Paz). Paz's language is instigative, intimating that people should be made to face a "hard reality" they are unlikely to seek out of their own volition. These words also suggest, however, that the artist possesses a strength and/or courage others lack, thus permitting her to face what others cannot. They cast the artist as the unflinching one whose task it is to make others see that which they would not. One difficulty is that this kind of "artistic courage" is often interpreted as either arrogance or insensitivity, or both. Explaining the decision to remove Paz's work, Queens Borough President Helen Marshall affirmed, "This is a time for healing, not opening wounds" (Bertrand, 5). The work is thus perceived as having precisely the opposite effect than that intended by the artist. Finally, whatever impulses we may have for understanding the situation are counteracted by more instinctual ones in which we seek to shield ourselves from the "hard reality" and search for the ways in which these things could never happen to us.

EMPATHIC UNSETTLEMENT: THE NEED (NOT) TO KNOW

Accusations of insensitivity imply the artist has neglected (or simply refused) to take into account the feelings of others. The same can also be said, however, for those critiques that label the artist as too sensitive, and thus unable to depict the harsh reality of the victim's experience. As such, the case of the falling people proves a litmus test of sorts. The extent to which we truthfully deal with the fact of the falling people reveals the degree to which we are prepared to consider our own vulnerability and mortality. Laura Frost, for her part, argues that the falling people are integral to the lessons we must learn from the event and that misrepresenting their experiences risks obscuring that which is most essential: "In treating 9/11 imagery gingerly, these artists and authors leave in place the myth of American invulnerability that the falling bodies call into question" (200).[2] Frost thus advocates for an unflinching gaze that will encompass all of the pain and suffering embodied in the figures of the falling people. She suggests that the repeated examination of the fate of these victims indicates a collective inability to incorporate them into a narrative and therefore any telling of September 11 is, by necessity, incomplete: "They continue to remind us that what we saw is not the whole story, and that the focus on sanctified images keep us from facing what lies beyond the frame" (200–201). The shattering and shocking violence of 9/11 is its principal and most elemental characteristic and representations of the event, the argument goes, must remain faithful and true to its most harrowing details. So when Frost speaks of "what lies beyond the frame," does she mean an unfiltered and unwavering gaze upon the full horror of the experience of the falling people? Must we search, then, for instances when artists have not treated the subject so "gingerly"?

Such examples are, admittedly, difficult to find.[3] Frédéric Beigbeder's *Windows on the World*, is one of the few novels to attempt a frank rendering of the events. Throughout the text, he strives to create images and observations that might communicate something of the traumatic experiences of the victims. At one point, for instance, he notes, "What no one said: everyone was vomiting" (119). Although this might strike the reader as a straightforward comment, it speaks to the fact that violence to the body is an unspoken element in many descriptions of 9/11. Blood, guts, shattered bones, bile, and vomit are rarely part of the discussion. Their evocation in Beigbeder's novel are part of the author's attempt to grasp something "beyond the frame," to use Frost's phrase. In the text, however, the author's alter ego repeatedly reflects on his inability to describe the full extent of the abomination: "Even if I go deep, deep into the horror, my book will always remain 1,350 feet below the truth" (119). The reference alludes to the fact that the writer will always remain alive and on the ground, at an insurmountable remove from those whose experiences he seeks to recreate. As such, any representation runs the risk of being treated as a falsehood. At the same time, Beigbeder claims to have no choice but to try and tell the story. As he acknowledges in his Author's Note, "The only way to know what took place in the restaurant on the 107th floor of the North Tower of the World Trade Center on September 11, 2001, is to invent it" (307). The knowing is never going to be more than imagining, because we can never truly *know*. But if he is going to invent the story of the last moments of these poor souls, he implies, then he will do his utmost to tell the whole and painful truth. For example, in a sentence found only in the original text, and not in translation, he notes: "Julian Schnabel observed that the sound the jumpers made when they hit was like melons exploding" (my translation, 155). There is a distinct brutality in this sentence, but also something amiss in its comparison of people to melons (no matter how accurate it might be). Attributing the metaphor to Schnabel, of course, relieves the author of some accountability. That Beigbeder excised the sentence from the translation, however, intimates some hesitation, and an awareness, as to how such a representation might be received and internalized by an American reading public. In the Author's Note, he recognizes that "merging fiction with truth—and with tragedy—risks hurting those who have already suffered" (307). Such a gesture reveals something about knowing the tolerance level of one's audience. Unlike Skarbakka and Paz, then, Beigbeder seems to have given some thought to the ways in which his novel might be received, particularly as a Frenchman writing about an American tragedy (I shall engage in a fuller discussion of the question of empathy in *Windows on the World* in chapter 3).

The desire to create these works of art and the corresponding desire to (self-)censor them are the two faces of trauma. The creation of the art depicting or representing the falling bodies and the visceral responses to them embody our conflicting responses to the event. As Dori Laub observes, "We are still involved with the ongoing struggle between an imperative need to know what it is that has happened to us all . . . and an equally powerful urge not to know, a defensive wish to deny the nature of the tear in the fabric of our shared lives" (204). Laub thus suggests that we are continually engaged in calibrating our responses to the traumatized other. For what precisely is to be gained from an unblinking and graphic depiction of these horrific ends? Is some unglimpsed truth made more accessible through an unflinching consideration of these brutal deaths? Is justice to the victims only truly done if one includes every aspect of their final moments? Does such an approach not risk alienating or distancing the reader/observer with an overabundance of otherness rather than allowing them to connect with the experience? What is, in fact, the best strategy for permitting the greatest degree of connection between the reader/observer and the experiences of those who died on 9/11? The challenge is finding an art that shakes us out of our complacency, makes us see the event anew, but does not cause us to turn away. It therefore should be an art that troubles, but not too much. It should be something "close enough" to the trauma to recall it, but not so similar as to evoke or elicit similar responses as those experienced during the original trauma. As such critiques of these representations often fall on one or the other side of the divide, either faulting a work for not doing justice to the event, or for resembling it so much that it actually re-traumatizes the viewer. Accusations are levied at these works for either being overly sensitive *or* not sensitive enough, for being too truthful *or* for providing a false representation, of offering a misguided alleviative *or* of re-opening wounds. In essence, these works are judged for *not finding the right balance*, for displaying too much or too little empathy towards their subject, or with those who will ultimately view the end result.

In language similar to Palumbo-Liu, Emy Koopman contends that a work of art concerned with representing trauma (in this case, a novel) is likely to elicit the same irresolvable and conflicting responses from its reader. Such a text, she argues, usually "evokes two opposed reactions, both of which are a result of the specific attempt to mimic trauma: the over-distanced reaction and the under-distanced reaction" (240). In Koopman's construction, an over-distanced reaction leads to under-identification, so that the experience of the traumatized other remains alien to me. An under-distanced reaction, on the other hand, leads to over-identification, so that I wrongfully feel or believe that I am "experiencing trauma [my]self through the upsetting [aesthetic] experience," and consequently fail or neglect to make a distinction between myself and the victim (240). So how does the artist alleviate or moderate these responses from the reader/viewer? What strategies is one to use to counteract the impression that one is advocating one or other of these responses? Again, like Palumbo-Liu, she suggests a vacillation between the two poles, never resting at either. In that way, both sameness and otherness are given their proper due. The task, in Koopman's opinion, is to carve out "a fruitful middle ground between a conventional engaging narrative which allows readers to understand the represented other, and disrupting techniques which make clear that understanding the other can never be complete" (237). Any genuine and successful interaction with the traumatic experience will make its awareness of its shortcomings clear, often literally demonstrating its inadequacies and inevitable failings. Endorsing a version of Dominick LaCapra's "empathic unsettlement," Koopman suggests that

> An ethical communication between text and reader in the representation of suffering would imply that the text offers the reader possibilities for empathy while confronting the reader with the fact that the suffering other remains other . . . there needs to be a balance between a narrative that engages the reader and techniques that disrupt (over)identification with the suffering character. (243)

Ideally, then, readers would continue to oscillate between these two poles, in a semi-permanent state of irresolution, satisfied (but not) with their limited (but still meaningful) empathic connection with the suffering other. In this vein, Koopman emphasizes that being an empathically engaged reader "does not simply mean trying to imagine [suffering] from the viewpoint of the victim . . . but taking responsibility for the failures, the perversities, in our imagination: our own weaknesses when we are faced with (imagining) the other's suffering" (248). In other words, a significant component of attempting to represent the traumatic experience is to acknowledge one's limitations and inabilities in creating an entirely satisfactory version of the event, and to recognize that the traumatized other remains on a plane never entirely accessible to one's empathic forays. Thus, Koopman contends, it is important that the writer visibly demonstrate his or her willingness to "let the other remain other."

Such a conclusion implies, however, that the author has still engaged sufficiently enough to give the reader a sense of the other's suffering, while refraining from appropriating, or assuming complete knowledge of, the other's experience. The artist must thus account for the very real possibility that he or she will be criticized for either empathizing *too little* or empathizing *too much*. This returns us to the impressions communicated by the work of art that lead the observer to form certain conclusions as to the adopted stance of the viewer towards the viewed. Such conclusions are derived, in part, from the agency the artist assumes in taking hold of the traumatic experience for his or her own ends. The artist's intentions are, as we well know, always open to misinterpretation. One way of countering such impressions, as we shall see, is to create an other through which the reader may observe empathy being deployed. Through this process, the artist illuminates the benefits and pitfalls of such an engagement, while also signaling to the reader/viewer his own awareness of the limitations of an empathic connection. The art forms of Skarbakka, Fischl, and Paz, however, do not easily allow for such an inclusion. Fiction, on the other hand, provides a forum through which multiple perspectives may be presented, and through which the empathic engagement of the author can be refracted through the engagement of others.

EXERCISING/MODELING EMPATHY

We should reflect, then, on how the work of art can model empathic engagement, both through its own imaginative interactions with the trauma, but also in depicting the reactions of others to the suffering other. Since we are predisposed to seeking that which distinguishes us from the victim (that would never happen to me because . . .), one role the artist might serve, then, is finding the means for pulling us back towards sameness and away from difference. In the literary text this is perhaps best effected by the creation of a surrogate through which the reader may witness the exercising of empathy and the obstacles inherent in the process. One might look, for instance, at the exercises undertaken by the narrator in Beigbeder's *Windows on the World* who seeks to physically reenact the last moments of the people trapped in, or seeking to escape from, the Twin Towers. In the process, the author's alter ego hopes to connect with the victims on an experiential level, but he never deludes himself about the level of sameness he establishes with the victims. Sitting on the 56th floor of the Tour Montparnasse, having placed himself in potentially the same hypothetically vulnerable position as those who died on 9/11, the narrator recognizes the limitations of his reenactment and of his imagination:

> If a Boeing were to crash below my feet, I would finally know what it is that has tortured me for a year now; the black smoke seeping from the floor, the heat melting the walls, the exploded windows, the asphyxiation, the panic, the suicides, the headlong stampede to stairwells already in flames, the tears and the screams, the desperate phone call. This does not mean that I do not breathe a sigh of relief as I watch each plane fly off into the white sky. (8–9)

In essence, the author concedes that though he may have the capacity to *imagine*, he cannot *know*. At the same time, he places some stock in the recreation of the physical circumstances the victims faced.

It is precisely this kind of activity that Alison Landsberg advocates in proposing a "radical politics of empathy," one that privileges an experiential approach to connecting with the traumatic past. She points to the Holocaust Museum and the manner in which its layout obliges its visitors to emulate some of the same actions and movements of those who were brought to concentration camps. Doing so, she argues, serves to elicit empathy from the visitor who is momentarily placed in the other's shoes. Landsberg similarly cites D-Day re-enactments and observes, "The popularity of these media events signals a widespread desire to experience history in a personal bodily way. They offer one way of making history into personal memory and thus advance the production of prosthetic memories" (74). Participating in these activities, Landsberg suggests, allows for the possibility of inhabiting a "transferential space" in which the viewer/participant "comes as close as possible to taking on the symptoms—the memories—of [the event] through which he did not live" (73). Beigbeder's narrator strives for a similar outcome by retrospectively placing himself in the physical circumstances of those with whom he seeks to empathize. At a later point in the novel, for instance, he notes that he "should have taken the stairs to see what it's like to walk down fifty-seven floors while the sky is on fire" (105). The premise is that in reenacting the bodily gestures of the victims he might also grasp something of their emotional reality. Though, as we have noted, he recognizes that all of his efforts will result in nothing more than a rough, and somewhat distanced, approximation. The presence of the text, however, would seem to indicate that he nevertheless has some faith in the possibility of connection.

And there appears to be some evidence for the possibility of a greater degree of empathic connection through the replication of physical gestures. Additionally, the mere fact of observing a behavior may elicit mental responses in the observer that resemble those of the observed. Freedberg and Gallese, an art historian and a neurophysiologist respectively, point to the existence of a Mirror Neuron System within the brain that triggers action simulation in response to actions observed: "the same neurons discharge when an action is observed as when it is executed" (200). This suggests that we are predisposed to feel with the observed. But we might take this a step further and suggest the possibility of such brain activity even when we are not witnessing the original event. In other words, reenacting for ourselves, or even observing (through reading) someone else in the process of reenactment, may trigger an empathic response. As Bennett observes, "For the memories of past subjects to be made vital—that is 'living'—in the full sense, they must in some way be inherited, opened up to empathic connection through their reembodiment in present imagination" (132). As such, one might presume that a work of art (a reenactment in its own right) might also instigate "embodied simulation" in the observer.

Similarly, Shoshana Felman suggests that the task of literary testimony is akin to an act of transmitting imaginative empathy. The role of the novelist becomes "to open up in the belated witness, which the reader now historically becomes, the imaginative capability of perceiving history—what is happening to others—*in one's own body*, with the power of sight (of insight) usually afforded only by one's own immediate physical involvement" (emphasis in text, 108). For not only is it often the case that the author models empathy for us (is this not the purview of the novelist, to know other minds?), or that as readers we are predisposed to empathize with the protagonist, but frequently the text provides characters who themselves are engaged in empathic behavior. Each of these approaches elucidates on the possibilities and limitations of such behavior. I will now examine two novels that specifically address the question of the falling people, but employ widely different strategies in their empathic engagement with the subject. The first, Helen Schulman's *A Day at the Beach*, presents a protagonist who seeks to meld her own experience with that of a falling person. The second, Don DeLillo's *Falling Man*, depicts an artist who explicitly reenacts the actions of the victims. Each novel seeks, through its chosen approach, to prompt the reader's own capacity for empathy in regards to the victims of the trauma.

Empathetically Unsettled 61

"I COULD HAVE BEEN HIM": SCHULMAN'S *A DAY AT THE BEACH*

Helen Schulman's *A Day at the Beach* is one of the few novels to fictionalize the witnessing of the falling people of 9/11 and its subsequent impact on the observer. The lives of Suzannah and Gerhard Falktopf are already in emotional turmoil as they awake in their Tribeca apartment on the morning of September 11. Their marriage is at the near-point of disintegration, and this is further complicated by the challenging care of their autistic son, Nikolai. Due to the proximity of their apartment to the World Trade Center (so close, in fact, that the North Tower obscures the view of its counterpart), they are shocked (and soon to be traumatized) witnesses to the events. Emerging from the shower, child in arms, Suzannah is assaulted by the vision played out before her:

> The apartment had big, industrial sized windows, so the changed world, the world still changing, stood as nakedly before Suzannah and her boy as they stood before it.
> "The birdies are on fire," Nikolai said.
> Suzannah watched the people fall from the wounded, burning tower, a huge gaping hole where the bomb must have gone off. There were several blazing human fireballs, then a man and a woman holding hands, the woman's skirt inflating like a flaming bell, an inverted tulip. (47)

A moment later Suzannah espies a falling figure whose impact on her will continue to grow throughout the day:

> And next, one man headfirst, in his shirtsleeves. Was that his tie floating behind him? He didn't take his tie off, thought Suzannah, before she put her hands over her son's eyes and turned him away. Why didn't he remove his tie before he dived? (47)

The falling man's tie serves as a symbol of his humanity, of the small decisions that make up a daily life. This particular detail captures Suzannah's attention and renders the man more fully human. The scene Suzannah helplessly observes sears "itself into her retinas" and she is troubled by her inability to unsee: "When she closed her eyes now, on the insides of her lids she saw that man diving, headfirst, tie flying . . . a scorched negative" (56). Having been caught unawares, Suzannah now has no choice but to work through that which she has witnessed. Despite the shock and surprise, however, she manages to focus on this particular detail, so that the event is fully absorbed as it unfolds before her. For this reason, her empathic connection with the falling man subtly (and subconsciously) solidifies throughout the day. He may be anonymous, but the tie positions him as an individual with a life of his own:

> She thought of *him*, the man in free fall framed outside her window, she thought of *him*, just hours before standing in front of his bathroom mirror, maybe in his briefs, maybe with a towel around his waist, tying his tie. Maybe his wife, or his girlfriend, maybe his boyfriend, had stood behind him, as she sometimes did with Gerhard—Gerhard hated wearing ties—and tied his tie for him. (72)

The passage is evocative, as the reader witnesses Suzannah's very real attempt to imagine a life for the victim, an existence entirely separate from her own. At the same time, the protagonist's moment of empathic imagination subtly shifts from expressing concern for the falling man and his partner, to a consideration of her failing marriage to Gerhard. One of the ironies with which the novel plays is the possibility that Suzannah experiences a greater degree of connection with the falling man than she does with Gerhard. The recollection of the moment between she and her husband is certainly not imbued with the same affection she accords to her burgeoning "relationship" with the falling man. In part, this is because the anonymity of the victim allows the protagonist to imbue him with the qualities that suit her needs. Throughout the day, Suzannah will relentlessly connect the experience of the falling man with her own. Such a strategy can, of course, lead to the establishment of common ground, and a greater understanding of the other. At the same time, however, we might consider the ways in which Suzannah's efforts to process her own situation come at the expense of any insight into the trauma undergone by the falling man. As Amy Coplan repeatedly warns, any attempt at ethical empathy is entirely dependent upon the maintenance of self-other differentiation (144). The more strenuously the observer seeks to identify with the other, however, the greater the risk of falling prey to "emotional contagion." In this scenario, an individual "catches" the emotions of another and subsequently imagines them as his own. When this occurs, Coplan concludes, the emotions of the other "are not experienced *imaginatively*; we simply experience them as our own. And cases of emotional contagion involve boundary confusion. When we 'catch' the emotions of another, it is as though we fuse with the other, losing our separate identity" (145). It should be noted that while there may be fusion, as Coplan suggests, the end result is typically a privileging of the viewer over the viewed.

This conundrum speaks to the situation faced by the novelist who seeks to represent trauma and offer the reader the possibility of empathic engagement with the experiences described therein. The author can either attempt to recreate the experience from the victim's perspective (requiring a fair amount of audacity with which few writers demonstrate). The alternative requires the writer to present the viewpoint of an observer who is confronted with making sense of the victim's trauma (a position in some ways analogous to that of both the author and the reader). The danger in the latter option lies in the real possibility of highlighting the traumatized spectatorship of the observer at the expense of the suffering other. Since novelists are necessarily, and somewhat naturally, concerned with the living, the dead often serve as impetus for change or to illuminate problematic aspects of the continuing life of the protagonist. The problem is further compounded through the possible implication (or merely the perception of implying) that the experience of the traumatized spectator is in some way commensurate to that of the falling person. Such a premium is placed on the identification of sameness as a prerequisite for empathy that its attainment is often stressed at the expense of allowing the empathized to preserve his difference.

Georgiana Banita, for instance, argues approvingly that in *A Day at the Beach* "a spiritual intimacy evolves that urges Suzannah as a witness to the jumper's suffering to also become a witness to her own" (95). This interpretation conceives of these actions as complementary—seeing the last desperate moments of an individual's life Suzannah awakens to her own plight. As noted, Schulman's protagonist is in such an emotionally volatile situation that she is perhaps more susceptible than most to connecting with the suffering other. At the same time, the reader may suspect that the author is using the emotionally laden historical moment as the means of instigating a consideration of the marital and domestic tribulations of her protagonist.[4] And Suzannah certainly exhibits a strong empathetic impulse throughout the novel, at one point imagining herself as someone in the South Tower hearing the messages to return to their offices (118), or later as a woman welcoming home the man she thought she had lost in the tragedy (120). Her strongest demonstrations of empathic engagement, however, are reserved for the falling man whose image and fate return to her throughout the day: "*I could be there*, she thought. I am lucky, lucky, lucky . . . I could have been *him*" (emphasis in text, 146). The recognition of sameness allows Suzannah to project herself into the victim's final torturous moments in the tower:

> What had he done in those final minutes before, that tiny bridge of time between the plane's impact and his jump, between all of his life and the astonishing, desperate feat he took to end it? Was there any time to contemplate his actions? Had there been a choice, even for just a second, of his doing anything else but? (173)

Suzannah comes to grips with the horror of the situation. She feels for him and yet, in the same moment a shift occurs so that their plights are now inextricably intertwined: "There must have been no choice for this man, this stranger that Suzannah now felt so inexplicably close to, closer to than anyone she actually knew really, anyone who still lived and breathed and populated this green Earth" (173). These words ring strange. Can Suzannah truly believe that her strongest human connection is now with a man she has never known and who lies dead in the rubble of the World Trade Center? Whether Schulman intends this or not, her protagonist certainly appears to project her own feelings onto the falling man, so that she is no longer understanding him but gaining greater clarity about herself. As the novel progresses, then, it becomes increasingly difficult to determine whether the protagonist's empathic impulse is engaged in order to connect with the situation of the victim or simply as a means of gaining some solace for her own troubled situation. Banita argues that Suzannah's "passionate rapport is energized precisely by the jumper's anonymity, so starkly opposed to familiar others" (104). But one might wonder whether it is precisely this anonymity that gives Suzannah *carte blanche* to attribute whatever emotions best suit her needs, and thus over-identify with the victim (or what Koopman refers to as an under-distanced reaction).

By the end of the novel, the falling man interjects himself into Suzannah's thoughts so that she has now become a passive receptacle: "*He swan-dived out of the blazing building and into her head*" (182). In a turnaround, the empathic connection has not led to her entering the experience of the victim (though she consciously attempts to do so), but rather it is he who enters *her* mind and becomes part of *her* experience: "*He was in her head and she was no longer alone*" (182). The novel certainly suggests a melding of sorts: "*They were falling together forever down the black hole inside her head*" (183). The reader is now witness to an involuntary and passive empathic engagement, since whatever self-other differentiation may have existed has been completely eroded. Banita, for her part, reads the novel differently, investing Suzannah with a degree of agency. She argues that Schulman's protagonist

> maintains a relationship to the falling man that fuses a sense of intimacy with the ethically serene acceptance of his death as the ultimate Other. Rather than reconcile herself to this loss, she continues to confer with him while remaining aware that her communication is mere ventriloquism. By entering into an imaginary 'duet' with the falling man, Suzannah thus concedes that her responsibility to him will never end or be fulfilled. (106)

Banita is right to point to "a sense of intimacy" in the empathic processing of Suzannah who seems, in fact, to exult in her witnessing, as though she alone was meant to connect with the doomed man. But Banita also contends that Suzannah is conscious of her ventriloquistic tendencies, thereby recognizing the extent to which the experience with the falling man is *not* mutual. Nothing in the text, however, suggests such an awareness. Schulman's novel does illuminate one obvious reality—the dead are, and will forever remain, inaccessible to our probing. If this is so, perhaps there is no novel that can be written about the falling people, only about our responses to them.

In encompassing the image of the falling man—the symbol of the trauma that was September 11—does the novel not go too far in divesting it of its terrible beauty? The answer to this question depends on whether we interpret Suzannah's act of empathy as aiding to make sense of the trauma or, and this seems more likely, in merely helping her come to terms with her crumbling marriage. The last time Suzannah thinks of the falling man, she has just thought about leaving Gerhard. She thinks to herself, "I am defeated . . . I am lost." This observation immediately leads into words from the falling man: *"We are defeated, he said to her as they fell, hand in hand now, in tandem. We are defeated and we are lost"* (200, italics in text). A degree of commonality is established, seemingly presenting Suzannah's "defeat" as in some way commensurate and "in tandem" with that of the falling man. What her "fall" shares with the plunge of the man in the tie, however, is far exceeded by that which it does not.

Suzannah meets the principal criteria for successful empathy through her openness to the possibility of connection. Witnessing the final seconds of the falling man's life, she does not turn away, but rather actively engages with the experience of the suffering other. But truly successful empathic engagement, it seems, is contingent upon one's ability to "let the other remain other." Ethical empathy, as Koopman suggests, "entails an affective sensitivity to the other's experience without ever confusing the other with oneself" (243). Similarly, Molly Abel Travis emphasizes the importance of "narrative distancing" as a strategy to keep readers at a remove from the trauma, so that self-other differentiation remains in place and that "too easy an empathy" with the protagonists is circumvented. Such narrative distancing is largely absent from *A Day at the Beach*, however. The wall separating empathizer from empathized is almost completely broken down so that empathizer and empathized have melded into one entity. So we might consider whether Schulman's novel falls short of achieving the right balance. Suzannah's complete connection with the falling man suggests there is no unsettlement, no lasting recognition of the ways his life is different from hers. The text reaches a level of sameness rendering the falling man's death—his otherness—almost void of its own meaning. The reader does witness empathy in action, but is left to witness a private moment, devoid of any larger significance. In the case of Delillo's *Falling Man*, as we shall see, the reader is placed at two removes from the falling people. The first layer of interference is the figure of Falling Man who reenacts the trauma of the victims. It is in seeking to make sense of Falling Man, that a principal character comes to empathize with both the falling people and those who witnessed their terrible fates.

DELILLO'S *FALLING MAN*

No American author seemed better suited to write the definitive 9/11 novel than Don DeLillo. His previous work, with its emphasis on terrorism, the power of the media, and the machinations of government, presaged the events and their aftermath. And just as the catastrophe was said to resemble a disaster film, many aspects of that day had already appeared somewhere in DeLillo's oeuvre. Even the cover of *Underworld* depicts the Twin Towers, their upper floors shrouded in clouds, the image of a dark bird almost ominously flying in their direction. No doubt DeLillo himself was aware of these readerly expectations, and this may have been cause for some trepidation on the author's part. It comes as no surprise, then, that *Falling Man* is a self-conscious and frequently metafictional text that focuses on survival *and* on the question of representation in the shadow of trauma. DeLillo gave some indication of the novel he might write in a piece published in *Harper's* in December 2001 entitled "In the Ruins of the Future." In the essay, he depicts a destabilized community searching for meaning, and outlines the ameliora-tory narratives constructed by the media and the government, all the while underlining their inherent insufficiencies. "We could not catch up with it," DeLillo observes (Ruins, 39). He then delineates the writer's role in relation to this national trauma: "The writer begins in the towers, trying to imagine the moment desperately. Before politics, before history and religion, there is primal terror. People falling from the towers hand in hand. This is part of the counternarrative, hands and spirits joining, human beauty in the crush of meshed steel" (DeLillo, Ruins, 39). DeLillo first broaches the topic of the falling people as a way of invoking the "primal terror" of that day, and ponders how their fates might contribute to a counternarrative to dominant reconstructions of 9/11. Six years later, *Falling Man* is his answer to that question.

The novel returns the reader to the world evoked in the article beginning with its protagonist, Keith Neudecker, emerging bloodied from the fatally wounded North Tower. Ash-covered, he stumbles to the apartment of his estranged wife, Lianne, and their son. From this point on, the novel sets out to catalogue a variety of responses to the event. In muted fashion, replicating the shock that follows trauma, the text provides the reader with insights into the manner in which the pain and suffering at the epicenter of the trauma ripples through and impacts the lives of a wide range of people. Keith begins an affair with a fellow survivor, eventually turning to the sureties of tournament poker. Lianne exercises her anger by physically assaulting a neighbor for playing music "located in Islamic tradition" too loudly. Their son and his friends scan the skyline for more attacks from "Bill Lawton." As one character observes, "Everything now is measured by after" (138). It may be too early to know what the new narratives may be, but these characters strive to create them nonetheless.

One significant obstacle is that sense-making abilities have been compromised as a result of the trauma. DeLillo subtly alludes, for instance, to the repressed portions of Keith's psyche. Throughout the novel, thoughts of Rumsey intrude upon the narrative (for it is only in the final pages that the reader learns of his death in the World Trade Center and of Keith's futile attempts to rescue him). And in the interactions between Keith and his fellow-survivor, Florence, the text affords glimpses of the lingering effects of the event: "If I live to be a hundred I'll still be on the stairs," she observes (57). In these ways, the novel effectively communicates the repetitive aspects of trauma and the shock that incapacitates the victim's ability to compartmentalize the experience. As Cathy Caruth observes, "the trauma consists not only in having confronted death but *in having survived, precisely, without knowing it.* What one returns to in the flashback is not the incomprehensibility of one's near death, but the very incomprehensibility of one's own survival" (64). The novel's conclusion further reveals the recursive loop in Keith's mind. The reader returns with him to the moment when the airliner strikes the tower, the ensuing chaos, and the gruesome horror of Rumsey's death. Additionally, the reader comes to realize just how closely Keith's traumatized state is linked to the fates of the falling people. Having failed to save his friend, he stares out the office window in time to catch sight of a man "falling sideways, arm out and up, like pointed up, like why am I here instead of there" (244). Keith's pain is thus aggravated by the vision of the falling man whose presence encapsulates the ineffable aspects of the event—a fact underlined by a shirt Keith sights "arms waving like nothing in this life" (246).

The last chapter also suggests, however, that no matter how much time elapses, the repressed always returns. For whereas the beginning of the novel finds Keith staggering away from the ruins of the towers, the ending plunges him once more into the building in the moments just prior to, and immediately after, the attacks. *Falling Man* thus enacts the idea that trauma is only understood retrospectively, if at all. Choosing the falling people as a focus of his novel, DeLillo reveals a desire to touch the awful truth through them. The narratives constructed after September 11, whether patriotic, political, or therapeutic, emphasize certain elements (those that help us cope and survive)—often to the exclusion of others (those that trouble). The images of the falling people (real as well as fictionalized) disturb because they offer no redemption, *and* because they resist incorporation into a soothing narrative. They are an explicit example of trauma's resistance to metaphor. As such, DeLillo's novel attests to the limitations of *any* counternarrative. The return to trauma at the conclusion of *Falling Man* makes clear that the intervening years (and the coping strategies contained therein) have helped only marginally, with memories of trauma continuing to fester within the community.

ART AS TERROR? TERROR AS ART?

The novel's title also refers to a performance artist named Falling Man whose presence in the text reflects a preoccupation with the falling people, and with the justification of any aesthetic reconstruction of those horrors. The character of David Janiak emphasizes the inevitable shortcomings of any representation of trauma, but also the desire to represent that is an inherent component of trauma. Falling Man leaps from buildings adopting stylized poses that recreate the images of the falling persons, briefly presented by the media on 9/11, quickly repressed, then relegated to the hinterlands of the Internet. At the same time, DeLillo's use of the Falling Man allows him to explore issues related to the aesthetic representations of this private/public trauma, but also to defuse the criticism leveled against representers of that trauma. The performance artist serves as a device through which DeLillo can acknowledge the potential controversy elicited by any work of art that chooses 9/11 as its subject, *including* his own novel. The author makes his awareness of such questions known when he metafictionally inserts a reference to an academic panel at New York's New School: "Falling Man as Heartless Exhibitionist or Brave New Chronicler of the Age of Terror" (220). Such a question could just as well be applied to the writer of the novel as to his fictional (re)creation.

In this way, of course, DeLillo's Janiak bears a strong resemblance to Kerry Skarbakka, though the reader is never afforded (as one is with the real-life artist) a rationalization or explanation for his performances. Because Falling Man is not a typical performance artist, since he violates the contract that normally exists between performer and audience. Typically, the audience is aware they are about to witness a performance (in fact, they have often paid for the pleasure). In essence, they implicitly give permission to the performer to do whatever he or she wishes (within the bounds of reason, though this may sometimes be open to debate). At the same time, this may defuse the performance of some of its power. For instance, Skarbakka's performances were announced and advertised, therefore eliminating the element of surprise/shock, at least for the majority of the audience. Such is not the case with Janiak, who in fact turns down an offer for just that kind of performance (222). Janiak intends to shock and surprise because this was part of the original experience he is replicating. It is that initial emotional impact, combined with the sight of his dangling figure, that will bring the morning of September 11 rushing back to the viewer. In other words, the element of "complicit discomfort" in which the spectator takes part is present in Skarbakka's performance, but absent from those of DeLillo's Falling Man. This can be explained as a desire to instigate a "primal" response on the part of the observers, something that more closely reproduces the reactions of the stunned onlookers from that September morning. Significantly, then, it is not Keith who beholds Janiak's performances, but rather Lianne who engages in the act of retrospective witnessing. Her first encounter occurs ten days after 9/11:

> He'd appeared several times in the last week, unannounced, in various parts of the city. Suspended from one or another structure, always upside down, wearing a suit, a tie and dress shoes. He brought it back, of course, those stark moments in the burning towers when people fell or were forced to jump. (33)

It seems clear that the objective of these performances is to shock the spectator, as he forces his audience to contemplate an image that has been erased from public view. The artist thus enacts an aggressive return of the repressed. Not surprisingly, then, Lianne's initial instinct is to flee the scene: "I had to get out of there," she tells her mother (33). Like many of the other onlookers, she feels assailed by what she perceives. Janiak, like the artists mentioned earlier, appropriates public space to force an engagement with his performance. Caught unawares, the audience is anything but receptive, and Lianne communicates the quality and nature of its response: "There were people shouting up at him, outraged at the spectacle, the puppetry of human desperation, a body's last fleet breath and what it held" (33). At that moment, the audience treats Falling Man as little more than a heartless exhibitionist, while Lianne's words signal the source of the discomfort—Falling Man presents an intimate moment, recreating the sheer vulnerability and desperation of one of the falling people. He has transgressed, choosing a victim's final moments as the impetus for his performance. One senses the despair of those unsure as to what precisely they are witnessing, trapped somewhere between current and past instances of anguished spectatorship. In this vein, John Duvall argues that "Falling Man's full performance is not a representation of the horror of 9/11, it is the horror of 9/11 itself" (162). Lianne's account certainly cites the performer for doing violence to the memory of the victims, but also to the already fragile psyches of those who survived the attacks.

Perhaps empathizing with Lianne's discomfort, a number of critics interpret Janiak's performances as deliberate assaults on the audience, as attempts to force members of his audience to relive those moments and thus retraumatize them. In this iteration, Janiak's actions are formulated as confrontational, violent and aggressive. And a correlation is thus implicitly established between the artist and the hijackers, the "performers" on September 11.[5] In the past, DeLillo has expressed a sort of writerly envy for terrorists who have replaced writers, and now appear to be the ones most capable of effecting social change.[6] And *Falling Man* is replete with terrorists. Among the nineteen 9/11 terrorists, we are privy to some of the thoughts of Mohammad Atta himself, but mostly to those of Hammad, a fictional terrorist also aboard Flight 11 that will crash into the North Tower. Additionally, the lover of Lianne's mother is one Martin Rudinger, whose real name may be Ernst Hechinger, and who may or may not have been a member of a leftist terrorist group (Baader-Meinhoff?) in Germany during the 1970s. Martin is now an art dealer and so the parallels between aesthetics and terror, a cherished subject of DeLillo's, are clearly established in the novel. The structure of *Falling Man* further strengthens this thematic connection with a proper name appended to each of its three parts. Parts I and II are entitled "Bill Lawton" and "Ernst Hechinger" respectively, while Part III bears the name of David Janiak. The linkage between these names is not immediately obvious, though each of these figures might be said to foment a degree of terror in their audiences, whether they be children, the German people, or simply passersby. Indeed, in a novel concerned with terrorists of all shapes and sizes, real and imagined, Janiak appears as one more iteration. His recreation of the falling people makes the link between art and the products of terror explicit. As noted, the observers of Janiak's "act" are unaware that they are about to be subjected to a performance they will be unable to *un*see. Thus they experience an initial shock not dissimilar to that of the 9/11 witnesses who were unsure that they were seeing living people plummet to the ground (many mistook the falling bodies for birds or furniture). Anker therefore asserts, "there is little doubt that the experiential vertigo and psychic fragmentation [Falling Man] cultivates enacts a form of terrorization" (477).[7] Having deemed the action the result of a desire for controversy and celebrity, she neglects to consider the possibility that such a gesture may be an attempt at invoking both individual and communal connection with the event.

Additionally, Anker deems that the intimations of a suicidal/sacrificial wish only confirm the solipsistic (and therefore self-serving) nature of Falling Man's actions. Late in the novel, Lianne stumbles across Janiak's obituary and discovers that "Plans for a final fall . . . did not include a safety harness" (221, 223). This might suggest an effort on the artist's part to truly approximate, or get as close as possible, to the experiences of his subject. Anker, however, construes Falling Man's intended final performance as a literal wish "to execute rather than merely enact his own suicide, meaning that his creations had all along been rehearsals of a pending death" (477). This interpretation suggests that *the* driving motivation is the artist's self. From this perspective, the gesture is seen as entirely egocentric with little or no thought given to its impact on the audience (beyond the recognition the artist seeks). In other words, the act is committed purely as an exercise in self-fulfillment, and is devoid of any communal intent. Anker pursues her argument about the preoccupation with self, contending that through "public spectacles that aggressively revisited the scene of terror" Falling Man "aimed to defray his own immanent unmaking, or to displace his finitude into fantastic illusions of exemplarity and consequence" (477). She thus identifies these performances as self-serving rather than altruistic. The artist is seen as entirely delusional, with an overblown sense of his own import. In this argument, short shrift is given to the notion that performer and audience might be involved in a reciprocal act. Again, we have returned to the place where the artist's intentions come into play. If, indeed, the artist is performing these actions solely for his benefit—preparatory assays for his own suicide—then these performances are nothing more than assaults on an unwary public. If, however, we conceive of these gestures as communal in nature, then they take on an entirely different hue.

THE ARTIST AS EMPATHIC CONDUIT

For might there not also be an intended positive outcome to these performances? Could Janiak's falls not simply be attempts to physically approximate and thus emotionally connect with the experiences of the falling people? In other words, can his performances not be seen as delivering sameness rather than otherness. This possibility is emphasized when the reader learns that Janiak worked with an ill-fitting harness and sub-par materials and, as such, actually suffered some degree of pain during each performance, bringing him one step closer to the traumatized other (220). Just as Beigbeder's narrator acknowledges that all of his efforts can never get him close enough to that which he seeks to imaginatively recreate ("my book will always remain 1,350 feet below the truth"), Janiak's actions lead the reader to infer that the performance artist also recognizes the inevitable shortcomings of his undertaking. His orchestrated "jumps" can only ever be pale simulations of those desperate and final moments undergone by the victims. Following this logic to its bitter end, the only scenario in which the artist attains a true point of connection is one in which a plane actually crashes into the Tour Montparnasse, or in which Falling Man leaps without a harness. The artist's attempts to "faithfully" recreate the victim's experience, however, are also meant to serve as objects of contemplation, providing the spectator/reader a degree of access to the victimized other.

At the same time, DeLillo's novel openly affirms its ambivalent and uncertain position in regards to such an enterprise, exposing its own urge to know while simultaneously recognizing the impossibility, or at least the inadequacy, of such knowledge. In fact, the novel warns against any interpretive assuredness through its consideration of the paintings of the Giorgio Morandi, the other aesthetic form accorded some prominence in *Falling*

Man, to which references appear in all three parts of the novel (12, 45, 111, 209). Lianne's mother owns two pieces, gifts from Martin, and so Lianne has had ample time to consider and analyze them. Her meditations are revealing and might serve, considering the statement's early placement in the text, as instructions (or at least qualifications) to the reader:

> What she loved the most were the two still lifes on the north wall, by Giorgio Morandi, a painter her mother had studied and written about. These were groupings of bottles, jugs, biscuit tins, that was all, but there was something in the brushstrokes that held a mystery she could not name, or in the irregular edges of vases and jars, some reconnoiter inward, human and obscure, away from the very light and color of the paintings. *Natura morta.* The Italian term for still life seemed stronger than it had to be, somewhat ominous even, but these were matters she hadn't talked about with her mother. Let the latent meanings turn and bend in the wind, free from authoritative comment. (12)

This passage is worth placing next to one describing Lianne's responses to Falling Man's performance:

> But the fall was not the worst of it. The jolting end of the fall left him upside-down, secured to the harness, twenty feet above the pavement. The jolt, the sort of midair impact and bounce, the recoil, and now the stillness, arms at his sides, one leg bent at the knee. There was something awful about the stylized pose, body and limbs, his signature stroke. But the worst of it was the stillness itself... (168, ellipsis in text)

Lianne's emphasis on Janiak's "stillness" creates a strong link between his performances and Morandi's paintings, the *still*-lifes, putting into question the viewer's capacity to interpret them. The last sentence of the first passage advocates, quite unequivocally, that readers should relinquish any striving after certainty, and simply accept the "mystery [they cannot] name" at the heart of these works. At the same time, the sentence hints at the existence of "latent meanings" to which the observer/reader might gain access, if only he or she resists the urge to categorize or draw conclusions. Each passage makes a point, however, of accentuating the significance of stillness. In the first, the text explicitly calls attention to the Italian term strengthening the allusions to mortality. The subject of the still life exists perilously in a timeless space between life and death. The painting's trajectory away from light and color into shadow, and the use of the word "ominous," imply Lianne's own movement towards darker matters—of which she does not speak to her mother. The second passage, meanwhile, suggests that it is in fact the static quality of Janiak's work that causes his audience the greatest discomfort. But why should this aspect be so troubling? No doubt this is due in part to the viewer's feeling of gazing upon the most intimate and vulnerable of moments. But the images of the falling people unsettle the viewer, as Karen Engle argues, because they freeze time, allowing for unfettered contemplation, but also for a potentially endless expansion of the imagination. As Engle notes, "This arrested moment, or movement between, hints at something far more terrible than death—something perpetual and incomplete" (16). The horrific significance of these images, that became still-lifes themselves, is amplified by the knowledge that death is imminent. The viewer is thus trapped in a state of endless anticipation, ever-aware of the violent ends awaiting those depicted. As Frost observes, "These haunting figures remain forever falling but never having fallen" (181). This "stillness," however, is something likely felt by the spectator but not the falling person and, as such, highlights the role played by the spectator. In many ways, then, *Falling Man* is more concerned with the reception of the trauma work than its representative qualities. In recreating the conditions of witnessing, Janiak may be violating the implicit performer-spectator contract, but the full impact of his gesture also depends on simulating the lack of control that witnesses felt that morning. In fact, the strong reaction to, and rejection of, his performances (and all other works depicting the falling people) emanate from an objection to being returned to such a vulnerable position. At the same time, the performance creates a simulacrum of the trauma allowing the spectator a moment of ambivalent, and differently troubled, reflection not afforded the original witnesses. This then becomes an opportunity for the spectator to recognize a vulnerability shared with both the victims and the witnesses.[8]

These performances, as Landsberg also suggests, "might actually install in us 'symptoms' or prosthetic memories through which we didn't actually live, but to which we now . . . have a kind of experiential relationship" (82). We might extrapolate, then, that the spectators experience Janiak's fall as in some ways their own—re-embodying to use Bennett's terms—and, in the process, move closer to "sensing" the experience undergone by some of the victims. In this vein, Sophie Oliver extols the virtues of performance art over other forms of representation. The problem with photographic representations, she insists, is that they remove the trauma from its context and thus handicap the viewer's ability to connect. These visual representations, Oliver suggests, are "frequently represented as anonymous icons of atrocity, while at the same time provoking an array of visceral, distancing responses that might range from fear and disgust to, in some cases, enjoyment" (121). The performance, on the other hand, recreates physical circumstances allowing the spectator to more genuinely connect with the originating experience. A performance, such as that of the Falling Man, allows for not only a cognitive, but also a physiological or bodily, *return to the event*:

> What is potentially "ethical" about this way of seeing is not only its call for a sense of response-ability towards the corporeal subject being viewed . . . but also, and crucially, the demand for the spectator's own self-conscious relation

to the (re)presentation, and the acknowledgement of his or her own embodiment as a performative presence in the moment of witnessing the other's trauma, even in cases of distant or mediated viewing. (Oliver 120)

In other words, performance art imposes and requires a greater degree of involvement from the spectator who, indeed, becomes part of the performance. And since the performance cannot exist without the audience, the latter becomes complicit in its playing out.

Oliver also points to the ephemeral quality of performance that further replicates some aspects of the traumatic experience. "Like trauma," Oliver observes, "performance is unrepresentable, uncontainable. The comparison is at once crude and potentially fertile; existing only in the moment of its happening, performance is always an enactment of loss, of the impossibility of retrieving the past" (125). That Janiak is not interested in being photographed or in turning his performances into publicized events, for instance, suggests that he intends his work to be ingested and analyzed in precisely this way. In essence, the performer interpellates the members of his audience to engage in unfolding and coming to terms with the trauma of the falling people—an action of which his performance is but the initiatory moment. As Oliver notes, the performance of trauma is "at the same time a political and ethical moment—political because it acts out a moment of rupture, ethical because it calls upon its spectators to join in the rehearsal of loss" (125). In these circumstances, spectating becomes an ethical obligation. Indeed, we might consider the ways in which the spectator becomes a receptacle, a kind of "preserver" of the performance:

> [Lianne] tried to connect this man to the moment when she stood beneath the elevated tracks, nearly three years ago, watching someone prepare to fall from a maintenance platform as the train went past. There were no photographs of the fall. She was the photograph, the photosensitive surface. That nameless body coming down, this was hers to record and absorb. (223)

Lianne's recollections suggest that Falling Man's performance has imprinted itself onto her memory/psyche. More important, the passage implies that Lianne has assumed a degree of ownership over, and some complicity with, the experience. She is the photosensitive material onto which the performance has left its mark; the experience now part of her.

In contrast to *A Day at The Beach*, then, *Falling Man* does not put forth a character who achieves symbiosis with the traumatized other. Lianne's empathy is a great deal less self-involved and more troubled. In fact, Janiak remains a mystery to Lianne:

> The man eluded her. All she knew was what she'd seen and felt that day near the schoolyard, a boy bouncing a basketball and a teacher with a whistle on a

string. She could believe she knew these people, and all the others she'd seen and heard that afternoon, but not the man who'd stood above her, detailed and looming. (224)

The passage illuminates one of the painful ironies of the falling people which is that the very thing that would seem to permit understanding—their accessibility—is in fact that which prevents it. Perhaps more interesting, however, is the extent to which Falling Man's impact translates for Lianne into concern for others rather than (her)self. She does not contemplate her own vulnerability, but rather that of others. The performance causes Lianne's mind to flash back to her husband and his colleagues, exposing a desire to understand the horrors Keith and others lived through that day: "But why was she standing here watching? Because she saw her husband somewhere near. She saw his friend, the one she'd met, or the other, maybe, or made him up and saw him, in a high window with smoke flowing out. Because she felt compelled, or only helpless, gripping the strap of her shoulder bag" (167). Falling Man thus creates a situation that enables the observer to empathize with the falling people *and* their witnesses. Viewed from this perspective, the performer models empathy for others. His actions cause Lianne's thoughts to move outward in an encompassing gesture of empathic communion with her fellow spectators.

Lianne's second experience of witnessing, in which she is present for Janiak's preparations, reveals this fellow-feeling even more clearly. Standing below the train tracks, unable to pull herself away, she anticipates how Falling Man's performance will be incorporated and internalized by others:

> She thought of the passengers. The train would bust out of the tunnel south of here and then begin to slow down, approaching the station at 125th Street, three-quarters of a mile ahead. It would pass and he would jump. There would be those aboard who see him standing and those who see him jump, all jarred out of their reveries or their newspapers or muttering stunned into their cell phones. (164–65)

In this moment, Lianne experiences a bout of anticipatory empathy for the members of the audience who are about to be waylaid by Janiak's performance. She actively imagines the respective experiences of the passengers on the train as it moves past Falling Man at various stages of his performance. At that moment, she is no longer simply watching the Falling Man, she is also watching others watch. In the process, Banita argues, Lianne and other spectators are accorded the possibility of "see[ing] beyond their own trauma, but also beyond the falling man himself, to an ethically potent acknowledgment of the presence of other viewers and their reactions" (71). Empathy here becomes the means of connection for all those trying to make sense of the falling people—Falling Man's performance has simply served as the catalyst (which may, in fact, have been his intention all along). The performance engenders a communal response through its recreation of the traumatic episode under different circumstances, allowing for greater self-reflection and connection with others. Janiak's reenactment reflects back onto the traumatized community that which the falling people most fully embody or represent—an all-encompassing sense of their own vulnerability. At the same time, individual members of Janiak's audience are made to recognize that they are not alone in experiencing these feelings, and that a bond exists, stronger that initially believed, between themselves and their fellow spectators.

And Lianne's moments of witnessing often seem to possess a communal quality of their own which reveals itself, for example, during her very first encounter with Falling Man. Looking up at his still figure, she thinks, "It held the gaze of the world. . . . There was the awful openness of it, something we'd not seen, the single falling figure that trails a collective dread, body coming down among us all" (33). The use of "we" and "us" certainly implies an awareness of a community recovering from a collective experience. Lianne's reaction includes an additional element—"something we'd not seen"—suggesting that the performance is contributing in some way to the recovery from the collective trauma. The text thus privileges the communal powers of the art work, then, over its ability to accurately reflect the experiences of the traumatized other. In contrast to her inability to relate to the Falling Man, for example, Lianne feels that she "knows" her fellow spectators and "all the others she'd seen and heard that afternoon" (224). While Falling Man remains the enigma at the center of his art, the dynamics of the performance, however, make it so that Lianne is able to connect with her fellow spectators and thus the traumatized community as a whole. The performance thus not only permits the spectators to see the event anew, but from a fresh different perspective. Eric Fischl's defense of his own aesthetic practices might well serve in justifying Falling Man's actions as well: "It's not about necessarily witnessing firsthand that makes the experience. Picasso wasn't at Guernica when it happened; Goya wasn't there on the firing line. This is what a culture looks to art for, to put image, or voice, or context to a way of rethinking, reseeing, re-experiencing" (Rakoff).

The notion of "re-experiencing" is worth contemplating for a moment, since few people are likely to consider the viewing of Fischl's sculpture or even Falling Man's performance as an exact reproduction of the original event. The spectator's experience will be qualitatively different from that undergone by witnesses on the morning of September 11. So it is the creation of this alternate space that opens up the possibility of contrasting both experiences, and in the process extracting or identifying that which distinguishes one from the other. In other words, the performance can be conceived of as the event's "other." Janiak's "jump" is not a person falling to his death, but remains close enough, as we have noted, to elicit similar responses. However, the individual who becomes aware that she is viewing a performance is not as transfixed by the scene unfolding before her and, as such, is able to contemplate her own responses as well as those of the other spectators around her. As Joseph Conte argues, the text counteracts our tendencies to view Falling Man as simply a representation by asking that readers

> evaluate the verbal description of his performance, the account of the crowd's reaction, and the interior monologue of a character who considers its meaning. In this fashion we as readers—rather than as onlookers once removed—are encouraged to enter the psychic terrain where victims, survivors, and witnesses of tragedy meet. (581)

DeLillo's novel presents this kind of scenario but moves this equation to another level, for the reader not only registers the effects of Falling Man's performance on Lianne, but also observes Lianne observing its effects on others. Lianne might thus be considered a "reader" in her own right, and strengthening the novel's empathic bond with the reader even further. Such a moment occurs near the end of the novel when Lianne rushes from her second encounter with the performance artist and chances upon a derelict on the street, staring up at the Falling Man: "He was seeing something elaborately different from what he encountered step by step in the ordinary run of hours. He had to learn how to see it correctly, find a crack in the world where it might fit" (168). Like the onlooker, we have all been forced to reconfigure our narratives. The performer, vacillating between the poles of sameness and otherness unsettles sufficiently so that the spectator recognizes her place within a still-traumatized community. Falling Man, suspended in mid-air, after the deadening jolt, elicits a "spontaneous commonality" in his spectators (and perhaps DeLillo's readers), offering all an opportunity to try to "see it correctly."

NOTES

1. See, for example, Lurie (44–50) and Engle (28–50), among others.
2. Elizabeth Anker also worries that "the containment of 9/11 within the psychic economy of the spectacle is ultimately a dissociative strategy that tempers horror with engrossment, with the end of muting 9/11's tragedies" (473). In other words, framing the event within the confines of an artistic piece means that, inevitably, the full power of the trauma will be lost.
3. Although the attacks on the World Trade Center was the most mediatized event in history, much of the mortality and human pain was excised or simply absent from the broadcasts. There are some who claim this is due to the small window of time that the Towers actually stood after impact, and to the total devastation that occurred in the wake of their collapse. But some record does exist of these moments. How could it not, with hundreds of people gathered at the site of the gravely wounded buildings, taking photographs and shooting video (to say nothing of the overwhelming presence of the media)? And yet when one turns to a historical record such as *Here is New York*, a collection containing hundreds of photographs

taken by both amateurs and professionals on that day, the evidence is scarce. The collection is subtitled *A Democracy of Photographs*, but one finds only a single representation of the gruesome reality witnessed by many while the Towers still stood. It shows the bloodied, severed foot of a woman, still shod in its shoes and stockings, lying in the street (264). Many of those fleeing from the Towers recount the hellish sights that awaited them as they peered into the plaza. And though over a thousand photographs (culled from over five thousand) were chosen to present the "most coherent sense of the whole," only a two-page spread is devoted to the falling people. The dead are almost entirely absent from the collection, represented only in two photographs that show the word "morgue," one spray-painted on a wall (363), the other on a piece of paper taped to a lamppost (513). See also the harrowing accounts in Dean F. Murphy's collection of oral histories, such as that of Ernest Armstead, an emergency medical specialist (149–155). Such is the situation for Marshall, one of the protagonists in Ken Kalfus's *A Disorder Peculiar to the Country*. He and another man are making their escape from the North Tower and, having reached the ground floor, they exit onto the concourse:

> Just as they were about to make their run, an object that was recognizably a woman in a navy business suit . . . thumped hard less than twenty feet away, and bounced and burst. Her shoes had come off in mid-fall and clattered emptily against the pavement a moment later. "Don't look," Marshall said. "For God's sake don't look." (Kalfus 16)

In two short sentences, the text graphically captures the "hard reality" of that day. Marshall's entreaty may be as much for the reader of the novel as it is for his companion.

4. In this vein, Carla Spivack argues that novels such as Schulman's "transformed the September 11 attacks from acts of political-historical significance into acts of their own private dramas" and as such they appear "to take the idea of world historical events as catalysts for [personal] rebirth at least somewhat seriously" (873).

5. Frank Lentricchia and Jody McAullife make the connection between artist and terrorist explicit when they observe: "In spite of their *intentions* . . . the suicide terrorists who struck New York may be said to have made—with the cooperation of American television—performance art with political designs on its American audience" (13). The success of terrorist actions depends on the widest possible audience. In this way, as many have noted, the media is complicit in propagating the fear that is the ultimate intent of terrorism. Solidifying their argument, Lentricchia and McAuliffe later suggest that we might conceive of Ground Zero as a work of art: "And the mainspring of this aesthetic experience is an absence, a rubble pit in lower Manhattan—that rupture in the perceptual field which marks the original art of the suicide pilots" (14).

6. The now-famous quote from *Mao II* reads: "There's a curious knot that binds novelists and terrorists. . . . Years ago I used to think it was possible for a novelist to alter the inner life of the culture. Now bomb-makers and gunmen have taken that territory. They make raids on human consciousness. What writers used to do before we were all incorporated" (41). And speaking to Lorrie Moore shortly after the publication of the novel in 1991, DeLillo similarly remarked: "Not long ago, a novelist could believe he could have an effect on our consciousness of terror . . . Today, the men who shape and influence human consciousness are the terrorists." (*New York Review of Books*, June 9, 1991).

7. Similarly, Laura Frost sees Janiak as engaging in "act[s] of art-terrorism" (Falling Man).

8. For these reasons, among others, Conte sees Falling Man as "a highly respectful figure of sacrifice and mournful meditation" (581).

Chapter Two

Otherness as Counternarrative in the Graphic Novel

Spiegelman, Rehr, Torres

Of the many traumas endured on the morning of September 11, one of the most immediate was our silent, helpless witnessing of the televised events. The distanced perspective, combined with the rapidity with which one calamity followed another, made comprehension near-impossible. All people could do was stare in disbelief. Soon disbelief was replaced by total shock as we realized the all-encompassingly cataclysmic nature of the event.[1] As Susan Faludi observes, "The suddenness of the attacks and the finality of the towers' collapse and the planes' obliteration left us with little in the way of ongoing chronicle or ennobling narrative" (64). In other words, the destruction was so devastating in its totality, that any attempt to find a story to tell seemed to be a desperate grasping at straws. And yet we had precious moments to take in the event and its horrific developments for ourselves, before the meaning-making process took over. The second tower had only just collapsed and we were already being told what it meant and what to think; the event was being "translated" for us. With each passing moment, the gap between event and interpretation grew. As Don Delillo proclaims, "The raw event was one thing, the coverage another" (38). Soon it would become difficult to distinguish September 11, or "9/11," from what we had seen broadcast on our television screens.

A lacuna at the center of this coverage was the very absence of the human element, its near invisibility. Thousands of people died that day, we merely witnessed the buildings imploding. A number of different factors contributed to this development. First, the sheer immensity of the Towers themselves guaranteed that we could barely glimpse the people trapped inside. Second, the very scale of the buildings required a long shot to give the viewer a full sense of the calamity. As Lilie Chouliaraki observes, "Long shots universalize. They abstract from indexical, context-specific meaning and foreground the iconic" (172). As such, we watched things unfold *from* and *at* a distance. Third, the sheer horror of the events, most particularly images of falling people (as examined in the previous chapter), soon elicited a reflexive self-censorship and the cameras pulled away. Finally, within a very short time (102 minutes) the devastation was so complete there were few survivors to film. Within hours, it became clear there would also be few stories to tell.

These factors may help to explain the responses to 9/11 cast in the form of the graphic novel. With its penchant for autobiography, the genre has demonstrated its capacity as a forum for the individual voice. This combined with its amalgamation of text and image, made the genre an attractive vehicle for testimony in the aftermath of disaster. The first person narratives in three graphic novels—Art Spiegelman's *In the Shadow of No Towers*, Henrik Rehr's *Tribeca Sunset*, and Alissa Torres's *American Widow* (illustrated by Sungyoon Choi)—bridge the gap between distanced mediation and real lives lived that day. Indeed, as we shall see, these texts express deep concerns and misgivings about the manner in which images were manipulated and presented to the public. As Jane Blocker observes, one of the functions of art is to question "the privilege and hegemonic power of official testimony" as well as "the politics of the ideal witness" (xxiii). As we shall see, the very structuring of the graphic novel—the willful interplay of text and image—highlights and problematizes the constructedness and purpose of these "official" narratives.

Less than three short months after the attacks, Don DeLillo identified the need for the proliferation of many versions of the events. Writing for *Harper's* in December 2001, he declared, "The narrative ends in rubble and it is left to us to create the counter-narrative" (34). He urged writers to step into the void, conferring upon them a degree of agency, but also making it incumbent upon them to create complexity where fixity threatened to take hold. DeLillo argues that 9/11 signaled a shift away from the narrative proffered by the technologically advanced West to that advocated by those who "want to bring back the past" (34). In the aftermath of the attacks, DeLillo declares, "the world narrative belongs to terrorists" (33). How people think about the world, and their place in it, is now determined by the actions of the terrorists. It also stands to reason, however, that the United States would seek to restake its claim.

DeLillo's use of the singular ("world narrative") implies that he envisions a struggle between two master narratives warring for supremacy. He thus addresses, in a different language, the vacillation between sameness and otherness to which Palumbo-Liu refers. In Delillo's version, an all-encompassing global narrative that would bind all peoples together is pitted against another which seeks to undermine the hegemonic tendencies inherent in these drives for sameness. So when he refers to "counter-narrative" he is actually speaking of emergent stories that serve to either complement or complicate these dominant strains. These are not so much conflicting as competing narratives, each jostling for attention and recognition. For instance, he points to the likelihood of alternate versions of the event springing up as time passes so that we will be left with "a shadow history of false memories and imagined loss" (35). And he anticipates the conspiracy theories that would proliferate after the event, pointing to the Internet as the source of another counter-narrative "shaped in part by rumor, fantasy, and mystical reverberation" (35). In other words, there exists the possibility of any number of narratives molded and emplotted to serve a variety of needs.

It is in this regard, DeLillo contends that the writer may have a role to play, delivering some of the emotional truth of that day

> The writer begins in the towers, trying to imagine the moment desperately. Before politics, before history and religion, there is primal terror. People falling from the towers hand in hand. This is part of the counter-narrative, hands and spirits joining, human beauty in the crush of meshed steel. (39)

Here DeLillo yearns for narrative that, unfettered by ideological concerns, can address the bare truths of that day. Such a parsing is not without its challenges, because though the reality of individual experience is a part of the horror, this counter-narrative is also inextricably linked to those narratives of perceived injustice and global inequities. As we shall see, these first-person narratives are inevitably swept up within the geopolitical realities of the event. This is an eventuality the narrators will seek to counter, with varying degrees of success. In a display of solidarity, and perhaps misplaced empathy for its citizenry, the government put forth a narrative of resilience (which the media quickly adopted). Expressing the need for a common front, the government put forth exclusionary narratives that left little to no room for disaccord or contrary opinion. These writers respond to, complicate, and sometimes reject, the messages of sameness and communal unity communicated to the American people by the nation's two principal delivery systems—the government and the media. They thus assert their otherness in the face of a driving force to create a national narrative of sameness. In *The Deliverance of Others*, Palumbo-Liu asks how otherness is communicated. In response, I present these graphic narratives whose principal objective is to assert otherness in the face of overabundant sameness (and idea also taken up, as we shall see in the next chapter, by a number of French novelists).

9/11 AS MEDIATED EXPERIENCE

For most of us, 9/11 was a distanced and mediated experience.[2] For this reason, among others, it retained a surreal quality. The many references and allusions to Hollywood movies arose in part because we experienced the attacks of September 11 through the same medium that had entertained us with various filmed fantasies about the end of New York, the United States, or even the world. That real terrorists, however, would actually use planes filled with people to crash into buildings, also filled with people, seemed as improbable as aliens destroying the Grand Canyon or the National Monument. And the only panacea for this sense of unreality was to listen to a media to whom we had relinquished the role of interpretation. This eventually led, however, to a greater sense of distancing and alienation since many of us harbored a nagging suspicion that this "official" version of events was not necessarily our own. For instance, E. Ann Kaplan speaks of stepping outside her Manhattan apartment, wandering around Union Square, and being exposed to perspectives different from the ones delivered by the media: "By contrast with what I witnessed locally, the male leaders on television presented a stiff, rigid, controlling, and increasingly vengeful response" (5, 13). Kaplan's observation highlights the manner in which a rush to signification inevitably misrepresents, reducing the complexities of meaning to assuage and placate immediate needs.

David Friend provides a description of the (perhaps unconscious) way the media took it upon themselves to create a frame—quite literally—into which the events of the day could be placed:

> As the event progressed, however, and the enormity of the death toll became clear, and the fulminating towers were no longer there to observe, television, as it always does, sought a way to mediate the moment passed, to reduce the infinite complexity to a single sight-and-sound bite. TV resorted to the instant replay and the neatly spliced videoclip. On air, the second plane, struck the south tower again and again, in flashback. The buildings disappeared in a blossom of gray, repeatedly, as a recurrent nightmare might haunt a trauma victim. In the ensuing days the clip would become the signature of the event: the streaking plane, the smoking towers, the death clouds attending the towers' collapse. (35)

Perhaps important to remember here is that those working in television were processing the information at the same time that we were, at least initially, and there was no clearer example than that of the anchors who were scrambling to make sense of things for us, and themselves. Friend is correct that television turned to its default position fairly quickly, particularly when the degree of devastation became all too evident. But in the initial moments, minutes, and even hours, what we saw reflected on the screen was the image of our own bewilderment and horror, acted out by those figures on television. The significant difference, of course, is that we have conferred upon these individuals the mantle of "official" witnesses. Acting as our surrogates, their words soon came to be our own. As Friend contends: "For many people the world over . . . on 9/11 the image, the footage, the movie *was* the event. For most of us, the picture was all we had, and ever will have, to signify it" (36). Though we give this little consideration, it is almost impossible to extricate our experience from what we witnessed on the screen and, similarly, from the narratives reiterated time and again during those endless hours of compulsive television-viewing. In essence, narratives became "fixed" largely through the presentation of looped images.

The problem for many was that the images did not, and could not, tell the whole story. In *Trauma Culture*, for instance, Kaplan voices her concern that "the 'realness' of 9/11 [was] being gelled into stock images, stock forms that would forever limit its meanings" (17). She contemplates how we might counteract this tendency, and wonders, "How could we keep the event open, fluid, specific?" (17). As a solution, she points to art as a means of "translating" trauma into forms that make the complexity and the unrepresentability of the experience communicable to others. She suggests that we must find a way to re-translate the mediated narratives, and that art affords us this possibility. What I argue here is that since the narratives were largely told using images, it stands to reason that a medium that incorporates both text and image might have better success with the "translation." The very structure of the graphic narrative raises questions about the limits of representation, for the panels capture a sequence of moments but also exclude an equal or greater number. In other words, the constructedness of the representation is made apparent through the reader's growing awareness of that which has been left out. As Gillian Whitlock observes, these narratives "are not a mere hybrid of graphic arts and prose fiction, but a unique interpretation that transcends both, and emerges through the imaginative work of closure that readers are required to make between the panels on the page" (968–69). The formal challenges posed by these narratives finally serve to create an empathic connection between reader and narrator, since both are implicated in meaning-making exercises. In the process, Whitlock argues, they also "require the reader to become a collaborator, engaging in an active process of working through" (969–70). Through the use of different strategies, then, these narrators seek the empathic engagement of the reader. For it is only through such a connection that they have any chance of communicating some of the reality of their traumatic experience.

THE TRANSLATION OF TRAUMA

Each of the graphic novelists examined here take up Kaplan's challenge and echo the sentiments expressed by Art Spiegelman: "I wanted to sort out the fragments of what I'd experienced from the media images that threatened to engulf what I actually saw."[3] Having been present at the event, each feels the urge to bear witness and provide their respective versions. Spiegelman's declaration, however, points to the obstacles facing the witness who seeks to turn experience into narrative ("sort out the fragments") and provide alternate perspectives that stray or differ from official testimony. John Durham Peters, for example, insists that the witness "has two faces: the passive one *seeing* and the active one *saying*" (26).[4] The text thus becomes the site where the narrator shuttles from one to the other. The time that spans between the moment of seeing and that of telling, however, impacts the degree to which the witness might be considered reliable: "Herein lies the fragility of witnessing: the difficult juncture between experience and discourse. The witness is authorized to speak by having been present at an occurrence. A private experience enables a public statement. But the journey from experience (the seen) into words (the said) is precarious" (Peters 26). First, of course, is the challenge of translating experience into words that will accurately reflect the event, and not to dilute or alter it in the process. Second, and this is particularly true of a large scale event such as 9/11, the witness is quickly inundated with images and memories that he or she may eventually have difficulty distinguishing from his or her own (did I actually witness the second plane flying into the building?). As such the witness must focus on and isolate the more personal aspects of the experience (that which was not observed by everyone), thus highlighting that which authenticates the telling.

In this regard, these graphic narratives strive to expand our visual recollection, providing alternative memories to those formulated by the media. In different ways and at different levels of magnitude, each author seeks to wrest control away from the dominant ideologies and insert degrees of nuance not to be found in the images broadcast, as well as the narratives constructed, repeatedly in the days and weeks following September 11. Additionally, they serve as venues for individual voices, counteracting the pervasive depersonalization of the calamity; they bring the reader into contact with lived individual experiences. In *The Limits of Autobiography*, Leigh Gilmore stipulates that trauma might be defined as "that which breaks the frame" and that "rebuilding a frame to contain it is as fraught with difficulty as it is necessary" (31). Gilmore's metaphor is particularly apt when discussing the graphic novel, which by its very nature entails the construction of a series of frames and, perhaps more interesting, frames within frames. As we shall see, each writer "frames" his or her narrative in a very specific way. Spiegelman constructs a metaphor of his own when he declares that he was "sorting through my grief and putting it into boxes," as a means of maintaining some control over it. Rehr concedes that he "had no choice but to create a love letter. A love letter to my family, a love letter to my friends and a love letter to the city we inhabit."[5] And Torres sees the purpose of her book as allowing her to "take control of the images" related to her personal trauma. These graphic novels also convey the complexity of emotions that follow an event that seemed to have no previous frame of reference.

One might stipulate these narrators feel compelled to bear witness because, like Spiegelman, they "saw it all live—unmediated." It is the mediation of the images, their very "colonization" as Blocker would say, to which these texts respond. Notably, these narratives are also extended exercises in self-portraiture or, one might say, in "self-imaging." Each writer seeks to bear witness by placing him/herself at the heart of a recreation of 9/11 in order to give shape to a traumatized self.[6] In Spiegelman's case, it becomes apparent that he feels agency was wrested from him not once, but twice: first, by the terrorists on 9/11, and then by his own government. One of his favorite devices in *No Towers* is to conflate the Bush Administration with the terrorists. Most famously, he declares that the hero of his tale is "Equally terrorized by al-Qaeda and his own government" (ISNT Panel 2). In the panel, Osama Bin Laden looms over the slouched figure with a bloodied scimitar, while George W. Bush stands opposite toting a six-gun in one hand and an American flag in the other. In fact, Spiegelman's text is perhaps more preoccupied with the machinations of his own government than with those of any terrorist organization. He conflates once more when he observes: "I had anticipated that the shadows of the towers might fade while I was slowly sorting through my grief and putting it into boxes. I hadn't anticipated that the hijackings of September 11 would themselves be hijacked by the Bush cabal that reduced it to a war recruitment poster" (ISNT Foreword). Spiegel man's play on the word "hijack" underlines the extent to which he attributes culpability to both parties. But he also uses the word to designate the appropriation of events in the fulfillment of an agenda.

At the same time, this is one of the more complicated panels from *In the Shadow of No Towers* for Spiegelman also includes a number of elements which point to his privileging his personal experiences of the event. For instance, behind the image of the sleeping figure of the protagonist (now in his guise from *Maus*) one glimpses a Missing Poster for Spiegelman's brain declaring that it was "last seen in Lower Manhattan, mid-September 2001" (Panel 2). While this is meant humorously, he nevertheless utilizes with questionable taste an iconic symbol of the event—the missing posters that proliferated around Ground Zero in the days after the attacks and which soon became one of the strongest, and most emotional, representations of the lives lost. But he is also not averse to referring to himself as a "heartbroken narcissist" revealing his awareness of his self-preoccupation.

These texts exist, as he suggests, "on the faultline where World History and Personal History collide" (ISNT, Foreword). As self-portraits, the texts also serve to broaden our conceptualization of the narrators. Spiegelman offers the most caricatural self-portrait, transforming into characters from the Golden Age of comics or his earlier work, *Maus*, at pivotal moments in his narrative. In the process, he communicates to the reader the sense of a fragmented self recuperating from trauma, as well as a conviction that much of the work of (national) mourning is still left undone. His successive panels, replete with recurring images of the "glowing bones" of the crumbling North Tower, reveal a repetition compulsion that Spiegelman contends is the proper emotional response to the trauma: "The pivotal image from my 9/11 morning—one that didn't get photographed or videotaped into public memory but still remains burned onto the inside of my eyelids several years later—was the image of the looming north tower's glowing bones just before it vaporized" (ISNT Foreword). *In the Shadow of No Towers* thus stresses the personal character of the trauma; he witnessed something not seen or reported by anyone else. Through the presentation of this "new" image, emphasizing the singularity of his experience, Spiegelman creates an opportunity for the reader to recognize the emotional impact of the event on the narrator, and to frame the event within a new context.

Henrik Rehr also accentuates the division between the personal and the political: "September 11th was a geopolitical event, but perhaps because I was so close to the destruction with both my children in harm's way that day, the attack has always had a much more personal context for me" (TS ix). His "love letter" recontextualizes the events, presenting them from his necessarily restricted, but more intimate viewpoint, blurring the line between public and private discourse. At the same time, he offers an introspective and honest accounting of the emotions—not always noble or compassionate—a great many of us felt in the aftermath of the attacks. His depiction of self and others contrasts sharply with the images of selflessness and bravery that filled our TV screens and newspapers. When disaster first strikes, his primary concern is getting his youngest son, Spence, to safety. Later, it is to reconnect with his wife and their other son, Dylan. When he learns the two are safe, his relief and joy are evident as he tosses a laughing Spence in the air (TS 35). This scene contrasts with an earlier moment when he recalls Dylan asking him whether he was sad when his father died. Lying awake after the conversation, Rehr realizes "that no matter how much I loved this boy, no matter how hard I tried to protect him from the harms of the world, I could never protect Dylan from the grief my death would impose on him" (TS 33). Rehr's unadorned expressions of anxiety and hopelessness stand in sharp juxtaposition to the many narratives of bravura and patriotic fervor. These expressions of "negative" emotions bear witness to the complexity of meanings and a wider range of feelings elicited by the events of September 11.

By reconstructing his experience that morning, and by jogging his memory for salient but also banal moments, Rehr instigates a similar action on the part of the reader. Early in the text, after the first plane has hit, he glances down onto the esplanade where people are standing staring up at the burning tower. Their behavior, he notes, "Made the whole thing seem somewhat ordinary" (7). The scene and the commentary communicate some of that shock felt by many. It also captures the degree to which people did not, could not, realize the magnitude of the event that had begun unfolding before their eyes. In this way, Rehr emphasizes the disconnect between individual experience and the images broadcast on television in the opening pages of *Tribeca Sunset*. Living in an apartment near the World Trade Center, he sees the whole thing unfold from his window. At the same time, his television, turned to CNN, plays the images with which we are familiar: the smoking towers and then, later, the rampaging dust clouds. In contrast, he peers from his window and sees people falling to their deaths. He draws the shades as a buttress to the horror of the events to which he is an involuntary spectator. Finally, however, the sounds of the crumbling towers oblige him to confront that reality. He returns his gaze to the esplanade, which is now empty, "covered in gray-white dust" (TS 9). All that is left is an abandoned stroller, a small detail that communicates the panic experienced by the onlookers in those frightening moments. The desolation of the scene brings the full horror home: "This is what nuclear winter must look like" (TS 9). The image of the vacant esplanade also captures a sense of the anxieties shared by many—that 9/11 might be the beginning of the end of everyone. The interplay of these two pages with their similar panel construction communicates the witness's sensory overload and his dawning realization as to the enormity of the events playing out before his eyes. At the same time, to recall Peters's distinction between passive seeing and active telling, Rehr's text literally illustrates someone taking hold of the images, and using them to work through the fear and helplessness (and later anger) he experienced in response to the attacks.

In Alissa Torres's case, the narrative works as a recuperation of self. She rejects the fixed image of the grieving widow so many people would foist upon her. She may very well be an American widow, but one complete with complex emotions that do not necessarily cohere with the national myth. She observes that "we were constantly bombarded by the same images over and over: the burning towers . . . 9/11 was such a graphic event. Just writing about it wasn't enough. I needed to take control of the images" (Minzesheimer). In fact, the title of the text immediately signals the attribution against which she will rail. The death of her spouse in the World Trade Center creates the prism through which she will be perceived, but Torres rejects the "colonization" of her experience for a larger purpose. As others have noted, the events were almost immediately seized upon and the emplotment of the narrative was transformed from one of irrefutable calamity to one of heroism and resilience. In the process, all those whose own experience might remind us of the more painful, and sometimes irresolvable, aspects of the tragedy were either pushed aside or made to conform to the new narrative. The 9/11 widows were thus seen not merely as figures of sorrow, the embodiment of our pain, but rather as proof of the nation's fortitude and determination. They became part of a hierarchy of grief created by the media: "The more fragile the wives seemed . . . the more formidable and potent their husbands. And the more dependent the better: a stay-at-home mom trumped a mere stay-at-home wife, and the most coveted 'get' on the media circuit was the stay-at-home mom who was pregnant on the day of the attack" (Faludi, 95). They became, in essence, official sites of mourning. Having suffered the greatest loss, they were cast as symbols of the nation soldiering on (their children, after all, carried the genes of their dead fathers).[7]

Torres turns the tables on this conceptualization by presenting herself as a very different widow from the one as which she has been cast. She refuses to see Eddie or herself as "heroes" and, like Spiegelman, will continue to grieve long after the moment others deem "appropriate." The depth of that grief is captured in the recurring image of Eddie's final moments. She repeatedly imagines him standing in front of a shattered window, gathering his resolve to leap: "You jumped. You said, 'Fuck it, I'm out of here.' And that was that. That was Day 1."[8] She revisits this moment three times in the text, once even imagining taking the fatal plunge with him (AW 55). Here Torres touches on a painful aspect of the survivor's trauma—the lingering uncertainty as to how their loved ones lived their final moments and how they met their ends. This uncertainty preempts the possibility of closure. As an active teller, however, she seeks to imbue her narrative with a certain degree of certitude, to varying degrees of success. This page thus encapsulates a great deal of Torres's struggle throughout *American Widow*, communicating the complex intermingling of the narrator's feelings of sadness and uneasiness, but also of abandonment and betrayal. Even Torres's use of the curse word distinguishes her narrative from other more carefully orchestrated responses. It communicates the narrator's feeling of abandonment and betrayal. In fact, she makes clear that her anger with him has grown rather than subsided. Near the end of the text, she thinks, "You told me, 'I want to turn 90 beside you.' But you didn't so that's how I got here . . . I am still so mad at you" (200). The use of Day 1 also suggests how Torres views her life beginning anew, though not for the better, after 9/11. The prevailing sense of isolation is accentuated by a second dominant image in the text, that of Alissa lying alone in the conjugal bed. Two full-page illustrations depict her solitary figure in bed: surrounded first by the heads of people voicing concern for her (AW 43) and second by the repeated calls from the Red Cross (AW 106). And a chapter is devoted to remembering their lovemaking in that bed; "High voltage traces of our lust and love flowed through our mattress nightly" (AW 121). She strongly senses Eddie's presence, but wakes up only to "make contact only with my own skin" (AW 125). These images convey the sheer depth of her grief and solitude, and explain her alienation from the "grieving" community. At the same time, it is not always easy to sympathize with the narrator, for there are moments in the text when it is difficult to determine whether she means to show how her frustrations caused her to lash out or whether she still wants us to side with her entirely. When a worker in the mayor's office gives her a diagram explaining the trajectory she must follow, she thinks, "Does grief make me look stupid or what?" and then lashes out at the worker, "Thanks. I don't need a flowchart" (61). She is so consumed by her grief that she fails to recognize the challenges faced by those trying to help her. Lesser challenges than her own, of course, but challenges nonetheless. At the same time, this narrative strategy communicates an authentic experience to her readers, no doubt making them more receptive to her plight.

GRIEF AND THE DELIVERY OF SAMENESS

Because in the immediate aftermath of the attacks, it seemed that every narrative had but one purpose. Such an example were the "Portraits of Grief" that ran in the *New York Times* between September and December of 2001. The impulse, of course, was honorable: to memorialize and highlight the qualities of each of the victims. This desire to "accentuate the positive," however, also created a lopsided view of the tragedy and some of its more permanent effects. Perhaps more significantly, the delivery system used to present these narratives—one of the most (if not *the* most) powerful and influential newspapers in the world—and the compounded effect of offering up these memorials on a daily basis for over three months, practically ensured that this "version" of events would dominate.

In examining the "Portraits," for instance, Nancy Miller queries their true purpose. She is troubled by the incompleteness of the portraits that seek to encapsulate the existence of those who died within a structured format. For not only do these memorials fail to communicate the complexity of the lives lost, they also neglect the experiences of the survivors that are inextricably and forever linked with the dead. She thus asks, "But are we mourning the loved ones who died—mourning *for* them? What about the survivors doing the mourning? What's really their story? If the portraits aimed at capturing individuals, could they also render the grief of those who remained to mourn their loss?" (42). As noted, the intention of these "Portraits" was to honor and mourn the dead, but they were also meant to bring solace. But, we might ask, solace for whom? In their persistent accentuation of the positive, these narratives sought to erase all traces of sadness. Whether consciously or not, they signal a desire to put an end to the hardship and pain, simultaneously implying the need to forego any lingering over unpleasant details. Finally, in the harshest reading, they ignore the fact that loss is still loss. As Miller observes, "we live in a culture whose rhythms push us to wish for the pain to end so that we can, as they say, move on. Closure implies another beginning—the door closes to reopen on another scene. Enough grief already" (44). The pain of the survivors was something we would rather live without; after all, its presence simply made living our own lives more difficult. Better to believe that time heals all wounds, and quickly at that.

But this desire went a step further. The "Portraits" were intended to make readers connect with the victims, to recognize a common humanity, but not necessarily a common mortality. The sheer suddenness and the horrific nature of the attacks had to be balanced by images of plentiful and positive lives. Counteracting the horror, however, meant shifting one's gaze too strongly in the other direction. The editors of the *New York Times* admitted as much when they expressed the hope that while the biographies presented a "map of loss," they would also produce a "map of fulfillment." It is with this conception that Miller takes issue: "Was it possible that no one who died in the attack on the World Trade Center was ever depressed; self-centered; without a passion; had a career that seemed stalled; or sometimes found life not worth living? . . . I could not perform the translation, identify with these lives from which all traces of unhappiness were banished" (46). It is interesting that Miller, like Kaplan, uses the word translation, suggesting that the words somehow failed to transmit or communicate the reality of those lives lost that day. In her critique of the limitations of these narratives, Miller expresses the wish for a more balanced (accurate?) representation of the aftermath of the attacks. Not every story can be one of fulfillment or renewal. In essence, she yearns for a counter-narrative that will also effectively communicate the pain and distress felt by those doing the real mourning.

If nothing else, Torres's narrative communicates this feeling of unresolvable grief and captures the more insidious trauma of a world moving on. The pain the survivor feels when looking at a world that seems no different, acts no different, from the way it did before the trauma. The pain of a world returning to "normal," while one's life has been irrevocably turned upside down. This was perhaps truer of 9/11 than any other recent event in American history, where each level of trauma (personal, local, and national) seemed to carry its own agenda and timeline, and thus was inevitably going to clash with the others. This complexity is communicated in an honest account of their relationship. In chapter 4, for instance, we are returned to the early morning hours of September 11. Lying in their conjugal bed, the coldness between the couple is apparent. We see a sleepless Alissa thinking: "I'm still so angry with you even if I don't want to be" (AW 29). Though we never learn the source of her anger, this moment creates in the reader the sense of being witness to a real-life relationship. Because Eddie is not depicted, like many of the people in the "Portraits of Grief," as a perfect soul leading a happy and uncomplicated existence. In fact, a pregnant Alissa contemplates leaving him. The type of narrative Torres offers was not to be found in *The New York Times*, and thus runs counter (but also complements) those stories that sought to heal and assuage. These texts are thus acts of narratorial reclamation of individual traumatic experiences after they had been subsumed within the narrative of national (and even local) trauma.

PERSONAL AND PUBLIC GRIEF

Indeed, the use of the graphic narrative format becomes a further means of representing that which has been over-represented in an unconventional manner. Speaking of a Holocaust survivor's testimony, Jane Blocker accentuates the need to look beyond empiricism, verifiable facts, and what we believe we already know. For her, the survivor's reenactment is "in these terms not a picture of the exterior world. It is rather, a picture of her own humanity, her own subjectivity lost in the trauma she experienced and regained in the process of verbally creating a picture of that trauma" (xix). These same observations could just as easily be applied to the efforts of these writers to create images of their own experience. Realizing they cannot represent the "truth" about 9/11, the writers seek an image to convey the emotional reality of the incident, to create pictures of their trauma. As such, each writer frames 9/11 as an individualized experience, metonymically implying the thousands of other stories that might be told.

Also apparent, however, is that each of these writers has a different level of emotional attachment to the event. Alissa Torres, having lost her husband, is the most deeply affected of the three writers. Her experience dictates that she will produce the most intimate and personal of these narratives. The positioning of both Spiegelman and Rehr means that each will be able to maintain a greater distance from the subject. And as someone not born in the United States, Rehr is perhaps less likely to have his nationalistic or patriotic heartstrings pulled. Consequently, the event will not carry the same resonances for him, nor will it seem as exceptional or unique an occurrence to him as it may have felt to many Americans.[9] A notable passage occurs when looking back, across the water, at the burning ruins of the World Trade Center, Rehr consciously connects the events of September 11 with a more personal trauma. The separation from his wife and one of their children causes him to recall the complications experienced by his wife during childbirth and the medically induced coma into which she lapsed for several days (TS 19–22).[10] Throughout the text, however, the personal keeps running up against the historical. Shortly thereafter, for example, Rehr overhears someone say, "This thing's bigger than Pearl Harbor." This contrasts, of course, with his personal circumstances: "Funny, she was putting the day in historical perspective. I had a kid missing" (TS 23). This moment reflects the text's principal concern, the impact of the event on individual lives. And children are at the forefront of his narrative, so that when Rehr contemplates his own death, his greatest concern is the world to which he will be abandoning his children. For Rehr, 9/11 is most significant in terms of the potential future it predicts. Also of note is his dawning realization that he is now part of a national, indeed global, event—something to which he is still adapting: "Peculiar thing about *being* the news. *Your* problems are suddenly somebody else's *product*" (TS 23). This comment touches on the idea of the media incorporating personal narratives as headlines, but also on the commodification of 9/11. Rehr's text highlights the disquieting realization that one's own story can be so easily appropriated to satisfy other agendas.

Somewhat in contrast to Rehr, and thus adding a layer of ambiguity to her narrative, Torres recognizes that being a national product is not without its benefits. In her first essay for *Salon*, she acknowledges that she has greatly gained from the happenstance of Eddie's death, and that if he had died in some other way, "I would not have found myself so high in the hierarchy of the nation's sadness and sympathy, a grieving widow with a post-9/11 baby, a newly minted American icon" ("Reluctant"). She recognizes that she and many other women (though, of course, there were widowers as well) have been recruited to play an integral part in the recovery process. And the text frequently underlines her problematic relationship with the community, for this is a role she neither asked for nor desires, particularly as it requires the observation of a very specific set of guidelines. In order to survive and care for her child, however, she will need help and must take advantage of the opportunities afforded her by her husband's death. In the same essay, she repeats a saying of Eddie's who was attempting to calm her worries about the upcoming birth and the financial constraints they would face. "Every baby is born with bread under his arm," he tells her. Torres observes, "As it turned out, the saying proved true: When our son was born in October, I no longer worked. But there was enough money to take care of all of our expenses, and the promise of more money to come. Eddie, who died on Sept. 11, became the bread under our son's arm" ("Reluctant," also alluded to in *American Widow*).[8] She is grateful and recognizes her "luck," but this in turn contributes to feelings of guilt. She compares her experience to having found a magic lamp, but one that came at a price. She imagines the magic lamp proclaiming: "Each wish fulfilled is a consolation prize that will make you feel more like a collaborator than a victim" (AW 99). Collaboration, used here for its negative connotations, communicates Torres's feelings of short-selling her own principles. It also means that she risks subsuming her narrative to the desires of the larger one. Because, paradoxically, the public want to help with the healing process, but they do not want to be confronted by the thing that needs healing. The solution, as Torres explains is to throw money at the problem: "America wants us to be OK, economically sound, happy and sane. If we're OK, somehow, by extension, all Americans will be OK too. It's America's way of healing" ("Reluctant"). But her method of mourning—extended, angry, emotional—does not correspond with the national agenda. By the six-month anniversary, everyone reckons she should be over it. "You're bad for my chi," her dogwalker tells her (AW 127). More significantly, she describes the way the community begins turning on the widows, characterizing them as opportunistic and greedy when they dared to contest the manner in which compensation funds were allotted (AW 136–37).

Of the three texts examined, then, *American Widow* most explicitly highlights the gap between personal grief and the mission of national healing. For the country, 9/11 will always be a day when American vulnerability became dreadfully apparent and people recognized that what happened to others (elsewhere) could happen to them (here!). For Alissa Torres, it remains the day her life was ripped asunder and irrevocably changed. Thus it is understandable that she would not respond similarly to commemorations or television programs replaying the most painful moments of her life. They commemorate something, but not her pain. She highlights this disparity in a panel depicting the headline from a March 11, 2002, newspaper: "9/11 TV: We Want it Raw" (AW 127). This sense of alienation reaches its heights when she walks by an electronics store in mid-August and sees a banner brightly declaring, "Just 21 more days!" (AW 184). *American Widow* is a consciously self-centered book, precisely because the true pain that people like Alissa Torres experienced is not something with which most of us were or are prepared to deal. As Charles Taylor observes, "by insisting on the solitary, isolating nature of grief, [Torres] is implying that the feeling of community was easier to grasp for those of us lucky not to have lost anyone" (Taylor). These moments of communal feeling were only cathartic for those spared any true pain. Without question, the trauma of 9/11 had a collective dimension. We may not have all considered ourselves victims that day, but we certainly felt we could have been. This realization, combined with the fear and uncertainty that followed, created a strong bond and a stronger sense of community. The belief that we all had an equal share in this tragedy, however, is an assumption that *American Widow* strongly contests.

To this end, Torres presents a well-meaning but overzealous post-9/11 community working every angle of mourning. Since there were so few actual survivors, the attention from the media and a host of charitable organizations necessarily turned to the surviving relatives. Torres speaks of the "hordes of volunteer therapists" who needed the victims to remain helpless "because they were so dependent on us to feel useful" (90, 91). Such is also the case when an organizer from a neighborhood German church invites Torres to a memorial, admitting all the other families are German, but that Torres is welcome because she is a "genuine American who lost someone. And someone with a post-9/11 *kinder*!" (AW 93). The most striking moment of disconnect occurs as the narrative approaches the first anniversary of 9/11 and, of course, her husband's death. She is invited to a women's forum where First Lady Laura Bush is scheduled to speak. Once there she is assailed by the media and surrounded by people who have very different motives for attending the event. The text's presentation of the speech—"God bless . . . blah blah . . . Libby Pataki . . . blah . . . God's will . . . Joyce Rumsfeld . . . Motherhood . . . Laura Bush . . . God Bless . . . Faith . . . United States . . . Heroes" (AW 201)—emphasizes the ubiquity of 9/11 buzzwords, and the control politicians now exert over the discourse. She thinks about the moment of Eddie's death and her baby crying in the next room. A stark contrast is thus constructed between the text of Laura Bush's letter celebrating the birth of post-9/11 babies ("we are grateful as well for the beautiful new lives that are gifts both to your homes and to our nation") and the opposing page depicting Eddie plummeting to his death. Torres's pain is made all the more real by a two-page collage of photographs showing a vibrant, smiling, and living Eddie (AW 198–99). The collision between World History and Personal History could not be clearer.

A similar disconnection from the community is felt and explored by Spiegelman. In his case, however, it is largely because he sees himself as the only one exhibiting an appropriate response—what he terms "a sky-is-falling tizzy"—to the tragedy (ISNT Foreword). *In the Shadow of No Towers* is a critique of responses to 9/11, but one that lays the blame more squarely at the feet of the Bush Administration. The longer we dwelled on the wound and the pain, the government's logic went, the weaker we would both become *and* appear. Immediate emphasis was placed on returning life to normal and on demonstrating how unaffected we were as nation. This aggressive logic undermined the possibility of fostering good will abroad, but also of any real engagement in self-reflection. Spiegelman extols the benefits of staying in the moment, of living with the trauma and its significance. "That's when time stands still at the moment of trauma . . . which strikes me as a totally reasonable response to current events" (ISNT Panel 2). Feeling compelled to witness, Spiegelman casts himself as a contemporary version of Coleridge's Ancient Mariner "doomed to drag this damned albatross around my neck, and compulsively retell the calamities of September 11th to anyone who'll listen" (ISNT Panel 2). The albatross in question is a bald eagle bedecked with a hat emblazoned with the Stars and Stripes. As the narrator speaks to the reader, the eagle interjects short phrases that encapsulate how the government "guided" the citizenry in the days after the event: "Go out and shop! Awk!" and "Be afraid!" By shopping we would reenergize the wounded economy, but we would also be demonstrating that we had put the event behind us. By being afraid, we would naturally relinquish some of our freedoms so that the government could better protect us. "Everything's changed! Awk!" the eagle declares. And the text depicts the community as far too willing to accept and follow the government's pronouncements. At one point, Spiegelman facetiously proposes the creation of an Ostrich Party: "Join your fellow Americans before it's too late . . . Rise up and stick your heads in the ground!" (ISNT Panel 5). Rather than using 9/11 as an impetus for real political change, the text charges, we let others dictate our responses for us.

THE NARRATIVE OF AN "UNCOMPLICATED WE"

In the process of delivering their first-person narratives, these representations also provide a fuller, and more critical, view of the post-9/11 community. They offer counterpoints to what one critic calls the "narrative of an uncomplicated 'we,'" pulling together during this time of unprecedented hurt, anxiety and fear" (Melnick 72). Stories of people looting or of profiting from the disaster obviously took a back seat to the tales of heroic and selfless acts performed on that day. And this is understandable, if only because the number of good deeds did exceed the bad. Nevertheless, the drive to convey the image of a unified and reborn New York (and, by extension, a nation) required an unbalanced, and some might say false, depiction of the events of 9/11 and their ultimate significance. Spiegelman, Torres, and Rehr each do their part in righting that balance.

For the first half of *Tribeca Sunset*, the community is depicted in a fairly positive light. In a six-page interlude, however, Rehr describes an encounter at Pier 94 with an acquaintance, Neil. Neil recounts two anecdotes that have a very different tenor than the first half of the book. In the first, he tells of sneaking back to his apartment near Ground Zero and coming upon two firemen looting a flat screen television from another apartment. In the second, he describes being mistreated by a landlord who hiked up his rents in order to profit from the disaster. When he arrives at his temporary apartment he discovers it is in a filthy state. He complains to the landlord, who replies, "Well, what are you gonna do, buddy? Go home?" Neil fires back, "You guys are real scumbags, you know that, running a lousy scam like this on the Red Cross! I'm sure they'll never see a dime of their 'security deposit'!" The landlord then screams, "What's it to you? It's not *your* dough" (TS 57). Neil recounts how he then stormed over to the landlord's office, knife block in hand, fully intending to stab the landlord to death. The anecdotes capture some of the complexity of the days after 9/11. The first that not everyone (not even every fireman) acted heroically or nobly on that day. The second that after the attacks most of us were filled with many emotions, some of which we would rather forget. The source of Neil's anger is clearly not the landlord, but the entire situation. In response to Neil's confession, Rehr admits that he has frequently fantasized about torturing and killing terrorists (TS 59). This recalls an earlier scene when Rehr is awoken one night by a thunderstorm and momentarily believes they are once more under attack. Unable to sleep, his mind anxiously wanders, but he admits that his "predominant emotion was anger." He then discloses, "There's a lot of ways to torture a terrorist to death, and I went over them *all* in my imagination" (TS 39). The panel shows a scarred and bruised foot in a pool of blood. Rehr's admission touches on the darker emotions elicited by the attacks, as does Neil's anecdote of near-murder.

In responding to what they perceive as inadequate, dishonest, and manipulative narratives, these writers engage in truth-telling exercises meant as rebukes and reformulations of them. By pointing to the flaws in our responses, as well as their own, the creators of these graphic narratives provide an authentic and truer representation of our working through of the trauma. As Charles Hatfield observes, these texts "privilege the most minute and shocking details of their authors' lives. It is this intimacy that authenticates their social observations and arguments" (114). It is also through the revelation of their humanity that these narrators are most likely to invoke empathy on the part of the reader. As Suzanne Keen notes, empathy is "a vicarious spontaneous sharing of affect" that "can be provoked by witnessing another's emotional state, by hearing about another's condition, or even by reading" (4). Narratives that give voice to the good and the bad, the weak and the strong, the cowardly and the noble, provide a greater possibility for accessing the truth of an event. The very act of creating such a text is also their means of coming to terms with the trauma. Indeed, one might posit there is something inherently affirmative in the act of witnessing. Each text certainly appears to confirm the beneficial results for each writer of having undertaken their respective projects.

CONCLUSION

Even *In the Shadow of No Towers*, which has been much-praised for its refusal to seek closure and its willingness to embrace the undeniable pain of the event, cannot resist offering some kind of consolation. Near the end of the novel, the narrator finds himself amongst a bunch of men sleeping. He bemoans their complacency and wonders, "Maybe they're right! Maybe the world stopped ending!" In the next panel, however, he screams "The sky is falling" rousing the sleepers. Finally, he settles down and notes, "Whew! Sometimes complaining is the only solace left! . . . ZZZZZZZ" (ISNT Panel 9). Having awoken others to the dire straits in which we find ourselves, the insomniac narrator may feel that his work is done. The panel reads not only as a justification of his method, but also an expression of hope that others will take up the cause. Spiegelman presents the final panel as outlines of the Twin Towers, offering his own memorial. Further evidence of the trauma loosening its grip is the image of the glowing bones of the Tower become less prominent with each successive page: "The Towers have come to loom far larger than life . . . but they seem to get smaller every day . . . Happy Anniversary" (ISNT 10).

For her part, Torres acknowledges that the writing of the text was a way for her to "work through" her trauma. *American Widow*, she says, "embodies my grief. I can open it and see this grief and remember it and remember Eddie. But I can also close it and live my life in the present tense seven years later and have a happy home for my son" (Minzesheimer). The novel ends with Torres escaping New York in September 2002, and vacationing in Hawaii with her son. But this sense of "moving on" is perhaps best encapsulated with the final image of the novel—a full-page panel of blue sky. This echoes the opening frame of the text, recalling the bright blue (and innocent) morning of September 11. In the final image, Torres and Sungyoon Choi go some way towards re-appropriating the notion of a happy blue sky we lost on that day. Henrik Rehr, on the other hand, discounts the possibility of affirmation, but does seem to laud human adaptability: "There's a lot of talk of closure and healing and whatnot these days. Pure nonsense. In my opinion, a wound this big doesn't close and heal, but if you're lucky, you can slowly get used to its presence" (48). The final page of *Tribeca Sunset* confirms this. It is Christmas day and a snowstorm falls on Manhattan. His family content and safe, Rehr recognizes that "The fierce, blind bloodthirst, which has haunted me since 9-11, is gone, has at last abated" (115). A serenity comes over him, and he concludes the book with the thought, "It's no small thing to find your place in the world" (115). Perhaps stronger corroboration still of life returning to New York, though, are the serene cityscapes Rehr sprinkles throughout *Tribeca Sunset*. These images, often full pages and sometimes two, depict a vibrant city that continues to live and thrive.

Rehr's image of the "open wound" is worth revisiting. First, because for more than ten years there existed an actual physical scar at the southern tip of Manhattan. Second, because the image conveys the sense that this is not an event we are likely to forget nor for which we can achieve closure. We can only try to come to terms with its continued presence and use this permanence as impetus for exploring its meaning. It is not something we can push aside, cover up, or transform into something more palatable, as some of the fixed narratives seek to do. This explains DeLillo's plea for counter-narratives. "We need them," he says, "to set against the massive spectacle that continues to seem unmanageable, too powerful a thing to set into our frame of practised response" (DeLillo 35). The objective of the counter-narrative, then, is not affirmation but acknowledgment of the immensity (sublimity?) of the event. As Rehr suggests, we can only adjust to the continued presence of the wound, incorporating but not assimilating it into our lives. It is now a painful part of our existence, our identity. That we experienced 9/11 visually, in a set of (eventually fixed) images, meant that the graphic form could lend itself to a reordering and (re)presentation of the events. In her review of *In the Shadow of No Towers*, Michiko Kakutani deplores the dominant tendency of turning to conventional narrative tropes as a means of representing the events of September 11. She points to Spiegelman's text as a rare example of a work of art "that makes no effort to contain or domesticate the surreal awfulness of that day" (Kakutani). The very unconventionality of the graphic narrative readily lends itself to the production of these alternate perspectives. For although "comix" have gained a greater degree of acceptance, the prospect of such a genre being used to represent and deal with serious issues/ events still has the capacity to jar the reader unaccustomed to such treatments. And while it must be noted that in contrast to the frenetic *No Towers*, both *American Widow* and *Tribeca Sunset* present more literal and earnest recreations of the events, each of the texts nevertheless depicts the ongoing presence of the wound and its lasting effect on individual lives. As James Brassett argues, the greater understanding of these tragedies depends on allowing the voice of the traumatized to be heard: "By focusing on these subjects, how they contest the meaning of their experiences, we might "learn from', rather than simply 'respond to' vulnerability" (24). These graphic narratives reveal different levels of trauma, but also individuals coming to terms with that presence in very personal ways. In the process, they give voice to a qualitatively different, and harder-won, resilience than the simplified flag-waving version propounded by the official engines of testimony. They exist finally as more complex, and thus potentially truer, testimonials to the events whose impact still resonates.

NOTES

1. This is also true of the crash site of United 93 in Pennsylvania, but not of the Pentagon which sustained substantial damage but remained standing.

2. Tellingly, in the first chapter of Torres's *American Widow*, an entire page depicts people all around the world telling others, "Turn on your TV," emphasizing the manner in which most people first experienced the events of that day (5).

3. Art Spiegelman, *In the Shadow of No Towers* (New York: Pantheon Books, 2004): Foreword. Subsequent references appear parenthetically in the text, cited as ISNT. Later, he observes that "he is haunted now by the images he *didn't* witness" (ISNT Panel 6, emphasis in text).

4. Charles Hatfield suggests that a similar transformation occurs in the creation of the writer's graphic persona: "Prerequisite to such caricature, it would seem, is a form of alienation or estrangement, through which the cartoonist-autobiographer regards himself as *other*, as a distinct character to be seen as a well as heard" (114).

5. Henrik Rehr, *Tribeca Sunset* (New York: iBooks, 2005): ix. Subsequent references appear parenthetically in the text, cited as TS.

6. Of the (at least) five graphic narratives written on the subject of 9/11, Spiegelman's *In the Shadow of No Towers* is the only one to have garnered any critical attention (aside from the odd book review). In fact, even in the extensive discussion of *No Towers*, reference is seldom made to these other texts. As the product of the author of the much-lauded *Maus*, it is natural that more attention would be paid to his text, but this disparity also indicates a general turning to perceived "experts" to best explain the trauma to us. But Rehr and Torres offer us very different texts, highlighting the possibility of innumerable responses to this tragedy. It is also worth noting that aside from the three works examined here, two others have been published in France: Sandrine Revel's *Le 11e Jour*, and Colin and Ciluffo's *World Trade Angels*.

7. Three years after the event, Debbie Amato, another 9/11 widow, noted, "The public wants you to live up to what they made you. . . . They don't really want you to move on" (Faludi 107).

8. Alissa Torres and Sungyoon Choi, *American Widow* (New York: Villard, 2008): 46. Subsequent references appear parenthetically in the text, cited as AW.

9. Rehr's "outsider" viewpoint is perhaps best communicated in a series of drawings entitled *September 12*. In one of these, for instance, an Arab man sitting in a reading room, addresses the reader in three consecutive panels; (1) "To the people of America, 9-11 was horrible, traumatic, and unprecedented." (2) "For most Arabs, it was just another day of hijackings, violence and random murder of innocent people." (3) "Now *you* know how *we* feel."

10. Sandrine Revel, a Frenchwoman, also uses an emotional touchstone to connect with trauma in *Le 11e jour* (*The Eleventh Day*). In her case she depicts the ghost of her dead brother appearing to her at key moments during the course of the day.

Chapter Three

French Fiction and the Utopian Potential of 9/11

In her introduction to *From Solidarity to Schisms*, Cara Cilano conceptualizes September 11 as a moment "characterized by unfathomable vulnerability and the possibility of a better future" (13).[1] She argues that the event, while traumatic, might have served as impetus to reconfigure American self-perceptions. Instead, she contends, the United States squandered the "utopian potential" of this moment. For while the country became the immediate beneficiary of world wide sympathy and fellow-feeling, in the months that ensued this goodwill was eroded by an American administration that succumbed to fear and anxiety, insisting on exercising its power unilaterally and flexing its military might.[2] Cilano remains optimistic, however, because she identifies European fictional discourse on 9/11 as emblematic of a desire for a melding of divergent positions. These narratives act as a productive counter-flow to American unilateralism, their critique intending to keep America's sense of itself unbalanced, thus providing fuel for self-reflection, analysis, and, most important, renewal: "Unsettledness is necessary in this conceptual framework, for the work of democracy is always in process, always aware of the stultification brought about by reification" (19–20). She further identifies a turning inward and a solidifying of boundaries, encapsulated in an emphasis placed on "home" that emerged in the wake of the attacks, and contends that this drive "entails a tightening of identifications intended to align people ideologically based on appeals to a manufactured sense of cultural nativity" (19). She advocates for a disruption of what she identifies as the reifying of nationalist imperatives at the expense of cosmopolitan or universalist ones:

> To be uncomfortable in one's home is, then, to take the time to acknowledge what is at stake in the construction of 'home'—both for oneself and, more urgently, for others—and to commit oneself to the endless reconstruction of 'home' so as to move toward greater inclusiveness and shared dignity. (Cilano 20)

Cilano posits these narratives of home as a principal obstacle in the quest to seize the utopian potential of the moment and, like others, calls for the dismantlement of the barriers standing between native and foreign, between us and them.

Of the European fiction written on the subject of 9/11 a substantial output has emanated from France; at least seven novels and two graphic narratives deal specifically with the cataclysmic events of that Tuesday morning in 2001. Four of these texts—Christian Garcin's *La jubilation des hasards* (2005), Didier Goupil's *Le jour de mon retour sur terre* (2003), Luc Lang's *11 septembre, mon amour* (2003), and Frédéric Beigbeder's *Windows on the World* (2003)—provide fertile ground for testing the soundness and validity of Cilano's hypothesis.[3] Each text demonstrates, in its own way, that the impulse to comment, to construct a counternarrative, emanates from a range of desires not so easily characterized: seeking to help the United States recover from the tragedy, critiquing American flaws and failures, responding to perceived demonstrations of uncritical collegiality towards the United States, or simply trumpeting French superiority. So we might question the degree to which the French response to 9/11 (and its aftermath) is reflective of a global reaction (from solidarity to schisms), and in what ways we might see it as expressing uniquely French concerns. A notable fact about these texts—with the exception of Frédéric Beigbeder's *Windows on the World*—is that they have not been translated into English. This inaccessibility may point to the extensiveness of American insularity, but it might also designate the true audience for whom these texts are intended. If the latter then these novels do not become part of a larger, global dialogue (as Cilano suggests), but rather serve to assert that which differentiates France from its American counterpart. And if these texts appeal primarily to French readers, it is because they speak of contemporary France itself, its self-proclaimed role as resister and regulator of the United States' global ambitions, but also its anxiety concerning its own decline or sense of growing inconsequentiality. So while this moment can be conceived as an opportunity for reconfiguring the geopolitical landscape, the question remains, is it being grasped with a genuine desire to improve global conditions or merely one's own standing on the international stage? I will argue that we can acquire some measure of the degree to which someone truly wishes to engage in this rapprochement, by reading literary output for signs of empathy or empathetic connection. Do these texts express empathy for the American situation? Are they imaginative attempts to genuinely feel the emotions of the Americans, to perceive the event from an American point of view? At the same time, we need to consider the ways in which the specific dynamics of Franco-American relations might handicap or limit the possibilities of empathy, on the part of the novelists, but also that of a French readership.

In *The French Way*, Richard Kuisel argues that the United States has long acted as "the foil for [France's] national identity" (7). His text, which examines Franco-American relations during the last two decades of the twentieth century, is subtitled, *How France Embraced and Rejected American Values and Power*, speaking to the tenuous relationship between France and its American counterpart.[4] This ambivalence derives in no small part from an underlying sense, felt by both countries, that they share more than either is willing to admit, so that, paradoxically, these very commonalities lead to the strongest oppositions:

> Rooted in history and lodged in the people's collective psychology was the conviction that the French, like the Americans, had a special global mission. For Americans it was the spread of democracy and free enterprise; for the French it was the *mission civilisatrice*. Such resuppositions were bound to clash. Or, put it another way, the Americans and the French are the only two people who believe everyone else in the world would like to be them. (Kuisel 353)

It stands to reason, as Kuisel suggests, that two universalizing missions cannot peacefully coexist. In other words, the "branding" of each nation bears such similarity to the other that the only means of highlighting one's own brand is to accentuate existing differences. Stanley Hoffman similarly argues that while the two nations have had their differences since 1945, it is "the rivalry of universalisms" that has given their opposition a "passionate inflection" (my translation, 65). This position is also taken up by Pierre Rosanvallon, who maintains that while there may be notable issues of style, method, and political consistency, the critical divide occurs between two versions of universalism, which he terms *dogmatic* and *experimental*, revealing his preference. He suggests that around the mid-nineteenth century, the United States reached a consensus about the notion of democracy, but this came "at the cost of sacralizing the democratic ideal, suddenly expunging it of its constitutive radical interrogations and its subversive potential" (Rosanvallon, my translation). Rosanvallon leaves no doubt as to which of the two approaches is truly universalist. The dogmatic universalism practiced by the United States is one that curtails freedoms and individual expression. France, for its part, practices a more radical, open, and renewable approach: "Democracy as religion on one side, democracy as experience on the other, these two approaches lead to very different conceptions about the universalist perspective" (Rosanvallon, my translation). In the end, the American approach has given rise to an "insupportable arrogance," in contrast to the truly experimental universalism practiced by France. Rosanvallon's assessment captures French feeling, expressing dismay and bewilderment that their uncouth and imperious cousin should experience a greater level of success in exporting its particular brand of universalism to the world.

American success is thus a two-edged sword. First, it highlights France's secondary status and, second, exacerbates fears about its diminishing relevance. As such France has turned to adopting strategies that oppose and counterbalance what they perceive as intrusive and self-serving behavior on the part of the Americans. This feeling is augmented when, with the dissolution of the Soviet Union and the end of the Cold War, the United States becomes the sole, uncontested superpower in the world, or "hyperpower." The antidote, as proposed by Jacques Chirac and others, is multipolarity, a system wherein power and influence are exercised more equally by a number of different constituents across the globe. But these oppositions, as noted, are also rooted in the desire to maintain national identity in the face of an unrelenting juggernaut that appears to swallow all in its path. For there obviously exists a far greater chance of preserving an identity in a multipolar (heterogeneous) world than in a unipolar (homogeneous) one. In fact, the adoption of the stance itself provided France with a measure of distinction. As Kuisel notes, "Responding to the hyperpower defined French foreign policy: constraining America and attaining self-reliance was the standard of measurement for the country's success and identity" (270). It may have been a measurement, but the results rarely seemed to be in France's favor. For while there may have been more than one universalism, and France hotly contested the unipolar vision of the United States, it was clear which country was reaping the greater benefits. Franco-American relations in the final years of the twentieth century revealed an increasingly insecure France whose prospects for regaining international prominence and influence seemed to be dwindling rapidly. Indeed, these years have been characterized as a fairly "depressed" moment in French political life. As Kuisel observes, "The French were in a defensive crouch and this defensiveness had its roots in what was often described at the time as the 'French malaise,' referring to a loss of confidence, a feeling of decline, a sense of waning independence, and a concern about vanishing national identity" (362).

Taking these factors into account, one could argue that the events of September 11, 2001, came at an opportune moment for France, bringing the world a little closer to Chirac's vision of things, reducing American power by exposing its vulnerability and, in the process, leveling the international playing field between the United States and other countries. At the same time the event played into France's increasingly pressing need or desire to distinguish (distance?) itself from the United States. In this case, the distinction served the twin goals of identity preservation and increased security (an awareness, perhaps, of the large Muslim population living on French soil). This pronounced emphasis on, and a drive to find, difference certainly undercuts any possibility of empathetic connection or common vision.

WE ARE ALL AMERICANS?

In reading these texts, then, one might expect to discover a continuum that extends from empathy (best expressed by the editor of *Le Monde*, Jean-Marie Colombani: "Nous sommes tous Américains") to antipathy for the United States (anti-Americanism, Americanophobia). That an event such as 9/11 should elicit such rapid criticism and condemnation from French quarters, however, certainly indicates a readiness to adopt an adversarial position. In this vein, Denis Lacorne argues that even before 2001, the French "were already of two minds, their empathy mingled with indifference, their admiration with doubts and distrust of the abnormalities of the American society" (Judt 38). The French reaction could also be explained as one which interprets Colombani's statement as a national endorsement of the American imperialistic approach to the world. But Colombani certainly intended the phrase as an expression of shared vulnerability, highlighting the fact that these attacks could happen to anyone. In fact, its intentions as an expression of solidarity are clear, as it alludes to the slogan used in support of Daniel Cohn-Bendit during the Paris student uprisings of 1968, "Nous sommes tous des juifs allemands." It is also worth noting that Colombani's essay is critical of the United States, pointing to the existence of a unipolar world as the primary reason for the hatred coming its way. In its growing insularity, and its newly acquired hyperpower status, he asserts, the American nation has failed to establish meaningful connections with the rest of the world, creating unstable conditions in which such barbarous events become an inevitability. Nevertheless, as we shall see, the phrase is frequently utilized or interpreted as an instance of unthinking and unabashed endorsement of American policies, attitudes, and values. This reveals an ingrained desire in some to *not* be connected to the United States in any way (even in the course of a single phrase), and goes hand-in-hand with an insistence that the event was the foreseeable result of American actions, and American actions only.

Colombani's emphasis on a shared vulnerability seeks to find common ground. In this way, it bears similarity to Cilano's call which, while referring specifically to fiction, is itself one of many responses that conceptualize 9/11 as a catalyst for positive change, often through the invocation of universalist principles. The event highlighted deep differences and divisions within the global community, leading to the proclamation of a "clash of civilizations." Such fissures can be mended, these advocates claim, through a renewed emphasis on the essential sameness of humanity, and certain concepts, or "cosmopolitan sentiments" as James Brassett labels them, which are proffered as antidotes to the "us versus them" narratives that proliferated in the wake of the event. Such an overt display of violence aimed at the other compelled a reframing and reconsideration of mutual vulnerability.

Engaging in these acts of feeling requires that we recognize some degree of sameness between ourselves and the suffering other. Sympathy—feeling sorrow when confronted with the suffering of another—is perhaps the easiest emotion to elicit under these circumstances. At times, however, it may be difficult to distinguish it from pity, and insinuations of superiority. Compassion, for its part, takes sympathy one step further by supplementing the emotion with a desire or willingness to come to the aid of the sufferer. The line separating compassion from empathy is harder to identify, and the terms are often used interchangeably. For instance, in "Compassion and Terror," Martha Nussbaum argues that compassion can only occur if we determine for ourselves that a person's "predicament is truly grave." This determination, she continues, "involves both trying to look out at the situation from the suffering person's own viewpoint and then assessing the person's own assessment" (235). It is not sufficient, in other words, to rely on our own determination of the gravity of the situation, we must also consider the different ways in which it might be considered grave by the other. Stressing repeatedly the challenges to compassion, Nussbaum contends that suffering can elicit this act of feeling, but "only insofar as we believe that the suffering person shares vulnerabilities and possibilities with us" (235). Or, conversely, that we share vulnerabilities and possibilities with them. In fact, Nussbaum seems to be suggesting that compassion is not possible without empathy. In the end, compassion does not completely fulfill the requirements of mutual recognition, since it implies a degree of inequality between observer and observed; by virtue of not being the one who suffers, the observer finds himself in a superior position. Empathy, while sharing this dispositional imbalance, comes closer to an understanding of the other's suffering through recognition that this pain could have been one's own. In this vein, Brassett suggests that while sympathy might be the most common response to the event, "the existential nature of vulnerability 'might' allow for the identification and nurturing of empathy as a more appropriate/powerful ethical sentiment" (24).

What finally distinguishes empathy from sympathy and compassion, at least the kind being considered here, is that it requires a conscious and willing effort on the part of the observer who must, to the best of his abilities, sublimate (if only momentarily) his own self in order to better perceive the world from the other's perspective. In this regard, Karsten Stueber argues for a distinction between basic empathy and what he terms "reenactive empathy." Basic empathy allows us to recognize another's emotion, but not the reasons for his subsequent behavior, and is thus insufficient. Stueber insists that only reenactive empathy will allow us to come to some conclusion about the actions of others since "only by using our cognitive and deliberative capacities in order to reenact or imitate in our own mind the thought processes of the other person—are we able to conceive of another person's more complex social behavior as the behavior of a rational agent who acts for a reason" (21). Engaging in this level of empathy opens the possibility of greater understanding not only of the other's thoughts, but also his actions.

Of course, empathy is not the only means of effecting a greater degree of inclusiveness, and it does have its limitations. It cannot replace direct interaction with the other (though it may have some impact on the quality of those interactions). And though we may use our imagination in an attempt to see what the other sees, we still have no guarantee that we really see as the other does. Consequently, we should remain aware of the dangers of presuming to know the other merely because we have attempted an empathetic engagement. As Julinna Oxley explains, there is always the possibility "that someone might merely project her own beliefs and thoughts onto others instead of correctly understanding the other's emotion" (32). Thus, exercising empathy requires a self-critical eye and an awareness of one's own motivations for engaging in the activity.

Despite these limitations and pitfalls, writers such as Oxley and Brassett nevertheless endorse empathy as a powerful ethical sentiment for navigating the current crisis. Through its emphasis on sameness and connection, it serves as a vehicle for diminishing misperceptions and erroneous conclusions, creating greater harmony between constituents. As Oxley observes,

> Empathy enables people to understand how others see the world, helps them to appreciate others' perspectives and connect with them emotionally, eliminates the perception of conflict between oneself and others, and makes possible the perception of similarity between oneself and others. (5–6)

The fictional responses to 9/11 would thus appear as ideal vehicles for allowing these writers to engage in some reenactive empathy. But the varied responses are not guided by these principles, instead, these French narratives seem intent on creating their own "us-them" scenarios, highlighting difference rather than similarity. They insist on emphasizing how unexceptional 9/11 was, pointing to other atrocities and man-made disasters throughout history. And compassion is forcefully withheld because these writers steadfastly maintain this occurrence was something Americans brought upon themselves. As a hyperpower, the United States is criticized in these texts for its arrogance, its unrelenting pursuit of material wealth, and its misapplication of military might. And much space is devoted to George W. Bush and his administration as embodiments of what Europeans fear most about the American nation: a frontier mentality combined with a thirst for violence, an apparent simplicity, a religious fervor, and a conviction that might makes right. That an American populace elected such an individual to office only served to corroborate that the citizenry had indeed succumbed to their own worst natures. As such, the American people are often targets of criticism in these texts, used as objects of ridicule, depicted as infantile, unsophisticated, regressive, with no capacity for independent thinking, blindly following the edicts of their newly appointed sheriff. As we shall see, expressions of empathy, when they do come in these texts, are reserved for the dead. The dead have paid the ultimate price, whereas the living continue to perpetuate the system that elicited these horrible attacks.

Finally, it is worth considering whether these texts contain expressions of mutual vulnerability.[5] This was the nature of Colombani's response. That the United States might be considered the "victim" in this particular instance, however, poses some particular challenges. Specifically, it raises questions about the directionality of empathy. Frequently when empathy is invoked, the focus is on a disadvantaged, oppressed, or brutalized other. But what if the other inhabits a space perceived to be superior to one's own? Is it in fact possible to empathize with a dominant force that suddenly finds itself victimized? It is easy to imagine that empathy will be attenuated in cases when the other is conceived as having lived a privileged existence, and of not having been particularly empathetic itself in its dealings with others. An empathetic response is further complicated if one believes that one's status in the world is contingent upon a comparative standing with a specific other. In that case, any diminishment or loss suffered by that other will most likely be received with some degree of pleasure rather than empathy. So this is not *schadenfreude* as such, but rather the perception that one's standing (in the eyes of others, on the international stage) is improved through the impoverishment of the other's. The emotion is thus contingent upon perceiving that one's influence and power is intimately tied to the highs or lows of the other.

So while the distinction are not always clear, these novels tend to use the events of September 2001 as an opportunity to raise some age-old griefs. As Tony Judt observes, many French books written on 9/11 are characterized by an initial "real or feigned regret" followed by an eventual "inventory of American shortcomings" (22). These events become the catalyst for emphasizing what sets France apart from the United States rather than searching for commonalities. Nationalist agendas and histories act as obstacles to cosmopolitan possibilities. This again raises questions about the "utopian potential" Cilano so optimistically believes might be attained through the reception of "outsider" texts. As my readings will show, the preconceptions of both the United States and France end up preventing the possibility of an earnest expression of American vulnerability (not framed or interpreted as justifications for exercising power) and/or of a true empathetic French response (unclouded by feelings of difference, inferiority, and/or superiority).

AMERICAN SHORTCOMINGS: CHRISTIAN GARCIN'S *LA JUBILATION DES HASARDS*?

The plotline of Christian Garcin's *La jubilation des hasards* is primarily concerned with reincarnation and the impact of ghostly presences in our lives. In the thirteenth chapter, however, the narrator-protagonist suddenly offers pronouncements on the subject of 9/11. The reader is not surprised since the protagonist has flown to New York to resolve some matters of business, and has accepted to write a piece on the city's recovery from the attacks. The commentary, coming as an intrusion in the novel, nevertheless reflects a seemingly irrepressible urge to opine upon the events of that day. The observations are certainly meant to shock the reader: "*Comme tout le monde j'avais vu en boucle les spectaculaires images des avions percutant les deux tours de Babel, et je ne pouvais m'empêcher de penser que, finalement, c'était assez réussi*"/'Like everyone I had seen the endless televised loops of the planes smashing into the two towers of Babel, and I could not help thinking that, finally, the attacks were quite successful' (91). Though the narrator professes to no interest in the subject, he still holds forth, acknowledging that his feelings are considerably different from those of the majority. Sounding much like Karlheinz Stockhausen (the composer who was maligned for his insensitivity), he admits that the execution of the attacks elicited in him "a strange satisfaction" which he labels as "*une sorte de satisfaction presque esthétique que je n'osais avouer à personne*"/'a kind of almost aesthetic appreciation that I did not dare admit to anyone' (92). He continues:

> *Je n'osais l'avouer à personne car parmi les gens que je côtoyais, personne à chaud ne me semblait pouvoir entendre cela. On mettrait aussitôt ces propos sur le compte d'un aveuglement salement idéologique, d'une détestation globale du système américain, d'une grande défiance—que je ne songeais certes pas à nier, même si tout était infiniment plus complexe, qui mêlait dans un même mouvement attrait et répulsion—à l'égard de la volonté hégémonique de ce pays, son cynisme politique, son inculture dominatrice, son idéologie exclusivement marchande, sa violence constitutionelle. L'heure était plutôt au consensus indigné, apitoyé, terrifié ou attristé, et mes propos n'eussent sans doute été considérés que comme des cyniques provocations, ce qu'ils n'étaient pas le moins du monde.* (92)

> I did not dare admit it to anyone, because among my acquaintances no one seemed willing or able to hear it. My point of view would be immediately shrugged off as blind malignant ideology, a globalized hatred of the American system, or simply distrust—remarks which I did not refute, even if everything was infinitely more complex, that mixed in the same dynamic was both attraction and repulsion—in regards to the hegemonic will of this country, its political cynicism, its dominant philistinism, its exclusively mercantile ideology, its constitutional violence. The mood of the hour was rather indignant, pitying,

terrified or sad, and my observations would have been taken as nothing more than cynical provocations, which they were not in the least.

The narrator never explains why these comments should not be viewed as provocations, nor does he ponder why others might view them as such. And though he gives cause for his repulsion, the purported reasons for his attraction are left unnamed. So while some of the critiques offered by Garcin's narrator may be legitimate—the attacks *were* a success and such attacks *have* occurred at other times in other places—they are tempered by his admiration for the accomplishments of the terrorists, and his lack of concern for the pain and suffering endured that day (and after). We find an insouciance in the writing, in the use of a language that can be perceived at times as (deliberately?) uncaring and insensitive. The use of the word "success" in describing the attacks, for example, indicates an emotional footing diametrically opposed to that of the majority of American citizens.

The comments and their style also reflect an impatience on the part of the narrator, directed at what he perceives as preferential treatment for the United States. One senses the text is meant as a counterbalance, intended to right what is perceived as disproportionate sympathy *vis-à-vis* the United States. For instance, Garcin's narrator strongly objects to the fact that French schoolchildren were asked to observe a minute of silence for the victims of September 11.[6] If such formalities are going to be observed, he argues, then all countries must be afforded the same recognition. This same level of outrage and bemusement characterizes the narrator's visit to New York. He berates himself for having any feelings about the event, as though they might legitimatize the plight of the victims. He arranges interviews for his piece, but holds little hope they will provide anything "new." His suspicions are immediately confirmed:

> *Comme je m'y attendais sans trop savoir pourquoi, il n'avait que de consternantes banalités à me dire sur les attentats, l'indescriptible horreur des attentats, l'héroïsme des pompiers morts pendant et après les attentats, les conséquences des attentats, l'inévitable, mais finalement marginale, et presque excusable, défiance à l'égard des musulmans américains après les attentats, l'extraordinaire solidarité du peuple américain à la suite des attentats, et la croisade, sans doute maladroite parfois, mais indéniablement justifiée, de l'administration Bush contre les terroristes organisateurs d'attentats. (111)*

As I had expected, without really knowing why, all [the interviewee] could offer me were dumbfounding banalities on the attacks, the indescribable horror of the attacks, the heroic firemen killed during and after the attacks, the consequences of the attacks, the inevitable, though finally marginal, and almost excusable, mistreatment of American Muslims after the attacks, the solidarity of the American people after the attacks, and the crusade, misguided at times, but undeniably justified, of the Bush administration against the organizers of the attacks.

The conscious repetition of the words "the attacks" (*les attentats*), recalls the media bombardments to which the world was subjected. But the narrator's tone also communicates his unwillingness to recognize how any of this is newsworthy; in fact, the repetition serves to empty the word of its traumatic significance. The passage conveys a palpable sense of boredom, and a conviction that Americans need to "get over" what happened to them on that day. And instead of connecting with the interviewee's struggle to communicate this harrowing experience, the narrator focuses on the "dumbfounding banalities" (*de consternante banalités*) produced in the effort. This language use betrays a host of other sentiments. Certainly, Garcin's narrator exhibits impatience, a caustic indifference, and a sense of superiority combined with an amazement at American naiveté. After all, did not everyone know that this day would eventually come? Did they really not see how the Towers might be perceived as a deliberate provocation? This sentiment is best emblematized in the frequent analogies made between the World Trade Center and the Tower of Babel. As I will demonstrate, a definite correlation exists between the manner in which these writers describe the Twin Towers (and their destruction) and the degree of empathy they exhibit towards their American counterparts.

Although known as a *provocateur*, Jean Baudrillard exhibits a representative attitude in his analysis of the events of September 11 and, specifically, the destruction of the Twin Towers. Much like Jacques Derrida, he argues that the implosion of the World Trade Center was nothing less than a "symbolic suicide," not caused by the terrorists (who did not imagine such an eventuality), but by a weakened system which, unable to support its "unnatural" position as the sole superpower, ends up "destroying itself, committing suicide in a blaze of glory" (4–5).[7] When the dominant system finds itself without an enemy, it turns on itself, seeking the weakest part of its own structure. In Baudrillard's words, 9/11 is evidence of *"triumphant globalization battling against itself"* (11).[8] This act of self-destruction symbolizes and reflects the unconscious will of all people (including Americans themselves) who desire nothing more than to see the hegemony of the United States overturned. Utilizing the metaphor of illness, Baudrillard theorizes that the destruction of the Towers was due to the people's innate resistance to expressions of hegemony: "Allergy to any definitive order, to any definitive power, is—happily—universal, and the two towers of the World Trade Center were perfect embodiments, in their very twinness, of that definitive order" (6). The American people, Baudrillard suggests, despise a superpower (even their own), and 9/11 is merely the expression of that hatred. As evidence, he points to enactments in Hollywood disaster films as overt demonstrations of this desire. He even implies that the people's disgust with the World Trade Center—"their secret desire to see them disappear"—contributed to their implosion. Finally, he argues that the national reaction to September 11 was disproportionate to the event, because of the American people's refusal to confront their own "unavowable complicity" (6). The use of the word "complicit" is telling, for it intimates conscious courting of an eventual backlash rather than ignorance of how actions may engender repercussions. The imputation of complicity, agency, and desire can be read as provocation and/or calculated indifference. But it also reflects a failure of empathy—the text reflecting the glee ("happily") the writer supposes others experience in witnessing and enabling a superpower's end.[9]

The same sentiments are echoed by these novelists who express their own insights about the symbolism and meaning of the event. The Towers embody a hegemonic hold against which the world reacts. In effect, the World Trade Center becomes the literal lightning rod for global dissatisfaction with the American (mis)management of worldly affairs. But in these texts, the Twin Towers come to symbolize a great deal more: world domination, excessive materialism, decadence, and a host of other sins. In Garcin's *La jubilation des hasards*, for example, the narrator acknowledges that his admiration for the attacks stems from the manner in which the Muslim terrorists manipulated Biblical symbolism: *"la Babylone moderne, ces deux impassibles tours de verre dressées fièrement à la face des humbles et des misérieux, tout cela abattu par le feu du ciel, c'était à la fois l'orgueil de Babel et la turpitude de Sodome et Gomorrhe qui étaient châtiés en direct"*/'this modern Babylon, these two impassive glass towers rising proudly in the face of misery, all brought down by fire in the sky, it was at once both the pride of Babel and the turpitude of Sodom and Gomorrah that were castigated live' (91). The invocation of the Tower of Babel asserts the manner in which the World Trade Center invited its own destruction. This symbolic reading permits the creation of a morality play signifying the punishment of arrogance, the emptiness of materialistic pursuits, a striking down of hubris, an inevitable loss of power. As with their biblical counterpart (which might be considered the first technological catastrophe in recorded history), the Twin Towers literally represent the apex of technological advances, while simultaneously throwing into relief their limitations and vulnerability.[10] The naiveté of the builders of the World Trade Center echoes that of those who constructed the Tower of Babel, men incapable of seeing that raising a structure to Heaven—an exhibition of both pride and decadence—might be perceived as an affront to God.[11]

THE PITFALLS OF CONSUMERISM: DIDIER GOUPIL'S
LE JOUR DE MON RETOUR SUR TERRE

The danger in stretching the Tower of Babel analogy too far, as Lawrence Schehr notes, is in creating strong correlations between the actions of the terrorists and those of a vengeful God (137). One might suggest, however, that this is precisely what Didier Goupil accomplishes in *Le jour de mon retour sur terre (The Day I Returned to Earth).*[12] The novel's overt symbolism presents a single tower from which the word "GOLD" is repeatedly beamed. When the Grand Tower is destroyed, the narrator observes that *"la ville venait non seulement de perdre le phare qui la guidait, mais son âme"*/ 'the city had lost not only the lighthouse that guided her, but her soul' (12). One can infer, then, that the edict which America follows, down to her very soul, is mercantile. Indeed, the indirect narration of the unnamed protagonist often blends with that of the implied author to present an ongoing critique of American consumerist and militaristic tendencies.[13] The protagonist's rejection of his former life, beginning with his refusal to answer his cell phone, his discarding of his briefcase, and his choice of homelessness, are meant to suggest the country has somehow lost its way. This is the novel's plot. A worker in the tower barely survives the attack and goes into a tailspin, rejects his former life (and all the capitalist trappings therein) and roams the streets around Ground Zero. Looking down at his ash-covered briefcase, he thinks: *"il lui sembla tout droit sorti d'un sarcophage, et appartenir à un autre temps, à jamais révolu"*/'it seemed to have been taken from a sarcophagus, and belonged to another time, gone forever' (29). The trauma has wrenched him free from the chains that bound him to a meaningless life. In this respect, Goupil's novel hints at the utopian, even Edenic, potential wrapped within the catastrophe. Later, the narrative explicitly connects the fate of the crumbling tower and his disengagement with an earlier materialistic self: *"Il n'éprouva pour sa part aucune haine. Ni même de colère, ou de peine. Il ressentait tout simplement un grand vide. Oui, un grand vide. Comme si quelque chose en lui avait disparu, s'était littéralement effondré"*/'For his part, he did not feel any hate. Not even anger, or pain. He simply sensed an emptiness at his core. Yes, a great emptiness. It was as if something in him had vanished, had literally collapsed' (54). The protagonist, however, appears to be the only person (until he meets his equally homeless and equally liberated soulmate) who recognizes the folly of his previous pursuits. So while the narrative exhibits some empathy for the dead, it accords little to the living. The multitudes are presented as blind followers whose steadfast devotion remains unshaken. The people not only want the Tower rebuilt, but feel *"comme orphelins des lettres géantes qui avaient si longtemps brillé à son sommet: GOLD . . . GOLD . . . GOLD"*/'like orphans of the giant letters that had once shone at its summit: GOLD . . . GOLD . . . GOLD' (112). They remain complicit with a system that brought retribution down upon their heads. The novel resorts to biblical analogy as a means of communicating the level of American hubris; Goupil also makes allusion to the Tower of Babel, and includes a biblical flood to hammer home the displeasure of the gods.

Rather than a cause and effect argument, however, or an analysis of political motivations, what is presented is something more closely resembling bad karma. Americans have acted so badly for so long that it has finally come back to haunt them. The terrorists, then, are not so much agents of an organization, but of much-needed change, controlled by an unseen force that seeks to right the balance of the world (the mastermind behind the attacks is called the Unknown). And the catastrophe serves precisely this function for the protagonist, allowing him to see his nation clearly for the first time: "*il était en train de comprendre que contrairement à ce qu'on lui avait appris, notre pouvoir ne reposait pas sur une simple affaire de sciences, d'industrie ou de finance, ni même sur une soi-disant supériorité nationale, mais tout bêtement au fait que de toute éternité, et en tout cas depuis l'antiquité, nos armées tuaient davantage et mieux que leurs rivales*"/'he was beginning to understand, in contrast to what he had been taught, that our power was not simply a matter of the sciences, industry or finance, or even of a so-called national superiority, but more simply that for all eternity, and at least since antiquity, our armies knew how to kill and in greater numbers than did their rivals' (48).

But the novel makes clear that the citizenry have not been privy to such an awakening. In this regard, the President is depicted not only as the perpetuation of their wishes and desires, but also as the physical representation of the isolationist and domineering impulses of the United States. The attacks provide him with "*une opportunité unique de nettoyer des contrées éloignées et hostiles, et d'étendre encore l'emprise de l'empire sur la planète*"/'the unique opportunity to not only destroy distant and hostile lands, but to strengthen the grip of the empire on the planet' (119). The novel thus makes plain the ways in which the United States has precluded the possibility for empathy through its aggressive military stance. Despite plagues of fire and rain, the President does not mend his ways, or contemplate what brought such misfortune down upon the people of his country. The unwavering determination of the nation, much lauded by its politicians, is seen here as a detriment, most ironically brought home in the depiction of the celebration surrounding the first anniversary of the attacks with which the novel ends. After a minute of silence, the President unfurls the coverings on a statue erected on the site of the attacks depicting a soldier in uniform grasping a gun in one raised hand and cradling a globe of the world in the other (158). With this startling image, the novel suggests that very little has changed. The nation, though slightly chastened, still clings tightly to its flawed principles. In contrast, the homeless and nomadic lifestyle of the protagonist and his partner is celebrated. The intimations to Adam and Eve are clear. The protagonist, as the title indicates, returns to earth, now cognizant of the folly of his earlier existence. He is prepared to begin anew. In this respect, the novels of Goupil and Luc Lang resemble each other. They both express a yearning for a return to a prelapsarian and Arcadian existence. Both texts imply that the pursuit of the American Dream has led the people of the United States astray, and that perhaps (and only perhaps) a catastrophe of this magnitude can awaken them to the error of their ways. Each novel suggests, however, that such hopes may be in vain.

BLIND ANTIPATHY: LUC LANG'S *11 SEPTEMBRE MON AMOUR*

Although it quickly turns to listing and attacking American shortcomings, Luc Lang's *11 septembre mon amour* begins with compassion, focusing on the voices of the victims and their loved ones on that fateful morning. Of these recorded voices, Lang himself observes that "a novelist could not have gone farther in the expression of cruelty and of empathy" (quoted in Obajtek-Kirkwood 213). And yet here he conveys all the pain and pathos of the situation, illuminating the boundless love expressed in this hopeless moment:

> *Un amour qui espère mais qui n'attend plus rien puisque c'est le néant qui vient, un amour sans désir assurément, qui voudrait vous transmettre une force, même si ce don vous inflige une douleur dont on ne guérit pas.* (15)

> A love that hopes but expects nothing more since nothingness looms, a love without desire surely, that wishes to convey strength, even if it inflicts a wound from which one never heals.

These opening pages are moving as they capture the pain and desperation, but also love, of those moments. The narrator empathizes fully with the plight of the people at both ends of the telephone line, trapped in an impossible situation.

Like Goupil, however, Lang's empathy is almost entirely reserved for the dead, who no longer have the capacity to offend. For the text outlines in a multitude of ways how the possibility for empathy is obliterated by the sins and misdeeds of the American people in the days after 9/11. In this same chapter, he imagines a library containing the lists of all "*les victimes civiles du XXe siècle jusqu'à l'aube à peine esquissée et déjà ténébreuse du XXIe*"/ 'the civilian deaths during the twentieth century right up to the barely risen and already darkening dawn of the twenty first' (26). This "universal library" would contain "*toutes les dispersions, disparitions, exterminations . . . tous les déchirements, de toutes les diasporas, de tous les genocides*"/'all the dispersions, disappearances, exterminations . . . all the rendings, all the diasporas, all the genocides' (ellipsis mine, 26) and, of course, all the names of those who perished on September 11. Having elicited sympathy for those victims, however, Lang concludes the chapter by identifying a manuscript already missing from the library: *"une sorte d'immédiat corrélat de celui du 11 septembre, le livre des victimes civiles afghanes, disparues lors des bombardements 'alliés' qui s'ensuivirent au cours de l'hiver 2001–2002"*/'a kind of correlate to that of September 11, the book listing Afghan civilian deaths, those who disappeared during the 'allied' bombings that ensued during the winter of 2001–2002' (27). In effect, Lang ends his elegy for the September 11 dead by reminding the reader that the United States (the word *allied* in quotes implying the participation of the ambivalent and the coerced) is responsible for much death and destruction.

Having traveled to Montana to research the Blackfoot (his previous work is entitled *The Indians*), Lang is on American soil the morning of September 11. The text recounts his impressions of the country, and its response to the event, during the week that follows. He tells of hearing the reading of names on a radio station on September 13 and of being truly moved because this mourning was done *"sans l'érection du drapeau national, sans l'aboiement d'un discours de guerre et de vengeance, sans le larmoiement de grand sentiments"*/'without raising the flag, without the barked discourse of war and vengeance, without the bewailing of grandiose emotions' (24). These same qualifications come to taint Lang's experience; flags, war, and nationalist sentiment are all on the horizon. The text thus details a dangerous progression, as the American people move from a natural response to the tragedy to a more vengeful and warlike one. No doubt it is difficult to feel sympathy for a nation you suspect will use a tragedy as the impetus for global invasion.

As with *Le jour de mon retour sur terre*, the text does not distinguish between the people and its government, and avers there is something endemic to the American character that has made this retribution inevitable. From his perspective, Americans are not only guilty of committing genocide, but of replacing an ideal approach to life (embodied by the Native-American) with one that is necessarily more debased. He enumerates American obsessions, including a wish to conquer the landscape and to *"refaire le Grand Canyon entre les tours de Manhattan, sculpter les Rocheuses avec le visage des présidents, bâtir des villes aussi vastes que le désert d'Arizona"*/'remake the Grand Canyon between the two towers in Manhattan, carve the Rockies with the likenesses of presidents, build cities as vast as the deserts of Arizona' (48). In contrast, the Indians lived on the land for hundreds of years and were so at one with nature, they left its appearance unchanged. But these natural beings had to be exterminated *"de toute urgence si l'on a l'ambition de faire de ce continent une société d'hommes libres"*/'as quickly as possible if our ambition is making this continent a society of free men' (49). Sounding very Baudrillardian, Lang contends that Americans have in fact wished this tragedy upon themselves, "*Est-ce pour s'arracher à cette culpabilité originelle, à ce temps premier où des hommes fondèrent une nation sur le socle d'un génocide, le génocide indien, s'entend . . .S'agirait de souffrir à son tour pour se débarrasser de ces cohortes de spectres emplumés qui hantent notre conscience d'hommes libres?*"/'to appease an original culpability, from a time when men founded a nation on the pedestal of a genocide, the Indian genocide of course . . . One must suffer in turn in order to rid oneself of these cohorts of plumed specters that haunt our consciences as free men?' (111).

A related sin is the country's inability to atone for (or even recognize) past wrongdoings. On September 12, Lang briefly espies the front page of the local *Missoulian* and the word "Japan." The sight "*me porte quelques dixièmes de seconde vers l'espoir d'une Amérique plus . . . plus quoi? N'ai pas les mots qui conviennent. Plus humaine? Plus miséricordieuse? Plus douée de mémoire? Plus humble?*"/'leads me to hope, for a few brief milliseconds, for an America more . . . more what? I can't find the appropriate words. More humane? More merciful? More gifted with memory? More humble?' (153). The use of these adjectives imply that Lang already believed the United States was lacking in humanity, mercy, memory, and humility. His "hope" quickly turns to disgust when he discovers that the word refers to Pearl Harbor, and not Hiroshima, as he initially assumed. For Lang, 9/11 should automatically cause Americans to recall the civilian deaths in Hiroshima and Nagasaki. Instead, the reference to Pearl Harbor serves to confirm America's warlike tendencies and its thirst for reprisals: "*Parce que nous voilà partis, tête baissée, dans le commencement d'une propagande occidentale guerrière telle que Double V Bouche et sa bande de porte-flingues choisissent de l'orchestrer. Nous sommes, quelle bonne blague, tous Américains, nous souvenant de Pearl Harbor!*"/'Because we are now implicated, head on, in the beginning of an occidental and warlike propaganda campaign, that W (*Double V Bush*) and his pistol-toting posse, can run any way they choose. We are all Americans in remembering Pearl Harbor. What a joke!' (158). Alluding to Colombani's statement, Lang makes clear he shares little with his American counterparts.

9/11 did momentarily raise hope in some that having been victimized, the United States would develop a greater bond with other victims (including, and perhaps especially, those *they* have victimized). But demanding this response from *any* victim in the immediate aftermath of a transgression seems exigent. Intent on seeing the U.S. as the oppressor, Lang cannot abate his condemnation during a moment of obvious victimhood. In his recalling Hiroshima (in the title's allusion to Marguerite Duras's famous work), Lang demands self-reflection and empathy from others. He does not, however, exhibit much himself. Attending a memorial held on a university campus for a professor killed in the plane that crashed into the Pentagon, Lang is taken aback by the innocence of the attendees:

Why? On est d'une innocence hagarde, on ne comprend pas le drame, l'ignoble attaque dont on est l'objet, pourquoi, mon Dieu, pourquoi? C'est une réelle émotion, profonde et sincère, enfantine et régressive, tout animée d'une identification personnelle au drapeau blessé et à la tragédie des victimes. Mon Dieu, ça pourrait être moi, moi, ma petite soeur, ma grand-mère, ma jolie fiancée, mon tendre père, quelle horreur! Mais quelle horreur! Une horreur personnelle, en rose larmoyant, pleine de bons sentiments aveugles et égocentriques, une émotion gluante et obscène, vu l'âge des participants. (188)

Why? They express a distraught innocence, not understanding the event, the vicious attack to which they have been subjected, why, God, why? It is a real emotion, profound and sincere, infantile and regressive, completely animated by a personal identification with the wounded flag and the plight of the victims. My God, that could be me, me, my little sister, my grandmother, my lovely fiancée, my dear father, what horror! A mawkish personal horror, full of blind, well-intentioned and self-centered sentiments, an obscene emotion, given the ages of the participants.

Even at such moments, Lang is incapable of resonating with the suffering others. He momentarily places himself in their thoughts, but adjectives such as "blind," "self-centered," and "obscene," reveal the commentator's true feelings.

Interestingly, Lang proclaims that *11 septembre mon amour* "is in no way anti-American, but it does attack the American administration" (Géniès). This is a stunning pronouncement for anyone who has read the novel.[14] This position does raise questions as to the extent to which anti-Americanism, particularly on the Left, has actually become *de rigueur* for the French intelligentsia. That Luc Lang is blind to his disgust may be indicative of this propensity. In his own defense, he points to the conclusion of his "novel" and his acknowledgment of American writers who have been an influence. But this concession comes too late and does far too little to counteract the images he has created throughout the book of American society as primitive, infantile, consumerist and, above all, violent.

MEASURED EMPATHY: FRÉDÉRIC BEIGBEDER'S *WINDOWS ON THE WORLD*

This knee-jerk reaction to everything American is the impetus for Frédéric Beigbeder's response in *Windows on the World*. In fact, he claims to have written the novel because he "was very annoyed by reactions like, 'After all, they asked for it.' I really didn't like this Frenchy-French aspect of anti-Americanism. I think you can absolutely criticize capitalism without criticizing the Americans. This is where I disagree with Luc Lang's book" (Géniès). The critique of Lang makes one of the book's objectives clear, and situates the text at the further end of the empathic continuum from *11 septembre mon amour*. Throughout the novel Beigbeder expresses his love for American culture: music, film, literature, Manhattan itself, but the ethos of Hugh Hefner and *Playboy* most of all (136–138). And in contrast to Lang and the other novelists, he readily identifies a number of parallels between France and the United States.

In fact, Beigbeder sets out to complete a twin act of literary empathy. First, he places himself in similar surroundings—the highest edifice in Paris, the Tour Montparnasse—in an attempt to reenact the experiences of the people in the World Trade Center. He strives to physically place himself in the shoes of the victims, at one point walking down the stairs of the Tour reenacting the exodus from the Twin Towers. Second, he extends this imaginative act of empathy by risking a fictional recreation of the events through the eyes of one of the victims, an American protagonist-narrator named Carthew Yorston. His ability to empathize will thus be put to the test as he presents events from a perspective that is both American and victimized. In fact, he is one of the only writers (of any nationality) to attempt such a reenactment. When victims are depicted in 9/11 fiction, their experiences are most frequently presented through the double filter of another character's attempts to imagine the victim's final moments. Beigbeder risks being accused of presumption, insensitivity, and perhaps worse, by placing himself directly inside the mind of an individual who has less than two hours to live. In the process, however, he creates a vision of what those unfortunate souls trapped in the blazing towers may have experienced.

Furthermore, Beigbeder exercises his empathic muscle in search of that which links him with his narrator and the American citizenry. And indeed there is a good deal of overlap between the two narrators. So much so that Kristiaan Versluys finds fault with the novel precisely because the reader has difficulty distinguishing between the Beigbeder-narrator and the author's American counterpart: "Since the feelings, ideas, and existential situations of each protagonist echo the other's, the binary expectations of the reader are frustrated. No dialectical tension develops, and the novel remains strangely monotonous or univocal" (135). While Beigbeder's approach has its limitations, it is clearly intended to smooth over the differences between Frenchman and American and to create a stronger link between cultures, which Versluys recognizes: "this assertion of a fundamental cultural unity is also a taboo-breaking challenge to the assumptions of the left-leaning French intelligentsia, whose anti-Americanism is inbred, automatic, and often hysterical" (137). The text's frequent references to, and emphasis upon, the commonalities between the French and the American people, indicate that its objectives vary considerably from the other novels presented here. For example, the novel is filled with a number of excisions meant to spare the feelings of its American readers. Another characteristic that significantly sets Beigbeder apart from his compatriots is his willingness to skewer his nation's pretensions: "As for the cultural exception that is France . . . it is not dead: it consists in churning out exceptionally tedious movies, exceptionally slapdash books, and, all in all, works of art that are exceptionally pedantic and self-satisfied. It goes without saying that I include my own work in this sorry assessment" (19). That he adds himself to the list serves to make the contrast with Lang and the others stronger. This act of self-criticism finds its most pronounced expression in a "Je m'accuse" section that stretches for three pages (and over forty individual items):

> I accuse myself of aesthetics without ethics.
> I accuse myself of having nothing in common with New York City except perhaps individualism and megalomania.
> I accuse myself of trying to please even in this self-accusation intended to parry the blows to come. (204–206)

Again, this acknowledgment of fallibility is a quality strikingly absent from the other French fictional considerations of the 9/11 incidents and its aftermath.

Nevertheless, Beigbeder is not blindly pro-American; he recognizes the nation's propensity for arrogance and self-centeredness. Early in the novel, the narrator declares, "That is the subject of this book: the collapse of a house of credit cards" (8). Reference is made to the World Trade Center as an economic symbol, but also to the fragility of a system—one which the events of September 11 highlighted. And the naming of the restaurant itself, *Windows on the World*, is seen as only "more proof of American condescension" (9). The scenes between the lustful stockbrokers trapped in the North Tower satirize materialist pursuits: "'When I think you'll never get to see my home cinema system . . . plasma screen the size of Lake Superior,' says the guy in Kenneth Cole" (154). Finally, the text is littered with political observations such as: "*Depuis le Onze Septembre, l'Amérique est en guerre contre le Mal. C'est peut-être ridicule mais c'est ainsi. Le problème, c'est que ce n'est pas son boulot. Elle pique le job de l'ONU. La démocratie planétaire ne doit pas être la propriété des États-Unis d'Amérique*"/'Since September 11, America is at war against Evil. This may be ridiculous, but it is so. The problem is that this is not America's job. She is scabbing the UN's job. Planetary democracy should not be the sole property of the United States of America' (301).[15] So while Beigbeder exhibits strong empathy for the United States and its people, it is tempered by an awareness of their foibles and shortcomings.

One might thus expect the text's many references to the Tower of Babel to be presented in the same spirit as those of Garcin and Goupil. In fact, the first allusion is made as the first plane crashes into the North Tower at 8:46 (55). Beigbeder's use of the Babel symbolism, however, is temperamentally different. After another mention of Genesis (82), Carthew Yorston wonders if he is in fact in the Tower of Babel and recalls an angry God who "does not approve of [the builders'] decision: man must not be prideful, man must not take himself for God" (117). The strong disapprobation of American arrogance is clear. But the text stresses that God does not actually destroy the Tower; he simply confounds the builders by conferring upon each a different language, leading them to abandon their project: "Divine punishment takes the form of preventing men from communicating with one another. The Tower of Babel was the first attempt at globalization. If, as millions of Americans do, we take Genesis absolutely literally, then God is opposed to globalization . . . God has set his face against New York" (117). The difference is that the novel does not in any way present this outcome as desired or inevitable. Instead, *Windows on the World* depicts the loss of the Tower of Babel, and by analogy that of the World Trade Center, as a missed opportunity. The punishment—preventing global communication—has no doubt led to a greater number of problems than had God simply allowed the tower's construction. And the global unity embodied in those Towers, with all its inherent flaws, is an ideal worth pursuing.

In fact, Beigbeder's text can be read as an effort to memorialize the Twin Towers (a true requiem). First, in its emphasis of the Tour Montparnasse as a "twin site" (*un endroit jumeau*), one might say a twin of the twins, and a physical recall of the World Trade Center. At one point he refers to the Tour as "the French equivalent of Ground Zero," but also acknowledges that it does not measure up to the World Trade Center, even noting that it will probably never be a target for terrorists (27). In the process, he concedes to the greater stature, in size and significance, of the American version. And in contrast to Baudrillard and Goupil who depict their destruction as an act of global necessity, Beigbeder makes it clear that one of the objectives of the novel is to grieve for these buildings: "The moral of the story is: when buildings vanish, only books can remember them. This is why Hemingway wrote about Paris before he died. Because he knew that books are more durable than buildings" (132). To this end, the novel memorializes the buildings through the physical manipulation of the text. The words are laid out on the page to represent two columns side by side, in the chapter entitled 10:28, the moment of the second tower's collapse (301). In this way, *Windows on the World* mourns the absence of the towers.

Just as the World Trade Center is juxtaposed with the Tour Montpartnasse, so too are American and French perspectives. This is most effectively communicated through the strategy of alternating the narratorial point of view between Beigbeder's alter ego and the American, Carthew Yorston. The adoption of an American character in *Windows* is a sharp contrast with that of Goupil, who transforms his alienated protagonist into a mouthpiece for critiquing the United States. Instead, Yorston embodies qualities that set him apart from, but also connect him with, the Beidbeger-figure. He also achieves a degree of recognition making him a figure with whom the reader can empathize:

> And so it happened: all those things I didn't understand, that I didn't want to understand, the foreign news stories I preferred to skirt, to keep out of my mind when they weren't on TV, all these tragedies were suddenly relevant to me; these wars came to hurt me that morning, not someone else; my children, not someone else's; these things I knew nothing about, these events so geographically remote suddenly became the most important things in my life. (107–8)

In this passage is a newfound (American) awareness of a cultivated ignorance, of a very real vulnerability, and of the extent to which events that happen on the other side of the globe can directly impact one's own life.

Admittedly, the dual perspectives come from the same implied author, but they reveal a conscious attempt to see things as the other might see them, to engage in re-enactive empathy. Through the novel's structure, Beigbeder creates a space in which the contrasted narratives play off each other. He even takes liberties with the fictional constructs of his text, so that, for instance, his narrator-persona and Yorston debate the significance of the falling people (148–49). As noted earlier, the alternating narratives serve to blur the cultural and national boundaries separating the two narrators. And this is made literally true when "Beigbeder" admits that he and Yorston shared an ancestor, making the latter a cousin. Revealing this to a waiter in a Times Square restaurant, he declares: "We do not hate you. You scare us because you rule the world. But we're blood relations. France helped your country to be born. Later, you liberated us" (299). As the novel reaches its end, a link between the two narrators is strengthened, reflecting the text's own philosophy about Franco-American relations. Maintaining this nuanced perspective, Beigbeder presents his own variation on "Nous sommes tous Américains": "If you go back eight generations, all white Americans are Europeans. We are the same: even if we are not all Americans, our problems are theirs, and theirs are ours" (296). Once again, we witness the need to address Colombani's declaration. Even Beigbeder's version, which accentuates a strong connection with the United States, modifies its intent by suggesting that we should not get bogged down in semantics, but rather strive, particularly in this moment of strife, to seek that which binds, rather than that which sunders.

CONCLUSION

The compulsion to modify or reject Colombani's remark is revealing on a number of fronts. First, it resists the implication that there is much that France shares with its American counterpart. Second, it seeks to avoid any suggestion of complicity with the American global enterprise. Third, it underlines the criticism that any notion of the West as a homogenous entity is misguided; there is more than one West, just as there is more than one Islam. As such, the conflation of the United States with Western ideology seriously neglects the West as it may be represented by France. Fourth, it reads the statement is as uncritical acceptance of all things American. That the comment elicited such responses suggests the varying degree to which the French may or may not define themselves in respect to their American counterparts.

As critics have noted, the United States squandered an opportunity; by acting in a fairly unilateral and hegemonic fashion, it "showed little, if any, understanding of the dignity, pride and fears of others, and of the way the fate and fortune of all peoples are increasingly tied together in our global age" (Held 57). The American response revealed an inability to recognize the global/internationalist implications of the event. As the first occurrence of its kind to occur on American soil, September 11 immediately elicited cries for revenge and increased protection. In order to counter apparent signs of vulnerability, and instead of recognizing how the event brought it closer to its counterparts, the United States sought once more to assert its exceptionalism. By the same token, however, other countries did not seek their strongest links with the United States, nor did they exercise their empathetic muscle for very long. Instead of eliciting compassion and empathy, the revelation (confirmation) of American vulnerability was seized as an opportunity to denigrate, critique, and emphasize the ways in which they were *not* connected.

Ulrich Beck, in presenting an image of the cosmopolitan world, illuminates the current dynamics of Franco-American relations:

> The world of the cosmopolitan outlook is in a certain sense a glass world. Differences, contrasts and boundaries must be fixed and defined in an awareness of the sameness in principle of others. The boundaries separating us from others are no longer blocked and obscured by ontological differences but have become transparent. This irreversible sameness opens up a space of both empathy and aggression which is difficult to contain. This is a consequence of both pity and of hatred—pity, because the (no longer heterogeneous) other becomes present in one's feelings and experience, and observing oneself and observing others are no longer mutually exclusive activities; hatred, because the walls of institutionalized ignorance and hostility that protected my world are collapsing. (8)

Beck's construction of course applies to all relations in this new geopolitical terrain, but the measures of sameness and difference will vary depending on which two nations are being contrasted and compared. In this configuration, sameness becomes harder and harder to deny, and one is obliged to work more strenuously to accentuate difference. And as Beck's explanation points out, this gives rise to a series of conflicting emotions, so that empathy and aggression now co-exist side by side. Faced with this "irreversible sameness," these French writers feel compelled to resist through hatred and aggression. Near the end of *Windows on the World*, the Beigbeder-narrator observes: "I truly don't know why I wrote this book . . . What else is there to write? The only interesting subjects are those that are taboo. We must write what is forbidden. French literature is a long history of disobedience" (295). What perspective does he believe French literature with its "history of disobedience" can add to what we already know? To what extent might we interpret defiance or resistance to American cultural hegemony, as "forbidden" or at least as some form of disobedience?[16] As counternarratives, these novels might be read as transgressive, as entering forbidden territory, though some of this activity is attenuated by the fact that if they are being disobedient, they are doing so to appeal to their French readership. (One might recall Chirac's dismal favorability ratings improving in the days following his opposition to the proposed invasion of Iraq in February of 2003). If these texts are written primarily for a French audience, then it is because they primarily address French concerns, proclaiming superiority and independence, while (un)consciously recognizing how deeply their national identity is now entwined with that of the United States.

In concluding, it is important once more to recall the historically constrained period in which these novels were published. The alacrity with which some of these texts were written, and then published, suggests that these French writers were not assailed by the same reticence as their American counterparts when addressing the topic of September 11. As I have noted, the moment also provided an opportunity to express opinions and sentiments lying just below the surface. As Schuerewegen contends, "The drama of the World Trade Center has also, one must admit, served as a release valve (*défouloir*) for French intellectuals" (150, my translation). For though the moment also reflected a global vulnerability, more attention was paid to the United States as victimizer than victimized. In these texts (theoretical and fictional), the critical focus remains firmly trained on the recipient of the attacks rather than the terrorists.[17] They reflect the suspicion that empathizing could be construed as condoning the American global agenda and that voicing such sentiments is tantamount to a violation of France's imagined sense of self. Any hope of attaining the utopian potential to which Cilano aspires is dependent upon the existence of constructive critique paired with an empathic connection, otherwise any possibility of internationalist cooperation is undermined. As such, we might contemplate the extent to which self-interest and questions of identity—personal, political, national—interfere with empathy, posing a considerable challenge to the utopian dream of a cosmopolitan world.

NOTES

1. I wish to thank the two anonymous reviewers of an earlier draft of this paper for their insightful comments and learned suggestions. Thanks also to two colleagues, Ian Dove and Greg Brown, for their thoughtful readings and instigations. Finally, my heartfelt appreciation to Jean-Claude Klein for his invaluable help in the arduous task of translation.

2. Tony Judt observes: "President George W. Bush and his advisers managed to make America seem to the overwhelming majority of humankind as the greatest threat to global stability. By staking a monopoly claim on Western values and their defense, the United States has prompted other Westerners to reflect on what divides them from America" (15).

3. Three other novels—Patrick Bouvet's *Direct* (2002), Y. B.'s *Allah Superstar* (2003), and Yann Moix's *Partouz* (2004)—certainly merit further study.

4. The titles of some recent texts reveal the paradoxical nature of the relationship between the two nations. For instance, Charles Cogan's *Alliés éternels, amis ombrageux* or Jacquelyn Davis's *Reluctant Allies and Competitive Partners* reflect two countries who seem to share a great deal, but between whom much friction persists.

5. See Brassett on the "politics of vulnerability."

6. Similar sentiments, expressed more forcefully, appear in Emmanuel Goujon's *Depuis le 11 septembre* (57).

7. Derrida suggests these events are the result of the nation's "autoimmunatory processes" which he defines as "that strange behavior where a living being, in quasi-suicidal fashion, 'itself' works to destroy its own protection, to immunize itself against its 'own' immunity" (Borradori 94). The metaphor has its merits. These terrorists were indeed United States–supported (in their struggle against the Soviets in Afghanistan), managed to live and train on American soil, and finally used the country's own technological advancements against it. Therefore, Derrida argues, "these *hijackers* incorporate, so to speak two suicides in one: their own . . . but also the suicide of those who welcomed, armed, and trained them" (Borradori 95).

8. Throughout Baudrillard's text globalization and Americanization are synonymous.

9. Another moment of projection occurs when Baudrillard's expresses his own disdain for the edifice: "In terms of collective drama, we can say that the horror for the 4,000 victims dying in those towers was inseparable from the horror of living in them" (45).

10. Kristiaan Versluys proposes that the linking of the World Trade Center with the Tower of Babel "reinforces the reading of 9/11 as an apocalyptic event" (140).

11. Of course, this comparison is not new. As early as February 1966, *The Nation* called the proposed World Trade Center "Manhattan's Tower of Babel."

12. Although Goupil changes key details (the attack occurs on a Monday, and there is only one Tower), he remains faithful to others (the attack happens at 8:46, and the President echoes Bush's exact words, "I hear you . . . The whole world hears you" [65]) creating a parallel world that is, and is not, Lower Manhattan in the final months of 2001.

13. Observations made by the narrator could well emanate from the latest terrorist missive; there are strong similarities between the text's overt criticism and that sent from the mastermind of the attacks: "la voix s'en prenait à la surconsommation et à la corruption qui rongeaient nos administrations, stigmatisant notre soif du profit et le pouvoir tout-puissant de l'argent"/ 'the voice took umbrage to our overconsumption and to the corruption of our administrations, stigmatizing our thirst for profit and the power of the almighty dollar' (70).

14. "Luc Lang does not like the American people and he demonstrates this a little too often, but worst, or the most astonishing, is that the author himself seems hardly conscious of the phobia haunting him" (Schuerewegen 145, my translation).

15. Citations in bold are from the original text in French not found in Wynne's translation.

16. In this regard, Meunier suggests being "anti" is a fundamental part of Frenchness, and that resistance is an innate quality of the French people (156). And Frédéric Beigbeder observes, "France has the same relationship with the United States nowadays as do the provinces with Paris: a combination of admiration and contempt, a longing to be a part of it and a pride at resisting" (18–19).

17. Aware they risk being accused of "blaming the victim," both Derrida and Baudrillard blur the lines between international terrorism (al-Qaeda) and state terrorism (U.S. Government). Derrida reminds us that the United States "was not always . . . on the side of the victims" (92), and Baudrillard argues we must conceive of the attacks of September 11 as an instance of "terror against terror" (9). Using such constructions, it is possible to frame the event as a response to the terrorism visited upon the rest of the world by the United States.

Chapter Four

"Toward These Uncanny Young Men"

Entering the Mind of the Terrorist

For a time following the events of September 11, it seemed that any understanding of the men who took part in these attacks could only emanate from the world of non-fiction. As such, Terry McDermott's *Perfect Soldiers: Who They Were, Why They Did It* was touted as the "definitive" telling of the lives of the men who became the 9/11 hijackers (Yardley); while another critic declared that it was "bound to become one of the most insightful books ever published about Sept. 11" (Weinberg). McDermott's text, however, cannot live up to the promise outlined in the latter part of its title. Since he must rely on facts, he can only tell us about what the hijackers did, not what they thought, therefore leaving the explanations as to "why they did it" ambiguous at best. We get a third-person narrative that leans heavily on the telling of others to construct an after-the-fact recounting. Since these otherwise mostly unexceptional men only gained notoriety after September 11, 2001—the day of their deaths—very few of their own words or thoughts are recorded. McDermott is therefore obliged to reconstruct and create a compelling narrative from the bits and pieces of rather uncompelling lives. This exercise is fated to only partial success and in fact leads to a glaring absence/aporia at the center of the text. For on more than one occasion McDermott acknowledges that he cannot really identify, nor describe, the moments, the triggers, that turned these unremarkable men into committed jihadists. Speaking of Ziad Jarrah, for example, the author admits that he is unable to identify "what lay behind [Jarrah's] change" to radicalism (52). A few pages later, in reference to another member of the cell, Zakariya Essabar, McDermott uses the words of a friend to arrive at the same conclusion: "[Zakariya] never explained to me why he changed" (66). So though we may have a better understanding of *who they were*, we are no closer to knowing *why they did it*. This still remains a strength of McDermott's book, as the text communicates the brutal truth that ordinary men such as these can commit extremely violent acts aimed at innocent civilians. But we never really understand their metamorphoses, rather we are only made aware that such transformations can and do occur. Since the credibility of a text such as *Perfect Soldiers* is contingent upon the author *not* indulging in inference, any attempt at representing the terrorist's inner life would only undermine its supposed veracity. And yet in his preface McDermott identifies such imaginings as essential components of the very book he has written: "A primary task—a great joy, too—of the journalist is to empathize, to try to understand the way the world appeared to the people being written about" (xvii). So while it is quite possible that Terry McDermott imagined viewing the world through the terrorist's eyes, the reader is offered no such access, seeing only the inexorable path of actions that will lead them to board those planes on September 11. We never understand how their respective (and divergent) views of the world came to mesh with those of religious extremism. What made the concept of jihad so alluring that they would forsake their lives for it? In *Terrorists in Love*, Ken Ballen similarly outlines the challenges and uncertainties of such an enterprise. And like McDermott, he points to empathy as "the key to opening up trust and getting behind the story" (xiii). More significant, he recognizes the need to "place [himself] in [the perpetrator's] shoes, no matter how evil the deed and uncomfortably close the fit" (xiii). The sentence construction is interesting, since it allows Ballen to allude to a degree of commonality with the terrorist to which we are unwilling or unable to admit. It is this reticence that an empathetic representation of the terrorist asks the reader to overcome.

This ideological reluctance, however, is something the novelist must also address, if he or she is to present a plausible portrait of the perpetrator's thoughts and feelings. Writing on the tenth anniversary of the attacks, Adam Kirsch bemoans a lack of good fiction on the subject, and attributes this in part to the fact that the experiences of the terrorists have been just as "inaccessible" to novelists as those of the victims. In the case of the latter at least, Kirsch notes, the reader is sometimes willing to entertain an attempt at representation. Not so, however, with the terrorist:

> Dostoevsky wanted his readers to say about the terrorists what Prospero says of Caliban in *The Tempest*: 'this thing of darkness I acknowledge mine.' It is this acknowledgement that the 9/11 terrorists cannot receive from American readers. This is not because of resentment or hatred, but because contemporary western literature does not understand, or believe in, the kinds of motives that drove them to commit murder-suicide. (Kirsch)

The failure of connection, according to Kirsch, therefore resides both in readers unwilling to acknowledge any human rapport between themselves and the terrorists, but also in novelists whose cultural disposition prevents them from accessing the world view of these extremists. The concept of terrorism as an act of altruism is likely to remain alien, if not offensive, to the targeted community, as will the notion of martyrdom. And yet an understanding of the terrorist's rationale is only likely to emanate from a narrative construction that presents a plausible "working through" of these central principles. When approached from this angle, it would seem that novelists are ideally positioned to undertake the exercise these writers of non-fiction like McDermott and Ballen extol.

And, of course, there is an ethical component to such understanding, as it opens up the possibility of examining the complex web of human relations that led to these catastrophic events. Indeed, since 9/11, a number of commentators have advocated the use of empathy as a way out of the impasse now existing in Western relations with Islam and, more specifically, Muslim extremism. For instance, Gayatri Spivak argues that all proposed solutions to the current crisis are contingent upon this capacity for empathy: "Unless we are trained into imagining the other, a necessary, impossible, and interminable task, nothing we do through politico-legal calculation will last" (83). Empathy acts as a bridging mechanism, allowing the parties to move beyond the application of judicial and political concepts, to recognition of a shared humanity, however tenuous it might be. As Spivak intimates, true empathy is not simply putting yourself in someone else's shoes, it is also recognizing how the other remains irretrievably *other*. But can the novel, through its representations of the radical and fundamentalist other, offer ways out of this ideological impasse? How might fictional texts aid the reader in moving "toward these uncanny young men," as Spivak calls them (89)?

This chapter juxtaposes a number of texts that present the final moments in the life of a terrorist who took part in the attacks of September 11—from the perspective of *that* terrorist. A short story by Martin Amis and a novella by Jarrett Kobek each offer the reader the musings of Mohammad Atta, considered by many to have been the leader of the hijackers. For their part, Andre Dubus III and Salim Bachi present entirely fictional terrorists who nevertheless take part in the actual event. I have chosen texts that purport to represent individuals who were involved in the 9/11 attacks, because I would argue that imagining the thoughts and actions of a person who actually took part in the horrific events requires a higher degree of empathy than does entering the mind of an entirely fictionalized terrorist playing a role in an entirely fictionalized event. It is a greater gambit on the part of the novelist who essentially proclaims an identification of sameness with a terrorist who perpetuated a very real act of horrifying terror. Novelists who connect with such a figure leave themselves open to accusations of insensitivity (to the victims) or of exculpation (of the terrorists). They are not afforded, to use Versluys's terminology, the "imaginative leeway" that John Updike allows himself in writing *Terrorist* (172). As such, I do not offer readings of two novels often included in this group. Slimane Benaissa's novel, *The Last Night of a Damned Soul*, presents in some detail the transformation and conversion of an individual to radical Islam. And the novel does communicate something of the communal realities of such trajectories. In the end, however, the novel cannot hew to the reality of the 9/11 story. At the moment of truth, Benaissa's protagonist deserts, and does not take part in the attack, almost as though the author has too much empathy for his protagonist to allow him to take part in such monstrous deeds. As for Updike's much-critiqued *Terrorist*, it is not included here for two reasons. First, it offers a fictionalized account of a plot to bomb the Lincoln tunnel, and thus evades direct connection with 9/11. Second, its plot concerns the transformation of an Arab-American teenager into a jihadist, shifting the focus away from global/external concerns to national/internal ones. In terms of his relationship with "America" and the United States, then, the other at the heart of Updike's novel is cut from a far different cloth than those presented in the texts studied here.

Dramatizing the inner life of a known terrorist, these texts illuminate the complexity of the radicalized mind, acting as a counterbalance to the popular image of a single-minded fanatic. Birgit Däwes thus observes that these novels serve to "complement and diversify the cultural memory of 9/11" (243). By focusing on this limit-situation, these writers clearly strive to capture the thoughts and motivations of an individual whose actions many may find incomprehensible. Their narratives exhibit a moving beyond the examination of the operations of terrorist groups and a striving towards an empathetic understanding of the individual who chooses terrorism as an expression of his or her identity. As such, these writers seek to tackle Spivak's "necessary, impossible, and interminable task." At the same time, these novelistic efforts raise a number of questions about narrative and its relationship with empathy: Is it possible to unconditionally inhabit the mind of the terrorist? Can common ground be established? In other words, can the writer find an accessible portal through which to connect with the thoughts of the terrorist? Or are texts about Islamic fundamentalists always going to be handicapped as outsider perspectives? Is literary skill enough to invoke the imaginations and motivations of the other who wishes one harm? And to what degree does the presence of threat (and consequent fear) incapacitate one's ability to empathize? Is empathy reserved for those with whom we share a connection? Or do we have a moral responsibility or ethical obligation to strive for empathy even in those circumstances when no connection appears to exist?

Through its aesthetic representation of the terrorist, creating a facsimile of sorts, the novel provides the means for overcoming (at least temporarily) the reader's ideological reluctance so that she might consider the terrorist in his full otherness. Natasha Walter takes this further when she suggests that we turn to the terrorist novel precisely because of the ways in which it questions received knowledge and challenges our assumptions: "we want imaginative understanding, not political positions; we want to get close to a fictional individual rather than stand in judgment over a real group; we want the challenge of speculation rather than the reassurance of certainty" (Walter). In other words, the possibility of empathetic connection between the reader and the terrorist is heightened by the fact that one approaches a novel with a different set of criteria, and a willingness to suspend one's instinctual resistance in the hopes of deeper understanding. And although the extent to which fiction can perform this function is up for debate, we seek out the novel because it affords a safe zone within which to contemplate, and thus assess, the actions of "real world" terrorists. In this regard, Richard Kearney observes that "Terror framed is terror defused" (130). Terrorist fiction thus offers comfort, in part because some degree of control has been exerted over the situation, and in part because the perpetrator has been incorporated into a narrative within which his actions now make some measure of sense (whether we agree with his rationale or not). And this is where the novel can provide a forum for entertaining the more threatening and uncomfortable possibilities of the terrorist's position. Just as *King Lear* affords the playgoer a safe zone from which to contemplate some of the more tragic aspects of the human condition, so the terrorist novel supplies an atmosphere in which to consider the perpetrator without feeling compelled to disavow any condoning of his or her motives. In removing the necessity for this distancing gesture, the novel increases the possibility of empathy and of understanding the terrorist other.

At the same time, the manner in which that life is communicated— through the construction of a coherent and logical narrative—signals to the reader the very real possibility that something may have been lost in translation. The novel's organizing principle thus guarantees the impossibility of subsuming the terrorist's otherness into a seamless narrative. As David Palumbo-Liu suggests, the novel's own "otherness" means that its representation of others "is itself of a nature entirely different from the world of experience, and while it brings us closer to others, it cannot or does not reach complete deliverance, so to speak. It stands alongside, or apart from life" (12). As such, the terrorist novel allows the reader to grapple with the alterity of the radical other, while conveying the unbridgeable gap that inevitably exists between self and other. Interestingly, Halpern and Weinstein argue that recognizing the other's humanity depends upon an acknowledgment of the immutable difference separating one from the perpetrator: "The work of empathy is precisely trying to imagine a view of the world that one does not share, and in fact may find it quite difficult to share" (581). This is particularly true of a moment when the otherness of the other is so emphatically declared. Because it was certainly the intention of the hijackers to communicate their otherness, and the ways in which that otherness had been so callously disregarded, to the citizens of the United States and the world. In this regard they succeeded, for Americans almost immediately set about outlining that which separated them from these extremist others. Under such circumstances any identification of sameness is doubly challenged. For if we impose limitations, if we believe there are individuals with whom we cannot empathize, or if there are others from whom we withhold it because we deem them to be unworthy, then the very idea of empathy loses much of its value. After all, merely identifying with one's similar offers only limited returns. A greater sense of one's self and one's place in the world can only be produced through sustained exposure to difference. For a seeking after sameness with the other, particularly a radical one, indicates a willingness for self-examination or criticism, something largely curtailed in the wake of the events.

THE SAMENESS OF THE TERRORIST

In response to this suppression, a number of writers have sought to illuminate the ways in which the antagonists in this crisis bear a striking resemblance to one another. Indeed, they suggest that it is not the terrorist's alterity that troubles, but rather his similarity. Not surprisingly, the call to recognize oneself in the perpetrator has often come from outside the United States. Jacques Derrida, for instance, observes,

> Those called 'terrorists' are not, in this context, 'others,' absolute others whom we, as 'Westerners,' can no longer understand. We must not forget that they were often recruited, trained, and even armed, and for a long time, in various Western ways by a Western world that itself, in the course of its ancient as well as very recent history, invented the word, the techniques, and the 'politics' of terrorism. (Borradori 115)

And so reluctance emanates from a feeling that we may be complicit in the current state of affairs, and that the techniques and stratagems of the terrorists are not so foreign to us after all. In fact, Derrida extends this argument suggesting that the terrorists are part of an "autoimmunatory process" whereby "a living being, in quasi-suicidal fashion, 'itself' works to destroy its own protection, to immunize itself against its 'own' immunity" (Borradori 94). In other words, the terrorists are not something apart, but a vital component of the organism, fostered by our own needs and insecurities. In a similar vein, Jean-Pierre Dupuy argues that the current conflict in fact emanates from an (unconscious?) recognition of sameness: "It is now on a planetary scale that the game of mimetic rivalry will play itself out, a game that binds the rivals all the more compulsively and tightly together even as they claim to have nothing in common" (42). We are now so intertwined, Dupuy contends, that we are not actually engaged in a clash of civilizations, but rather in the midst of "a civil war within a single global civilization, which has come into being kicking and screaming" (42). From this perspective, the fundamentalisms of Islam and the United States are not vastly different. In other words, this is warring so as to impose one's version of a similar thing. Finally, Slavoj Žižek, with his usual aplomb, takes this one step further, suggesting that, "Every feature attributed to the Other is already present at the very heart of the USA" (43).

These declarations of similarity are intended to lessen the divide created between "us" and "them" after the events of September 11. The more otherness is effaced in the pursuit of sameness, however, the more confident the subject may feel in expounding upon the thoughts and actions of the other. Because any empathetic engagement is open to the accusation of being nothing more than an exercise in colonization, since it often masks our assumptions, as well as our presumptions, about our relationship with the other. In seeking to empathize, then, we should be careful to establish "what we can know but also what we, perhaps, ought not to assume we have the right to know" (Lather 19). These observations certainly apply to the novels under consideration, because each novelist, to varying degrees, can be accused of presuming to "speak for the other." So while engaging in this act of ventriloquism certainly suggests that the writer (and by extension the reader) is working through difference in an attempt to understand the other, another possibility is that he is merely foisting his conceptions of the terrorist onto his fictional creation. We can thus question whether he is actually seeing the world through the terrorist's eyes, or simply creating a terrorist who peers through his. As Linda Alcoff observes, "the practice of speaking for others is often born of a desire for mastery, to privilege oneself as the one who more correctly understands the truth about another's situation" (29). As such, a very real danger exists of the novelist falling prey to feelings of superiority. Because there are instances when the pursuit of knowledge can be perceived as a transgression, as a violation of personhood. Patti Lather quotes Doris Sommer who observes that the empathetic gesture is often "an appropriation in the guise of an embrace." To which Lather adds, "This is how empathy violates the other and is part of the demand for totality" (19).

But does this necessarily have to be the case? Must we relinquish any attempt at understanding because we risk the possibility of imposing our views upon the other? Do we simply accept that full and complete empathy is impossible (as with the struggle to represent trauma) or do we still strive, no matter how flawed and inadequate our attempts may be? Because in extreme situations such as these, there is a predisposition towards difference, with a greater investment being made in accentuating that which sets us apart from the other. It is in these very situations, I would argue, that an attempt at rapprochement should be made. For though criticism leveled at empathy and its advocacy of sameness is not without merit and should awaken us to our propensities, we can safely predict this will not be the predominant reaction of American readers when confronted with a depiction of the terrorist. In fact, antipathy is the more likely response. For, as we shall see, there are any number of reasons why one might be inclined to dehumanize the hijackers, perhaps the most salient being that the attacks of September 11 were blatant demonstrations of dehumanization themselves. The terrorists exhibited very little regard for the innocent victims who suffered at their hands. Finally, the actions which brought these individuals to the world's attention were also their last. As such, for many, they exist only as disembodied and ghostly presences, lost amid the ashes of their self-destruction.

As such, this chapter will examine these four texts for the ways in which they do, or do not, humanize the terrorist. How is the otherness of the terrorist dissipated, and in what ways is it solidified or maintained? These texts thus illuminate the interplay between the drive for sameness and the urge to foreground difference. The terrorist cannot simply be presented as alien, as entirely other, since this obstructs the possibility of fellow-feeling. Nor should the impression be given that the thoughts of the terrorist have somehow been completely appropriated. In other words, the text should still communicate, or at least intimate, what makes the other *other*, alluding to that which resists incorporation within its narrative. As Lather observes, "A recalcitrant rhetoric is about inaccessible alterity, a lesson in modesty and respect, somewhere outside of our desire to possess, know, grasp" (Lather 19). Engaging in empathy must be approached as a means of acknowledging otherness, not effacing it. As such, a useful critical strategy would identify probable or potential tensions between the text's implied objectives and the rendering of the terrorist's mind. For we tend to think of empathy as something reserved for the challenged and the downtrodden (revealing its hierarchical propensities), not for those who have acted violently or actively sought to harm us. Fiction, engaged as it is in the depiction of other minds, is confronted directly by this dilemma. As Birgit Däwes notes, an empathetic connection with the mind of the perpetrator is complicated by the positioning and the roles of empathizer and empathized in this dynamic: "Since representation always involves issues of hierarchy and power, the adoption of the perpetrator's perspective is highly problematic." This problem is further compounded, Däwes concludes, by the fact that on 9/11 "the staging of the hijackers' image was an integral part of the traumatic effect" (242).

In this configuration, the novel becomes a means of (re)transmitting that image. Certainly, in the reading of these texts, we find the traces of a tension between wanting to condemn or discredit the terrorist, and seeking to humanize or establish an empathetic connection with him. As Däwes observes, "The hijacker is both a projection screen for our desire to externalize the Other (tempting us into seeing it as a caricature, making it grotesque, laughing at it) and a reflective device which makes us see precisely those desires in the Other—a mirror in which this desire for the abject returns" (257). And so, we might ask, what distance is created or bridged by the narrative voice? Does the text's narrative stance improve or hinder the reader's understanding of the motivations of the terrorist? In other words, what degree of accessibility does the text provide the reader? If we accept the notion of reconciliation, to return to Halpern and Weinstein for a moment, then we must seek ways of rehumanizing the figure of the terrorist whose horrific actions have understandably led to his being dehumanized and demonized. Again, this does not mean forgiving, or even accepting the actions of the perpetrators, but rather adopting an ethical position that allows access to the other's anger, frustration, and despair. These all-too-human emotions no doubt contribute to the actions of the suicide bomber, and require their due consideration. In this sense, we might read the texts to analyze the degree to which the worthiness of the terrorist's claims, as well as that of his or her emotions, are either minimized or given their due accord within these texts. In other words, we can read each novel in terms of its capacity for remaining in a state of, or at least tolerating, ambivalence.

"THE DETESTATION OF EVERYTHING": MARTIN AMIS'S "THE LAST DAYS OF MUHAMMAD ATTA"

For though these texts create the impression of unfettered access to the terrorist's thoughts, this is not always effected as a means of drawing the reader closer to the protagonist. Instead, the terrorist is sometimes depicted in such a way as to encourage disengagement or even disgust. This is the case with Martin Amis's "The Last Days of Muhammad Atta," whose tone and language contribute to maintaining a wide berth between the implied narrator and the terrorist-protagonist. The objectives of the narrative—condemnation and marginalization of a representative figure in the 9/11 attacks—quickly become apparent. To this end, the story presents the terrorist's body as rebelling against him; Atta has suffered from constipation, overwhelming bouts of nausea, and searing headaches for months. That this occurs during the period in which the plans for the attacks were hatched and formulated is a fact surely not lost on the reader. It is as though the body rejects the mind's machinations, inflicting what punishment it can. Thus, Atta is first seen, in the shower, struggling unsuccessfully to remove a hair from a bar of soap. He then ignominiously slips on a shampoo packet, landing on his coccyx. Finally, he labors in vain to move his bowels "while disused gastric juices bubbled up in the sump of his throat. His breath smelled like a blighted river" (95). The writing has a dark comic bite, and while this mishap and the bodily ailments could serve to "humanize" Atta, they are presented unsympathetically, thus diminishing him (and his purported ambitions) in the eyes of the reader.

Due to the repeated broadcasting of his name and the haunting passport photograph (often identifying him as the leader of the group), Mohammad Atta is by far the most recognizable of the nineteen hijackers. Certainly, his visage came to represent and embody any number of things for many Americans: anger, evil, the unknown other. It was the image most frequently latched upon by the media to embody the hatred of the event.[1] And, indeed, the story plays on this infamy, describing Atta's inability to look upon his own countenance because, as the implied narrator suggests, he is painfully aware of the emotions it reveals: "The detestation, the detestation of everything, was being sculpted on it, from within. He was amazed that he was still allowed to walk the streets, let alone enter a building or board a plane" (95–96). In this way the text corroborates the reader's feelings, since Atta feels much the same about his visage as they do.

Any searching after rational explanations for Atta's actions, however, is finally squashed by the assertion that he "detests everything." This, in fact, is the main objective of the text: to emphasize the extent to which the suicide bomber is not driven by any kind of higher calling. To this end, the narrator tells the reader quite bluntly: "Muhammad Atta was not religious; he was not even especially political. He had allied himself with the militants because jihad was, by many magnitudes, the most charismatic idea of his generation. To unite ferocity and rectitude in a single word: nothing could compete with that" (99). But is this sufficient reason for wishing to kill oneself? While this construction of the terrorist signals the search and desire for some unifying principle through which to live one's life, it also reads as a construction. The text negates any consideration of the altruistic or communal motivations the suicide bomber may harbor, instead painting Atta as a loner, a misogynist, *and* a misanthropist, a hater of humanity whose sole desire is to initiate a perpetual cycle of death. And by focusing on a single terrorist, Amis's text, like many of the others, tends to accentuate the individual over the communal, thus offering a particularly Western spin on Oriental actions. And, of course, the behavior of an individual suicide bomber is more easily discounted (labeled irrational, evil, insane) than the sustained actions of a larger group of men working together towards a communal goal. Amis's Atta is presented as anything but communal—an individual whose declared "core reason" for participating in the attacks is to unleash a cycle of never-ending death and destruction: "Killing was divine delight. And your suicide was just part of a contribution you made—the massive contribution to death"

(118–19).[2] This particular construction of the suicide bomber requires us to consider the question of nihilism or the existence of a destructive urge. For instance, late in the story, Atta contemplates with pride the competitive nature of his relationship with another terrorist, Marwan. He concludes that their relationship works because it is based "not on jihadi ardor so much as nihilistic insouciance" (113). Again, the elimination of any political or religious motivation primarily serves to undermine the objectives of the terrorist. He is driven not by a desire to redress wrongs, or to make a better world; rather, he is compelled by the drive for self-annihilation and the obliteration of all life. Atta becomes a figure of pure negation, with not a single redeeming feature.

In contemplating justifications for these actions, however, we cannot entirely discount the possibility of just such a motive. In a scene from Christopher Nolan's *The Dark Knight*, a film filled with echoes and allusions to September 11, Bruce Wayne/Batman struggles to make sense of the Joker's motivations since money appears to hold no attraction. He tells his butler, Alfred, "Criminals aren't complicated. . . . Just have to figure out what he's after" (The Dark Knight). Alfred, in turn, replies with an anecdote:

> With respect Master Wayne, perhaps this is a man that *you* don't fully understand, either. A long time ago, I was in Burma. My friends and I were working for the local government. They were trying to buy the loyalty of tribal leaders by bribing them with precious stones. But their caravans were being raided in a forest north of Rangoon by a bandit. So, we went looking for the stones. But in six months, we never met anybody who traded with him. One day, I saw a child playing with a ruby the size of a tangerine. The bandit had been throwing them away. (The Dark Knight)

This prompts Bruce to ask, "So why steal them?" To which Alfred answers: "Well, because he thought it was good sport. Because some men aren't looking for anything logical, like money. They can't be bought, bullied, reasoned, or negotiated with. Some men just want to watch the world burn" (The Dark Knight). In essence, Alfred is stating that in such an instance, Bruce Wayne is simply wasting his time trying to understand. This is certainly the message communicated in Amis's text, and we might even concede the possibility that Atta may have been one of these men (though of this we cannot be certain). Representing him as such, however, immediately curtails the consideration of other possibilities, or other explanations in which issues of complicity and culpability might come into play. The combination of satiric portrayal and attributions of nihilism serve to make Atta an entirely dismissable figure.

Similarly, Birgit Däwes reads the story as an expression of antipathy, one that "sarcastically dismantles any heroism that jihadist ideology might construct" (255). Our readings diverge, however, since she nevertheless contends that Amis's text exhibits moments of empathy towards Atta ("however entangled and grotesquely decorated"), reaching their climax in the poetic description of the terrorist's perception of his own death (255–56). The narrative records Atta's final fleeting thoughts, and we see that his fatal flaw is to recognize the beauty of living only during the final milliseconds of existence:

> And where was the joy he thought he had felt—where *was* that joy, that itch, that paltry tingle? Yes, how gravely he had underestimated it. How very gravely he had underestimated life. His own he had hated, and had wished away; but see how long it was taking to absent itself—and with what helpless grief was he watching it go, imperturbable in its beauty and its power. Even as his flesh fried and his blood boiled, there was life, kissing its fingertips. Then it echoed out, and ended. (120–21)

We feel Atta's anguish, but this moment entirely undermines the notion of the enraptured terrorist attaining paradise or a better world, indicating only the "helpless grief" with which he watches his life force being extinguished. This may be a form of empathy, but it can also be read as a refusal to allow the terrorist to derive even an iota of pride or pleasure from the action he has just committed. We might also wonder whether the glimmer of humanity the text accords Atta is a demonstration of sympathy towards its subject, or whether it is another means of punishing Atta in his final living moments. Does the circular quality of the narrative not suggest that Atta is being made to relive, and will relive, this moment of anguish for all eternity? Because if this is empathy, it is short-lived. Amis's story undercuts the possibility of feeling anything for this unfeeling man. In this respect, it cannot be faulted; in terms of veracity, it hews closely to what has been reported about Atta. He was unwavering, humorless, and one-dimensional. Terry McDermott, for instance, quotes others who describe Atta's "complete, almost aggressive insularity" and that he was "reluctant to any pleasure" (25–26). Lawrence Wright, for his part, highlights Atta's "extreme rigidity" and his immovable hatred of women and Jews (346–47). Using Mohammed Atta as a representative figure, however, guarantees an un-nuanced reading reflective of its un-nuanced subject. For although these aspects of his personality were in evidence, it becomes clear that focusing on this particular individual conveniently suits the objective of the text, which is not so much to provide a realistic portrait of its human subject, but rather to undermine the tenets of Islamist extremism.

THE PATHOS OF THE TERRORIST: ANDRE DUBUS III'S *THE GARDEN OF LAST DAYS*

In contrast, Andre Dubus III's *The Garden of Last Days* offers a less claustrophobic depiction of the terrorist. Taking place in the days leading up to September 11, the novel presents the terrorist in interactions with both infidels and some of his fellow conspirators. Offering the alternating narratives of three different protagonists, one of whom, Bassam al-Jizani, will soon hijack an airliner and crash it into the World Trade Center, the novel also provides the reader a variety of encounters with otherness, not merely that of the hijacker. Instead of isolating the narrative of the terrorist (as Amis's text does) the novel incorporates and presents his story as one among many. The text thus achieves a measure of empathy through its alignment of Bassam with the other lost souls it presents (April, A. J., Lonnie). Like the others, Bassam stumbles through life, clinging to a sense of disappointment, dissatisfaction, and failed ambitions. As Banita observes, "Dubus's narrative nurtures empathy precisely through the equal subjection of both ordinary poor Americans and Saudi Arabian terrorists to a set of social forces that alienate and impoverish both groups" (Banita, Middle, 215). The novel thus utilizes a democratizing effect that enables the reader to gain some access to the terrorist mind.

Interestingly, Dubus asserts that the writing of the novel led to a number of realizations about the essential sameness of people, and the false dichotomization of good and evil. As a result, he contends that he has "a hard time believing in good people and bad people" (Skemp). In other words, Bassam is no different from the other characters—he simply behaves badly. The novel thus establishes a continuum within which a number of "bad" behaviors are exhibited. Here the author demonstrates an empathetic impulse, seeking to create a paradigm which includes, and thus humanizes, the terrorist. The problem with such a conceptualization, however, is that it requires conceiving of mass murder as simply "bad" behavior, albeit at the far end of the continuum. The writer is thus faced with the difficulties of presenting the sameness of an individual whose "differences" threaten to wash away all other considerations. Thus, maintaining a balance between empathizing and condemning is fraught with challenges, of which the writer remains aware. During another interview Dubus recalls his reluctance in approaching the subject. He concedes that any treatment of the events of 9/11 requires coming to terms with the actions of the terrorists and their underlying rationale. He notes, however, that he "just did not want to write from the POV of one of these men; I did not want to go there emotionally, and I wasn't sure I could reserve my judgment of him enough that he would show up, not as I want him to look, but as he is" (Johnson, 20). In other words, the writer is conscious of the ways the terrorist might be transformed in the process, that his incorporation within an American narrative might erase his alterity. No doubt as a consequence of this ambivalence the text veers between ventriloquizing Bassam's feelings and thoughts, while repeatedly expressing its understandable desire (obligation?) to censure his actions.

But is it possible to have it both ways? Can a text truly balance empathy for the terrorist with the urge to condemn? Faced with the chasm that stretches between himself and the extreme other, the novelist resorts to found knowledge, to that which is generally known about members of radicalized groups. This approach, however, tends to efface all marks of individuality, leaving only conventional representation. In other words, the unknown is described through the known (to use Gray's formulation), so that what emerges is a familiarized, sometimes stereotypical, version of the unfamiliar. This certainly describes the nature of much of the criticism leveled at *The Garden of Last Days*. The following appraisal, for instance, is typical: "for all the Arabic words and phrases [Dubus] deploys Bassam seems to be the stereotypical resentful, sexually frustrated fanatic with a giant inferiority complex *vis-à-vis* the infidels" (McInerney). Janet Maslin similarly criticizes the novel for its empathetic shortsightedness contending that it "would have been a vastly better book if Mr. Dubus had an unusual understanding of Bassam's nature" (Maslin). Both critics read the novel as having diluted the otherness to the point of inconsequentiality. These critiques, among others, thus raise doubts as to whether the terrorist represents an "excessive otherness" the novel cannot hope to represent (Palumbo-Lui, 29), and if such attempts are fated to communicating a merely solipsistic rendering of the other. We might consider such assessments too categorical and that their focus on the shortcomings of the text neglects the ways in which the text succeeds. For though one might accept that *The Garden of Last Days* ultimately fails to convey the terrorist's humanity, we can nevertheless contemplate those strategies that manage to intimate an otherness existing beyond the scope of the text.

The novel's ideological inclination towards its subject is signaled by the setting in which the novel begins, and where it will remain for nearly half of its pages: the Puma Lounge, a seedy strip club in Florida. In doing so, the novel picks up on news stories that circulated shortly after 9/11, suggesting that some of the hijackers had actually frequented a strip club in Daytona Beach—an apparent and glaring contradiction (paradox) with their religious devotion. As we shall see, this is one of the strategies the text utilizes to undermine the mission of the terrorist while simultaneously emphasizing his all-too-human frailties. This particular setting, combined with the varied narratorial perspectives, allows for a more complex understanding of the terrorist. For example, the reader's impressions of Bassam are not limited to those pages providing his point of view; they are also shaped by the perspective of April, a stripper who dances for him in a private booth. So while we may not be privy to any great revelations or disclosures in the prolonged interaction between Bassam and April, the text communicates and illuminates the elusiveness of the other for either side. For just as many cannot fathom the motivations of the terrorist, Bassam is at a loss when faced with the actions of a woman who removes her clothing for the pleasure of others. Throughout his time with April, he constantly questions, probing for a clearer understanding of what compels her to act as she does. He repeatedly offers her more money in the hopes that she will clarify her reasons for engaging in such activity: "Explain to me why you do this and I give these to you as well" (106). He also demands to know her real name (her stage name is Spring), and continues to press as though glimpsing the true April will provide the key to comprehending these Western others ("kafir") with whom he is at war.

Making April a stripper allows the text to communicate the obstacles faced by others when trying to comprehend us. In her discussion of "strategic empathizing," Suzanne Keen introduces the notion of a "bridge character" whose function is to serve as a buffer between the reader and a protagonist with whom the novelist feels the reader may have difficulty identifying (487). In other words, the bridge character's responses to the other serve to modulate those of the reader. This is not quite the role April serves, for although she may experience brief flashes of compassion for Bassam, she keeps him at a distance, both from herself and the reader. For instance, she repeatedly thinks of him as the "little foreigner" and that he possesses "a meanness in him she could feel" (82).Though as the evening progresses, this attitude does soften somewhat: "She wasn't afraid of him anymore. She almost felt like reaching down to run her fingers through his hair, comfort him the way she would her own child" (172). The word "almost" is significant here because it reflects the text's reluctance to exhibit even a fleeting moment of empathy for the eventual suicide bomber. In the end, Dubus uses April to express some pity, but mostly disgust, for Bassam. In this way, the text reveals its own tensions in regards to the terrorist's humanity, while mirroring the uneasiness experienced by the terrorist tantalized by, and yet alienated from, that which he will eventually seek to destroy.

For it is Bassam's interactions with April that come closest to shaking the foundations of his hatred for the West. His visit to the strip club is cut short when she discovers that her daughter, who was being babysat at the club, has gone missing. Hearing April's anguished cries after her daughter's abduction Bassam is reminded of his mother grieving the death of his brother. The similarity troubles him: "how can this kafir love and fear losing in the same way as a good wife and mother under the Creator in the birthplace of Muhammad? How can this be?" (282). Recognizing resemblances naturally breaks down barriers so that Bassam is confronted by the sameness of the other. Further tensions emerge when his antipathy for his potential victims occasionally transforms into empathy. At times, Bassam even finds himself thinking affectionately about these others despite himself:

> But what is worse is what he never would have known as he hardened and purified himself in training, as he prayed steadfastly in tents and motel rooms and autos, that he would like these kafir, that he would like Kelly and Gloria and Cliff, and yes, this April who calls herself Spring. (259)

These propensities serve to problematize the stereotypical image of the terrorist as a ruthless fanatic with nothing but the killing of innocents on his mind. His attraction to alcohol and loose women (both symbols of a degenerate West) intimate a complexity to which Bassam himself is not willing to admit. On more than one occasion he suspects he is lying to himself, that he truly desires that which he claims to despise. But, as John Dufresne observes, "everything Bassam denies himself is precisely what makes him human and compelling" (Dufresne).

The terrorist is thus humanized through his inability to reconcile his desire to destroy that which he also desires. Most frequently, this is represented through his continued attempts to repress sexual yearnings. Exposed to degenerate American life on a daily basis, Bassam must gird himself against the urges aroused in him. Frequently, this is achieved through the invocation of Allah, the depiction of America as the den of Shaytan, and a sense of righteousness fostered by the belief that he has been empowered by the Koran to kill the unbelievers (here Dubus and Amis overlap). Often, however, he simply resorts to violent ideation, imagining the murder of those whose promiscuous lifestyle perturbs him. At these moments, the novel illuminates the dehumanizing ideation that enables an individual to carry out such horrific acts. Staring across at two strippers sitting at the bar, to whom he is obviously attracted, Bassam

> makes himself think of cutting their throats, how the short blade must be forced into the skin below the jaw. The artery there. He does not care if they feel pain, for anyway it will be brief, and he does not worry of their souls burning for they have brought it upon themselves. But to kill bodies he has never lain with—this is what weakens him. (230)

Bassam's struggle not to think of these women as sexual beings is resolved through imagining their violent deaths, reflecting the deadly rationale used in carrying out the suicide mission on the World Trade Center. Like a number of other moments in the text (437, 461), the passage implies that part of the terrorist's anger emanates from a frustrated desire, a cultural incapacity to partake of that which the West has to offer. Birgit Däwes reads *The Garden of Last Days* in this way, arguing that Bassam is presented as the embodiment of "the Islamist . . . driven mainly by a repressed desire for the West"

(270). But this analysis tends to simplify his attitudes towards those against whom he will commit an act of unspeakable violence. For while the attribution of terrorist hatred to unfulfilled yearning could be read as American hubris—they want what we have, and are angry merely because they don't have it—Dubus's depiction of life in the Florida panhandle is certainly not flattering, nor does he paint a very desirable version of the pursuit of happiness. The juxtaposition of the narratives of lost souls in the novel thus offers a continuum in which Bassam al-Jizani's actions are simply the most extreme among a series of other desperate acts (stripping, taking your child to a strip club, child kidnapping). The extremity of Bassam's actions may set him apart, but he still shares a number of defining characteristics with other characters in the novel. Jay McInerney suggests it is a "sense of victimhood," while Janet Maslin sees it as "anger" and "inner turmoil."

The text further accentuates the terrorist's alienation by demonstrating that Bassam's sense of radical disconnection is not reserved merely for American others. Near the center of the novel, the reader finds the longest section of those devoted to Bassam. These ten pages unequivocally present the chasm that opens up between the prospective suicide bomber and the material world. Returning from the jihadist training camp, Bassam and his comrades find that their old friends only "wanted to race, to smoke, to gossip, to stay baboons" (254). In Bassam's eyes, these acquaintances have been vanquished by their attraction to the West: "Karim, standing before them in his Nike cap and T-shirt and jeans, his shiny cell phone in his hand, he was already lost" (254). From the heights of his newly found devotion, he can only look down at his former friends as damned souls who will soon suffer the torments of hell. The best he can do is offer them his pity and "leave it to the Most Merciful to spare [them] from the fall to Jahannam" (255). In this way, the text communicates the energy and conviction of an individual now imbued with a sense of purpose soon translated into a sense of superiority. This ascendancy is communicated ("baboons"), as though, having been selected for this mission, the jihadi is now privy to a knowledge, and a clarity of vision, unavailable to those who are now lost or asleep. He alone sees things as they truly are: "Since he'd become a jihadi, living among his family was like living in a dream except in the dream everyone else is sleeping while you are awake. They sleep and they do not know they sleep. His mother did not even know she was no longer awake with the Creator as she should be" (258–59). These passages reveal a progressive alienation and isolation, not only from the world of the kafir, but also from one's immediate circle and community. This increased estrangement is no doubt a necessary part of the evolution of the suicide bomber. Since it may take months before he is eventually called, it is only by severing all ties, earthly and familial, that he can steadfastly proceed to his designated end.

The novel soon makes clear, however, that it does not endorse Bassam's perspective. Having dismissed his friends and members of his family as lost, he then turns his attention to his father of whom he feels "ashamed," since the latter has also succumbed, "forgotten the Creator, the Mighty, the sustainer and Provider" (257). But their interaction is a telling one, since the father is presented as a knowledgeable and credible contrast to Bassam's fervency. At one point, for instance, when the son proclaims to his father that he has learned the Truth, the other replies, "And what is the Truth, Bassam? Who can know the Truth but Allah?" (255). Although Bassam acquiesces to his father's question, it nevertheless remains apparent that he feels his Truth to be the truer one. But the plot of the novel is engineered so that the only criticism Bassam receives for his jihadist inclinations comes from his father, from within the Islamist world: "You have never been a bright boy . . . so you must listen to me carefully. Jihad is this: it is a struggle within yourself, that is all. It is the struggle to live as Allah wishes you to live. As good people. Do you understand? As good people" (256). The implication is that Bassam, through his lack of intelligence, has been lead to misinterpret jihad (a "lower meaning of it," his father tells him) and has embarked on a flawed course of action. This misinterpretation means that he will not live, nor will he be good. Which is, finally, how the novel judges him and, by implication, how it wishes him to be judged by the reader.

For all its attempts to connect with the radicalized other, then, *The Garden of Last Days* remains a text that shies away from offering any justification for the hatred and anger expressed on September 11 (even from the mouth of the terrorist). And though it resists depicting him as delusional, the novel nevertheless disparages Bassam's aspirations to heroism or martyrdom by repeatedly suggesting that his repressed sexuality is in fact *the* driving force behind most of his actions. This is emphasized through the detailed description of Bassam's botched attempt at sexual relations with a prostitute—he ejaculates prematurely—on the night before they are scheduled to leave Florida for their predetermined meeting with destiny. The piteous tone with which the prostitute consoles Bassam serves to make him little more than a figure of pathos in the reader's eyes. Finally, this undermining is compounded by April's assessment of Bassam, offered in the closing pages of the novel. When asked, after the attacks, what he was like, all she can say is that he was "Like a boy. Just some drunk and lonely boy" (526). This pithy reply reveals very little, though it may in fact reflect precisely what the reader feels he or she truly knows about the suicide bomber. Somewhat ironically, then, a novel that has run for nearly six hundred pages implies that, ultimately, very little is to be gained from any striving after answers when it comes to the terrorist mind. Both Amis's short story and Dubus's novel reveal a contempt for the terrorist. The reasons for these horrific actions are not contemplated, but rather depicted as the meaningless gestures of frustrated and confused individuals. The following novels, however, offer more complex depictions of the terrorist mind. Though that is not to say these are stable minds—Jarett Kobek's Atta and Salim Bachi's Seyf are characters on the verge of existential breakdowns. These texts, however, plumb more deeply into the interiority of these troubled figures, seeking to comprehend the radical logic of the terrorist. At the heart of the novelist's quest lies the question of self-annihilation and the deathly rationale (however flawed and irrational it may seem) that leads individuals to act as these nineteen men did.

TERRORISM AS CRITIQUE: JARETT KOBEK'S *ATTA*

In Amis's story, realism is sacrificed for the sake of satire and condemnation. Consequently, "The Last Days of Muhammad Atta" fails to satisfy the desire to understand the terrorist. For though pleasure may be derived from seeing the terrorist debased, readerly intuition tells us that detailing the reasons for these acts of extremity will require a more painstaking and detailed untangling of the multiple strands that make up the terrorist's personality. So that even in the case of the apparently one-dimensional Atta, pat conclusions or stereotypical depictions fall short in rendering the reality of the suicide bomber. Relatedly, Stephen Holmes underlines the difficulty in pinpointing a singular motive driving the terrorist:

> Resentment at unfair personal treatment and indignation at elite selfishness were no doubt mixed promiscuously together, in his mind, with religious distress at disobedience to God's will. Such a blurring of personal frustration, political protest, and religious convictions make it very difficult, if not impossible to demonstrate the specifically *religious* roots of Atta's commitment to jihadist violence. (140)

Because, from what we know, Atta was also outraged by instances of injustice, particularly when carried out by the dominant powers (whether that be in the United States or Egypt). On another, but no less significant level, he was pained by what he perceived as the desecration of cities through modernization, and more specifically the appearance and proliferation of skyscrapers (Holmes 139, 141). In this case, then, the targets chosen for destruction on September 11 aligned perfectly with Atta's own hatreds. As Daniel Brook conjectures, "when Atta was told he would lead a mission to destroy America's tallest and most famous modernist high-rise complex—the apotheosis of the building type he dreamed of razing in Aleppo—he may have felt the hand of divine providence at work" (Brook). Brook's observation points to the complex intermingling of motivations and griefs roiling within the terrorist's mind. We might say, then, that al-Qaeda fortuitously provided Atta with the opportunity and the means to exercise/exorcise both his religious and secular indignations.

In his novella, *ATTA*, Kobek sets out to dramatically represent this admixture of religious and secular motivations swirling within his protagonist. He identifies his novella as a "psychedelic biography" in which "a good 90 to 95 percent of the book is true. The 5 percent that's not is wildly untrue" (Wedell). So while he claims to have adhered to the known facts, the writer also acknowledges a role in shaping the reader's perceptions of the subject. A lengthier text than Amis's, it uses the space to elaborate upon the idiosyncrasies and contradictions of Mohammed Atta. It also offers a far less insular portrait of the terrorist, allowing other characters to provide commentary and alternative perspectives to those proffered by the protagonist.

The most salient of these idiosyncrasies is Atta's proclaimed relationship with the surrounding architecture. Early in the novel, he announces that he hears, and is conscious of, a constant "humming" which he identifies as "the sound of buildings talking" (10). A little later, he notes that "The city itself speaks. The buildings scream. I alone hear the words" (25). The meaning of these private messages, and a subsequent theme of the text, is the horror and oppressiveness of contemporary architecture. On first sighting the Twin Towers, for instance, Atta expresses his dismay: "Solid rectangle erections of architectural arrogance, total modernist faith in the ability of buildings to shape lives, of the architect's belief that he can control his vision and utilize it towards good" (16). Such notions are not only misguided, Atta concludes, they are also harmful, since this type of architecture "rapes the landscape, rapes lives around the building" (16). In these passages, Atta reflects a humanity and empathy of his own. For although trapped within a conservative and traditionalist viewpoint, his statements obviously reflect a concern for buildings and fellow human beings victimized by modern theories and ideologies. And Atta's perspective here bears a good deal of similarity to that voiced by a number of Western critics. These exhibitions of fellow-feeling from the terrorist certainly offer an entry point for empathy on the part of the reader. For whereas focusing on religious fundamentalism or jihadist philosophy may alienate a Western reader, the highlighting of Atta's loathing of modern architecture actually serves to create a point of connection. For instance, it is no secret that a good number of people regarded the Towers (at least prior to their destruction) as twin monstrosities blighting the landscape of Lower Manhattan. In his reading of Kobek's novel, John Cotter similarly proposes that Atta is "humanized by the disgust we share with him, disgust for the bad architecture of American motels, the coldness of metropolises" (Cotter). Cotter suggests that empathy for Atta's point of view is thus elicited through the ongoing architectural critique presented in the novel, and that establishing such an area of potential agreement provides the reader a higher degree of accessibility to the terrorist than a text that merely seeks to condemn. A further point of connection with the reader is established through the hybrid narration of the novel. The chapters in *ATTA* alternate between the protagonist narrating his own story and chapters presenting the perspective of an omniscient third-person narrator. This narrative strategy moderates the impression that the author is attempting to "speak for the other," since this juxtaposition of viewpoints conveys an uneasiness with a narrative that would attempt to encompass the entirety of Atta's perspective. The utilization of third-person narration also allows the text to establish some distance between itself and its subject, while grounding the story in the few facts that are known about one of the chief engineers of the 9/11 attacks.

The protagonist, however, remains an enigma both to the reader and to himself. A section devoted to a potential romantic attraction reveals just how painfully self-unaware Atta truly is. On one of his excursions to Aleppo, he meets a Palestinian woman named Amal. Narrating this chapter Atta introduces her to the reader as follows: "Amal, Amal, Amal. Tell me brother, how do you describe the whirlwind?" (64). The question reveals the emotional turmoil his encounter with Amal has initiated. On their first meeting she has the audacity to touch his hand. When he complains to a friend about how "forward" she is, the friend explains that she is simply interested in him. Atta discounts this possibility. He claims to "have no attraction for her" but returns to her office daily, ostensibly to review records (65). And against his better judgment, he agrees to visit her one evening at her home. Atta's uncertainty and discomfort are likely to garner some sympathy from the reader; at the same time as his rigidity deflects those feelings. Amal tells a story about Harun al-Rashid's court from *A Thousand and One Nights* and, like Scheherazade, she cuts the story short in the hopes that Atta will return the following night to hear its continuation. Despite these signals, he remains unsure as to her intentions or desires. He leaves that evening, never to see her again. In this episode and others, Atta demonstrates that he is as equally oblivious to the feelings of others as he is to his own. A character so bereft of insight is hardly likely to provide the reader with the necessary indices to make sense of the protagonist's actions. As such, the true reasons for Atta's conversion remain a mystery. What little we know we glean indirectly from comments made by others, primarily his father, much as it is in Dubus's novel. Parental figures offering assessments on their son's progress towards extremism is thus a recurring motif in these texts. At times representing tradition, at others a more relaxed and less extreme approach to Islam, the figure of the parent is used as a vehicle for critiquing the choices of the protagonist.

In the case of the real-life Atta, it has been hypothesized that the dynamics of his family life contributed to his metamorphosis. The academic and professional success of his two older sisters (one practices internal medicine, the other is a professor of zoology) seems to have placed enormous pressure upon the young man's shoulders. This situation was further exacerbated by the strict attitude and constant criticism he received from his father. Kobek's novel picks up on these relationships, depicting a patriarch frustrated and confounded by the behavior of his son: "There is madness in him. I should have never paid for his Hajj. Look how he comes to us, with the beard of a mujahadeen" (85). Telling his son that he is not "the type" to become an extremist, Atta's father declares that he is "not a fool who throws it all away on holiness, on the hope of prayer, on throwing stones at pillars. You are educated! You are upper class! You are one of us, you little thing!" (93). Atta later concedes to the reader that he did not undergo a transformation at Mecca: "I, Mohamed el-Amir, stand on the plain of Ararat, the moment of Hajj, and I feel nothing" (94). So, either is father is right, and Atta has not undergone the stereotypical conversion of the fanatical believer, or religion is not the principal motivation for his actions. Because others do observe a change in Atta and he will, in fact, do just what his father thinks he should not: become a stone and hurl himself against the pillars of Western arrogance, despite his upbringing, his education, or his social standing.

Perhaps more important to the reader's assessment is the contrast offered between the perspective of the terrorist-protagonist and one of his fellow conspirators. This other terrorist acts as a foil, someone against whom the reader can take the measure of the protagonist. This contrast, of course, can impact the reader's empathetic connection in a number of ways. We should thus be aware of the use of juxtaposition as a strategy for influencing one's openness (such as it is) to the protagonist. In three of the texts examined (Dubus is the exception) Atta's philosophy and attitude are specifically set against the otherness of Ziad Jarrah, a member of the terrorist cell who adheres to a far looser interpretation of Islam and who, to the former's eyes at least, repeatedly succumbs to the temptations of the West. The reason the figure of Jarrah is used as a foil for Atta in these various texts is because he "was by any accounting an unlikely candidate for Islamic warrior" (McDermott 49). While contrasting Atta with Jarrah certainly serves to highlight the former's extremity, it also raises questions about commonalities and dissimilarities between the various members of the terrorist cell. Now it is in fact possible that the degree of difference between the members was minimal and all traces were erased by the time they set out to complete their mission, but this nevertheless suggests a variety of individuals coming together for a common cause. The diversity humanizes the terrorists, presenting them as distinct entities with their own struggles and motivations. The notion of us and them is certainly destabilized by the presentation of a variety of individuals who only loosely make up a group we might refer to as them.

Kobek's novella addresses this idea, presenting Atta as confounded and deeply perplexed by what he perceives as irreconcilable differences between Jarrah's way of being and the demands of jihad. "Imagine we are equals,"

Atta thinks, "though one is righteous and the other a sex maniac rank with Western corruption"(124). When Jarrah, sensing the other's displeasure, asks what is bothering him, Atta replies:

> How different we are. You have known one woman, probably more. You indulge in cigarettes and alcohol and drugs. These things should prevent you from being here. And myself? I am a different model. I deny myself false pleasures, avoid sins of the jahili world. I have never known flesh nor drunkenness. Yet here we are, equal before our muhajid brothers. I think about this and wonder why? (124)

Atta finally accuses the other of superficiality and of "revel[ing] in haraam," in essence questioning his true belief in the cause for which they will soon give their lives. It is clear that he is incapable of coming to terms with Jarrah's contradictions. Jarrah's retort, on the other hand, reveals that he understands Atta's mindset all too well, and that the unwavering self he presents to the world hides many things: "You have your haraam, worse than mine. Haraam of the soul, a thing that winds within your mind . . . I am different. I keep no secrets. Perhaps our muhajid brothers recognize the power of a person who speaks the language of sinners. Perhaps . . . the brothers want a man who is truly of this world" (125). Jarrah alludes to the darker side of Atta, hinting at repression, but also that the organizers might have sought some kind of balance when they formed a group of individuals containing individuals as disparate as Mohammed Atta and Ziad Jarrah. Jarrah's repeated use of the word "brother" suggests that, in his mind at least, they are still united, despite their differences. In these interactions, Kobek manages to humanize Atta a little, as he does by presenting the terrorist a someone with typical issues, such as familial pressures. The fullness of Kobek's portrait thus moves Atta, if only briefly, back into the realm of the human.

That Jarrah identifies himself as "a man who is truly of this world," however, also implies that Atta is not. Jarrah suggests that by embarking on this mission Atta, and perhaps some of the others, have removed themselves from the human arena. Interestingly, much the same language is used in other novels in describing Atta who is depicted as a man whose "mind was in the upper skies" (DeLillo 80), or as someone "already beyond this world" (Dubus 25). This naturally complicates the possibility of empathetic connection because the terrorist who is not of this world, much like the one who kills himself and others out of "nihilistic insouciance," provides very little material with which to decipher and, more important, grapple with the reasons and motivations behind his actions. He remains an enigmatic, one-dimensional, figure of only limited interest. And even if we accept Atta as a man who simply "wants to watch the world burn," we still need to account for the behaviors and motivations of eighteen other men. Indeed, these novels do not make Atta out to be representative at all. In fact, at this point, the otherness of

Jarrah actually appears more intriguing and worthy of examination. Because an incontrovertible fact about the nineteen men who hijacked jetliners and crashed them into the World Trade Center, the Pentagon, and a field in Pennsylvania, is that they were not a homogeneous group themselves. In fact, one of the mysteries of the event remains how this disparate group of individuals managed to remain committed to this singular action over such an extended period of time. Humanizing the terrorist is important, not merely as a strategy for self-preservation, through the anticipation of his next move, but, more importantly, as a way of connecting with his issues and grievances (which, under other circumstances, might have been *our* issues and *our* grievances) and thus instigating a search for potential solutions.[3] These extreme actions may never make complete sense to us (hence the frequent attribution of "irrational" when discussing the terrorist's motives), but a reading of these texts provides a grain of connection, an acknowledgment that these men were of this life, even if it is one we sometimes have difficulty recognizing.

Before turning to our final text, it is best to take a moment to recognize an underlying impulse behind much Western writing to discount the validity of the terrorist's agenda. This propensity reveals a reluctance to accept that the terrorist may have acted while in full control of his faculties or that he may have been driven by motivations whose foundations bear some similarity to our own. This is not the same as arguing that one person's terrorist is another person's freedom fighter, but it is advocating for a consideration of the ways in which these actions might be formulated in the mind of the potential suicide bomber. In other words, an extensive and honest contemplation of the terrorist's act requires that gestures typically conceived as acts of aggression, *also* be reframed as evidence of the individual's generosity, selflessness, and sacrifice for the welfare of his community. Having been victimized, however, it is understandable that those in the West would be unwilling to listen to any narratives of reciprocal action or of shared responsibility. And yet an understanding of the terrorist's rationale is only likely to emanate from a narrative construction that presents a plausible working through of these central principles. As Robert Pape observes, "the homicidal dimension of the act should not cause us to overlook an important cause leading to it—that many suicide terrorists are killing themselves to advance what they see as the common good" (180).[4] For though the suicide bomber may harbor personal motivations (revenge, renown, meaningfulness), the act of sacrificing one's life "demonstrates publicly that a cause larger than any personal interest or wish is at stake" (Holmes, 147–48). Suicide thus serves a tautological purpose; its very occurrence invests the cause with the ultimate justification—it is so important that people are willingly giving up their lives for it.[5] Recognizing such a fact, however, runs counter to a narrative constructed on the dichotomy of good versus evil. For in this iteration, these are no longer individuals intent on the slaughter of innocent civilians, but young men who, misguided or not, sacrifice their lives in the hopes of bringing some measure of relief to their ailing communities.

But what mental contortions must a victim undertake in order to imagine the perpetrators as victims? Can we, as Butler implores, look beyond our own victimization to recognize the victimization of others? Such a position depends first on the extent to which one is willing to accept that the situation of the other is not entirely his responsibility nor of his own making. Second, that the other is not wholly to blame for his condition, nor that he be expected to resolve the problem on his own. And finally, that a specific set of circumstances as well as the actions of others (including, most likely, our own) have contributed in some way to an unbearable and unjust situation. Butler therefore contends that any illumination of current dynamics is contingent upon envisioning "not only how [American imperialism] is experienced by those who understand themselves as its victims, but how it enters into their own formation as acting and deliberating subjects" (11). In other words, that we should make a concerted effort to know and feel how *we* are experienced by the other. Any such exercise, as I have pointed out, requires a kind of role reversal in which we attempt, as much as is humanly possible, to put aside our own feelings and consider those of the other. Any such direct identification, however, almost immediately elicits in the empathizer a prevailing anxiety that explanation might be (mis)taken for exoneration; and it suggests an awareness that an argument offering anything less than outright admonition embarks on the slippery road of equivocation. This is an understandable and natural sentiment: no one wishes to be seen as forgiving (to say nothing of supporting) actions that are unequivocally unforgivable. But this "condemnation imperative," as Ghassan Hage calls it, has slipped into most of the intellectual discourse pertaining to these events. He contends that under these conditions, "It is difficult to express any form of understanding whatsoever, even when one is indeed also condemning the practice. . . . Only unqualified condemnation will do. And if one tries to understand, any accompanying condemnation is also deemed suspicious" (67). In these circumstances, any considerations of motivations, to say nothing of social or political drives, is severely handicapped. As is, Hage insists, any possible identification of solutions to this geopolitical problem. Because even outright condemnation of the gestures of these men on any number of levels does not immediately or necessarily negate their reasons for committing said actions. In other words, while we can categorically maintain that their means do not justify their ends, this judgment does not invalidate their ends entirely. For unless we maintain that every suicide bomber is insane, or has been hoodwinked into committing an act that no otherwise sane person would ever commit, then we must question, as Hage suggests we do, why so many individuals continue to consider this a viable course of action. For even if these are merely the acts of desperate individuals who can conceive of no other recourse but ending their lives, we might still ask ourselves what conditions contributed to this state of affairs and what part we might play in alleviating such despair.

"NOT A ROBOT PROGRAMMED FOR TOTAL DESTRUCTION": SALIM BACHI'S *TUEZ-LES TOUS*

I now turn to *Tuez-les tous*, a novel written by an Algerian writer, that presents the thoughts and movements of a terrorist-protagonist on the day before the attacks. In the novel, Salim Bachi adopts an alternate path, seeking to confound and problematize our notions of the terrorist by presenting an individual who does not conform to stereotype and whose motivations resemble no others. When asked why he had made his protagonist a reluctant fundamentalist, Salim Bachi answered,

> It was primarily novelistic temptation. A committed Islamist did not leave me much room to maneuver. It was difficult to bring the character to life. To write this novel I needed a human being and not a robot programmed for total destruction. That's why *Tuez-les tous* remains a work of fiction and not an essay on the genesis of a terrorist, nor on September 11 as an historical event. (Temlali, my translation)

Bachi's reply suggests his novel intends to offer a more complex portrait than that usually afforded the terrorist. When he observes that he "needed a human being" as his protagonist, he is acknowledging the necessity of unequivocally depicting a character who accomplishes his suicide mission, but who nevertheless exhibits characteristics or qualities with which the reader can identify. Bachi assumes the reader will perceive the otherness of his protagonist (indeed, will come to the text with that preconceived notion), and therefore his challenge is to communicate the possible, and unexpected, areas of sameness that protagonist and reader may share.

To this end, *Tuez-les tous* (*Kill Them All*) presents the agonized thinking of a terrorist protagonist whose namelessness allows him to represent the seemingly endless stream of young men willing to give their lives in the search of meaning, community, and identity. He calls himself "No one" (*Personne*), is then referred to as "Pilot" by members of the group, and is finally given the *nom de guerre* Seyf el Islam (sword of Islam) by the organizers. As much as the novel highlights the representative qualities of its protagonist, however, it emphatically accentuates the question of otherness by offering an alternate construction of the terrorist, one that veers from conventional depictions in a couple of significant ways. First, Seyf is an unbeliever, thus moving the novel away from any convenient religious explanations or rationalizations. Second, the text circumscribes the notion of the individual as subsumed by the collective; Seyf displays contempt for Western civilization (Paris, the Enlightenment, the Towers) but also for the organization for which he will purportedly give his life. It is these problematic and paradoxical qualities that give him the shapings of a real life. Unlike some of the other fictional representations, he is not defined by intransigency or fanaticism. He does not believe in God or the Organization. If God does exist, he expects that "He will spit in my face." As for the Organization it is made up of "hypocrites," with the "effeminate Saudi" being the worst of all (134).[6] Having undermined the two most obvious motivations for such actions, Bachi forces the reader to look anew and reconsider the criteria by which the otherness of the terrorist is defined and determined.

From the beginning the novel makes clear that faith is not a determining factor for Seyf:

Orphelin, il avait erré à Paris, la ville lumières éteintes. Puis il avait été adopté par l'Organisation. Il suivit leur enseignement dans la mosquée où on le laissait dormir, lui qui n'avait plus ni feu ni leu. Ils l'avaient nourri, protégé et il avait grandi, devenant immense par son incroyance et sa détermination.

Orphaned, he had roamed through Paris, city of lights out. Then he was adopted by the Organization. He followed their teachings in the mosque where they let him sleep, he who had neither hearth nor home. They had fed and protected him, and he had grown, becoming immense through his lack of faith and his determination. (29)

Unlike the terrorists depicted in other texts, then, he fosters no illusions about the heavenly paradise that purportedly awaits him and his compatriots. Even if religious justification did hold some solace, Seyf's own knowledge of the Koran prevents any such construction, his thoughts repeatedly invoking the following passage: "*Car celui qui a tué un homme qui lui-même n'a pas tué . . . est considéré comme s'il avait tué tous les hommes*"/'Whoever kills a man who has not himself killed . . . it is as though he has killed all humankind' (67). He therefore accepts that his transgressions cannot, and will not, be forgiven: "*il savait pertinemment qu'il allait tuer des croyants dans les tours, pas seulement des adorateurs du veau d'or noir ou vert, mais des croyants sincères, plus sincères que lui, et un seul, un seul suffirait à sa peine éternelle*"/'he knew absolutely that he was going to kill believers in those towers, not just the worshippers of the golden calf, but true believers, truer than he, and just one of them, a single one, would suffice to guarantee his eternal damnation' (64). In this case, Seyf's realization of his own guilt, of committing a sin, complicates the reader's understanding of the suicide bomber's motives.

Traditional explanations of suicide bombing argue that if religion fails to provide the impetus for such action then motivation is to be found, logically, in belonging to an extremist group and acting for a cause greater than oneself. Ideology gives the individual's life structure, while the organization offers a community within which one's life begins to make sense. The alienated and disenfranchised individual is thus provided with an identity, through his inclusion in the organization, but also within the greater community on whose behalf the organization claims to act. But Seyf's entrance into the Organization, while bringing him comfort, is anything but smooth. In fact, he demonstrates a disdain for "the Saudi" (a not so veiled reference to Osama bin Laden), and for his fellow combatants who fail to assuage any of his doubts: "*Dieu sait et tu ne sait pas*"/'God knows and you know nothing,' they tell him (67). Consequently, Seyf steadfastly rejects the insularity of the Organization, repeatedly rebuffing, for instance, the attempts of other members to hail him as their "brother" (33, 68, 89). He recognizes that he shares little of their philosophy and, indeed, sees their vision as both backward and morally questionable: "*Ils se trompaient, on ne revenait pas aux origines, ce n'étaient plus que légendes que les siècles glorifient, et ces idées de pureté de la religion, de la race, étaient aussi dangereuses que celles des nazis*"/'They were wrong, one could not return to one's origins, these were nothing more than legends sanctified by the centuries, and their ideas of purity of religion, and of race, were as dangerous as those of the Nazis' (71). Their inability to entertain any form of uncertainty alienates Seyf further, so that he finds himself in an existential quandary much like Hamlet, to whom the text frequently alludes. And like Hamlet, Seyf is haunted by the spirit of his dead father:

> *Ils s'aveuglent, mon fils, on ne revient jamais à la pureté originelle, elle n'a jamais éxisté. Et sur son corps même, le corps saint du Prophète, ils se disputaient déjà pour savoir qui prendrait sa succession. I'l n'y eut jamais de pureté.*
> *Mais il ne reste rien, père, rien.*
> *Nos ancêtres ont bâti les Pyramides. Fondé Carthage.*
> *Mais Carthage brûle.*
>
> They are blinding themselves, son, we never return to original purity, it never existed. And on his very body, the body of the sainted Prophet, they fought over the rights of succession. There never was any purity.
> But there is nothing left, father, nothing.
> Our ancestors built the Pyramids. Founded Carthage.
> But Carthage burns. (71)

The figure of the father (as with Dubus and Kobek) is a pivotal but complicated character in Bachi's novel. For though he is cherished by Seyf, who shares some of his views, he is also depicted as downtrodden, too accepting of slights, and blind to the flaws of the Western civilization, of which he is a ardent proponent. Indeed, it is at his urging that Seyf leaves Algeria for the supposed limitless possibilities of France. As such, while he exerts some influence on his son, the reader is nevertheless cognizant of these limitations. More important, in contrast, we sense the limbo in which Seyf finds himself, feeling neither his father's optimism nor the extremist's blind conviction. He thinks of the Saudi and his lieutenants as *"le démon et ses djinns"*/'the demon and his djinns' (133) and as *"d'anciennes taupes qui s'étaient brouillées avec les Américains pour d'officielles raisons—occupation de l'Arabie saoudite— et d'obscures et officieuese histoires de fric. Lui savait tout cela. Pourquoi, alors, les suivit-il?"*/'former moles who had broken relations with the Americans for official reasons—the occupation of Saudi Arabia—and obscure and unofficial questions of cash. He knew all this. So why, then, did he follow them?' (29). Though the answer to this question is never explicitly stated in the text, the narrative implies that while the Organization has failed to imbue his actions with meaning, it has nevertheless provided him with the means of expressing his disillusionment with the life of this world.

These factors contribute to making Seyf a different kind of terrorist. He has reached an existential impasse, in part because he does not really believe the world can change. If this is all the world is, and all it will ever be ("there is nothing left"), then might as well end it. Imbued with this rationale and thoughts of imminent extinction, he undertakes an interior dialogue with God and Satan, intermingling verses from the Koran, haunting memories of his father, related allusions to *Hamlet*, recollections of his life in Paris with all its attendant deceptions and disappointments, his subsequent entrance into the Organization, fruitless interactions with Khalid and the Saudi in Kandahar, a brief but joyous interlude in the South of Spain, and the final stages of preparation. All of this is presented as an unrelenting jumble in his mind.[7] And as the novel progresses, the use of punctuation becomes increasingly arbitrary, contributing to the sense of a mind on the verge of becoming unhinged. Because to the very end Seyf remains uncertain as to the validity of his chosen path. Of course, these depictions of the uncertainty of the terrorist may be soothing to the reader who may console himself with the terrorist's lack of conviction. After all, if the terrorist is not that committed, then surely his reasons are not that strong. On the other hand, these hesitations reveal a human side of the terrorist, destabilizing the image of the suicide bomber as a brainwashed, unthinking automaton merely doing the bidding of his superiors. It is through this kind of depiction of the terrorist that the text may overcome a reader's ideological reluctance. In contrast to the other texts which present realist and fairly linear narratives, Bachi attempts to communicate the chaos and confusion, the repetition-compulsion, and the relentless assessing and justifying, that are likely to occur in the mind of someone on the verge of self-destruction—no matter how valid the cause may appear to be. For this is not mere suicide, but the committing of a monumental crime against humanity.

Seyf's commitment to his mission, however, emerges from a conviction that humanity has thoroughly lost its way. He dates the beginning of this downward spiral to the year 1492, that of Columbus's "discovery" and, more significantly, of the expulsion of the Moors from Spain: *"Grenade tombait aux mains des mêmes rois qui avaient armé les navires des Génois et permettait à l'Occident de s'étendre au-delà des mers, de conquérir et d'inventer un nouveau monde"*/'Granada fell into the hands of the same kings who had armed the ships of the Genoese permitting the Occident to extend its reach beyond the seas, to conquer and invent a new world' (119). The vanishing of Arab Andalusia, an emblem of pluralism and cultural tolerance, represents for Seyf the loss of inclusiveness and a turn towards fragmentation. The United States, with its superpower status, symbolizes the current disequilibrium in the world, with New York as the epitome of injustice:

> *New York était la ville des Iniquités*
> *le World Trade center le symbole*
> *de l'orgueil démesuré de l'Amérique*
> *et du saccage du monde*
> *les tours, les démons Gog et Magog*
> *Qu'il faillait abattre*
>
> New York was the city of Inequities
> the World Trade Center the symbol
> of the excessive pride of America
> and of the plundering of the world
> the towers, the demons Gog and Magog
> That had to be demolished. (presented as such in text, 101–2)

As in this passage, *Tuez-les tous* frequently depicts the United States as oblivious to, and unconscious of, the ways in which its actions are reacted to, or perceived, as impositions or dictates. In its arrogance and continued displays of disdain for others, the United States presents itself as the antithesis of the pluralistic society for which Seyf yearns, and thus as an ideal target. The novel does attempt, therefore, to truthfully represent the anger felt by the terrorist for his intended victims. Riding in an elevator in his hotel, and imbued with the knowledge of what is to come, Seyf suddenly feels contempt for the people around him. He thinks of himself as an entomologist observing insects:

> *ils l'avaient contaminé, il s'était prêté à leur jeu, le monde entier s'était prêté*
> *à leurs manigances et lui, eux, ne voulaient plus mourir et vivre sans jamais*
> *s'apercevoir que tout cela était vain sans croyance, sans Dieu, que leur soif de*
> *conquête, leur ponctualité au travail, l'ardeur avec laquelle ils s'abrutissaient*
> *à la tache, cette ferveur à détruire ceux qui ne leur ressemblaient pas, le*
> *conduisait à les haïr, et s'il avait pu faire sauter l'ascenseur à cet instant il*

n'aurait pas hésité, mais l'idée que demain il atomiserait des dizaines d'ascenseurs, les deux tours démoniaques, cette idée le calmait.

they had contaminated him, he had taken part in their game, the entire world had taken part in their machinations, and he, they, no longer wanted to die and lived without ever contemplating that all this was pointless without faith, without God, that their thirst for conquest, their punctuality at work, the ardor with which they set themselves to the task, their fervor for destroying those who did not resemble them, led him to hate them, and if he could have blown up the elevator at that moment he would not have hesitated, but the thought that tomorrow he would atomize dozens of elevators, the two demonic towers, this idea calmed him. (101)

In moments such as this, Seyf makes no distinction between the nation and its citizens who are depicted as thoughtless ants moving through their respective days, never questioning the political philosophy to which they so faithfully adhere. In essence, Seyf responds to those fundamentalist aspects of the American psyche, the belief in their own exceptionalism, and their inability to comprehend why anyone would not want to be exactly as they are.

It is ironic, then, that Seyf's hatred for the West emanates from its apparent unwillingness to accept him into his folds. For in contrast to the other terrorists who strive to keep the new country at arm's length, he truly embraces the notion of a new culture and a new identity. As such, when assimilation fails, Seyf's feelings of betrayal are all the more palpable, particularly in regards to his relationship and marriage to a French woman: *"Tout avait commencé pour lui quand il avait désiré devenir l'un des leurs en épousant l'une des leurs"*/'Everything had started for him when he had desired to become one of them by marrying one of them' (141). In his eyes, her acceptance of him as a partner conferred legitimacy upon his struggle to integrate. This sense of belonging is shattered, however, when she makes the choice to abort their unborn child: *"Ils vivaient ensemble dans un miniscule studio et il croyait avoir trouvé une patrie, lui l'Emigré, un lieu et un feu, mais elle l'éteignit et il accepta. Il l'accompagna et assista au crime, à la mort de son espoir et des son avenir"*/'They lived together in a tiny apartment and he thought he had found a home, he the Immigrant, a hearth and a fire, but she extinguished it and he accepted it. He accompanied her and abetted the crime, the death of his hope and his future' (40). Their relationship endures, but the abortion signals its eventual end. His feelings of complicity in these events only fuels his despondency about a hypocritical West that, despite its own liberal and democratic proclamations, will never accept him as one of their own.

It is in its depiction of these injustices that *Tuez-les tous* comes closest to offering a plausible explanation for Seyf's hatred of the West. Arriving in the birthplace of the Enlightenment, he anticipates, like some many other immigrants, partaking of the limitless possibilities his adopted country claims to offer. He is soon dissuaded of this dream, however, and becomes a disillusioned soul, prey to the whims of every racist cop and functionary:

> *Il avait quitté son laboratoire parce qu'on le traitait comme un rat un travailleur au noir et les flics chaque année le regardaient de travers parce qu'il ne venait pas du bon endroit du monde, c'était un sous-dévelopé, et un sale enfant de putain de flic inculte se croyait supérieur à lui, un sale enfant de putain d'alcoolique qui battait ses enfants se permettait de le juger.*

> He had left the lab because they treated him like a rat, a worker in the shadows, and every year the cops would eye him warily because he did not come from the right place on earth, he was an underdeveloped, and a moronic son of a bitch cop thought himself superior, an alcoholic son of a bitch who beat his kids felt free to judge him. (45)

Through repetition the text communicates the effects of the endless onslaught of racism and discrimination, the constant badgering and humiliation compounded through its relentless (and sometimes thoughtless, but not) usage. Over the course of four pages (44–48), for instance, the text recounts three similar versions of an encounter between the protagonist and two gendarmes who have stopped him for no justifiable reason:

Je travaille.

Combien d'heures par semaine?

Je travaille dans mon labo.

Tu ne comprends pas, il faut te le dire en quelle langue? Y a des lois, ici, en France.

Il se retourna vers sa collèque, une blonde grasse et décolorée, et lui dit: "Ils ne savent même pas répondre à une question simple et ils font des études."

Je ne travaille pas je ...

Quoi?

J'étudie et je suis payé par mon directeur de recherches.

C'est légal, ça?

Tout ce qu'il y a de plus légal monsieur.

Alors revenez avec une autorisation de votre directeur et alors on étudiera votre dossier.

I work.

How many hours a week?

I work in my lab.

Do you not understand, in what language do we have to speak? There are laws, here, in France.

He turned toward his colleague, a fat blemished blonde, and said: "They can't even answer a simple question and they go to school."

I don't work I . . .

What?

I study and I get paid by my research director.

That's legal?

As legal as can be, sir.

So come back with an authorization from your director and we'll review your file. (45–46)

The repetition of the scene conveys the accumulated effect of such moments upon the individual. In the process, it probably elicits a combination of empathy and dread from the reader, who both feels for the protagonist but also recognizes that the accrual of such incidents will lead the protagonist on his eventual path of destruction. From this perspective, Paris is in no way the "city of lights" but rather the "city of lights out" (*ville lumières éteintes*).

These experiences, and not Allah or bin Laden, eventually compel Seyf to act as he does. The text communicates to the reader a sense of the innumerable "slings and arrows," the injustices that have contributed to the protagonist's (self-)hatred and nihilism. The significance of such encounters in the development of a radical extremist cannot be understated. Ghassan Hage, for instance, argues that while a "culture of martyrdom" may lead an individual down the path to terrorism, it cannot do so without a predisposition on the part of said individual (79–80). This condition is usually obtained when that person feels he or she is living a meaningless life—a feeling exacerbated when one is singled out repeatedly for humiliation. As Hage observes,

> Humiliation is the experience of being psychologically demeaned—treated like less than a human being, by someone more powerful than you, without a capacity to redress the situation. This is experienced not only at a national level . . . [but also] at a personal level: being shouted at, abused, searched, stopped, ordered around, checked, asked to wait, "allowed to pass," and so forth. (82)

As Hage makes clear, the humiliation experienced by Bachi's protagonist is a common symptom of the life of the transplanted and dislocated young man. Seyf, like many others, had been led to believe that if he forsook his land, his community, and his family, that his adopted country would reward him with purpose and untold riches. Instead he finds alienation and rejection. He also discovers that this land of supposed opportunity—this same land that deems him unworthy—is one steeped in hedonism, decadence, rampant materialism, and promiscuity. The individual is thus simultaneously exposed to a world that has prospered in ways his homeland has not, but that (to his eyes) lives a thoroughly indecent and sinful existence, permitting itself transgressions the likes of which he would never even dream. So this other existence has its temptations, as we have noted, but it also endows these young men with feelings of superiority, if only because they believe they will be spared the anguish of Hell which awaits the infidels.

Placed at the interstices of two cultures, and exposed to a world that raises significant doubts about, but just as strongly confirms, the rightness of his upbringing, the dislocated individual becomes the battleground for warring impulses. As a number of writers have observed, it is no surprise that the radicalism of these individuals often increases *after* their exposure to the West.[8] Residency in a Western country creates culture shock and unresolvable tensions, irrevocably changing these individuals, so that they are not comfortable living in either place, becoming "limbo men" to use Stephen Holmes's phrase—not at home in Europe or the Middle East (153). But how does this alienation turn into hatred and anger? How does this purgatory not of their own making eventually lead to their lashing out against the host country? The displacement of these individuals, and their subsequent alienation, make them particularly susceptible to the lures of radicalism. This cultural dislocation, a product of ever-increasing globalization, is further amplified by a host country which, concerned with preserving its cultural identity, highlights the immigrant's difference, illegitimacy, and consequent ineligibility.

Instead of accepting their subjugation in this new community, as Arjun Appadurai observes, some of these men come to equate their mistreatment to that suffered by all Muslims across the world. In this way, they "begin to identify themselves with the cellular world of global terror rather than the isolating world of national minorities. Thus they morph from one kind of minority—weak, disempowered, disenfranchised, and angry—to another kind of minority—cellular, globalized, transnational, armed, and dangerous. This transformation is the crucible that produces recruits to global terrorism" (112–13). So whatever else the West (and the United States more specifically) may have done, it becomes the focal point for a profound dissatisfaction with the current state of world affairs. Thus, the resentments seem to obtain traction and a greater degree of focus in the "crucible" of Western society. Bachi's novel comes closest to communicating this painful process and the West's own complicity of which it is no doubt unaware. For all its humanizing of its protagonist, however, *Tuez-les tous* still falls short of providing a terrorist with whom the reader can readily identify. In large part this is due to the singular nature of Seyf's religious rebellion, but also to the mental instability communicated through the text's rambling and repetitive narrative.

CONCLUSION: THE RELUCTANCE OF THE NOVEL

In the end, not one of these texts provides an entirely unabashed, pro-terrorist narrative. For though they are not hampered by the historical record (they take it and leave it as they wish), they all exhibit a measure of discomfort with their unfiltered and unbalanced presentation of the terrorist that, by necessity, fails to pay equal attention to the victims. As such, each of these novels exhibits, in its own way, a need to undermine the motivations of the terrorist, and delegitimize whatever reasons he may harbor. Sometimes, it is simply by showing that neither the political or the religious agenda is in fact the terrorist's primary motivation. Instead, it is the "nihilistic insouciance" of Amis's Atta, or the sexual frustration of Dubus's Bassam. Or a critique of Western architecture that progressively degenerates over the course of Kobek's novel, so that Atta's mind is eventually filled with an incomprehensible buzzing ("ZzZz zZ zZzz zZzzZZ z zz zzz zzzz ZZ") as he flies a commercial airliner into the North Tower. Even Bachi's novel, which presents a fairly complete, albeit stylized, image of the terrorist's inner life, undercuts that vision by imbuing its protagonist with motivations with which very few readers are likely to connect—a rebellion against a God that would allow such a world to exist. And even those readers who might identify with such a cause are likely to deem Seyf's mutinous gesture horrifically excessive.

An essential part of the terrorist's equation is that his actions be framed and perceived as justified acts of retribution, carried out in the hopes of righting past wrongs, of raising awareness of the injustices perpetrated against them, and/or of making others suffer as they have been made to suffer. Any narrative aspiring to truthfully render the mind of the terrorist must strive to give these elements their due consideration. Only in this way can a text begin to communicate the complex dynamics of victimization involved in any suicide mission. Highlighting ways in which the reader might think about the terrorist (and his community) as victimized certainly increases the possibility of eliciting sympathy, and a greater degree of openness, on the part of the reader. Such imaginative connections are possible, but only if the reader feels that the sins previously committed against the perpetrator are greater than, or at least equal to, those which he in turn commits.

With the events of September 11, of course, such a correlation is unlikely, and this is certainly not the case with any of these texts. Amis's Atta bitterly recalls an incident when fellow Muslims were discriminated against by a female flight attendant, Kobek's version rails against the encroachment of modernity, while Bachi's Seyf carries a list of grievances, the foremost being his rejection and humiliation at the hands of a French society that will not accept him as one of their own. The degrees of victimization pale considerably in the face of the immensity of the horrors these men will commit. Dubus's Bassam comes closest to harboring a personal reason for his actions, blaming the contamination of the Muslim world by the West for the death of his brother, Khalid, who meets his end drag racing his Grand Am through the Saudi desert while listening to David Lee Roth and drinking Coca Cola. Again, none of these events provide sufficient cause. Admittedly, personal grievances are often compounded with social, political, and religious ones, but none of these texts presents a convincing case for the initial impulse that would lead an individual to mete out cataclysm and extreme horror. In other words, these texts fail to put forth terrorist-protagonists whom the reader might momentarily consider as victims in their own right. Nor do these characters think of themselves in such terms (Bachi's protagonist comes closest). In fact, they are far more likely to evince feelings of superiority towards their potential victims, as Bassam does with April, than they are to conceive of themselves as oppressed. Empowered by their mission and the knowledge they possess of the upcoming disaster, they view their unsuspecting victims in a condescending and disdainful light.

So why do these novels avoid communicating the victimization of the terrorist? Perhaps they fear being accused of creating moral equivalency between the 9/11 hijackers and their victims, or that this blurring flirts a little too closely with legitimizing the actions of the terrorist-protagonist. One wonders, therefore, whether the novels in question are not affected by the same "condemnation imperative" to which other forms of discourse on terrorism have been subject. Such an argument is in fact put forth in an extensive study of the relationship between the novel and terrorism, by Robert Appelbaum and Alexis Paknadel, which notes that the narratives found in terrorist fictions are almost always—and quite understandably so—on the side of the victims. These texts are inevitably constructed in such a way as to elicit sympathy from the reader for the victims, and a commensurate degree of contempt for the terrorist. They further note that this is even truer after the events of September 11, and point to a "sea change" in the writing of subsequent terrorist fiction. This tendency, as Appelbaum and Paknadel note, is not without its effects:

> Without necessarily making overt arguments, or having characters make overt arguments, about the political or moral legitimacy of the society to which terrorism's victims belong, the novels recruit us to the side of the victims, terrorizing us along with them, and in so doing implicitly enlist us against the perpetrators, rendering illegitimate the terrorist's political aims often even without stopping to say what they are. (422–23)

Such narrative constructions thus curtail any striving after understanding. The novel's focus on the act of aggression necessarily shifts readerly sympathy and empathy away from the figure of the terrorist. Indeed, resorting to an act of violence simultaneously discredits the position of the terrorist while tacitly legitimizing that of the victim:

> by focusing on the injuries caused or threatened by terrorist violence, in making the meaning of the violence its violation of everyday life rather than the expression of political or social conflict, most of these novels demand that we assent to the illegitimacy of the politics on behalf of which terrorism is deployed and by the same token, though perhaps more on the level of affect than idea, that we assent to the legitimacy of the side against which terrorism is deployed. (Appelbaum and Paknadel 423)

Even when the novel presents the narrative from the perspective of the terrorist, thereby providing the optimum conditions for the reader to connect with, or glimpse the rationale of, the terrorist's grievances, those points of connection are often undermined or discredited through, and by, the violence perpetrated by the terrorist. So, paradoxically, whatever critique of the victim's position is implied in the thoughts and actions of the terrorist is rendered illegitimate by the violence it has engendered.

The treatments of the terrorist in these novels raise the question as to whether it is possible to write from the perspective of the Other who wishes one harm. It is as though by becoming perpetrators (and, admittedly, this is a question of definition) these individuals irrevocably renounce any previous claims they might have had to being considered victims. From this standpoint, the perpetrator, through his suicide and the taking of innocent lives, has both literally and metaphorically removed himself from humanity. Difficulties in empathizing are further compounded by one's response to the terrorist's own apparent disregard for the humanity of others. Such dehumanizing gestures make the rehumanizing of the terrorist all the more difficult. As Richard Kearney suggests, expressing empathy still requires a degree of pardon or forgiveness on the part of the victim—something which he recognizes as an improbable task: "How do we forgive our enemies? And how do enemies forgive themselves (and us)? Who has the power to forgive? And who the right? Is forgiveness of terror possible? And even if possible, should we still attempt it?" (135). In response, he notes that there is no obvious gain for the victim in forgiving the perpetrator. Finally, Kearney acknowledges that he has "no answers for these questions," but still believes "that the more we understand the evils and causes of terror . . . and the more we work through the traumas of such terror, the closer we may get to making impossible pardon that little bit more possible" (135). And it may very well be that certain acts are unforgivable (although Derrida argues that forgiveness can only truly exist if there is no such thing as the unforgivable). But when Kearney refers to "making impossible pardon that little bit more possible," perhaps he is not alluding to forgiveness so much as a more empathetic understanding of the conditions ("causes of terror") and the states of meaninglessness that could lead a fellow human being to act in such monstrous fashion. In this formulation, neither side can be said to be seeking after mutual vulnerability, as Judith Butler implores we all must do. And perhaps she is asking for too much when she declares that one must rise above one's own victimization and understand the victimizer's own vulnerability. However, Butler is referring more precisely to that of the community the terrorist claims to represent, rather than to the individual terrorist *per se*. So while the nature and gravity of the perpetrator's actions have made the possibility of forgiveness a nearly impossible task, we might nevertheless seek to determine the social and political conditions that have made such actions possible. Because these actions take on a different sheen when they are framed as serving altruistic purposes, as a form of extreme communication meant to awaken the world to the injustices suffered by the community.

One way out of this impasse, then, is to shift the focus from the individual terrorist and train our attention on the community on whose behalf these men and their organizations claim to act. In this manner, we can move away from private motivations towards public and political concerns, thus creating conditions for evaluating the degree to which these actions might be thought of as altruistic or serving a purpose that extends beyond the satisfying of any personal desires. As Schaefer observes, "It is in that group context that terrorists' rational calculus makes sense, as the benefits of terrorism are generally those of the group and not of the individual" (Schaefer). In other words, these actions seem irrational to Western audiences because they continue to interpret them through the paradigm of individualism, not considering the communal motivations that serve to foment and sustain these suicidal ambitions over long periods of time. The Western tendency to privilege the rights of the individual is directly reflected in these narratives which focus on private motivations. The terrorist-protagonists are portrayed as disenfranchised individuals who take part in the attack for largely egotistical reasons.

Even *Tuez-les tous*, which devotes some space to the interactions of the members of a terrorist cell, includes a protagonist driven by his private demons and most decidedly *not* by the rationale of the Organization to which he belongs.

These novels thus reveal as much about fragile Western psyches as they do about the minds of radical extremists. As Däwes suggests, these texts disclose "more about the location of their origins (i.e., non-Muslim, Western writers) than about their actual theme. Rather interestingly, they subvert—at least for the most part—conventional projections of villainy and expose a remarkably profound unease at the heart of Western identity" (248–49). In other words, the perception of the other remains trapped within a solipsistic and limited point of view. If the novel is to serve as a vehicle for opening dialogue, however, then novelists should confront their own propensities for focusing on the individual in all his or her idiosyncratic splendor and turn their imaginative capacities to delineating the ways in which people within a community are simultaneously, but also differently, affected and impacted by the conditions in which they live. In this way, among others. the imaginative reconstruction the novel undertakes, however flawed, can serve as a model for our own investigations and soundings into a world which, though brought into dramatic relief by the events of September 11, remains as elusive as ever, globalization or not.

NOTES

1. For this same reason it is Atta's eyes that stare out at the reader from the cover of the paperback edition of McDermott's *Perfect Soldiers*. Again, there are dual implications here: that Atta was a perfect soldier, and that reading the book will shed some light on why Atta, the most demonized of the terrorists, acted as he did.

2. In an interview with *Newsweek*, Amis observes that Atta "was in it for the killing, and I think that's another underestimated consideration: killing people is obviously terrific fun. It's a crude expression of power to kill people, and it's arousing."

3. Carine Bourget contends these departures "make us see 9/11 not just through the eyes of the actual hijackers . . . but through those of other potential hijackers as well, thereby drawing attention to the social conditions that breed terrorism" (157–58).

4. Gambetta similarly proposes that we consider these actions as expressions of extreme altruism carried out in cold blood (ix), and suggests that while we may "instinctively think of altruism as doing purely good deeds, altruism and aggression are not antithetical" (270).

5. Suicide becomes, as noted earlier, the ultimate act of validation. In this vein, Avishai Margalit suggests there is one other motivating factor in using suicide as a means of attacking one's foes: "Vengeance through suicide bombing has, as I understand it, an additional value: that of making yourself the victim of your own act, and thereby putting your tormentors to moral shame" (Margalit).

6. All translations of the text are mine.

7. As Abderrahmane observes, the text "shuttles back and forth between a hazy past and an imminent future with its promise of liberation, disintegration, and nothingness" (Abderrahmane, my translation).

8. See, for instance Lawrence Wright's *The Looming Tower* (344).

Chapter Five

"Selective in Your Mercies"

Privilege, Vulnerability, and the Limits of Empathy in Ian McEwan's Saturday

As we have noted, a number of critics, including Judith Butler and Gayatri Spivak, have outlined a greater need for empathy, most specifically from those who were targeted on that day. The logic of this argument is that those who were victimized should use their newfound vulnerability as a means of connecting, or "resonating" (to use Spivak's term) with the other (or "all the others," as Levinas might put it). Butler's wish is that this altered state of being—a new sensitivity to the very fragility of individual and communal lives—will lead to a deeper understanding of the value of *all* lives: "To be injured means that one has the chance to reflect upon injury, to find out the mechanisms of its distribution, to find out who else suffers from permeable borders, unexpected violence, dispossession, and fear, and in what ways" (Butler, xii). The fate of the victims that day points to the "precarious life of the Other," Butler observes. She insists that one should not simply be concerned with one's own vulnerability (and the fear and anxiety elicited by that knowledge), but with that of others who live parallel and equally, if not more, vulnerable lives. For her part, Spivak argues that all proposed solutions to the current crisis are contingent upon one's ability to discover a capacity for empathy. She suggests that seeking either revenge and/or justice necessarily limits one's capacity to know the other. Spivak creates a dialectic between epistemological and ethical ways of knowing, and argues for a move towards the latter:

> Epistemological constructions belong to the domain of law, which seeks to know the other, in his or her case, as completely as possible, in order to punish

or acquit rationally, reason being defined by the limits set by the law itself. The ethical interrupts this imperfectly, to listen to the other as if it were a self, neither to punish or acquit. (83)

But is it possible to "imagine" this unencumbered other, free of the attributions his or her actions have invited? In Spivak's construction, empathy requires that we separate ourselves from the pain caused, and the threat posed, by the violent other. And circumstances are further complicated by the recognition that there is no immediate path to recovery because, as Jacques Derrida suggests, the power of terror lies not in what has happened, but in the eruption of fear for what *might* happen: "We are talking about a trauma, and thus an event, whose temporality proceeds, neither from the now that is present nor from the present that is past but from an im-presentable to come" (Borradori, 97). It stands to reason that an ever-present sense of vulnerability and fear do not present an ideal situation in which to empathize with, or find compassion for, the other, no matter how vital such an exercise might be. And yet, as Butler and Spivak argue, it is precisely at this time that the need for empathy is greatest.

Ian McEwan's *Saturday* endorses precisely the kind of scenario to which these theorists allude. The novel illuminates a desire to empathize, to recognize its importance, and expresses an assuredness in the civilized individual's capacity for forbearance, understanding, and magnanimity. The protagonist, already existing in a state of heightened alert, is confronted by an other (a street tough named Baxter) in whom he recognizes anger and hatred, but also suffering—optimal conditions for the exercising of empathy. The novel's dynamics, however, inadvertently demonstrate the problematics of such a gesture. For while *Saturday* may declare the need for empathy and extol it as a cornerstone of Western, secularized society, the text simultaneously reveals how easily its application is constructed and perverted. The protagonist's display of empathy, in contrast to Butler and Spivak, does not translate into a coming together of opposites, but rather exemplifies the extent to which such an exercise may serve subjective and instrumental, rather than altruistic, ends. In fact, I want to demonstrate that engaging in empathy, particularly in circumstances in which there exists a power differential, often serves to create a false sense of connection in which the empathizer is then freed to foist convenient attributions upon the empathized. In the case of *Saturday*, as we shall see, the possibilities for empathy are overridden by the protagonist's desire to protect the lives of his family, but also to doggedly maintain his privileged status. The novel is too hopeful, in part because it neglects to address the ways in which a lack of understanding of the other (and also how that lack is perceived by the other) may prove detrimental to its own future. The fears Perowne expresses are, in part, indicative of an unwillingness to accept any outsider perspective, or to consider how the treatment of the other may highlight flaws of the privileged system within which he luxuriates. The seemingly benign and benevolent actions of the novel's neurosurgeon thus emphasize the blindspots of privilege and the co-opting of empathy to assert a superior moral stance over that of the other. This is strengthened by the novel's use of free indirect thought, which presents a narrative closely resembling interior monologue. But the indirect narration is also meant to provide the reader with a sense of the difference between Perowne's sensibility and the ethos of the novel, and thus prevent the reader from identifying uncritically with the protagonist. More often than not, however, it is difficult to distinguish the protagonist's thoughts from those of the implied narrator. As such, the narration is fairly solipsistic in nature and reveals the challenge facing anyone who seeks to step outside of himself in order to truly know the other.

As such, the dialectics of *Saturday* suggest that a retrenchment of differences, rather than a recognition of shared vulnerability, is the more probable response to violence. And the novel acknowledges the complexity of these dynamics when it indicates that the motives for exercising empathy are not always altruistic. About midway through the text, for instance, Perowne is shopping for ingredients for his special fish stew when he is suddenly troubled by the sight of living crabs and lobsters in crates. He thinks to himself:

> This is the growing complication of the modern condition, the expanding circle of moral sympathy. Not only distant peoples are our brothers and sisters, but foxes too, and laboratory mice, and now the fish. [He] goes on catching and eating them, and though he'd never drop a live lobster into boiling water, he's prepared to order one in a restaurant. The trick, as always, the key to human success and domination, is to be selective in your mercies. For all the discerning talk, it's the close at hand, the visible that exerts the overpowering force. And what you don't see . . . (McEwan, 128, ellipsis in text)

The passage suggests that the capacity for empathy (or "moral sympathy") has concrete limitations. It also stipulates that if one is in fact being "selective," then one is likely to choose the proximal and recognizable as objects of empathy and turn away from the remote and the unfamiliar. The key notion, or what the narrator calls the "trick," is to possess the ability to be "selective in your mercies." This, the text tells us, is "the key to success and domination," suggesting that empathy must be used sparingly, and instrumentally.[1] Perowne thus admits that the exercising of empathy frequently implies inequality between empathizer and empathized. This certainly runs counter to Spivak's notion of "resonating" with the other as a means of creating fellow-feeling and positive action. In this construction, empathy becomes a tool for identifying the other's weaknesses and turning them to one's advantage. This is one of the few moments when Perowne acknowledges the existence of a differential between the empowered and the powerless. Paradoxically, this imbalance, combined with the privilege in which Perowne luxuriates, proves a major stumbling block in achieving the kind of empathic connection necessary for any lasting resolution to the current conflict. While Perowne fails to consider his contribution to the inequities that afflict someone like Baxter, the threat the latter represents understandably exacerbates the unlikelihood of any empathic feeling. In this way, the novel captures the polarities at work in any navigation of the post-9/11 world.

For despite these feelings of dread which refuse to be repressed, Perowne clings to optimism about contemporary Western civilization and its tenets. He even imagines his successors enviously contemplating this age: "the future will look back on us as gods, certainly in this city, lucky gods blessed by supermarket cornucopias, torrents of accessible information, warm clothes that weigh nothing, extended life-spans, wondrous machines" (McEwan, 77). Perowne's admiration for the modern world is unequivocal. He even pauses to praise the contemporary kettle-making as proof of advancement: "What simple accretions have brought the humble kettle to this peak of refinement: jug-shaped for efficiency, plastic for safety, wide spout for ease of filling, and clunky little platform to pick up power . . . someone had thought about this carefully, and now there's no going back. The world should take note: not everything is getting worse" (68). Perowne revels in the material trappings of progress; the Mercedes, the shops, and even the kettle, all exist as evidence of irrefutable forward movement. Not once does he stop to consider the cost of such progress, or the inequities it is bound to engender. Indeed, the World Trade Center was chosen as a target specifically in relation to its symbolic representation of Western economic hegemony (among other things). In other words, the very objects that he identifies as markers of evolution and superiority ("gods"), others consider instruments of their oppression. Perowne's belief in the 'rightness' of his position is buttressed by the economic and technological successes he sees flourishing before his eyes: "Such prosperity, whole emporia dedicated to cheeses, ribbons, Shaker furniture, is protection of a sort. This commercial wellbeing is robust and will defend itself to the last. It isn't rationalism that will overcome the religious zealots, but ordinary shopping and all that it entails . . . Rather shop than pray" (127). Underlying this line of thinking is the assumption that no one could possibly refuse, or want something other than, the bounties of the Western world. And the final clause explicitly solidifies the dichotomy Perowne constructs in his mind between late-capitalist and religious cultures. In this sense, the novel can be read as an expression of faith in the creative process, *and* in the creation of a secular counternarrative to whatever delusional construction slouches toward Bethlehem. In other words, the novel is meant to stand as affirmation in the face of devastation and ongoing fear. Perowne's thoughts may shuttle between the poles of anxiety and optimism, but the text repeatedly asserts both the wonders and the perseverance of his world.

WHEN THE BACKDROP IS FEAR

The opening of *Saturday* is well known to many readers. Unable to sleep, the protagonist, Henry Perowne, walks to his bedroom window in time to see a flaming airplane descending upon London. He immediately flashes back to 9/11: "Everyone agrees, airliners look different in the sky these days, predatory or doomed" (McEwan, 15). The burning plane (initially perceived by Perowne as an apocalyptic comet) hijacks the already edgy post-9/11 reader into a heightened state of anxiety and a twitchy consciousness of looming threats in the unfolding of this particular day in the life of a British neurosurgeon. Although the event has no impact on the plot, it announces just how pervasively the attacks of that September morning hover over the narrative.[2] The novel thus lands squarely on a sense of vulnerability, as well as a preoccupation with the preservation of Western cultural values *and* material trappings in the face of a seemingly unreasoning and intractable foe.

Henry Perowne is not alone, of course, in experiencing the event as a massive jolt to established priorities (if only temporarily), bringing certain preoccupations to the fore: the frailty of "civilized" order, the tenuous and skewed grasp of the historical moment, the imminence of destruction. Meandering through Perowne's perambulations and thoughts over the course of a single day (February 15, 2003), *Saturday* depicts a world seemingly teetering on a precipice. From allusions to 9/11, to the inclusion of an anti-Iraq War demonstration, to the home invasion at its climax, the novel highlights the apparently countless forces threatening to destabilize or destroy the protagonist's happy existence. Perowne lives in a "community of anxiety" whose fears have been amplified and become more pervasive in the post-9/11 world (McEwan, 180). He spends a great deal of time both contemplating his good fortune *and* fearing it will all be taken away. Early in the novel, in a moment of blatant foreshadowing, Perowne walks by his front door and thinks, "Such defences, such mundane embattlement: beware of the city's poor, the drug-addicted, the downright bad" (37). The pause allows him to briefly reflect on those worse off than himself, but only briefly. They represent, more than anything, a danger to him and his family.

It makes sense that Perowne, a neurosurgeon who witnesses the fickleness of fate on a near-daily basis, should be prone to this diffuse anxiety. As he looks at the doors to his supposed safe haven, he knows they are no match for the press of random intrusions—a flimsy partition between civilization/order and unpredictably emergent chaos. He eventually identifies the source of his percolating anxiety:

it is in fact the state of the world that troubles him most, and the marchers are there to remind him of it. The world probably has changed fundamentally and the matter is being clumsily handled, particularly by the Americans. There are people around the planet, well-connected and organized, who would like to kill him and his family and friends to make a point. The scale of death contemplated is no longer at issue; there'll be more deaths on a similar scale, probably in this city. Is he so frightened he can't face the fact? (80)

Despite the semblance of reflection in this passage, Perowne's musings are devoid of self-appraisal—of even the slightest consideration of complicity or responsibility.[3] He and his world are innocent bystanders caught in an irrational and ill-managed conflict. His admission of foolishness refers only to his nagging fears of destruction. Ways in which he may have contributed to, or benefitted from, local and global inequities pass unexamined. And Perowne's luxuriant penchant for reflection never alights on the potential betterment of a wildly inequitable world. To him, the world is near-perfect as it is. Following a consciously rhapsodic meditation on his Mercedes, Perowne sits listening to Schubert and thinks, "At every level, material, medical, intellectual, sensual, for most people it has improved" (77). There is no ambivalence or hesitation in his decidedly Western musings. Even Perowne's own use of the qualifier "most" does not elicit reflection on those who might be excluded.

Baxter's appearance, occurring moments after this thought has crossed Perowne's mind, would seem timed to generate this kind of an amendment on the latter's part. Even in the face of danger, however, Perowne refuses to contemplate why he and his innocent family might be the targets of anyone's anger. This conviction remains steadfast even in the face of imminent danger and is in turn confirmed by the manner in which the threat is neutralized through two decisive actions. The first is the protagonist's daughter (naked and pregnant) fending off Baxter by reciting Matthew Arnold's "Dover Beach." The second is the protagonist performing emergency surgery on the same assailant. In both instances, the novel celebrates the power of civilization, through Art and Science, to ward off, and maybe even civilize, the barbarians at the gates. Perowne's decision to "operate" on the threat proclaims the superiority of a "civilization," whose perhaps most distinguishing feature is its ability to empathize—the real difference between "us" and "them." The threat, however, is not accorded the same degree of importance. The antagonist is never provided an opportunity to offer an alternate cultural conceptualization (unattractive though it may be) or to voice a grievance against perceived injustice (ill-conceived though its expression may be). The threatening other is simply the embodiment of a defective, irrational stance that is the product of arrested intellectual and emotional development. The novel can thus be read as a conversion narrative in which the aggressor is altered by his exposure to those very qualities he seeks to destroy. As such, it becomes an exercise in wish-fulfillment, with the forces of creativity—embodied in a pregnant poet, no less—ultimately, though somewhat ambivalently, vanquishing those of destruction.

Saturday presents an unapologetic view of Western life and wealth, marred only by fear and anxiety about its tenuousness in light of seemingly uncontrollable and random threats. Perowne wavers between displaying his own single-minded faith in the worlds of reason and capital, and expressing his concerns about their inability to hold the barbarians at bay: "And it's at this point he remembers the source of his vague sense of shame or embarrassment: his readiness to be persuaded that the world has changed beyond recall, that harmless streets like this and the tolerant life they embody can be destroyed by the new enemy—well-organized, tentacular, full of hatred and focused zeal." (76). In his mind, a future narrative may tell of a rational and advanced world subsumed by an irrational and backward one. The imbalance in the reflection is also revealed in the use of the adjectives "harmless" and "tolerant"—he never stops to ponder the possibility that his opponent might not perceive these "streets" in the same way. And whenever Perowne does contemplate the antagonists, it is to express amazement at their inability to appreciate the wonders of his world. Magali Cornier Michael asserts that *Saturday* presents a post-colonial male attempting to exert some control over the world (primarily through work, domestic rituals, and family), but who fails to recognize the degree to which that control is constantly subverted. Such a reading makes possible the interpretation of the novel as an examination of the instability of the First World faced with new and unknown forces. However, as we shall see, the ending of the novel validates Perowne's approach. Yes, the threats are real and many, but they are nothing in the face of reason, family, and love.

"CRUEL, WEAK, MEANINGLESS": *SATURDAY*'S UNEQUAL OPPONENT[4]

Saturday thus reflects a nervously hopeful conviction that the West's Manichean conflict is ultimately with a severely mismatched opponent. Although its foes possess the capacity to cause significant harm, the intellectual and moral superiority of the West would seem to guarantee an advantageous conclusion. Perowne's many reflections assert the pointlessness of these opponents: "In the ideal Islamic state, under strict Shari'a law, there'll be room for surgeons. Blues guitarists will be found other employment. But perhaps no one is demanding such a state. Nothing is demanded. Only hatred is registered, the purity of nihilism" (McEwan, 34). The West is portrayed as generative, creative, and rooted in the preciousness of the now (i.e., life-affirming) while its adversaries promote ascetic survival, reserve their utopian visions for beyond the grave, and seek the mindless destruction of deviations from their plans (i.e., life-denying). The surgeon might serve their survival purposes, but the guitarist is dispensable, if not dangerous. Perowne places little stock in the dreams of the foes of rationality and progress: "Out in the real world there exist detailed plans, visionary projects for peaceable realms, all conflicts resolved, happiness for everyone, for ever—mirages for which people are prepared to die and kill. Christ's kingdom on earth, the worker's paradise, the ideal Islamic state" (176). For Perowne, this is the axis of delusion, more so than evil, in its strongly polarized view of the contemporary condition. But it is also the source of a feeling that looms throughout the novel about how easily things may be destroyed. The text frequently juxtaposes the wonder of creation with the rapidity of destruction. Perowne finds beauty and meaning in the minutest of creations: "it's one of those cases of a microcosm giving you the whole world. Like a Spode dinner plate. Or a single cell. Or, as Daisy says, like a Jane Austen novel" (27). He is also aware of how easily it all might be taken away. Late in the novel, for example, he thinks about the rapidity with which they were able to pack up his mother's house: "It took a day to dismantle Lily's existence" (McEwan, 284). The same kind of juxtaposition is present in the thoughts concerning the Perowne family itself, certainly one of the most cherished creations in the novel. Perowne's own children are creators, a poet and a blues guitarist (the novel provides appreciations of each of their talents), and the epitome of all he holds dear. As such, they present the most vulnerable target in his existence. As one critic observes, the Perownes "represent the very flower of Western civilization—decent, thoughtful, productive, cultivated, deeply, fundamentally good. And yet, it is eighteen months after the Twin Towers. Are such humane values enough to safeguard them in a world in which one can never know, hardly even guess, from where the blow will fall?" (Dirda).

In *Saturday*, the blow falls in the form of Baxter, a street tough with whom Perowne has an altercation following a fender bender. As McEwan tells Charlie Rose, "It is as if this character has materialized out of [Perowne's] fears" (Rose). On one level, the events of 9/11 served to coalesce a pre-existing and diffuse unease around an identifiable source, whether it was Bin Laden, al-Qaeda, or "terrorists" in general. Similarly, Baxter gives form to Perowne's generalized anxieties. For though he presents an immediate danger to the protagonist, his family, and home, he also embodies a potential cataclysm that looms throughout *Saturday*: to London, to Britishness, to Western civilization, and more. And though McEwan may react to this binary reading of the novel, his objection is revealing: "I am not writing an allegory here. I am not making [Perowne] stand for something. But, nevertheless, just a little or maybe a lot below the surface in his confrontation with Baxter is an echo of the confrontation of the rich, satisfied, contented West with a demented strand of a major world religion" (Birnbaum). While the comment alludes to inequities and perhaps the West's indifference to the suffering of others, it does not offer a balanced perspective. The West may be "rich and contented" (not flaws in and of themselves), but the opponent is depicted as simply "demented." And though McEwan appears to both deny and confirm writing an allegory, it is close to impossible to read the novel (at least at this juncture in history) in any other way. The home invasion alone contains many parallels with September 11: the unexpected attack, the innocent victims, the perpetrator's need to avenge a wrong the victim is unaware of having committed. The parallels are too evident not to read *Saturday* as a commentary on the conflict between the West and fundamentalist Islam, or between civilization and supposed barbarity, frightening though these polarities may seem.[5]

As the novel presents it, however, the confrontation is fought by unequal adversaries. On one level, the conflict is portrayed as that of brute force versus intellect. On another, it is between civilization and barbarism. From Perowne's viewpoint, the situation is patently perverse; he cannot conceive why this might be anything more than a traffic accident for Baxter. He alternately thinks of the incident as a "trivial matter" (81) or simply as an "urban drama" (86). This relative unconcern stems from Perowne's inability to contemplate Baxter's pre-history or whatever baggage (emotional or social) his nemesis might be bringing to the confrontation. The reason Baxter is such an ineffectual threat in *Saturday* is that the novel never reflects upon the legitimacy, or even the perspective, of the threat he is meant to echo. The significance of the conflict at the heart of the novel would have been strengthened by the occasional reference to those possibilities existing beyond the scope of Perowne's blinkered perspective. This lack of consideration is further compounded by a very conscious diminishment of the opponent's capabilities. As someone who has worked in the Emergency room, Perowne is all too aware of the menace Baxter poses. The novel, however, undermines the danger in a number of ways. First, through physical description—"five foot five or six perhaps" (McEwan, 84)—that emphasizes slightness and lack of power; second, by descriptors that highlight the intellectual (and maybe even human) distance separating the violent instigator from the cultured, educated man. This is further compounded by Perowne's characterization of Baxter as "simian" and with "vaguely ape-like features" (99). In a novel that highlights the progress and sophistication of Western society, the assailant is thus portrayed as step or two behind, evolutionarily speaking. So while the reader might be inclined to interpret these descriptors as indicative of worrisome limitations on the part of the protagonist, the novel never questions his valuation of Baxter. Instead it resolutely confirms it at every step of the way.

The most salient feature, however, is the illness that simultaneously incapacitates Baxter while privileging the surgeon's perspective. Perowne quickly surmises that Baxter suffers from Huntington's Disease and uses this knowledge to embarrass him. Publicly humiliated, Baxter acquiesces quickly to the probing questions, and the "power passes" to Perowne without much of a struggle (McEwan, 96). And the existence of Baxter's illness undermines the possibility that he might have any other more complex justification for behaving as he does—a rationale that might offer a critical perspective of Perowne's assured stance. Baxter is meant to embody the menace to all that Perowne holds dear, but the novel does not furnish him with any legitimate reasons for his actions. He is simply cast as someone to whom life has dealt a bad hand, quite randomly and without human implication. Most tellingly, as with those who would enact violent solutions, he is afflicted with an "illness" that prevents him from thinking rationally—a biological rather than a social problem.

Baxter's condition nevertheless makes him unpredictable and dangerous. During this first encounter, Perowne receives a blow to the ribs, leaving a considerable bruise. This occurrence, in itself, might lead to some consideration of the illusion of invulnerability with which we cloak ourselves. It is precisely this type of encounter with the other with which Butler is concerned in *Precarious Life*. She returns to the idea that being awakened to one's own vulnerability should cause one to contemplate it as a condition uniting us all. To understand that conflation, Butler argues is

> to be awake to what is precarious in another life or, rather, the precariousness of life itself. This cannot be an awakeness . . . to my own life, and then an extrapolation from an understanding of my own precariousness to an understanding of another's precarious life. It has to be an understanding of the precariousness of the Other. (134)

And although Butler recognizes that the response for which she advocates is the less likely of the two, she nevertheless holds out hope for such an eventuality. But she would also no doubt concede that such action is dependent on the good intentions of the empathizer. Again, McEwan's novel would appear to offer the ideal conditions within which such recognition might take place. After all, at practically the same moment that Perowne is made aware of the precariousness of his situation, he senses the vulnerability of his opponent (though their conditions vary in kind). In this situation, then, according to Butler's schematics, Perowne is presented with an opportunity to connect with the vulnerability of the other, and his medical experience makes him an almost ideal candidate for doing so. Instead, he acts in a diametrically opposed fashion, exerting his professional superiority to take advantage of Baxter's vulnerability and extract himself from the perilous situation. As an act of self-preservation, then, Perowne's treatment of Baxter is completely justified, but it also highlights the difficulties in meeting Butler's prescription.

He may be well-equipped to identify his antagonist's vulnerability, but to expect that he will embrace it when his security and well-being are at risk is perhaps asking too much of any individual. The manner in which he engineers his escape, however, can be questioned. The revelation of Baxter's "secret shame" is a deliberate attempt to belittle and demean him in front of his subordinates. This will be a part of Perowne's impoverished learning curve. However, it is only after the fact, prodded by his son, that he recognizes he should have done more to understand Baxter (154). In fact, Baxter remains largely hidden or absent for significant stretches of the novel, reflecting how invisible and/or incomprehensible he is to Perowne.[6] And given the novel's ideological predisposition, he is inevitably cast as a rather impotent threat who is humiliated, vanquished, and, ultimately, rendered unconscious. He ends up a figure of pity rather than of terror, first defeated by a man of Science, then struck dumb and harmless by Art—the menace held at bay by two pillars of Western civilization.

This pivotal scene of a pregnant Daisy reciting "Dover Beach" extols art and creativity as symbols of sophistication and advancement (as something transcending ourselves), but also as indications of superiority over the "armies of the night." But the scene appears so improbable that it demands examination.[7] Perowne even wonders, "Could it happen, is it within the bounds of the real, that a mere poem of Daisy's could precipitate a mood swing?" (McEwan, 229). Of course, it is not Daisy's poem, but one of Matthew Arnold's. Nevertheless, the novel certainly answers in the affirmative. At that moment, we are meant to believe that Baxter's wonderment—"You wrote that. You *wrote* that" (McEwan, 231)—overrides his appetite for mayhem and destruction. This voluble display of aesthetic appreciation also suggests that the chasm separating Baxter from Perowne may not be as wide as the latter supposed. It is also meant to imbue Baxter with an air of mystery and force Perowne to reconsider his assessment, but only insofar as the former demonstrates an appreciation for something which the latter (and the text itself) holds dear.

Interestingly, the novel seeks to depict Henry Perowne as someone who neither understands nor appreciates the beauties of literature. The point is stressed a little too persistently, in order that Daisy's recitation surprise not only Baxter, but also Perowne himself. Baxter's act of appreciation is meant to stand as the "difference" with which Perowne the pragmatist connects. But this comes across as a false construction, for though Perowne may be a neurosurgeon, and his wife a lawyer, the couple is surrounded by a family of artists. Meanwhile, literary allusions proliferate the text, often coming from the mind of Perowne himself (McEwan 2005, 126, 131, 159). In this regard, the novel demonstrates a degree of disingenuity, for even if the protagonist professes insistently that he is no reader of literature (the form *par excellence* for exhibiting empathy, for entering the minds of others), he nevertheless belongs to, and reflects through his actions, a world that values these qualities. These are reflected most clearly, as we shall see, in his agreeing to operate on Baxter, a gesture in which his empathy for his assailant is meant to shine through to the reader of *Saturday*. For despite the terror Baxter unleashes on his family, the protagonist maintains his rational and compassionate self. In this way, he enacts Butler's wish for alternative responses to violent action (Butler, 10, 17).

Having been alerted earlier to Perowne's philosophy of selective mercy, however, the reader might contemplate how he conversely uses empathy to dominate the other. In this regard, Patti Lather warns that we need to remain cognizant of the ways in which empathy might be manipulated or applied for non-altruistic purposes. Pointing to the patriarchal and imperialistic sides of empathy, she notes that recent objections to empathy raise questions "about what we can know but also what we, perhaps, ought not to assume we have the right to know" (19). For are there not instances when the pursuit of knowledge of the other can be perceived as a transgression, a violation of personhood? Lather quotes Doris Sommer who observes that the empathic gesture is often "an appropriation in the guise of an embrace," to which she adds, "This is how empathy violates the other and is part of the demand for totality" (19). In other words, empathy is sometimes invoked under false pretenses. Instead of being utilized to come to terms with and understand the other's difference, it is used to subsume alterity under an all-encompassing sameness. We might conclude, then, that Perowne only connects with Baxter, acknowledges similarity, when the latter exhibits a way of thinking he recognizes and esteems. For that instant, Baxter's "difference" is erased and he proves himself open to conversion; he shifts from being a troubling and unpredictable other to a civilizable entity. Order is restored because Baxter's presence no longer problematizes that which Perowne cherishes.

RESONATING WITH THE (VIOLENT) OTHER

Some critics, however, point to Baxter's poetic appreciation as the act that opens Perowne's eyes to the possibility of communality with this outsider. Hillard contends, for instance, that "Baxter becomes the catalyst for Perowne recognizing, if not realizing, a wider community from which he has shielded himself. The dawning sense of mutuality comes ever more insistently in the final scene of the novel" (192). And Wall suggests that perceiving Baxter's appreciation of the poem "allows Perowne to recognize . . . that [he] is human, not animal" (785). Both Wall and Hillard similarly argue that Perowne undergoes some kind of conversion through his witnessing of the power of literature at work. In other words, as he observes the flowering of Baxter's imagination, his own expands to include Baxter as more than a dehumanized other. These readings depend upon accepting that Perowne and Baxter have experienced simultaneous epiphanies—different sorts, but epiphanies all the same. But if this is a moment of communality, then surely we should read in Perowne's thoughts a rapprochement, a greater understanding of the other. In wishing to accentuate the communal, however, both Hillard and Wall ignore the neurosurgeon's descriptions of Baxter's "general simian air" and as something less than civilized (88). Perowne stops short of empathy, pitying Baxter rather than putting himself in his place.

Perowne proves himself incapable of making that leap, in part because he identifies himself as a "professional reductionist" (McEwan, 281). So that when he does focus on the issue of the haves and have-nots, his training and specialization inevitably lead him to biological formulations, rather than political or socio-economic ones. In an early scene, he looks out onto the square and spies a young woman whom his medically trained eye identifies as a drug addict. He contrasts her with his daughter who will be shortly arriving at the house:

> It troubles him to consider the powerful currents and fine-tuning that alter fates, the close and distant influences, the accidents of character and circumstance that cause one young woman in Paris to be packing her weekend bag with the bound proof of her first volume of poems before catching the train to a welcoming home in London, and another young woman of the same age to be led away by a wheedling boy to a moment's chemical bliss that will bind her as tightly to her misery as an opiate to its mu receptors. (63–64)

While the thinking reveals an awareness of the disparities that surround him, it is almost immediately undermined by his professional training—the same dynamic that characterizes Perowne's interactions with Baxter. The stark contrast in the life situations of these two men certainly invites the reader to consider the possible reasons for such inequity. But *Saturday*'s plot, complete with an antagonist afflicted with his own biological misfortune, allows the protagonist to steadfastly maintain his way of thinking. In other words, the existence of the illness trumps any other explanation for Baxter's actions. Facing his assailant for the first time, Perowne adduces, "The misfortune lies within a single gene, in an excessive repeat of a single sequence—CAG. Here's biological determinism in its purest form. More than forty repeats of that one little codon, and you're doomed" (McEwan, 94). Baxter's behavior merely confirms what Perowne already knows—this is a question of dumb genetic luck—and thus never shakes the latter's bourgeois certainty. For while the text does allude to the ways in which one tends to stigmatize the other, reducing the adversary to a singular trait such as "evil" or "fanatical" or simply "sick," this act of stigmatization is not viewed critically. In the case of *Saturday*, this scientific reductionism not only enables Perowne to protect his family, but also to eventually "save" Baxter.

As such, there always remains a suspicion of superiority in Perowne's interactions with Baxter. Even when he acknowledges the latter has experienced something he has not, he devalues the significance of the experience, noting that the poem "touched off in Baxter a yearning he could barely begin to define" (288). One might interpret this sentence to suggest that Baxter cannot appreciate the poem on anything more than a primitive level. And critics have ignored the palpable condescension in the way Perowne thinks about Baxter's experience: "Baxter finds nothing extraordinary in the transformation of his role, from lord of terror to amazed admirer. Or excited child" (231–32). Though the novel's indirect narration sometimes blurs the line between Perowne's thoughts and those of an implied narrator, it is unlikely that Baxter would think of himself as "an excited child." These are Perowne's words. And from that moment on, Perowne effectively establishes a professional, objective distance from his adversary, as though observing a test subject. When Baxter allows Daisy to dress and impulsively claims the book of poems for his own, Perowne concludes, "It's of the essence of a degenerating mind, periodically to lose all sense of a continuous self, and therefore any regard for what others think of your lack of continuity" (232). He thus attributes the threat of physical violence to a "degenerating mind," rather than to Baxter's earlier humiliation, or to the possible affront a disadvantaged individual might feel when confronted with the affluence and good luck embodied by the Perowne family.

These conceptualizations inhibit thoughts of mutual experience, so that during those few moments when Perowne does make an attempt to apprehend Baxter's perspective, the empathy he exhibits is largely in the service of self-preservation. For instance, at the moment of the break-in, he strives "to see the room through [Baxter's] eyes, as if that might help predict the trouble ahead" (213). An empathic connection would require that Perowne see himself from the other's perspective—perceiving his privilege and apparently near-perfect life reflected back to him through that prism, and having some feeling for the sense of injustice Baxter might be experiencing. Such a connection also depends on one's ability to recognize the limitations of that understanding. He remains unable to assess, however, how his stance of superiority—through which he identifies and utilizes Baxter's vulnerability but denies his own—has contributed to the current conflict. Having been exposed as vulnerable, not once but twice, Perowne ignores his shared humanity with Baxter, striving to reestablish the illusion of his impermeability. For while Perowne's "percolating anxiety" certainly suggests he is aware that both he and his family are vulnerable, there are sufficient mechanisms in place allowing him to pursue his existence as though they were not. The intrusion of Baxter and his subordinates momentarily breaks through that veil, but Perowne's existence solidly rests on this foundation. The solution to the disparity that divides the two adversaries may well lie in Perowne's ability to embrace his vulnerability, but this is not easily managed when one is in the ascendant. Primacy of standing or place is not so readily relinquished, particularly when it has been placed in jeopardy. One is more likely to witness the struggle to preserve the "mundane battlements." In this way, among others, Perowne's actions bear some similarity to that of the United States, which used its dominant position and force after 9/11 in an attempt to eradicate any suggestion of weakness.

It comes as no surprise, then, that Perowne's awareness of the inequities finds its fullest expression only at the very moment when order and control are reestablished. As he watches Baxter tumble, he thinks

> he sees in the wide brown eyes a sorrowful accusation of betrayal. He, Henry Perowne, possesses so much—the work, money, status, the home, above all, the family—the handsome healthy son with the strong guitarist's hands come to rescue him, the beautiful poet for a daughter, unattainable even in her nakedness, the famous father-in-law, the gifted, loving wife; and he has done nothing, given nothing to Baxter who has so little that is not wrecked by his defective gene, and who is soon to have even less. (McEwan, 236)

As we shall see, there are faint traces throughout the latter part of the novel suggesting that Perowne experiences sympathy for Baxter's situation. But sympathy differs in very significant ways from empathy. The act of sympathy, of feeling sorry for the other, implies differential positioning between sympathizer and sympathized. The sympathizer's non-suffering condition in fact liberates him or her to feel for the other's piteous state. Such dynamics do not allow for an empathic connection, since the sympathizer inevitably remains in a dominant position in relation to the sympathized. This seems particularly true in the case of Perowne, whose professional expertise enables him to predict the arc of Baxter's illness and his eventual untimely death. This medical knowledge cannot but make Perowne sympathetic to Baxter's plight. At the same time, it serves as a distancing mechanism since it prevents the neurosurgeon from acknowledging mutual vulnerability. As Julinna Oxley observes, "sympathy involves direct concern for another person as a subject distinct from oneself" (17). So it is sympathy, and not empathy, that he demonstrates in his decisions not to press charges and to operate on the injured Baxter. Nevertheless, the reader may well ask from whence do these magnanimous gestures emanate and why at this moment? As Richard Brown notes, "For the most part there is little to cause us to question Perowne's defensive and, in the final stages of the novel, ethically mature and 'forgiving' perspective on this aggressive assailant" (87). But he points to the same self-conscious moment during Baxter's tumble, and observes, "For all the sense of relief at a real danger to domestic security averted, there is something awkward and uneasy in the contrast between the powerful and powerless here" (87). As Brown suggests, it is natural that these feelings should emerge when the threat has been vanquished, but it also demonstrates that Perowne's diluted form of empathy is only possible as long as the power structure is preserved and all threats have been neutralized. At the same time, the text nevertheless suggests that Perowne, despite the near-rape of his daughter and near-murder of his wife, feels remorse for his treatment of Baxter ("he has done nothing, given nothing to Baxter"). These feelings of guilt, as well as the eventual benevolence he demonstrates towards his assailant, do suggest some misgivings about his own actions, including suspicions that he should have exhibited a greater degree of compassion. The text thus continues to extol empathy as a defining trait of the evolved and progressive individual.

INSTRUMENTAL EMPATHY

Indeed, once the home invasion is over and Baxter has suffered his injury, there is a distinct change of mood in the novel. Grammaticus, the grandfather, remarks to Daisy, "I actually began to feel sorry for that fellow. I think, my dear, you made him fall in love with you" (239). This indicates that even during the confrontation, Grammaticus experienced a sense of pity for the man who broke his nose moments earlier. And Theo asks the investigators whether his father and he might be charged with something; revealing a fleeting sense of complicity in the way events have unfolded. But the fear and anxiety brought on by Baxter's violence do not lead the Perownes to contemplate a mutual vulnerability they might share with their assailant. The family, though shaken and perhaps traumatized, emerges more or less unscathed from the ordeal. The family's recognition of Baxter's appreciation of the poem (and the poet, according to Grammaticus) overshadows whatever terror he may have elicited. As they continue to process the events of the evening (while enjoying their interrupted dinner), even Perowne expresses surprise at what he calls his "shift in sympathies"—"What weakness, what delusional folly, to permit yourself sympathy towards a man, sick or not, who invades your house like this" (239). That he and his family permit themselves these kindlier feelings intimates an awareness of their privileged standing in contrast to their assailant. This is no longer (if it ever was) a conflict between equals, and the novel itself reflects this transition, for Baxter's significance to the plot diminishes rapidly once he has been defeated, now serving only as the object through which Perowne demonstrates his rational magnanimity.

This raises a significant question concerning the significance of trauma in *Saturday*, and the degree to which the protagonist has been altered by the troubling events of the day. Butler argues that a proper response to grief and trauma occurs "when one accepts that by the loss one undergoes one will be changed, possibly for ever. Perhaps mourning has to do with agreeing to undergo a transformation (perhaps one should say *submitting* to a transformation) the full result of which one cannot know in advance" (Butler, 21). Butler contends that we are not in control of the ways we are affected by trauma nor can we decide on the best way to emerge from it. Her words, however, do suggest a degree of agency on the part of the traumatized. Only by *agreeing* or *submitting* can a transformation occur. And while Butler concedes that a willingness to be transformed by trauma may not necessarily be typical, she holds out hope that some will act counter to their impulses. But Henry Perowne is not one of these people. No such transformation occurs on his part. In fact, he remains remarkably consistent throughout, clinging to his role as professional reductionist. Unable to conceive of a system better than the one in which he lives, he will do everything in his power to preserve this "fantasy." And in its very construction, *Saturday* itself communicates this desire for a return to a former order—the novel ends much as it began, with Perowne looking down meditatively on the (unchanged) world from his bedroom window.

The invasion certainly seems to have had little impact on Perowne. Emotional responsivity is left to Rosalind; she feels "Angry. . . . And terrified still. . . . I feel they're in the room. They're still here. I'm still frightened" (273). She shakes uncontrollably while Perowne fulfills the part of the reassuring husband. She wants Baxter punished while he remains calm and rational, not revealing his plans to have all charges dropped. This contrast within the couple allows the novel to further accentuate the divide existing between the rationalist Perowne and the home-invader Baxter whose "spooky uncontrollable emotions were driving him" (276). The juxtaposition is perhaps most striking during the scene of the operation which is written as an ode to work. Perowne appears as a man consumed by the task at hand, whereas Baxter is literally reduced to a faceless figure on the operating table at the surgeon's mercy. However, the degree to which he fails to consider Baxter—the man who mere hours earlier savagely held a knife to his wife's throat and intended to rape his daughter—is surprising. Surprising, perhaps, but not necessarily unlikely. For as Kelly Oliver observes, recognition of one's vulnerability often leads to denial or, worse, the domination of the other, so that his or her vulnerability overshadows one's own: "it is the fear and denial of our own vulnerability that causes us to hate and exploit the vulnerability of others" (93). These dynamics are at work in *Saturday*, as Perowne's exploitation of Baxter's illness, albeit justified, is also the means for preserving his privileged position. The novel thus runs counter to Butler, since it reveals how a First World position necessarily precludes the ability to admit to ourselves that our vulnerability is equal to that of others. For do not the comforts and illusions provided by the West mostly serve to obscure or occlude this possibility? While connecting with the vulnerable other is an admirable act, most would not opt to live in a state of permanent vulnerability (however true that reality might be), choosing instead a life that maintains a sense of security and stability (however tenuous it might be). In this regard, Perowne's actions permit the maintenance of a power structure wherein individuals like Baxter are made subservient. His insistence on seeing Baxter's situation as "blind luck," for instance, serves to perpetuate the divide, endorses Perowne's rationality, and finally warrants his condescension towards his adversary.[8]

So Perowne's flaw is not one of empirical recognition; indeed, one might note that he is remarkably quick at identifying the other's vulnerability. This does not, however, put the novel's opponents on the same footing, for though Baxter and Perowne may be equally vulnerable, they are not equally dangerous—nor are they equally powerful. This power imbalance practically guarantees misperception and misunderstanding. As Oliver suggests, greater levels of privilege lead to greater degrees of deniability about one's vulnerability. And perhaps the issue is that Perowne conceptualizes his weakness as qualitatively different from Baxter's. In fact, he seems to recognize the vulnerability of the other more readily than he does his own, privilege providing a shield, or battlement of sorts, against such awareness. In turn, this becomes a barrier preventing any mutuality between the antagonists. Those who argue for empathy's relevance contend that the mere act of consciously striving to empathically engage with the other leads to greater awareness on the part of the empathizer, both in terms of the other's difference and one's capacity to assimilate that difference. Peter Rosan, for instance, contends that engaging with the other creates a "sense of wonder" in the empathizer, brought on by an apprehension of "a kind of unknowing" (120). Rosan further argues that consciously recognizing the limits of possible knowledge about the other should cause the subject to relinquish his "presumed sense of mastery or competence in the situation" and, in the process, become "open to the mystery of what is unique to or unknown about the other, as well as himself" (121). Finally, such an experience should instill in the empathizer both a sense of "knowing naiveté" and humility in the face of such obvious limitations (126).

But what if instead of undermining one's assuredness in apprehending the other, engaging in empathy conversely leads to the belief that one has mastered the challenge posed by the other's existence? In how many cases will one accept the limitations of one's viewpoint and in how many will one conclude that one has gathered sufficient information to make an educated determination about the other? Perowne certainly feels that his experience and training provide him with the requisite tools to "know" Baxter. For though he expresses doubt about a number of issues throughout the novel, he never does so in terms of his assessment of Baxter and his condition. Perowne may be surprised at the aesthetic appreciation he exhibits for the poem, but otherwise there is very little ambivalence about the ways in which he thinks about the other. And though the text's narration occasionally reveals the gap existing between reality and Perowne's assumptions about the control and order he actually wields in his life, this does not extend to the actions of Baxter and his associates. Tellingly, he even anticipates the possibility of further violent action (if not the home invasion necessarily) when he repeatedly senses that he is being followed by a red BMW during his shopping excursion (McEwan, 142, 148, 156). Thus, he fails to evince surprise when Baxter bursts in upon their soirée. In fact, he takes it all in quite rationally: "It is, of course, logical that Baxter is here. For a few seconds, Perowne's only thought is stupidly that: *of course*. It makes sense" (213). Perowne seldom feels, nor does the text imply, that he has "misread" his opponent.

So the challenge lies not in recognizing the other's humanity, but rather in how this knowledge impacts attitudes and actions towards the other. Perowne's response to Baxter thus illuminates the dangers in placing too much faith in empathy. Pleas for empathy are most frequently directed at those who find themselves in dominant positions *vis-à-vis* the empathized. As such, empathizing can often be interpreted as another form of colonization. Certainly one risks being accused of misguided presumptions—the very act of engaging in empathy contributing to an inability to distinguish between what might be a correct perception of the other and the possibility that one is merely seeing the other one wishes to see. And, as Oliver's argument suggests, the mere use of empathy and the recognition of the other's vulnerability does not guarantee that one will appeal to the better angels of one's nature.[9] In fact, she asserts the opposite is more often the case, contesting whether mutual recognition will even lead to just treatment. The problem is that despite the empathic connection, violence still occurs: "We can recognize [others] as humans in both an epistemological and a political sense and still torture them and kill them" (Oliver, 105–6). Certainly, Baxter's predicament after his fall gives Perowne pause and forces a limited recognition of his own potential for violence. But he hesitates only briefly before agreeing to operate on Baxter, and thoughts of retribution do not cross his mind. The text makes clear that Perowne would be perfectly justified in seeking vengeance. For instance, Rosalind later admits that she "wanted [Baxter] to die," and that when she spoke of revenge, "it was [her] own feelings [she] was afraid of" (274). Perowne, however, is exempted from making any such comment; the closest he comes to an admission is when he considers the impoverished life Baxter will lead after the operation: "By saving his life in the operating theatre, [he] also committed Baxter to his torture. Revenge enough" (288).[10] Conveniently, this is also a form of revenge from which Perowne can wash his hands. Again, a power greater than his own determines Baxter's fate. As the end of the novel makes clear, Perowne is on the path to forgiveness, conscious that his beneficent attitude towards Baxter may not please everyone, especially Rosalind. It is worth pointing out, however, that the plot of the novel strongly enables this possibility of forgiveness. For while the Perownes have suffered a trauma, it could have been much worse. One can imagine a very different reaction and outcome had Baxter actually raped Daisy or killed Rosalind. Nevertheless, Perowne's rationality and morality allow him to end the cycle of violence and to begin the healing process.

Having not killed Baxter (though he very well may have), Perowne finds himself in the advantageous position of being able to recognize Baxter's vulnerability. This does not make a kindred spirit of Baxter, however; he remains someone whom Perowne literally looks down and "operates" upon. Later, as the patient recovers, Perowne peers in on him noting, "Sleep has relaxed [Baxter's] jaw and softened the simian effect of a muzzle. The forehead has loosened its habitual frown against the outrageous injustice of his condition" (McEwan, 270). Baxter is depicted as a figure of pathos, and in both instances, the power remains clearly in the neurosurgeon's hands. Furthermore, the return of the word "simian" indicates there has been no degree of leveling between the antagonists.[11]

CONCLUSION

Saturday points to the larger limitations of a Western empathy trapped in its own solipsistic conception and perspective of the world. Perowne may experience a "shock" when he witnesses Baxter's aesthetic appreciation for poetry, but this does not instigate any serious reevaluation of himself or his position on any number of issues. He attributes Baxter's aggression to bad luck and thus has no need to investigate further. This is akin to labeling the terrorists as evil, insane, or demented—once this is accomplished there is no need to understand their actions. Similarly, Perowne thinks of Baxter as "a special case—a man who believes he has no future and is therefore free of consequences" (McEwan, 217). By making Baxter distinctly other—"a special case"—Perowne liberates himself from having to analyze what they might share and how his own existence may have some impact on the lives of people not unlike Baxter, who are legion rather than exceptions. In the end, then, Baxter is presented as a figure to be pitied more than feared. This is problematic. If the other is conceptualized as a figure of evil, or a figure of pity, there is little hope for empathy.

Michael identifies Perowne's "inability to shed his privileged perspective" as the flaw that ultimately prevents him from empathizing with Baxter (40). But the novel does not offer a critique of privilege. In fact, the ending would seem to exalt in the glories of Western society, most particularly in an operating room replete with Angela Hewitt's "wise and silky playing" of the Goldberg Variations (McEwan, 257). Under these conditions Perowne performs his surgical magic. In an interview with Zadie Smith, McEwan declares that he was aware of the criticism likely to come his way for having created a character who so obviously luxuriates in his good fortune. He insists that any criticism coming from other Westerners is more or less hypocritical, that they benefit from the same things Perowne does: "That's why I had him gazing at the locks on his door, thinking about the bad people, the drug dealers who want to get in—there's an embattlement. They're on the other side. You block these people out of your world picture" (Smith, 56–57). But Smith persists, noting that he is "saying that happiness is based on unreality or a bubble of unreality." McEwan responds, "It's a kind of framing, yes. But great things are achieved within that frame" (57). McEwan's words, here at least, suggest that one may be no more capable of empathy than those seeking violent solutions. He also implies that the "frame" is necessary in order to create great things, that if we spend too much time contemplating the miseries of the world we will find ourselves paralyzed. While it would be disingenuous to deny that we do not all engage in varying degrees of avoidance, the novel illuminates the benefits of such an approach without acknowledging the costs (which often remain out of sight). So though the novel denotes the ways in which Western empathy is hampered by privilege, it nonetheless cherishes the foundations upon which this privilege rests. The novel's narrative voice remains enraptured with the wonders of modern life, including the protagonist's mastery of contemporary neurosurgical procedures. Perhaps another way to conceptualize this is to say that the text highlights social inequities through the positioning of a protagonist who is so obviously on the side of privilege that the disparities are brought into sharp relief, but it contends that the structure ("a framing") in which this privilege has flourished (with all its inequities) is still the best thing we have.

Painfully aware of these societal circumstances, Butler acknowledges the shortcomings of such an engagement:

> Not only is there always the possibility that a vulnerability will not be recognized and that it will be constituted as the 'unrecognizable,' but when a vulnerability is recognized, that recognition has the power to change the meaning and structure of the vulnerability itself. (43)

In this configuration, however, Butler addresses only those moments when the other's vulnerability is not recognized, or not granted, recognition. She places greater hope in situations in which the subject willfully seeks to empathize and connect with the other. She does not consider, as Oliver's critique points out, the possibility of using the empathic gesture as a path to domination. It is precisely this outcome that *Saturday* (unwittingly) presents. For, as noted, Henry Perowne is ideally equipped to identify the vulnerabilities of the other. In fact, his professional reputation depends on it. It is all the more telling, then, that in his final reflections on the day he should think of Baxter as "meaningless" (McEwan, 276). Baxter's reaction to Perowne's humiliation may be violent, erratic, and possibly out of proportion to the slight he suffered, but it is surely not meaningless—least of all to Baxter himself. For though the possibility remains that he is misguided and wrong, the determination of "meaningless" should be only be attributed (if ever) once adequate consideration has been given to probable cause and effect. The reasons Baxter undertakes his actions may not be justified, or necessarily clear, but this does not signify they are without meaning.

Perowne's mistake is to come to his conclusions about Baxter based solely on the latter's violent gesture, never giving much thought as to the source of his "destructive energy." Butler recognizes this as a central problem in the resolution of any violent encounter. She warns that

> to take the self-generated acts of the individual as our point of departure in moral reasoning is precisely to foreclose the possibility of questioning what kind of world gives rise to such individuals. And what is this process of 'giving rise'? What social conditions help to form the very ways that choice and deliberation proceed? (16)

In labeling Baxter as "meaningless," Perowne refuses or neglects to contemplate the conditions that might give rise to such an individual. This stems from the confidence he places in his ability to diagnose the violent other. Here we might invoke Suzanne Keen's notion of *false empathy*, and suggest that Perowne has fallen victim to "the self-congratulatory delusions of those who incorrectly believe they have caught the feelings of suffering others from a different culture, gender, race, or class" (Keen, 159). And the text itself corroborates these delusions by remaining resolutely in the present, paying no attention to Baxter's history prior to the event. And the text's unidirectional perspective fails to provide sufficient data for the reader to accurately evaluate the validity of Perowne's conclusions concerning Baxter. As such, the narration of *Saturday* in this case unequivocally privileges Perowne's viewpoint, even if it occasionally undermines his certainty. Baxter is presented from Perowne's perspective, and never the other way around. Thus, the novel highlights the inequitable aspects of the empathic gesture, pointing to its colonizing impulses. In this vein, Keen notes that "the directional quality of empathy offends because an empathizer feels with a subject who may or may not be empowered to speak for herself, to correct misconceptions about her feelings, and to refuse the pitying gaze" (162). In this respect, *Saturday* remains unaware of the ways in which its striving for empathic connection and a curtailment of violent response has effectively quieted the voice of the other.

With its subtext of the war on terror, *Saturday* advocates for the superiority of a Western perspective, with its ability to adopt a pluralist perspective and in its capacity for forgiveness. Nevertheless, the privilege of the West, as well as its technological and economic dominance, weaken its capacity to connect with the less fortunate, but more desperate, other who seeks to redress past wrongs and equalize global footings. The novel stands, then, as an artifact of Western complacency and mystification, highlighting the extent to which Western society remains incredulous that others might wish for its destruction and perplexed about the reasons driving that wish. Early in the novel, Perowne concludes that "the pursuit of utopia ends up licensing every form of excess, all ruthless means of its realization" (34). This observation emanates from a man who is, in almost every conceivable way, content with his life. By presenting a protagonist who inhabits his very own utopia, and an antagonist crippled by illness, the novel raises doubts, not always intentionally, about the possibility of meaningful reflection and understanding. In his privileged position, Perowne cannot imagine the need for something more or other. *Saturday* thus exists primarily as an artifact documenting a Western insouciance surprisingly tenacious, even in the aftermath of 9/11.

NOTES

1. Interestingly, in studying the similarities between the discourses of George W. Bush and Osama Bin Laden, Vaheed Ramazani notes that they are "above all, similarly marked by a resolutely selective capacity for empathy" (Ramazani, 121).

2. McEwan has repeatedly admitted as much, claiming that *Saturday* was "written in the shadow of the event" (Caminada).

3. McEwan tells Charlie Rose that he explicitly gave Perowne a happy life, so his protagonist would be liberated from thinking about the small things and thus have time for contemplating weightier issues (Rose).

4. This is, in fact, one of Perowne's final assessments of Baxter, whom he identifies as "cruel, weak, meaningless, demanding to be confronted" (McEwan, 276).

5. James Wood sees the novel as "stag[ing] a conflict between liberal decency and illiberal menace" (Wood).

6. In a note, Elaine Hadley observes, "This is decidedly not Baxter's novel—Baxters rarely, even now, have novels about them, and his confirmed case of Huntington's disease, although in its early stages, only renders him more definitely beyond the investments of this sort of fantasy of Victorian liberalism—but he yearns for the fantasy even so" (Hadley, 100–101).

7. A number of critics have derided the plausibility of this scene. One critic goes so far as to call it "histrionic silliness" (Szalai, 89). Another concedes, "Such things do happen, I suppose, but more often in novels, alas, than in life" (Dirda). And if works of literature are so effective in fending off impending danger, David Orr facetiously asks, "should we start outfitting the New York Police Department with pocket editions of *Sonnets from the Portuguese*?" (Orr).

8. Heidi Butler argues that Perowne fails to empathize because he is committed to preserving his privileged status: "He not only subscribes to, but thrives on the social master narratives that essentialize other characters and position Perowne as the novel's dominant white male" (Butler, 102).

9. Indeed this is precisely the assumption McEwan makes about the 9/11 terrorists in an essay written days after the attacks: "If the hijackers had been able to imagine themselves into the thoughts and feelings of the passengers, they would have been unable to proceed. It is hard to be cruel once you permit yourself to enter the mind of the victim. Imagining what it is like to be someone other than yourself is at the core of our humanity. It is the essence of compassion, and it is the beginning of morality" (McEwan, Only love). McEwan infers that if only the terrorists had been enlightened enough to recognize the glories of our civilization (and those who live in it), they would never have acted as they did. But surely it is not difficult to imagine someone being cognizant of all this (and, maybe, *because* of all this) and still imagining, and wishing for, the destruction of the other.

10. Critics have attributed various levels of agency or malice to the act of operating on Baxter. Hadley, for instance, sees it as an "act of liberal detachment," (Hadley, 97) whereas Hillard argues that in operating on his assailant Perowne "returns invasion for invasion" (Hillard, 194).

11. The novel constructs a false sense of connection between the two men when the hospital staff twice refers to Baxter as Perowne's "friend" (McEwan, 252, 253).

Chapter Six

The Otherness of Islam in Amy Waldman's *The Submission*

If one follows the argument of Judith Butler and others to its logical conclusion, then those most likely to empathize with the vulnerability of others would be those who were made to feel most vulnerable themselves. Using Erickson's notion of the "geography of disaster," expressions of empathy for others should thus be at their strongest at the epicenter of the catastrophe. Early on, this certainly seemed to be the case. Spontaneous demonstrations of unity were pointed to as evidence of burgeoning fellow-feeling. And perhaps one of the most vociferous arguments for the ways in which the catastrophe engendered stronger feelings of unity between people was that of the image of a Manhattan (and its people) transformed practically overnight. Ordinarily cantankerous and anti social New Yorkers were now depicted as thoughtful, compassionate, and caring about their fellow citizens. Thus, New York was a city suddenly transmuted, at least momentarily, into a softer and gentler version of itself. Perhaps more striking was the sense of communality that arose between neighbors, but also complete strangers, on the wounded isle. E. A. Kaplan, for instance, points to the ubiquity of flags, on cars, in windows and storefronts in the city (though this phenomenon soon spread throughout the rest of the country). She suggests that while these flags primarily represented "a newly engaged patriotism," they were also used "to indicate empathy for those who had lost relatives and friends, and a shared trauma about the shock to the United States" (9). Kaplan's writing testifies to the idea of a city altered by the event. So she speaks of the "togetherness" she felt in the city, where everyone "looked at each other as if understanding what [they] all were facing" (9). And she finds expressions of communal feelings are particularly strong in the gatherings in Union Square where people reveal a need to share grief, in all of its forms, with others. Looking over the various shrines and tributes, Kaplan perceives a strong strain of empathetic and fellow-feeling: "despite all the differences in perspectives that the artifacts showed, an apparent commonality reigned in the form of respect for differences within a whole (the events) that we shared" (12). Kaplan's vocabulary suggests a breaking down of barriers between people and a generalized burgeoning of mutual feeling.

As we now know, this sense of togetherness was not to be long-lasting. Nor was it to be universal. One witnesses, for instance, a visible shift in sentiment when one considers those victims of the attacks who were not American, and who hailed from over sixty different countries from across the globe (estimates range from three hundred fifty to five hundred). As David Simpson observes, many who perished "were indeed foreign nationals, who imagined a kind of global diversity"—a notion fostered by the mere fact of working in the World Trade Center, a hub of the globalized marketplace. Here were citizens of the world working side by side killed in the pursuit of the same goals and, most tellingly, being killed because of it. If ever empathy might be easily accorded, this was surely such an occasion. It soon became apparent, however, that these "foreigners" were not to be accorded the same reverence as American victims. In the end, as Simpson points out, these individuals were not "produced as representatives of a united world consciousness or universal human condition so much as made secondary characters in a distinctly American drama" (62). As the days progressed, the event was no longer presented as a global tragedy, but increasingly as an American one. The erasure of the international or global aspects of the event effectively eliminated a number of avenues for cosmopolitan sentiment. Because instead of being framed as an occurence in which all people should have a vested concern, September 11 was soon conceptualized as a crime perpetrated against the United States and all the country stood for (all that made it "exceptional").

As such, to use Judith Butler's terms, not every life was equally grieved. And nowhere was this truer than in those undocumented workers who had the misfortune to be "employed" in the World Trade Center on that Tuesday morning (as many as one hundred, according to some estimates). If such a tragedy should make us aware of the vulnerability of those less fortunate than us, then one would presume that such fellow-feeling would likely occur foremost with those living nearest to us. Such, of course, was not the case. Instead, the opposite occurred, with these individuals receiving no recognition, as though they had never existed. In this vein, Sturken argues that the media coverage of the event "established a hierarchy of the dead, privileging the stories of public servants, such as firefighters, over office workers, of policemen over security guards, and the stories of those with economic capital over those without, of traders over janitors" (272). These undocumented workers present a paradox of sorts. For although they were thought of, on the one hand, as "non-Americans," on the other they were killed while supporting the American way of life (if only by working and paying taxes). So although they were killed for the same reasons as the corporate traders and business people that day, they nevertheless remained unrecognized. These notes of discord, and their undermining of a possible unity, reveal that the widespread impact of tragedy and trauma is not in and of itself sufficient to bring about greater levels of mutuality. For if a sense of kinship and compassion cannot be generated at the site of the tragedy itself, what hope is there for making such connections with others living at farther reaches of the globe?

It is to the contested site that I now want to turn my attention, before offering a reading of a novel explicitly concerned with issues of memorialization. After all, nothing seemed more likely to command agreement, or to awaken fellow-feeling, than the construction of a monument dedicated to the memory of those who lost their lives on September 11. The challenge, as David Simpson observes, is to erect a memorial that speaks to communal and individual grief at the same time. He indicates that such monuments "must somehow signify and acknowledge the idiosyncrasies and special qualities of each of the dead, so that each death is not simply merged with innumerable others, without allowing those idiosyncrasies to disturb or radically qualify the comforting articulation of a common cause and a common fate" (2). The vacillations within Simpson's sentence itself communicate the need for the maintenance of equilibrium. The challenge for the memorial, then, is to speak to (for?) all while not subsuming otherness in the pursuit of some homogenizing vision. Of course, constructing anything at Ground Zero was bound to be problematic since many of the remains of the victims had not been recovered and were unlikely to ever be. As such, the site was consigned as "sacred ground," primarily by the grieving families, but also by politicians and the media. Such a designation severely curtailed what could be built there. On another front were entities primarily concerned with the amount of prime real estate the memorial was likely to swallow up at the heart of Manhattan's financial center. Many also feared that the memorial would engage in an eternal looking backward to the moment of trauma, halting any forward momentum. The monument would not communicate the country's resiliency, nor its determination to get back on its (economic) feet, but rather would keep the city, and the nation, mired in melancholia. In this iteration, Ground Zero would forever exist as a reminder of the nation's moment of weakness—a site of destruction rather than rebirth.

The greatest source of debate for most people, however, was not whether a memorial should be built at Ground Zero, but rather what kind. The number of interested parties expressing competing interests meant that it would be impossible for a single memorial to meet everyone's needs. A further point of contention involved what we might call a hierarchy of survivors—those who possessed the greatest capital (often related to degrees of grief) and thus could dictate how things should proceed. As Marita Sturken observes, the construction of the memorial is "a highly contested issue" that raises a fundamental question: "To whom does the site of Ground Zero belong—to the city, the port authority, the developers, the families of the dead, the architects who reenvision it, the tourists, the media, or the nation?" (321). Sturken's question about possession of the site highlights the degree to which Ground Zero, in its vast emptiness, symbolizes different things for different people. Because the converging needs to both rebuild the site *and* to memorialize the dead would prove to be far more divisive than initially believed. In fact, it seemed almost impossible to predict or imagine the endless permutations of disagreement that arose around the future of Ground Zero. As Sturken notes, "the different factions have found their place, so to speak, in opposition to each other rather than by working together" (259). What the site meant to developers or to architects (who had now been provided a blank canvas upon which to construct their work) and what it meant to relatives of the dead were two very different things. The affected area of the city existed simultaneously as a site of memorialization and reconstruction—in some ways diametrically opposed impulses. And while this is certainly true for any number of sites of destruction, what differs with the space in Lower Manhattan, is the length of time in which it simultaneously existed as both. As a result, Sturken observes, Ground Zero became a place "of intense emotional and political investments, a highly overdetermined space . . . inscribed by local, national, and global meanings, a neighborhood, a commercial district, and a site of memory and mourning" (311–12).

Contention about the meaning of the site reached a fever pitch in the summer of 2010 when people learned of a proposal to build an Islamic cultural center in close proximity to the World Trade Center site. Interestingly misnamed (since it was neither a mosque nor at Ground Zero), the furor surrounding the proposal became known in the public arena as the "Ground Zero mosque controversy." The misnaming not only reveals how painfully misinformed people were about Islam, but also how many individuals insisted on connecting Islam with the attacks. The building plans elicited a number of predictable responses—the majority in opposition to the center's presence so near to "sacred ground"—but these reactions can be characterized by placing them into one of three categories. The largest group, or at least the most vocal, contended that such an edifice would be an affront to those who perished on September 11 and to the surviving members of their families. The center would also serve to mark the place (read *celebrate*) where radical Islam perpetuated an act of unspeakable violence against the United States and the people of New York. As Jeanne Kilde observes, some people now felt as though "an Islamic building was claiming the space and, in the view of some, 'triumphing' over the site" (305–6). The opposing view argued that allowing the construction of the center would demonstrate the tolerance of the United States even in the face of such violence. Such a gesture—the recognizing and cherishing of religious freedom—would also allow the gap between Muslims and non-Muslims to be breached. "What is great about America, and particularly New York, is we welcome everybody," declared Mayor Michael Bloomberg, "and if we are so afraid of something like this, what does it say about us? Democracy is stronger than this. And for us to just say no is just, I think—not appropriate is a nice way to phrase it" (Barbaro). Finally, a third group contended that the center should be built, but pleaded for the builders to demonstrate both restraint and sensitivity by placing the center at some tasteful remove from the site of the tragedy. Prominent New York leaders, such as Governor David Paterson and Archbishop Timothy Dolan, advocated for an alternate location. In an interview for CNN, Paterson posited that "If people put their heads together, maybe we could find a site that's away from the site now but still serves the area" (Goldman). While this may appear, at first glance, as the most reasonable position, it is actually a "compromise" that undermines its very stance. It is safe to suggest, for instance, that no such objections or alternatives would have been raised if someone had proposed the building of a synagogue or church near the site. The controversy not only illuminated the susceptibility of Ground Zero to being hijacked and made to symbolize different things. Unfinished and overdetermined, the site existed as a kind of *tabula rasa* on which a multitude of narratives might be written. The furor also made clear that nearly nine years after the attacks, many Americans still harbored fears and suspicions about their Arab and Muslim counterparts. The proposal for the Islamic center was doubly troubling, as Kilde points out, because the sacred ground of the site was "now understood to be threatened not simply by something profane but by the very enemy who had originally defiled it" (305).

The proposed solutions to the mosque controversy reveal the extent to which the presence of Arabs and Muslims within American borders now made a substantial segment of the population fearful, suspicious, and uncomfortable. In effect, the invitations to move the Islamic center underscored the degree to which Ground Zero was now intended to be reserved for a select few, and any attempt to broaden or complicate these arrangements was sure to be met with resistance, particularly in respect to Arab and Muslim others. Kilde, for instance, finds this apparent attempt at compromise nothing more than disguised discrimination:

> Perhaps more pernicious than outright Islamophobia, this perception of vulnerability and subsequent calls for 'respect,' both informed and achieved by spatialized social processes, are in effect a measure of the distance that Islam and American Muslims are from being viewed as fully American. (307)

So despite the fact that leaders such as Rudy Giuliani pleaded with the population not to resort to racial violence, Arab and Muslim Americans were now viewed and treated with suspicion. Individuals who had been mostly "invisible" to the majority now came under heightened scrutiny. Armed with a cursory knowledge of Islam, if any, many people confounded and associated all Arabs and Muslims with the radical fundamentalism of the terrorists and al-Qaeda. Furthermore, Islam was generally projected by the media as a religion largely based in violence and whose ideologies were fundamentally incompatible with American values (freedom, democracy, etc.). A large number of Arab and Muslim-Americans immediately became suspect merely because they shared one thing with the terrorists: religion. As a result, they faced deportation, interrogation, indefinite detention, surveillance, hate crimes, defacement and destruction of personal property, and various other forms of discrimination. As Besheer Mohamed and John O'Brien point out, the terrorist attacks helped to revive "a handful of widespread and durable misconceptions about Islam and Muslims within American society" (62). The first of these contends "that there is a natural and abiding association between religious Islam and terrorist extremism." A second related idea is that Muslims are "more prone to support terrorism than others." While a third notion maintains that "Muslims with higher levels of religious commitment are more likely to hold extremist views" (62). 9/11 merely served to exacerbate anti-Arab and Muslim sentiments that had been promulgated long before the towers fell. The reaction to the cultural center proposal reveals that, a decade after the attacks, Arab and Muslim Americans continue to be viewed with intense trepidation and suspicion, despite any number of pronouncements to the contrary. So while there is little doubt that a good many Americans now possess a greater knowledge (and perhaps understanding) of Arab and Muslim others than they did prior to September 11, 2001 (including those living among them), we might question whether this newfound awareness has actually manifested itself as increased empathy for this demographic.

WALDMAN'S *THE SUBMISSION*

The debates surrounding the ultimate purpose(s) of the memorial, as well as those concerned with the treatment of Arab and Muslim-Americans after 9/11, testify to the cracks and fissures existing in the supposed national consensus presented by the Bush Administration and much of the media. Amy Waldman blends these fractious issues into the plot of her novel, *The Submission*. The text depicts the siege mentality that existed in the aftermath of the attacks, and the subsequent emphasis placed on the need for all citizens (perhaps all New Yorkers first, but eventually all Americans) to project a unified front. This was effected largely though the construction of an "us" in response to a perceived "them." In other words, high levels of vulnerability and fear led to an all-or-nothing philosophy that demanded that one assert one's belonging to one group or another. There was no room for nuance or contradiction. No consideration was given to those who might not so easily fit into these new designations.

But too much otherness exists in the world, even among close-knit communities, to imagine that any such devising could ever be maintained for an extended period of time. As we have noted, depictions of a united nation soon began to show signs of strain. In this regard, the premise of Waldman's novel is a reasonably simple, though effective, one. The author imagines the fallout (political, emotional, social) from an anonymous selection process in which a Muslim architect is chosen to design the 9/11 memorial. One of the text's accomplishments is the manner in which it captures the competing impulses at work within the traumatized community. In this strained and shocked atmosphere, the site of the wound becomes both a rallying point and a source of discord. What might normally engender communal agreement soon instigates a series of heated debates within the supposedly unified community. After all, a united front presumes a common response to the attacks. The musings of the chairman of the selection committee, Paul Rubin, however, reveal how such machinations work to mask any number of fissures and contradictions already at play within the wounded community itself:

> The trauma, for Paul, had come later, when he watched the replay, pledged allegiance to the devastation. You couldn't call yourself an American if you hadn't, in solidarity, watched your fellow Americans being pulverized, yet what kind of American did watching create? A traumatized victim? A charged-up avenger? A queasy voyeur? Paul, and he suspected many Americans, harbored all of these protagonists. The memorial was meant to tame them. (13)

In this intriguing paragraph, Waldman characterizes a variety of responses from the American populace. More interesting, however, is the suggestion that each of these responses may coexist within the same individual. The various embodiments Paul imagines reflect the complicated relationship the survivors have *vis-à-vis* those who died, and the extent to which said relationship determines the measure of one's Americaness. The final sentence posits the memorial as a salve—a deliverer of sameness—turning everyone into the same kind of American. The use of the word "tame," however, implies warring reactions and impulses that must be harnessed—a function the memorial is intended to fulfill.

Because even before the identity of the designer is revealed, strong disagreement already exists about the design and the purpose of the memorial itself. The very titles of the two competing submissions—The Garden and The Void—make their aesthetic intentions clear, and each elicits its advocate. Claire Burwell, a widow of the tragedy and the appointed representative of the grieving families on the jury, endorses The Garden because of its beauty. She sees it as a place "where the widows, their children, anyone—can stumble on joy" (5). In essence, Burwell argues for a space not defined by death. Her opponent, the artist Ariana Montagu, advocates instead for The Void which she identifies as a "truer" representation of the tragedy, and thus a more fitting memorial for those who perished. She contends that, "The Void is visceral, angry, dark, raw, because there was no joy on that day" (5). A disservice is being done to the dead if the memorial simply becomes a space through which people stroll, or sit and eat their lunches. As mentioned earlier, there were many who considered Ground Zero to be nothing less than "sacred ground," so that any transformation of what was now essentially a gravesite would not be welcomed or tolerated. As a place where many had met their untimely ends and from which their remains might never be recovered, the site must be left undisturbed. Others, on the other hand, argued that leaving the site as is would be viewed as a concession—a constant reminder of national and personal vulnerability. Instead, the site should be rebuilt, trumpeting the country's resilience, while still engaging in commemoration. Evident in these two positions are the opposing impulses of sanctification and celebration.

The heated debate at Gracie Mansion, two years after the attacks, addresses a number of related questions: Who is a memorial primarily intended to serve, the living or the dead? Is it meant as a place of contemplation for those who survived, or as ever-present reminder of the tragedy that took place there? For their parts, Burwell and Montagu agree on the need for a memorial. They disagree, however, on the role it should play. Montagu's stance strikes Burwell as nihilistic and anti-therapeutic; "You have something against healing?" she asks. To which the artist responds, "We disagree on the best way to bring it about. I think you have to confront the pain, face it, even wallow in it, before you can move on" (5–6). Montagu seems to suggest that they want the same thing, and that it is simply a question of means. But there is no overlap in their arguments; the women maintain their oppositional stances. Again, this reveals how even a gesture with universalizing intentions can still elicit contrasting and competing positions. If agreement cannot be reached on this issue, what hope is there for any kind of consensus on more controversial ones? Later, when the voting reaches a standstill, the chairman, Paul Rubin challenges the jurors, "How can we ask this country to come together in healing if this jury can't?" (11). At the same time, we might ask whether it is truly beneficial and necessary for the country to "come together" and if this is the best approach to the working through of (national) trauma. One could argue that this emphasis on national unity, on the presentation of an unbroken front, has actually proven detrimental to the healing process, privileging some voices to the detriment of others.

"THE PROBLEM WITH ISLAM IS ISLAM": THE QUANDARY OF A MUSLIM DESIGNER

The notion of a country banding together, however, is revealed as a fantasy the moment the seal on the envelope is broken and the identity of the designer becomes known. The furor that erupts, and the outrage connected to the name of Mohammad Khan, at once makes clear how little the wound has actually healed, but also the extent to which Arab and Muslim-Americans are now viewed with nearly as much suspicion and anger as al-Qaeda operatives. As a number of reviewers were quick to point out, Waldman's novel presaged, or bore a striking similarity to, a number of events that came to pass. Prior to the cultural center controversy, however, one might have imagined that the emotions surrounding 9/11 had become less raw, less volatile. In this age of rapidly moving events—where nothing remains in the media's crosshairs for very long—it may have been possible to believe that the significance of the terrorist attacks had already begun to fade. Waldman acknowledges, for instance, that in the process of writing she became worried as to whether her novel depicted an exaggerated response. Would the community really react in such dramatic fashion to the announcement that a submission from a Muslim had been chosen as the design for the memorial? "For a couple of years before, I actually had started to doubt if it would really be a big deal if this guy won. But when the Ground Zero mosque controversy exploded, I thought, 'no, I'm right'" (Derbyshire). The protests of the summer of 2010 signaled not only that Waldman was correct in her assessment, but that feelings continued to run high in regards to anything connected to the events of September 11. In light of the controversy, the novel's depiction of the furor surrounding Khan's selection rings even truer.

For many characters in the novel, the construction of a memorial whose design is Muslim in origin is the equivalent of creating a "victory garden" for the jihadists. After all, Ground Zero is also the final resting place of the nineteen terrorists, a fact rarely discussed or acknowledged. As such, suspicion grows that Khan's design may in fact be a tribute to the martyrdom of the attackers rather than a memorial to their victims. For although the "Garden" is not an obvious affront, the predominant assumption remains that Khan shares more with the victimizers than he does with their victims. It is of no consequence whether Mohammad Khan is a practicing Muslim or not (he is not), or whether he is an American citizen or not (he is). The population's lack of knowledge about Islam short-circuits their capacity to contemplate any other scenario. In their minds, all Arabs are Muslims, all Muslims are Islamists, and all Islamists seek the destruction of the Western world. Any commonalities Khan may share with his "fellow" American citizens are overshadowed by his Muslim background. It makes no difference whether these thoughts are rational or not—the existence of a link between the designer and the violent otherness that wreaked havoc on the city serves to seriously handicap the possibility of any empathetic connection. So if Khan's design is an attempt to bridge the gap between Islam and the West, his efforts produce the opposite effect. Groups such as Save America from Islam and the Memorial Defense Committee are not moved by his attempt at rapprochement or reconciliation (130). The identity of the designer trumps the design, and calls increase for Khan's removal from the competition. No attempt is made to really understand Islam, or to discriminate between the majority of its followers and those entranced by its more radical versions. This general sentiment is best captured in a line from Alyssa Spier's column: "The problem with Islam is Islam" (106).

The novel also highlights how this connection is further hamstrung by the (mis)information propagated by the media. *The Submission* is insightful (due in part to Waldman's journalistic background) in outlining the disproportionately significant role the media now plays in shaping (and perhaps even distorting) public opinion. Although occasionally verging on caricature, the character of Spier reveals the extent to which personal ambitions often overpower professional ethics, and the degree to which much of the media is invested in fomenting dissent than in creating consensus. Spier's presence in the novel may also cause the reader to consider the processes through which the media either help or hinder us in navigating or negotiating the surfeit of otherness with which we are bombarded every day. For how is the public supposed to get a solid grasp of that unknown, distant other when forces strive to (mis)inform for their own political, if not nefarious, purposes? The debate surrounding Mo's selection (and that of the Ground Zero mosque as well) reveals a lack of knowledge, if not a degree of ignorance, about the other that is further exacerbated by the proliferation of misinformation on the Internet, but also through the popular media.[1]

Additionally, the media exerts its influence through other discursive delivery systems in communicating and accentuating Khan's otherness to their readership. First, the novel presents an appraisal of Khan's design by the architectural critic for the *New York Times*. Among other things, the critic identifies the work as imbued with Eastern, and perhaps even Islamic elements:

> One does not know, of course, if these parallels are exact, or even intentional—only Mr. Khan can answer that, and perhaps even he was unaware of the influences that acted upon him. But the possible allusions may be controversial. Some might say the designer is mocking us, or playing with his religious heritage. Yet could he be trying to say something larger about the relationship between Islam and the West? (115)

The critic's assessment encapsulates a number of the conflicting responses elicited by the jury's selection. The principal point of contention, however, remains the extent to which Islamic elements have been incorporated (knowingly or unknowingly) within the work and to what end. In a second instance, the novel offers a commentary on Khan's selection written by an editor at the *New Yorker*. Treading lightly so as to not insult the sensibilities of any of the magazine's liberal readers, the editor asserts, "Mohammad Khan has absolutely, unequivocally every right to proceed with his memorial" (124). Having voiced the opinion of everyone who considers individual rights to be the backbone of American society, however, the editor then abruptly shifts his argument, "The question is whether he *should* proceed" (124). This stance not so subtly indicates a preference for Khan not proceeding with his design. Because, without actually saying it, the editor maintains that the designer, as a Muslim-American, should have the perspicacity and the wherewithal to recognize the sensitivities of those others he might be offending. In this configuration, the individual must submit to the will of the majority and withdraw from the competition. There is no apparent recognition on the editor's part that making such a demand actually runs counter to the very tenets American society seeks to uphold. Finally, and tellingly, the editor criticizes Khan for his unwillingness to explain his intentions, Again, he acknowledges that the designer has every right to do this, but contends that "to insist that any questions about his influences or motives are offensive is to answer the anguish of the victims' families with coyness" (125). The editor's approach is problematic because it points to the liberties of the individual and then, effectively, pulls them away.

Those positing for the possibility of empathy in the aftermath of the attacks would contend that the degree to which the design incorporates Islamic elements should have no bearing on whether to build or not. And, in fact, others might maintain that this should be all the more reason *to build it*. The irony, of course, is that Khan's otherness cannot be accommodated within this supposed gesture of inclusivity. Because no matter how many arguments are made as to the non-extremism of the vast majority of Muslims, the recently victimized population is seemingly unable, or unwilling, to make that distinction. In demanding an explanation from the designer, most people are effectively seeking a disavowal, if not an outright rejection, of Islam. So that instead of grasping these moments as opportunities to demonstrate tolerance and empathy—of connecting with the other—the critics of Mohammad Khan's design and the "Ground Zero mosque" alike, lean in the opposite direction, failing (or refusing) to recognize how either of these constructions could stand as symbols of reconciliation. As with the proposal for the Islamic cultural center, the selection of Khan's design provides an opportunity to accentuate sameness and promote commonality in the wake of the attacks. *The Submission* highlights how such opportunities are ignored or missed.

MUSLIM = TERRORIST

Perhaps the greatest hindrance to restoration of communality was the visceral need to identify an enemy following an event that elicited unprecedented levels of fear, uncertainty, and vulnerability in the American populace. Thus, much like the tens of thousands of Japanese-Americans who immediately became suspect and were sent to internment camps after the surprise attack carried out by Japan on Pearl Harbor, so too are Muslim-Americans differently viewed and treated in the wake of the attacks of September 11, 2001. Although this comparison can be problematic, it does highlight certain commonalities between the two events. Most notable is the fact that the element of surprise was utilized to enact violence. The act of terror immediately creates a fearful and suspicious populace now on alert for "others" who might wish to do them harm. As a result, and although they had been granted American citizenship, first Japanese-Americans and then later their Muslim counterparts, are envisaged as potential enemies simply waiting for the right moment to strike. Seemingly overnight, then, they have been transformed from same to other—from being considered "one of us" to becoming "one of them." Of course, such turnabouts undermine the supposed acceptance of others upon which American society prides itself. As David Simpson observes, "The relatively comfortable pluralism within which we have been living, whereby other cultures have come to be accepted in their own terms as long as they subsist at some distance from (or peacefully within) our own, was shattered by this event's confrontational negation of any ethic of tolerance" (6). That which separates Muslim-Americans from the majority is now emphasized to the detriment of that which they share. Such a sudden shift in perception is likely to have a jarring and alienating effect on members of the ostracized group, no doubt impacting conceptions of self and identity.[2] The sense of unbelonging was magnified after 9/11. For his part, Mohammad Khan responds to such maneuvers with an understandable mixture of outrage and befuddlement. Not surprisingly, he rejects any invitation to prove his Americanness. But the attacks have created a "need to know" in the majority, and Khan's silence simply fuels their suspicions. When the planners seek an explanation (or perhaps, more accurately, reassurance) as to the motives behind his design, he declines to provide any, contesting that no such demands would be made of a non-Muslim designer. Unsure as to where his sympathies (loyalties?) lie, his critics have been primed to assume the worse. Invariably, attempts are made to more explicitly link Khan and his work with terror.

Khan's new social standing is made readily apparent to him just days after the attacks when he is pulled from the line at LAX. His name alone is enough to set off alarms. And although explainable, the actions of the airport officials are nevertheless a clear case of racial profiling. The first question

Khan is posed reflects suspicion and doubt on the part of the agents, "So you say you're an architect?" (24). The very phrasing presumes deceitfulness and conscious efforts at concealing his real identity. The interaction also makes plain these men are incapable of seeing Khan as anything but "other," their queries intended to concretize difference:

> "Do you love this country, Mohammad?"
> "As much as you do." The answer appeared to displease them.
> "What are your thoughts on jihad?" (25)

Khan's attempt at deflecting this line of questioning and of creating a connection between himself and his interrogators is met with annoyance. They are resolved in associating him with radical fundamentalism, asking questions that only a week earlier would have seemed preposterous:

> "Know any Muslims who want to do harm to America?"
> "None. I don't know any Communists either."
> "We didn't ask about Communists. Do you believe you'd go to heaven if you blew yourself up?" (26)

Khan's allusions to the Cold War, and the House on Un-American Activities, are lost on the officials, whose questioning not so subtly moves from asking about relationships he may have with extremists to whether he himself has ever entertained radical ideology. One senses Khan's frustration, but also his disbelief as the incident plays itself out. That Islam—a part of himself to which he has, by all accounts, paid very little attention—should now be his defining characteristic is both unsettling and alienating. He barely contains his anger at having to suffer these indignities. He allows himself to be photographed and fingerprinted though the very fact of being touched by an agent ignites in him "a brief flare of fury, an impulse toward violence" that he quickly subdues (28). On his return home, he realizes they have "pillaged" his suitcase, increasing his "bitterness" towards those with whom he supposedly shares citizenship and nationality.

In a second instance, Khan somewhat surprisingly agrees to be interviewed by Lou Sarge, a right-wing radio host whose show sports the tagline "I Slam Islam" (41). Perhaps the architect believes his appearance will provide a platform for asserting his sameness. The host's questions, however, immediately make apparent how he intends to "frame" his guest and deliver his otherness to the listening audience:

> "So what did you feel, really feel, the day of the attack?"
> "I felt devastated, like all of us. Like a hole had been blasted in me."
> "That sounds pretty bad," Sarge said. "It must have been like finding out your brother is the Unabomber."

"No, that's not what I meant." (188–89)

While Khan attempts to construct a sense of communality by asserting that the event affected him in the same way it did "all of us," Sarge seeks to position him as an other whose reactions to the attacks were qualitatively different from that of most people. He implies the latter's devastation and dismay came from the discovery that Muslims had committed the act rather than the fact that thousands were killed that day. And when he asks Khan to tell his listeners how he "really" felt, he intimates the designer is hiding his true emotions about the event. Much of the interview, then, is geared towards convincing Khan to divulge his real self and his real desires.[3] Sarge begins by probing for the origins of the design, asking the architect, "where'd you get the idea?" When Khan responds that he felt a garden was the symbolically appropriate choice, Sarge jumps in:

> "Got it. So is it, actually, an Islamic garden?"
> "It's just a garden."
> "A martyr's paradise?"
> "It's a garden."
> "A jihadi playground?"
> "It's a garden."
> "A joke on the American people?"
> "Excuse me? The American people include me."
> "I mean, if I were Muslim—it hasn't been an easy couple of years for you, I'm guessing, you know, maybe you're a little bit peeved, maybe you're thinking, let's just slip this under the radar."
> Mo was so furious at the assertion, and at the kernel of truth it contained, that he couldn't speak for a moment. (189)

Sarge's questions enumerate the suspicions harbored by many, that Khan's memorial is intended to serve Islamic purposes rather than American ones. Engaging in faux empathy, the host pretends to imagine himself as a Muslim, but only in the hopes of inciting his interviewee into admitting that anger and frustration were the principal motivators behind the development of his design. For his part, Khan offers guarded and perhaps disingenuous replies, volunteering generic observations about the interplay of life and death which do nothing to allay suspicion, or illuminate how his submission best serves a community seeking to memorialize its dead. And he protests too much in repeatedly asserting that "It's a garden," as though no other explanation is needed. The two men are working at cross-purposes, so there will never be any understanding or real empathy between them. Sarge presses for a damning admission, while Khan, naturally feeling unsafe, raises a number of barriers to protect himself against that eventuality.

It makes sense, of course, that Khan would not wish to be identified with a group now being ostracized and demonized. Just as it is understandable that he would lack any desire to be forcefully linked with Islam which, up to this point, has had little or no significance for him. At the same time, these encounters instill a combativeness within him. In negatively accentuating that which is still an undeniable part of his self, they cause him to reconsider and explore those aspects of himself more fully. Khan recognizes "a kernel of truth" in Sarge's statements, though there is a good deal of ambiguity as to which of the radio host's assertions has elicited this (internal) admission. Is the "kernel" to be found in the fact that Muslims have a right to be angry, having been betrayed by the country to which they had pledged allegiance, because of the actions of a few men? Or is it that Khan has actually limned his design with messages meant to undercut the patriotic message of the traditional memorial? What remains difficult to gauge is Khan's comfort level with that kernel. He seems capable of admitting its presence to himself, in private, but not to anyone else, as though doing so would amount to some kind of concession on his part. During the airport interrogation, for instance, Khan strenuously objects to any implication of sameness between himself and the terrorists. Later, however, in the privacy of his home, he allows himself to contemplate potential commonalities:

> These men who had given vent to their homicidal sanctimony had nothing to do with him, yet weren't entirely apart. They represented Islam no more than his own extended family did, but did they represent it less? He didn't know enough about his own religion to say. He was the middle-class Muslim son of an engineer, a profile not all that different from some of the terrorists. Raised in another society, raised religious, could he have become one of them? The question shuddered through him and left an uneasy residue. (29)

Under different circumstances, Khan suspects that he might very well have been one of them. The "uneasy residue" serves as an apt metaphor to explain Khan's own problematic relationship with the Islamic aspects of his identity. The situation creates tensions within Khan, who remains ambivalent about his ties to Islam, but whose combative spirit compels him to adopt positions counter to those the majority of Americans wish to impose upon him.

This ambivalence is further exemplified in his decision to observe Ramadan, for though he might imaginatively frame it as a gesture of solidarity with his fellow Muslims, Khan admits, "The truth was he didn't know why he was doing it, why his first act each day was abstention, and this uncertainty harbored so many others, even as it was born from them" (185). Something he cannot readily identify incites him to embrace this side of his identity more fully. What he does recognize, however, is his need *not* to conform. The fasting for Ramadan, he later concedes, "would suit him less well in a Muslim country, where it meant conforming not defying" (186). Defiance becomes a defining characteristic of many of Khan's interactions with the American other. His response to being profiled, then, is to embrace his otherness, those aspects of his person that led to his being marginalized in the first place. Refusing to conform to their wishes, he continues to instigate and provoke, "testing" his fellow Americans by sporting a beard—an act that intentionally heightens rather than diminishes his resemblance to the nineteen hijackers. Later, deciding to shave, he admits to himself that he had "grown the beard to play with perceptions and misconceptions, to argue against the attempts to define him" (213). If Khan is prepared to use the fasting of Ramadan, or the mere growing of a beard, as "provocation," is it not possible that he might use his design for similar purposes? After all, the creation of the memorial comes after his humiliation at the airport, the passing over at his firm, his visit to Kabul, and any number of other incidents where the majority communicate how they feel about the Arabs and Muslims living in their midst. Might the memorial not be intended as a reaction to this discrimination, since Khan often does more to raise suspicions than to alleviate them?

An air of mystery, for instance, surrounds the circumstances of the design's submission. He never reveals his reasons for entering the competition, and tells no one he is doing so. It is possible, as he claims, that this silence was a product of his wanting to do something for himself, but this justification fails to convince. And if Khan is not being secretive, then why does he omit to tell the architectural firm with which he is employed, or to alert his closest associate (and future business partner), of his intentions? (107). A more likely explanation is that he was not oblivious to the impact the selection of a Muslim designer (albeit an American one) would have on the general populace. His subterfuge about submitting indicates a desire to keep certain things hidden, including the possibility that the memorial is meant to stand as a political statement with a variety of motivations. First, he intends his work to act as a healing gesture, one that will help bridge the divide between Americans and Muslims the world over (including those living within the nation's borders). Second, he submits the design purely out of self-interest, as a way of advancing his career. Third, he does in fact harbor ulterior motives, intending to exact some measure of satisfaction by undermining the memorializing process. These categories are not mutually exclusive, however, and it is therefore conceivable that he simultaneously entertains each of these motivations, to varying degrees. After all, his situation does make him same *and* other; he is Muslim *and* he is American.[4]

At this juncture in history, however, the two designations are seen as incompatible by the majority of the American population. Khan's Islamic ties (however limited they may be) would inevitably place the Eastern characteristics of the memorial in relief, forever reminding attendees of the tensions between the West and the Muslim world. The Islamic echoes of his Garden would guarantee that the political context of the event would never be far from anyone's mind. The remote possibility that it could be a "victory garden," would forever color the ways in which the memorial was perceived. And even if Khan has not created a "martyr's paradise," his connections with Islam cast the memorial in a different light than if it had been created by anyone else. In the eyes of many Americans, a monument created by a Muslim would inevitably recall the nineteen men who perpetrated violence against their country.[5] Khan's design, like the proposed mosque, would unsettle because it would bring perpetrator and victim, intentionally or not, in close proximity to one another.

GRIEVING WIDOW AND AGGRIEVED DESIGNER

Despite the political firestorm, however, there are many who support Khan's selection, most notably Claire Burwell. She is, in fact, his most ardent advocate. And so the eventual dissolution of their apparent entente underlines even more painfully the difficulties and limitations in creating a strong empathic bond between self and other. Burwell's metamorphosis—from empathizer to exasperated widow who ends up asserting Khan's otherness—encompasses a complicated trajectory. Because Khan and Burwell begin almost as comrades-in-arms, for it is she who first convinces a number of jurors to select his Garden as the memorial, and who forcefully urges them to forge ahead even after the designer's identity is known. The selection of a Muslim, she argues, will "send a message, a good message, that in America, it doesn't matter what your name is" (18). This is, as the novel repeatedly shows, wishful thinking. Because in the present context, whether Burwell wants to admit it or not, Khan's name *does matter.*

Burwell nevertheless works hard to maintain her convictions. At first, it is the doubts expressed by others against which she fights. We see how their opinions and needs progressively impinge upon her own decision-making process, and on her capacity to empathize with Khan's point of view. Finally, she struggles with her own qualms about the challenge that Khan himself poses. The novel charts the arc of Burwell's waning conviction in the face of his adamant refusal to either explain his design, or to dissociate himself from the actions of the terrorists (to say nothing of condemning them). And an accrual of small moments causes the distance to grow between Burwell and the designer. At a press conference, for instance, she feels he smiles inappropriately, causing her to wonder about his true feelings towards those who died and the relatives left to grieve (115). That same day, articles in the *Times* and other media sources begin to signal the possible presence of Islamic elements in the design. She sleeps poorly and her uneasiness deepens: "The possibility that his garden was meant to eloquently, wordlessly bolster believers lapped with oceanic insistence at the edge of her thinking" (117). Misgivings she would not have entertained about a non-Muslim designer worm their way into her mind, wearing down her conviction to the point that, in the end, she finds herself in the minority, demanding that the architect withdraw from the competition. She is forced to admit she could not tolerate living with the possibility, however remote, that the memorial might stand as a political statement, or worse. Because, like a good many others, Burwell is deeply invested in the meaning of the memorial. So much so that even when she asserts that selecting a Muslim designer sends "a good message" to the country, she still seeks to control the content of that message. This desire eventually hampers her capacity for entertaining divergent perspectives. She may recognize the value in having a Muslim designer, but only within certain limits. He can build his memorial, as long as he guarantees there are no subversive subtexts to his work. Discussing the role of Claire, Keeble argues that the novel "condemns the hypocrisies of the character who is an embodiment of liberal middle-class values" (169–70). In this way, the conditions Burwell and others seek to impose on Khan bear a sharp resemblance to the stance adopted by the supposed moderates who argued that an Islamic cultural center in Lower Manhattan was a good idea, as long as it was built a suitable distance from Ground Zero (thus invalidating the spirit of their approval).

Khan and Burwell thus reach what might have been an evitable impasse. He fails to see why she must know his motivations, and she cannot fathom his reasons, given the heightened circumstances, for not not divulging them. The text is finally not very optimistic about the possibility of comity or fellow-feeling. If the architect and the widow cannot reach an agreement, the novel suggests, it seems unlikely anyone else will. Their strongest instance of empathic connection occurs, ironically, at the very moment they both recognize the impossibility of agreement. Paul Rubin has brought them together for what he hopes will be a consensus-building moment. In his mind, the widow will ask the questions she most needs answered, while the architect will proffer appropriate words to allay her fears and doubts. Nothing of the sort transpires. Khan refuses to entertain her queries, contending they are only being asked because he happens to share a religious background with the terrorists who attacked the United States. Frustrated by her persistent treatment of him as other, he challenges her to question her thinking, "Wouldn't you assume that any non-Muslim who entered the competition thinks the attack was wrong? Why are you treating me differently? Why are you asking more of me?" In response, Burwell exclaims,

> "Because you are asking more of us!" she said. "You want us to trust you even though you won't answer questions about your design—what it means, where it came from."
> "But you are only asking those questions because you don't trust me."

"And I don't trust you because you won't answer, so we're stuck." She smiled, and to her surprise so did he. If they could recognize, even laugh at, this bind, she thought, her antagonism easing, they could escape it. (270)

Such hopes, however, prove to be in vain; they are in a bind from which they are unable to extract themselves. Khan remains resolute in his refusal to answer, but also in his unwillingness to acknowledge why people might be fearful, or why the thought, however far-fetched, that his design might be a shrine to the terrorists, is a notion many people would find unbearable. Burwell, for her part, refuses to demonstrate the "faith" that Khan demands of her (271). The end result of their interaction is a sense of betrayal and keen disappointment on both sides. Khan is wounded because people, and most particularly Burwell, refuse to unconditionally accept his place as one of their own. By repeatedly insisting that he make his intentions clear, Khan's questioners strengthen his resolve to do precisely the opposite. On her side, Burwell feels hurt because the architect neglects to acknowledge her pain, or recognize that her honoring of her dead husband's memory requires that she know exactly what his memorial seeks to "represent." In the end, Burwell concedes that she has no right to ask, but also admits that she *must* know.

THE OTHERNESS OF MOHAMMAD KHAN

Burwell's frustration with Khan is likely to mirror that of many a reader of *The Submission*. Waldman clearly opts for keeping readers in a state of irresolution similar to Burwell's, in which they remain unsure as to the true reasons for Khan's determined silence: rigorous principles or hidden motives. As Waldman tells an interviewer, "With [Khan] in particular I came to believe a certain amount of mystery was essential, because in a novel partly about trust, it allows, or forces, the reader to enact the central drama of the book—to decide if they do or don't trust [Khan], and why" (Lawless). Undergoing a similar experience to that of the grieving widow, the reader is likely to feel some empathic connection. At the same time, this positioning should cause readers to examine the nature of their own desires for uncovering his "mystery." With whom do they empathize and why? Are they really immune to the suspicions Burwell comes to harbor? In other words, the onus is placed on readers to question their own misgivings about Khan. For there is no question that Khan, despite being Muslim-American, is the other of the novel. This alone should give the reader pause. Just as the otherness of Arab and Muslim-Americans was heightened after 9/11, so too is the designer's. Waldman thus creates a scenario where ambivalence exists on both sides. The grieving community, full of suspicion and mistrust, cannot see Khan as anything other than a representative of that which seeks to do it harm. Khan, for his part, is unwilling to compromise even a little on his principles. At the same time, the text implies that the humiliations and provocations Khan endures would be justification enough for creating a memorial with hidden and subliminal messages. And having witnessed the designer's combativeness, it is certainly not inconceivable that the design was intended as a challenge to the supposed inclusivity of American society. The end of the novel suggests that Khan, despite his protestations, may not have been the indifferent Muslim he claimed to be. First, we are provided with a complementary version of an earlier episode recounted in the novel, which casts Khan's design in a different light. Second, the plot flashes forward twenty years, permitting the reader to assess the ramifications of the events recounted in the novel from a distanced perspective.

Mysteries surrounding Khan certainly deepen in the final pages leading up to the novel's epilogue. The text suddenly introduces, without preamble or transition, additional details concerning his visit to Kabul in early 2003, a few months after his design is selected. Although a description of this trip appears early in the novel (44–47), the moment is revisited, without explanation, providing a more intimate and internalized portrait of Khan's experiences in Afghanistan. The placement in the text of this unexpected flashback is likely to put the reader on alert as to its potential significance. The earlier passage described Khan's reactions to visiting a Muslim country and to other Westerners who treat him with barely veiled racism. Now we find Khan in a deep state of communion with the surrounding elements. Experiencing a moment of sheer vulnerability (submissiveness?)—he is shown being subjected to a severe bout of diarrhea, desperately searching for a place to relieve himself—he first glimpses the "patch of green" that is the Bagh-e Babur, the famous Babur Gardens of Kabul. Depressed at the physical state to which war has reduced the city, Khan is immediately drawn to the site: "The jumble on the hill broke abruptly at the garden's rear wall, which demarcated an entirely different landscape, one marked by symmetry, order, geometry" (279). The reader may think that she has read that sentence before; the evocation of the Babur Gardens strongly echoes the words used to describe Khan's own design early in the novel: "The concept was simple: a walled, rectangular garden guided by rigorous geometry" (4). The scene certainly suggests that commonalities and, more important, affinities exist between Khan's work and that of the Mogul creators of the garden in Kabul. One now recalls Khan's supplications to Lou Sarge—"It's just a garden"— and recognizes the extent to which this hid the designer's true feelings about his design. The passage also occurs immediately after Claire Burwell acknowledges that Khan "shouldn't have to say what the garden is, or where it came from" (277). Thus the novel not so subtly hints at the provenance, however indirect, of Khan's creation. For, after all, is it not possible that the Islamic aspects of the design were unconscious, just as the reasons for his other actions often remained a mystery to Khan himself.[6] The fact that he never mentions these experiences—not when asked about his trip to Afghanistan, nor when pressed to discuss any possible influences—raises suspicion as to their true significance. Receiving these revelations so late in the text, however, the reader is likely to infer these experiences play some part in the development of Khan's design.

The novel's epilogue only serves to add another layer to the "mystery" surrounding Mohammad Khan. The section begins with the architect once more demonstrating his intransigency. A Kuwaiti prince, for whom Khan has designed a palace, now wishes to add a grandiose lawn. The architect's response is revealing: "The landscaping isn't an accessory, it's part of the design, so you take all or none of it" (285). This is still the same Khan, twenty years later, unaltered by the memorial experience, sticking steadfastly to his aesthetic principles. In the meantime, he has become a "global citizen," American in name only, although the Museum of Modern Art offers a retrospective on his work entitled *Mohammad Khan, American Architect* (286). The relationship between Khan and the United States is irreparably strained. He does not attend the retrospective and feels compelled to emigrate from a place where "he had found himself reinvented by others" and move to a country—in this case, India—where "his name was not a liability" (292–93). The tenor of his recollections nevertheless suggests that some of these emotions continue to resonate and that he still sees himself as the victim of unjust treatment. These feelings, combined with an absence of anything resembling guilt or remorse, imply that that the design was never intended as a "victory garden" for jihadists. And the first part of the epilogue certainly paints Khan as a man more sinned against than sinning. The country that mistreated him has now moved forward, recognizing and freeing itself from the intolerant frenzy with which it was gripped in the aftermath of the attack: "Today most Americans thought as he had, but at the time his stand had been lonely" (287). In hindsight, the country should have accepted the design, and Khan's repeated assertions that it was intended to help in the healing process, at face value.

At the same time, the novel refuses to offer such obvious closure. Thinking of the MoMA retrospective Khan recalls a section entitled "Unbuilt," exhibiting his drawings and plans for the memorial, and the reader connects with the pain and frustration this remembrance no doubt causes the designer. What we soon discover, however, is that Khan has in point of fact built his memorial—only it is now significantly altered and has found a home in the garden of "some rich Muslim—a sultan or emir or something" in a Middle Eastern country (296). That a Muslim commissioned Khan to finally build the memorial to the attacks, albeit altered, on his land *and* that the designer agreed to such a "re-location" may give the reader pause. Is this an act of reconciliation, an exhibition of the tolerance Americans lacked, or does the garden actually speak to Muslims in some of the ways Khan's critics initially suspected? And once more, as with the first version of the memorial, the text will provide little to no insight into Khan's rationale for constructing this new iteration.

Interestingly, the reader experiences this discovery through the eyes of Claire Burwell, whose son has filmed the site while interviewing Khan for a documentary on the controversy surrounding his submission. Watching the video, Burwell is convinced that the new configuration is entirely of Khan's making, since she has experienced his intractability firsthand and knows he is unlikely to bend his vision to suit someone else's whims. His interaction with the Kuwaiti prince at the opening of the final section certainly reinforces this notion. And so, the original upended steel trees communicating the chaos and brutality of the attack remain. These symbols are surely not what the emir would have wanted, and reflect the designer staying true to his vision, Burwell thinks.[7] She is therefore shocked when the camera pans the walls of the garden, and she espies passages from the Koran now in the place where the names of victims would have been. Substituting verses for the names of the victims is such a "loaded" maneuver that it is difficult to imagine Khan not experiencing at least some hesitation, if only from an aesthetic perspective, before forging ahead. For although he is entirely within his rights to make such changes, the transmutation of the design nevertheless reveals an insensitivity and disregard for the totemic value of the names. Of course, it is possible that the verses selected are intended to perform a healing or conciliatory function, but what they actually say is not revealed. Burwell nevertheless responds to the erasure of the names with incredulity and dismay. That Burwell should react in this fashion is understandable. She experiences the palimpsest created in her mind's eye—the names written over and replaced with Arabic script—as an act of transgression.

Because names and naming play a significant role in *The Submission*. The novel's opening sentence reads: "The names," Claire said. "What about the names?" (3). And it ends with Burwell's son revealing to his mother how he has strategically placed pebbles inscribing his father's name at the foot of Khan's altered memorial in the Middle East. What also becomes clear is that the act of naming means something very different for Burwell and Khan. And their respective relationships with this gesture reveal the chasm currently lying at the heart of American society. For Burwell, naming serves to validate her husband's existence. Her privileged status, however, also ensures that her relationship with the names is an uncomplicated one. There is never any question about Calder Burwell finding his rightful place on the memorial. Khan's experiences after the attacks, on the other hand, guarantee that he cannot share Burwell's relationship with the act of naming. In fact, the gap separating widow and designer is made evident from their very first meeting, when Burwell exults about his design. Her declarations imbue Khan with more empathy than he may actually possess: "How did you know that a memorial that wasn't just bleak was exactly right for us, for who my husband was?" The question assumes the architect commanded an emotional connection with the victims *and* their grieving families. "I felt like you got inside my head," Burwell declares (112). But the narrative reveals that she is mistaken in these attributions. Khan, only half-listening to her, recognizes that the names "had become, for him, just another design element" (112). Of course, the names can never hold the same meaning for Khan as they do for Burwell. At the same time, this apparent lack of empathy tells us something about the relationship between the artist and his delicate subject.

At the same time, naming for Khan is an exercise fraught with potential perils and humiliations. After all, his own name has been the source of many of the troubles he faces. It is the sight of his name that first alarms the jurors on the selection panel, that gets him profiled at the airport, and that perhaps contributes to his being overlooked for promotion. The treatment he receives accentuates his otherness, robbing him of any illusions of belonging he might have entertained. On more than one occasion, for instance, the desire to erase his name is voiced. At one point, the chair of the selection committee suggests that perhaps the name of Khan's firm's might be used instead of his own, effectively rendering the designer invisible (63). And the people who protest against his submission worry that "Khan's name, and his paradise, would torment them" for the rest of their days (119). Finally, as we have noted, he claims to have left the United States so that he could live and work in a country "where the name Mohammad wouldn't be a liability" (292). For no matter how hard he tries, he possesses too many characteristics that set him apart from "us" and that identify him with "them." For example, Nadine Naber suggests that the treatment of Arabs and Muslim-Americans after 9/11 occurred "through the association between a wide range of signifiers such as particular names (e.g., Mohammed), dark skin, particular forms of dress (e.g., headscarf or a beard), and particular nations of origin (e.g., Iraq or Pakistan) as signifiers of an imagined 'Arab/Middle Eastern/Muslim' enemy" (278). That Mohammad Khan can be turned, seemingly overnight, into a racialized other, undermines the myth of a unified country. His "signifiers"—most specifically his name—guarantee his continued treatment as other, eventually causing him to flee the country. In this light, then, Khan's "erasure" of the names can be interpreted as an act of resistance, a form of commentary on the inequality embedded in the significance accorded to names and the ways they are used to perpetuate notions of otherness.

It is worth noting here that the problematics of naming (or not) and its role in the creation of otherness is further explored and solidified in one of the subplots of the novel, the story of Asma Anwar. Claire Burwell is not the only grieving widow in *The Submission*; Asma also loses her husband, Inam, on the morning of September 11. This is where the similarities end, however. Burwell is a wealthy woman who moves in the right circles, whose voice is heard loudly and often after the attacks. Asma, on the other hand, lives in the country illegally (like her husband), has little money, and no voice (though she eventually gets both, for a brief moment in her tragic life). Because when Inam, an undocumented worker at the World Trade Center, perishes that morning, for all intents and purposes, he vanishes from the face of the earth. This was the case, as noted earlier, for perhaps as many as one hundred individuals who lost their lives on 9/11. Since they did not have papers and were not listed in any ledgers, they had no rights. The same, of course, applied to their surviving relatives. While others have the value of their spouses measured in the millions of dollars, Asma cannot even get someone to admit that her husband existed, including his employer. Even in death, these individuals are denied the slightest modicum of equality, for to do so would be to legitimize their presence in the United States. Those in charge of the recovery process thus refuse to acknowledge the existence of such individuals: "The undocumented also had to be uncounted, officials insisted. The consulate could not abet illegals, even posthumously" (70). This proves an alienating experience for Asma, who blames herself for having convinced her husband to take a job at the World Trade Center. Instead of establishing themselves, of "moving higher" in American society, Inam's demise solidifies their invisibility: "How could you be dead if you did not exist?" Asma wonders (70). She assumes that certain democratic principles apply equally to all those who work hard. That Inam is to have no place on the memorial undermines such thinking. Such an act, Asma believes, "would be the final repudiation of his existence—as if he had lived only in her imagination. He had to be named, for in that name was a life" (77). But Inam is doubly unwelcome—first as a Muslim, and second as an illegal. In this case, the *not* naming serves as a deliberate and exclusionary tactic.

Because an accepted, and often unquestioned, premise of a memorial such as the one created in remembrance of 9/11 is that each death is of equal value. The supposed inclusivity of the memorial, its globalizing potential, is put into question by the experiences of Asma and her dead husband. After all, should all lives not be equally grievable? That exclusions were made, however, might cause us to question the rationale that guides the construction of such memorials. They should cause us, as Butler argues, "to ask about the conditions under which a grievable life is established and maintained, and through what logic of exclusion, what practice of effacement and denominalization" (38). Butler thus pushes the reader to consider the ways otherness is constructed and maintained, even as unity and brotherhood are being proclaimed. In the wake of the attacks, otherness became problematic. Ignited by the realization that terrorists had lived in their midst for months, and sometimes years, before carrying out their dreadful deed, Americans became hyper-conscious of a set of others, particularly Arab and Muslim others, whose presence now caused discomfort and suspicion. As smoke rose from the wounded site, images emerged of both the archetypal victim, and the archetypal perpetrator, of the attacks. The existence of people like Mohammad Khan and Asma Anwar should serve to problematize such archetypes. The fact that it does not, offers a telling commentary on the distance that still needs to be traveled before the country can attain those principles of tolerance and acceptance it so heartily professes to endorse.

CONCLUSION

Might we interpret the proposal to build an Islamic cultural center near Ground Zero as the expression of an unconscious desire to provoke debate or instigate dialogue? In other words, might the unspoken intention not be to force a response in order to gauge the extent to which the country has modified its attitudes towards its Muslim brethren. In the process, the absence or presence of the Islamic cultural center becomes commensurate with the absence of presence of inclusivity. In this vein, we might consider the parallels existing between this proposal and Khan's submission. Each of these requires that the nation stands by its principles. In an ideal world, of course, there would be no need for such things. The country and the city would accord each citizen equal status. The reality, however, is that the nation continues to struggle in its relations with its Arab and Muslim citizens. For at what point must statements declaring the value of diversity and acceptance of Arab and Muslim-Americans actually be put to the test? Should the United States not be held accountable for its pronouncements, and for the benevolent image it so steadfastly projects to the rest of the world? For although 9/11 is clearly a limit-situation, is it not precisely in such circumstances that the strength of one's convictions can truly be measured? Khan's submission demands a response. Just like the growing of his beard (on a lesser level) or his alteration of the memorial to incorporate Koranic verses (on a greater level), we should consider whether his submission is presented as a test of inclusivity which the country ultimately fails. Waldman observes that the end of the novel is, "about loss— the first, most devastating, which gave rise to the novel and the events in it; but also what was lost—or thrown away—by all of the characters in the wake of that initial loss. There's some redemption in the ending, but not a lot, and that has seemed the harder choice for some readers" (Lawless). In a way, one might say that the tragedy of the event is in the greater loss enacted in the shadow of the first loss (in this way, we might conclude, the terrorists accomplished part of their objective). *The Submission* alludes to the opportunities opened up by the event, and to those not taken. Waldman remains vague as to where the redemption occurs, but suffice to say that it is small in light of the manner in which the novel's plot ultimately unfolds. Creating a memorial to the victims of the attacks that contained

Islamic elements would have been an ideal way to demonstrate the country had not been swayed by the terrorists. It would also have indicated recognition of the common mortality and humanity shared with the majority of Muslims throughout the world. A similar argument was put forth during the Ground Zero mosque controversy—that allowing the construction of the Islamic center would lead to a greater sense of togetherness. Such an ideal, the novel makes clear, is not so easily reached. Instead of being the impetus for greater displays of empathy and inclusivity, as some had hoped, the events of 9/11 lead to stronger outbursts of mistrust and discrimination within the very city where the tragedy occurred.

NOTES

1. As the subject of these missives, Khan is astonished at the variety of information fabricated about him: "Facts were not found but made, and once made, alive, defying anyone to tell them from truth. Strangers analyzed, judged, and invented him. Mo read that he was Pakistani, Saudi, and Qatari, that he was not an American citizen; that he had donated to organizations backing terrorism" (126). As real-life counterpoints, one might recall the number of people who continued to believe, despite abundant evidence to the contrary, that Saddam Hussein was directly responsible for the 9/11 attacks or that Barack Obama was in fact Muslim.

2. This experience is not uncommon for those living the immigrant experience, as Steven Salaita observes: "Often accused of dual sympathies, Arab Americans feel sometimes as if they are removed (of their own accord) from the Middle East, but equally removed (not of their own accord) from the United States" (153).

3. Repeated insinuations, and sometimes assertions, are made throughout the novel that Khan is being deliberately deceitful. This is eventually interpreted as an Islamic trait when people at the press conference accuse him of committing Tagiya—the practice, sanctioned in the Koran, of lying about one's religious beliefs on those occasions when one faces possible persecution. References to Tagiya also occur in the *New Yorker* review (125), and in Asma's musings about demanding compensation from the American government (132).

4. Khan is in a constant state of vacillation, particularly when he is explicitly labeled as Muslim: "I know I should have thought about this before I agreed to the ad—but to be out there as a part of a MACC campaign identifies me so thoroughly as a Muslim when I've been arguing I shouldn't be defined as one. It looks like I'm trying to have it both ways." To which his girlfriend (and the lawyer representing him) observes, "Aren't you?" (174).

5. The same rationale was used in the vetting process for the 9/11 memorial and in the controversy surrounding the Ground Zero mosque. Any design that sought to problematize or question, or that failed to promote the notion of the United States as blameless victim, was unlikely to gain any traction. As Simpson observes, "No design that offered explicitly to trouble any of these besetting rhetorics would be likely to be approved; any challenge to the hegemonic language of good and evil will have to be covert and implicit" (78).

6. Khan's inability to recognize influences, or his unconscious use of them, is suggested during the Sarge interview (190), but also in the *New Yorker* review (125).

7. Earlier in the novel, Khan expresses feelings of personal instability and that this event has caused him to change constantly. Laila responds that he "underestimates [his] own solidity" and observes that he is in fact "intact . . . like [his] steel trees" (155).

Chapter Seven

Communal Trauma?

The Wounded City in Hunt and Lethem

In *The Rhetoric of Terror*, Marc Redfield emphasizes the intensely mediated nature of the catastrophe that was 9/11. The sheer audacity of the attack served to magnify heretofore untapped feelings of vulnerability which were then hyper-magnified by the protracted treatment of the media. Redfield argues, however, that not all people were equally traumatized and, in fact, that some were not traumatized at all: "For those who had the protection of distance, the September 11 attacks were not 'really' traumatic; they were a spectacle: a famously, infuriatingly cinematic spectacle" (2–3). Thus, he coins the term "virtual trauma" to designate the experience undergone by the majority, those not directly impacted by the events. Early on, Redfield defends the use of the term, contending that virtual is "not at all a synonym for insignificant or nonexistent" (3). And yet, later in his text he claims that September 11, by virtue of its virtuality, is "a kind of trauma without trauma" (30). In contrast, I would suggest that it was precisely the highly mediated nature of the event which guaranteed a collective impact on a great number of people (as the terrorists fully intended). And Redfield's analysis neglects the more diffuse, and less readily apparent, symptoms of trauma. We may not want to call it "trauma," in deference to those who suffered far worse fates, but the events of September 11 certainly exerted a palpable change in the fabric of American society. People were more fearful, anxious, and depressed in the ensuing weeks and months . . . and may still be more than a decade later.

In a recent issue of *PMLA*, Laura Tanner argues, in effect, that the manner in which most people were exposed to the event increased the likelihood of widespread trauma. Her position is grounded in the notion of the ever-increasing role screens play in our lives and the extent to which we live in a world where they "have been literally and theoretically incorporated into perception at the level of lived experience" (60). She suggests that critics such as Redfield, instead of giving credence to reports of individual trauma, resolutely interpret such expressions as products of a nationalist frenzy created in the aftermath of the attacks. Furthermore, these writers largely discount the possibility of communal trauma based on the notion of proximity, either in terms of being part of, or directly impacted by, the event. Those who merely watched it, they argue, experienced a significantly lesser form of upheaval. But what these approaches "fail to register," Tanner suggests, "is the increasingly complex ways we experience embodied subjectivity, as well as public life, through the mediation of screens" (59). The line separating lived from virtual experience has been blurred to the point that the experience of witnessing a real-time event on television may not differ significantly, on an affective level, from that of an eye-witness standing on the street below.[1]

In fact, we might stipulate that Redfield and Tanner dispute the extent to which the mediation impacted the event's effect on those who witnessed it at a remove. After all, mediation suggests that something has come between the spectator and the thing observed; by the time it reaches us, it has already been digested and filtered. While some of this is no doubt true for 9/11, we can also point to the fact that the rapidity with which events unfolded on that morning largely negated the possibility of such filtering:

> The twin towers were a world-building, appreciated within a world-culture. They were the scene of a world-event, presented within a drastic compression of time. Never before had the expression 'in real time,' used by mediaticians to signify simultaneity and synchrony, been more appropriate than on that day. (Andrieux and Seitz, 115)

As such, we might say that the event came to us mediated, but not. The television did not buffer the viewer from the shock, rather it exposed the viewer's vulnerability to that shock. For although brief, in contrast to other historical traumas, the minutes between the impact of the planes and the collapse of the buildings allowed for a stunned contemplation of that newly exposed vulnerability and what the future might hold.

But how does one gain a sense of the collective or cultural effects of a trauma? Aside from taking a measure of the number of people affected (and how broadly does one cast that net?), or surveying people asking them to self-report on their levels of fear and anxiety, what other means do we have at our disposal for assessing the impact of a disaster on a given community? When such events occur, Kai Erikson argues, we need to contemplate what he terms the "geography of disaster." In other words, the catastrophe plays itself out in and across actual space, sending shock waves throughout the affected area. As Erikson explains, "A map of the disaster would begin simply enough with an epicenter, a point in space called Ground Zero, but from there things spread outward almost endlessly" (353). Again, the impact of the disaster is most readily apparent at the site of impact, but less so as one attempts to decipher signs in the populace. This does not mean they are not there, as Erikson points out: "beyond that perimeter is a vast territory, stretching as far as the mind can see, where people nonetheless feel that they were witnesses *to*, victims *of*, even actors *in*" the event (354). Similarly, Trimarco and Depret observe that "Even if the sense of national trauma was constructed through media accounts and shaped by political agendas, this does not mean that people did not experience it, or make it any less real to people scattered throughout the United States who suffered anxiety, nightmares, and general fear" (36). Such arguments, of course, raise questions as to what one means by "community," and how broadly one wishes to establish the parameters of one's definition. It also invokes issues related to an "imagined community" and the extent to which individuals imagine themselves belonging to a clearly demarcated group or other. In this vein, for instance, therapist Karen Seeley stipulates that the event itself not only affected a great number of individuals, but that the mere act of witnessing of others being impacted, was in and of itself impactful:

> Contrary to conventional conceptualizations of mental disturbance as individually located and owned, the attack's psychological repercussions were shared both within and across communities and spread as if contagious. September 11 was a collective trauma not only in the sense that it damaged the bonds of community, but also in the sense that it was experienced communally. (275)

Seeley thus suggests that communal trauma emanated not simply from enduring the trauma as it occurred, or perceiving others being traumatized, but also through living in the aftermath of the events when the pain and suffering flowed throughout the community.

But again what evidence can be collected for making an argument for the existence of communal trauma? Beyond self-reports of trauma, one should uncover and examine physical manifestations or signs that reveal the network of suffering to which Seeley alludes. One potential avenue for exploration is to look at the ways we speak and write about the city and its buildings in the aftermath of the attacks. The quality of these interactions surely tells us something about how the trauma is lived and experienced as people struggle to come to terms with both an altered landscape and a transfigured conception of the city. I contend that the communal aspects of the event were heightened by the "relationship" people had with the structures chosen for destruction, both before and after the attacks. Similarly to Tanner, then, I point to an aspect of the trauma's manifestation that has not been sufficiently considered. Just as our relationship to screens opens up other possibilities for being negatively affected by the event, so too, I argue, do our connections to surrounding buildings (and the attributions we confer upon them). September 11 was thus also traumatic due to the affiliations (real and imagined) people fostered with the landscape, and the city within which these structures existed. As many others have noted, the targets selected for destruction on 9/11 were chosen primarily for their symbolic value. The thousands of deaths were incredibly tragic and painful but they were also, in some ways, collateral damage, serving to make the terror real for those who survived. The primary intent of the attacks was to demonstrate U.S. vulnerability by boldly destroying architectural icons constructed to trumpet precisely the opposite (that is, economic and military might).

In *The World Trade Center: A Monumental Target*, Andrieux and Seitz point out that one of the assumptions upended on that autumn morning was the inviolability and permanence of iconic structures or landmarks (and, by extension, some version of one's own inviolability and permanence, if only through the existence of these structures). The mortality of the city, and its potential extinction, were made apparent. Additionally, attacking and destroying structures that were symbolic in the first place guaranteed the action would acquire a deadly symbolism of its own. Similar motivations guided the actions of the Taliban in March 2001, when it undertook to demolish the Bamiyan Buddhas in Afghanistan.[2] Of course, the attacks on the Twin Towers and the demolition of the Buddhas were very different events in significant ways: no one died in Afghanistan, the Taliban repeatedly announced the imminent destruction of the statues, and their surroundings differed considerably, one existing in a rural valley, the other in a thriving metropolis. Similarities emerge, however, when we consider the motivations behind these acts. Most of all, of course, they were carried out for their symbolic value. And the structures themselves were also, quite notably, two sets of twins, with one shorter than the other. The World Trade Center and the Buddhas were both perceived as impurities to be washed away; physical insults to the True Word. And much like the Buddhas, the Towers seemed to grow in significance with their destruction.[3] Writing of the statues, Charles Freund observes, "There's nothing like a staged spectacle of barbaric destruction to transform otherwise obscure artifacts." While no one would have characterized the Twin Towers as "obscure," there is no question that since their construction they had been regarded by many as faceless, bland buildings, with little to no redeeming value.

All of that changed at 10:28 AM on September 11, 2001. From the moment they no longer existed, attachment to the Towers began to grow. And I want to suggest that this sympathetic bonding is due in no small part to our capacity to empathize with a building, a landscape, or even a city. We display affective responses to the (urban) landscape, but also, it stands to reason, changes to that landscape. For although these are inanimate objects, it is possible to feel for them, to care for them (beyond what they might mean to someone's sense of self), and that the more someone experiences such feelings, the greater the likelihood of being traumatized by their destruction or sudden alteration. As Judith Greenberg observes, "We relate to objects even before we have a concept of identity; we ground ourselves in space. A profound dislocation is created when part of our landscape is missing" (25). As Greenberg suggests, one's sense of identity is inextricably linked to the space within which one moves, so that the obliteration of salient parts of this environment is bound to have a direct and personal impact. So we might also think about the city having been altered by trauma, so that New York is also a victim worthy of empathy.

And it stands to reason that in identifying ourselves with certain buildings (or simply feeling that connection), we cannot but humanize them in some way. Indeed, the desire to personify the Towers was made evident within hours of their collapse. There were any number of missing posters or postcards dedicated to the Towers themselves, referring to them in human terms, such as the "handsome twins," among other things.[4] And it is precisely such imaginings that lead to stronger feelings *for*, and identification *with*, the buildings. In many ways, anthropomorphism is an act of empathy, or an effort to find those points of sameness that link (my)self with the other. For though I remain fully aware that these objects are inanimate, they have such a presence in my life that I cannot help but imbue them with human characteristics. One strong indication of this affective attachment to architecture is the extent to which the discourse of September 11 readily embraces the anthropomorphizing of these structures.

Such a gesture is present, for instance, in Mark Wigley's "Insecurity by Design," which begins with the following description: "A very tall building absorbs a plane and collapses after 105 defiant minutes, having watched its twin suffer the same fate" (69). Personification is readily apparent here, with the North Tower observing, and empathizing with, its sibling's plight before finally succumbing to its own wounds. And, in fact, a number of writers, including Wigley, have argued that an emotional connection to the buildings was augmented by the twinning of the towers. Terry Smith, for his part, contends that the doubling of the buildings actually served to humanize the structures and soften much of the criticism elicited by their construction: "Indeed, to some, the pairing of the buildings raised warm and fuzzy feelings toward their coupling, twinning, sharing—senses that permitted human identification with them. For some architects and critics, the two towers seemed to mitigate the shortcomings that would have been condemned in a single building of this design" (119). Smith thus suggests that the "twinning" of the structures actually served to counteract their minimalist coldness, and thus permitted empathic connections that might not otherwise have occurred.[5]

These feelings were further complemented and amplified by the sheer magnitude of the Towers and their pronounced daily presence, practically guaranteeing their eventual incorporation into a citizen's sense of self or identity. Hence, as Wigley suggests, we may experience the destruction of a familiar edifice in the manner of a bodily wound:

> to lose a building is to lose not simply an object that you have been living in or looking at but an object that has been watching over you. And when our witnesses disappear, something of the reality of our life goes with them. People are really grieving for themselves when they grieve for buildings. (71)

Wigley's contention that "something of our life goes with them," is open to interpretation, but it seems to suggest that while something of the old reality remains, a new one has also been created. There was the reality embodied by the presence of the Towers, and now there is the reality embodied in their absence. Wigley also reveals an awareness of his own anthropomorphizing propensity, and that of others, when he observes that the towers are repeatedly,

> described with the same terms used for suffering people . . . In all the improvised memorials and media coverage, images of the towers' faces share the same space as images of the victims' faces. The buildings became victims, and in so doing victimize those who watch them suffer. (72)

So both people and buildings were victimized, and this conflation to which Wigley alludes suggests that any understanding of the event will require an apprehension of the Towers as victims and the city as a traumatized other.

Perhaps most significant, then, was the extent to which the event altered what Manhattan represented and its subsequent impact on those people who identified themselves as New Yorkers (one might extrapolate further to those who saw Manhattan as quintessentially American, and the degree to which the event thus affected them directly as Americans). Of course, when a particular structure is also laden with symbolic significance, its destruction serves as a commentary on all those for whom it served as a symbol. In this regard, Neil Leach puts forth a proposition similar to Wigley's. Uniting Lacanian theories of identity-formation and Christian Metz's analysis of the cinematic viewer, he suggests that a kind of "mirroring" occurs between the observer and the building upon which he or she gazes. Leach identifies "a twofold mechanism of grafting symbolic meaning onto an object and then reading oneself into that object, and finally seeing one's values reflected in it. The environment must therefore serve as a kind of 'screen' onto which we would 'project' our own meaning, and into which we would 'read' ourselves" (174). Following this line of thinking, the violence perpetuated against the World Trade Center (and thus the city) becomes violence perpetuated against the selves of its citizenry. This link between human bodies and the city's "body" is perhaps nowhere better reflected than in the frequent use of the word "wound" to describe the condition of Lower Manhattan, and Ground Zero specifically, after the attacks. Its usage necessarily implies the existence of a body—a living organism—upon which harm has been inflicted.[6] Using anthropomorphic language, for instance, David Harvey diminishes the severity of the attacks, thinking of the wound itself as "relatively trivial," as no more than the "metaphorical equivalent of a broken bone" (37). But it is not simply that Manhattan now bears a visible scar, a product and reminder of the violence perpetuated against it, but that something is now tangibly *missing*, with the scar serving as a manifest reminder of that absence. As such, a more apt "metaphorical equivalent," I would suggest, is one that likens the destruction of the towers to *the loss of a limb*. Indeed, we might consider whether New York was not suffering (and may be still) from a version of phantom limb pain, perhaps best symbolized by *The Tribute in Light* used in commemoration, but also by the preserved footprints of the Twin Towers which serve as focal points in the current memorial. Each of these memorializing gestures suggest that people remain aware of the empty spaces once filled by the Towers, and that these spaces at the tip of the island are still invested with a negative energy. The concept of phantom limb pain is thus entirely appropriate here since it helps us understand the ways in which absence can be most painful in its very presence.

As noted, a unique aspect of this tragedy was the rapidity with which these imposing, and seemingly inviolable, structures were present one moment and entirely absent the next. As Sturken observes, this raises "the question of materiality. How could those buildings, those objects—those people—suddenly be gone?" (312). This psychic shock creates warring impulses in which a strong desire to restore their presence runs up against the need to acknowledge their absence. These restorative impulses are also readily apparent in a variety of works which imaginatively seek to invoke the Towers while mourning their disappearance. Perhaps the earliest example is the cover of the *New Yorker* from September 24, 2001, drawn by Art Spiegelman, which offers the viewer a darkened page on which the figures of the towers are faintly visible. The image is reprised for Spiegelman's *In the Shadow of No Towers*, whose title also reflects the notion of presence through absence. Indeed, the graphic memoir attests repeatedly to the phantom presence of the buildings long after their destruction. And certainly, it is the destruction of the towers that traumatizes Spiegelman, the text reading as an attempt to memorialize (immortalize?) them. The final panel of the memoir shows the Towers restored through the physical manipulation of the images on the page.[7]

The emphasis placed on recovering the physical immanence of these structures does seem to imply a greater connection or empathy with the buildings themselves than with those who perished within their walls. As Marita Sturken observes, the *Tribute in Light* "was intended to pay tribute to the dead. But one could not help feeling that it was really the loss of the towers that the light memorial mourned" (319). Sturken's comment reveals an ongoing relationship people had with these buildings, one strengthened by their untimely, and thoroughly unexpected, demise. These examples all suggest that the absence of the towers still exerts a powerful force on many while resisting any easy incorporation within a narrative structure. In this vein, Claire Kahane contends the event forced "us to acknowledge the reality of disintegration and annihilation through the very materiality of the ash and the debris raining down on Lower Manhattan and, more uncannily, through the *absence* that it left behind, the sheer space a powerful reminder of the event" (110). Absence thus becomes a fundamental part of the event—the absence of towering buildings that had become integral to the landscape, the absence of survivors to tell their tales, and the absence of corporeal selves to mourn. Similarly, in her study on what she terms "traumascapes," Maria Tumarkin envisages modern ruins as

> counterparts of the dead. They are shreds and fragments of dead matter, material culture violated and left to rot. Just like the dead, ruins lure and repel in equal measure. While the dead cannot be fully cast away from our minds, ruins too are an inescapable presence in our public spaces. (173)

This "inescapable presence" continues to manifest its hold on the populace. For Tumarkin, these traumascapes "emerge as spaces, where events are experienced and re-experienced across time. Full of visual and sensory triggers, capable of eliciting a whole palette of emotions, traumascapes catalyse and shape remembering and reliving of traumatic events" (12). In such spaces, as Tumarkin intimates, the line between past and present is blurred. The past exerts its own power, in part through an absence that weighs the present down. In these conditions, one is prevented from living solely in the present, constantly forced to remember the past and, consequently, the fragility of the present within which one lives. So that the witnessing of the event, and the experiencing of its aftermath leaves, as Christine Muller calls it, "a residue of unresolved unsettlement" (48). After all, if one's past can be eradicated, turned to rubble, is there much hope that one's present will exert any greater degree of permanence?

This sense of a twin reality, of living parallel lives, was drastically heightened in the aftermath of the attacks and in the ensuing months. In fact, one might argue that the prolonged dispute about what should ultimately stand or not stand at Ground Zero is in fact a debate as to which of two realities should be given prominence at the site. Should it be a memorial that invariably recalls the death and disaster that took place at the site, a firm foothold in the past? Or should it be shining new towers and buildings reflecting the city's resilience and its abilities to continue as the economic powerhouse everyone wants to be, a clear gesture to the future? Can it be both things simultaneously and what would be the effects of such a bifurcated approach? A reading of fiction that accounts for New York as a traumatized entity in its own right and, by extension, of all those for whom the city and its buildings possess some symbolic and/or affective value, will perhaps offer new ways of considering the traumatic impact of terrorist attacks (and other violent incursions) on vulnerable populations. And fiction that expands its focus from individual trauma and pain to incorporate a metropolitan outlook may also avoid some of the pitfalls outlined in much of the criticism dealing with post-9/11 fiction. In order to illustrate this point, I will briefly examine two recent critiques before turning my attention to a couple of novels that offer a perspective on a new Manhattan.

RECUPERATIVE STRATEGIES AND IMAGINATIVE STRUCTURES

In *After the Fall*, Richard Gray argues that most fiction has been essentially incapable of communicating our post-9/11 condition, of representing the "unresolved unsettlement" to which Muller alludes. As a result, Gray pleads for an "enactment of difference" which is "not only the capacity to recognize that some kind of alteration of imaginative structures is required to register the contemporary crisis, to offer testimony to the trauma of 9/11 and its consequences, but also the ability and willingness imaginatively to act on that recognition" (29–30). The problem, as he sees it, is that most of the fictional works concerned with the events of September 2001, "simply assimilate the unfamiliar into familiar structures" (30). A second critique arises in a review of a recent exhibition of photographs in commemoration of the tenth anniversary of the attacks. Edward Rothstein notes the evocation of "almost private sensations" which leads him to wonder whether "these impulses have just metastasized and that, given strength by the events of the last decade, they prevent us from daring to commemorate and comprehend rather than simply remember." Rothstein expresses some surprise that these planned events communicate "that Sept. 11 [is] still something to be remembered rather than interpreted, still an event that could only be invoked as a series of traumatic memories, not a historical event to be understood and put into context. . . . The private details of grief still overwhelm any sense of public meaning" (Rothstein).

In different ways, then, these writers both bemoan the lack of a larger context within which to frame these events. Gray urges the creation of "imaginative structures," seeking new forms to contain the trauma. Rothstein contends that the focus has rested solely on individual pain and needs to be broadened to access the more "public" resonances and meanings of the event. Taking a cue from these critiques one might seek texts that provide unfamiliar structures, or treat 9/11 in an unanticipated way. As Jenny Edkins observes, linear narratives that seek to re-inscribe trauma often fall short. An alternative, she suggests is "that of encircling the trauma. We cannot try to address the trauma directly without risking gentrification. We cannot remember it as something that took place in time, because this would neutralise it" (Edkins 15). As we shall see, one such narratological strategy approaches the event through indirection, thus allowing the text to communicate some of the more diffuse aspects of the trauma referred to earlier. In terms of Rothstein's demand for "public meaning," a fruitful line of inquiry would focus on fictions situated in New York, but whose subject is not specifically 9/11. An examination of the manner(s) in which these novels tangentially incorporate, or allude to, the event in the narrative is bound to offer some insight into the lingering effects of the event on the community.

Indeed, the attacks of September 11 came as such a shock and surprise that many people questioned their previous assumptions about the reality of their existence. As E. Ann Kaplan observes, "The events radically altered my relationship to New York, to the United States qua nation, and produced a new personal identity" (2). And like Kaplan, many wondered whether they actually knew the world in which they were living. This sense of being betrayed by appearances was perhaps most sharply felt in those expressions of incredulity related to the weather that Tuesday morning in September, almost as though this bluest of skies had conspired with the hijackers in order to provide the greatest possible element of surprise (as we shall see, weather plays a significant role in Lethem's novel). This led numerous people to proclaim that the attacks had come "out of the blue."[8] Was there, in fact, an alternate reality in which this event actually made more sense? Was the New York they thought they knew merely an illusion, or was there, in fact, another New York revealed by the attacks? Kaplan suggests that her

> immediate physical world had changed dramatically with the disappearance of the Twin Towers from my daily visual landscape at the end of Broadway and their reduction to a mountain of smoking wreckage sending acrid air into our apartment. My relation to the public sphere was also changed since New York City, and the United States as a nation, both were destabilized as concepts. (2–3)

One might wonder about the degree to which a sense of a double New York emerges in the wake of the attacks, with a traumatized New York on one side and a (seemingly) untouched New York on the other. Did an over-emphasis on recovery and resilience, on emphatically creating the perception that the city was not brought to its knees by the attacks, lead to a kind of collective schizophrenia?

The unexpected collapse of the Twin Towers creates an uneasy commingling of warring impulses, revealed in the tensions raised in attempting to maintain a diametric approach—one in which the dead are honored and given their due, but which also seeks to forego any indication of weakness, proclaiming survival and unwavering resolve. David Simpson identifies these impulses as "the upward and downward components of the site as a whole" which transforms Ground Zero into "part grave site and memorial and part commercial and civic morale-booster" (71). The event led to a twinning of responses, wherein each was equally acceptable, or equally unacceptable. Simpson, for instance, identifies the paradoxes apparent both in Daniel Libeskind's rhetoric about the rebuilding of the World Trade Center and in the criteria set forth for the creation of the memorial:

> There was the same tension between commemoration and celebration, the same bizarre insistence that the disaster and its implications are at once global and specifically national ("American" values are also "universal"), the same demand that remembering the dead be conjoined with the evocation of an upbeat future. (75)

As Simpson implies, a desire to accomplish seemingly opposed objectives created a kind of liminal zone wherein people remained unclear as to the best way to proceed. Could one still be strong while acknowledging vulnerability? Could one honor the dead while advocating for the restoration of capital pursuits on what some now considered sacred ground? Could one consider oneself a liberal, progressive person while harboring doubts and suspicions about the swarthy individual seated two rows back in the airplane?

It is within this discordant complex of discordant and entangled ideas and practices that the residents of Manhattan continue to live in the wake of the disaster. Trimarco and Depret suggest an analogous dynamic when they question the use of the "graveyard" trope in reference to Ground Zero. A more appropriate one, they contend, is the graveyard versus the carnival, in which each one is "entirely unable to exist without the other" (39). The site is thus neither one thing nor the other, but both, with citizens existing in a kind of post-traumatic limbo. Metaphorically, as we shall see, this leads to the contemplation of the existence of one or more New Yorks. One might say that the attacks turned the city into an "other" for many of its citizens. It was no longer the permanent, impervious structure on which they could rely. Rather it was just as vulnerable as they and, as such, now something somewhat strange to them. This strangeness was compounded by the fact that the city no longer physically resembled itself.

Gray suggests that the events are made more bearable through their assimilation within familiar structures. In other words, the unfamiliarity is tamed through the use of recognizable forms. He is so invested in highlighting the uniqueness of the event (and the corresponding need for a unique form of representation) that he fails to recognize the power of the uncanny, of inserting the unfamiliar firmly within the familiar, an aspect that made the events of September 11, 2001, we might argue, truly terrifying. Gray's critique of post-9/11 fiction also depends too heavily on the unfamiliarity of the event, and fails to recognize those aspects that made it all too familiar to New Yorkers (and others). The most obvious example is that similar scenarios had been presented/imagined in any number of Hollywood films and, as such, the traumatized spectators (both eye-witnesses and television viewers) experienced a powerful and eerie sense of *déjà vu*. So that these spectators might be said to be startled but not, shocked but not, since there was something dreadfully recognizable about the terror being perpetuated before their eyes. A more accurate fictional representation, then, would account for the defamiliarization and instability caused by the event, presenting a structure that offered the reader the usual and unusual, the known and unknown, in uneasy balance.

As such, we might look to a strain of post-9/11 fiction that elects not to address the tragedy head-on, but rather seeks meaning through indirection and allusion. Such an approach allows the novelist to illuminate the ways in which the event has now been incorporated or contextualized but also, conversely, repressed or compartmentalized. In other words, in reading these novels, particular attention might be paid to the types of tensions raised through specific references, allusions, parallel constructions, or even obvious circumvention, of the event when the plots of these novels are not specifically about 9/11 (at least on the surface). Might we look at the ways the event is incorporated into a narrative and what the manner of incorporation tells us about how we are coping, recovering, and adjusting to that event? At the same time, an attempt should also be made to examine the ways in which the event resists incorporation. As we shall see, the New Yorks depicted in both Laird Hunt's *The Exquisite* and Jonathan Lethem's *Chronic City* are entirely recognizable, yet infused with unfamiliar elements that serve to destabilize the reader. This instability and defamiliarization might be said to replicate or mirror that felt by the citizens of Manhattan whose environment remains remarkably unchanged on the one hand, and irrevocably so on the other.[9] Each novel addresses the uncanny through a consideration of these twin, or alternate, realities. Through the use of literary and metaphorical devices, they also intimate the after-effects of the trauma, and the lingering impact on the quality of the lives of those living in the shadow of no towers. An uneasiness, a sense that both life and the city have been made uncanny, is communicated through their depictions of Manhattans that are, but are not, the city with which everyone is acquainted.

THE DOUBLENESS OF TRAUMA: *THE EXQUISITE*

Laird Hunt's *The Exquisite* takes the idea of doubleness probably as far as it can go. Not only does it present a double plot, with characters assuming twin roles, it self-consciously raises the possibility of two New Yorks. Furthermore, the city is presented as an entity of many different guises. On the second page of the novel, for instance, New York is referred to as "a city of subtle simulacra, of deceptive surfaces, of glib and phantom shimmerings" (2).[10] Through its emphasis on doubleness, and its use of both direct and indirect allusions to September 11, the novel creates a world in which both protagonist and reader experience a good deal of instability and unsettlement. The novel offers two alternating narratives, that may or may not have any connection with each other. In the first, the protagonist, Henry, makes the acquaintance of Aris Kindt and becomes involved with some questionable people, including a tattooed beauty named Tulip. In the second, Henry is hospitalized (perhaps from injuries suffered when he was hit by a flower truck, or perhaps for emotional and mental issues, or perhaps for both). There he is cared for by a Dr. Tulp, and visited by Mr. Kindt (the same one?), who may also be hospitalized. The reader, much like Henry, is unsure as to which of these narratives is real (or if either entirely is). And questions of authenticity, as well as those concerned with the validity of individual perception, are sprinkled throughout the novel. This destabilizing gesture is further compounded by the fact that the reader experiences these dual realities filtered through Henry's troubled and unreliable psyche.

How Henry arrived at this particular juncture is never entirely clear, and the degree to which he is responsible for his current predicament is equally vague. Did his disinterest in his girlfriend's passions (French poetry, fashion) cause her to leave him? Did he in fact beat up a restaurant owner who refused to hire him? Did he abandon his aunt during a health crisis, leaving her to die alone? And, finally, did he murder Mr. Kindt? These events occur prior to, during, and after the unnamed disaster downtown. By leaving it so unnamed, the text relies on the reader supplying his or her own post-9/11 anxieties to the atmosphere of dread that pervades *The Exquisite*. We are also left to wonder as to the impact this event may have had on Henry himself. Some reviewers are unequivocal in suggesting a direct connection between the attacks and Henry's present "condition." Matthew Tiffany observes, for instance, that "the narrative unfolds in such a way as to leave questions in the reader's mind as to what role that day might have played, unwritten, in Henry's life" (Tiffany). And although such an event is never actually mentioned in the text, another sees the collapse of the towers as "the catalyst for Henry's descent into homelessness and fractured self" (Jewell). The text, however, deliberately obscures such easy connections, and it is more likely that the tragedy in Lower Manhattan merely exacerbates Henry's already fragile constitution. His homelessness appears to predate the events of September 2001, but they further weaken his tenuous hold on reality and increase his sense of living in an unsure world. And a good deal of what Henry relates (his relationship, the troubles with his dentist, accumulating debt and avoidance of collectors) suggest a degree of personal instability. So we might consider the ways in which the external world has come to mirror the internal one. The events had some impact on all, but the severity depended on the individual, as Henry's case illuminates.

The ongoing presence of that horror and its infiltration into the psyches of the populace is suggested in a number of indirect, and not-so-indirect, allusions to September 11 sprinkled throughout *The Exquisite*. Henry makes explicit reference to "the gaping hole" (17), "the horror downtown" (76), and "the steaming ruins" (153), but never specifically mentions a date, terrorism, or the World Trade Center. Nevertheless, thoughts of the tragedy are never very far from the surface—and they burst forth in the novel, often when least expected. That so little needs to be said in order for the reader to make connections with 9/11 also reveals the extent to which the mere evocation of New York City, and Lower Manhattan especially, still connects to a network of associations in the reader's mind between the city and the tragedy of terror. References to the "horror" are always made in passing, and Henry never lingers to ponder the meaning(s) of the event. The degree of repression exhibited by Henry and others—the willful refusal to openly contemplate the event's significance—signals to the reader the extent to which the occurrence still wields a powerful and emotional force over the populace. Early in the novel, for instance, while viewing anatomical sketches of an arm, Henry offhandedly observes that "I thought first of Manhattan and the deep hole that had been punched in it" (12). There appears to be no ostensible reason for Henry to have that particular thought. A little later, attempting to remember an early moment in his homelessness, Henry returns to the image of a damaged arm. He recalls that it was during a time when "the gaping hole—in what I heard someone standing outside St. Mark's Church call 'the arm of the city'—was still horrifyingly fresh, and the air was still stinging everyone's eyes, and you saw people going around like death's heads with their goggles and respirators on" (17).

Aside from the anthropomorphic quality of these imaginings (something to which I shall return), the text thus communicates the uncanniness of the event, primarily through its unannounced intrusions and eruptions. At one point, for instance, Henry wanders the streets of the East Village, and suddenly notes, *à propos* of nothing at all, "and you stop for a time and think about verticality, then compromised verticality, then rubble, about steaming ruins, about vanished buildings" (152–53). Again, no explanation is offered, but the reader is not really in need of one. A number of such references are slyly inserted in the text, revealing the prevalence of thoughts of death, decay, and destruction in the wake of the "events downtown." And so the action of the novel unfolds, punctuated occasionally by an allusion to the disaster, assuring, in part, that its presence is never far from the reader's mind. During the chapters concerned with Henry's hospitalization, for instance, he is visited by the apparition of his dead aunt. When he asks her why she has come, she replies with a question of her own, "You know anything about these buildings falling down?" (96). Her question, though irrelevant, does illuminate Henry's unconscious thoughts—his own feelings of instability, anxiety, and doubt. But they also serve to create an atmosphere of dread within the text, something of which Henry is only dimly aware. It is as though the characters seek not to think about the events, or at least not accord them any importance, but the existence of the ruins still manages to intrude, in large part precisely because they have become part of the collective psyche of the city. Repressing thoughts or any contemplation of the "horror downtown," however, is also a part and parcel of a more generalized denial of vulnerability and mortality. Such efforts to repress are usually rewarded, as Freud tells us, with unexpected eruptions and visitations. This is best exemplified in the text in Henry's vision of two New Yorks.

TWO NEW YORKS

A little more than halfway through the novel, an entire chapter is devoted to Henry's theory of two New Yorks. The first New York is the one of the everyday jostling and negotiating with the rest of the humanity on the island. It is the New York that "smacks you in the face and maybe you laugh a little and people walk down the street and trucks blow their horns and you are happy or maybe you are not, but your heart is beating" (152). There is a sense of life and vitality in Henry's descriptions of the first New York. It is the New York with which the reader is readily familiar. The second New York is the one that troubles, making its presence felt during moments of trauma. What *The Exquisite* underlines, however, is that this vision is not a product of catastrophe, but rather that its existence is made visible during and after cataclysmic events. It is the city's dark and deathly double, whose presence is suspected, perhaps intuited, but only rarely confirmed. Henry's first glimpse of New York's "other" occurs immediately after he has been struck by the flower truck. He sees it flitting across a puddle on the street: "and you were on your hands and knees leaning over and there it was, or there you were, in those vast lands of the other city, the other New York, pale and scary, but not for long" (154). Henry's vision of the vibrant city's other serves as a symbol of the disintegration and decay inherent in the life of any metropolis. Parts of the organism that is the city are always bound to fall into disrepair, from a sidewalk to whole neighborhoods. Often these indicators draw little attention since they are an accepted part of the continual evolution of the city. The disaster downtown, however, highlights the tenuous existence of structures thought of as permanent. Henry's knowledge of the second New York mirrors the awareness of permeability, vulnerability, and mortality brutally foisted on the populace of Manhattan on the morning of September 11.

However, the city, as *The Exquisite* makes clear, is not just structures, it is also people. After a brutal altercation, in which he is beaten to within an inch of his life, Henry once again catches sight of the other city:

> You said to yourself, o.k. fine, all right, that's it, good-bye now, time to vanish, let's cruise. And you did. You left and wandered both alone and in company, walked arm in arm with yourself and with a couple million others, up and down the windy, gleaming streets of the necropolis, New York number two. (154)

The vision of the necropolis stands in sharp contrast to its vital counterpart, touching on the carnival/graveyard juxtaposition to which Trimarco and Depret refer. Any reference to burial grounds is naturally going to elicit in the mind of the reader connections with Ground Zero. As Andreas Huyssen observes, "A whole part of Manhattan had been turned into a cemetery, but a cemetery without identifiable bodies and without graves—a death zone" (158). The image of a "death zone" gives some idea of the thoughts that were percolating through the minds of many of the inhabitants of the traumatized city. The dead of 9/11, however, are only the most recently arrived in the second New York, so that Henry glimpses "a couple million others" residing in the necropolis. In normal circumstances, the dead exist behind a veil, obscured by the first New York, only emerging in moments of trauma. 9/11 is different, however. As the text's allusions to the event suggest, the awareness of the "horror" is so strong, maintained through a variety of reminders, that a consciousness of the second New York remains a near constant for the citizens of the city. This is certainly true for the hospitalized Henry: "Little windows that opened onto this New York number two were of course omnipresent on the ward" (154). Since the hospital is situated near the site and dump trucks are constantly driving by on their way to the novel's version of the Fresh Kills Landfill, the patients of the hospital are continually reminded of the disaster: "Always there were the sirens coming or going and the sound of sledgehammers and saws and earthmovers in the distance where they were removing rubble" (82).

The necessarily prolonged exercise of reconstruction meant that there was no way to move on quickly from this event. For although the cleanup was carried out in a very efficacious and rapid manner, the process could not be anything but too slow, especially for Americans who generally would rather not contemplate the past. The debate about what actually should be built, or not built, at Ground Zero served to decelerate the impetus to fill in the gaping hole in Lower Manhattan and any attempt to sublimate, if not erase, the memory of the trauma and the revelation of new found vulnerability. The living are thus reminded that they share the city with dead, whose presence is felt more or less strongly at various periods. In the aftermath of 9/11, the dead exert a stronger immanence, particularly because many remains are still unrecovered and are likely to forever be a part of the site, because of the ash that floated over and covered the city in the weeks after the catastrophe, and because of the remains that continue to be discovered more than a decade after the event—on a bank roof, in a manhole. And the ruins that continued to smoke weeks after the event, combined with an uncanny and unidentifiable smell, created a sense of permeation as the ash floated endlessly down upon the city. Certainly the idea that one has ingested the dead is an uncanny feeling. That parts of another, however microscopic, may now be containted with one's own organism, is a troubling and unsettling thought.

The coexistence of these cities is strengthened when Mr. Kindt, listening to Henry's theory, infers the existence of sixteen million versions of the city. Henry corrects him, stating that there are only two New Yorks which everybody shares:

The one contains the other, I said.

The larger the smaller, or is it the other way around?

I don't know.

It is nevertheless a lovely notion, he said. All cities must be wrapped in a doubling embrace.

And all people, I said.

Yes, Henry, of course, we are all of us wrapped in the darkened shadow of our afterselves. (156)

The language in the passage is appropriately vague; one is left to interpret what Kindt means by "wrapped in a doubling embrace," though it does suggest the city always exists in the presence of its uncanny other—a vision of its ruined self that remains an ever-constant possibility. That Kindt reuses the word "wrapped" in reference to our "afterselves" points to a connection between cities and people, particularly in respect to a foreknowledge of extinction brought on by moments of trauma—as Henry's experiences make clear. It is in those moments of physical duress or danger, when one shuttles between life and death, or wherein the tenuousness and fragility of existence is made painfully clear, that the existence of the second New York comes most vividly into view.

RITUAL NEGATION

It is only natural to expect that people would seek some way to relieve or at least attenuate this overbearing knowledge. In *The Exquisite* this finds metaphorical expression in a mock-murder service in which Henry is enlisted by Mr. Kindt and a mysterious associate, Cornelius. The service allows citizens to experience the circumstances of their own murders without actually dying. These acts of terrorism, the text implies, have aroused a particular set of impulses in the survivors still living in the wounded city. Cornelius introduces Henry to the idea, noting that "There is a real need, it would seem, a deep seated impulse following the horror downtown. An impulse that manifests as desire" (76). When Henry questions whether "desire" is actually the right word, Cornelius replies, "We offer the modalities to perform an act of ritual negation. One is able, on one's own terms, to say no" (76). The text thus suggests that people feel so destabilized in the wake of the events, so shaken by the fact of not knowing when the next attack might come, that they are willing to take part in the staging of their own (fake) murders in order to experience some modicum of control.

For his part, and despite assurances from Mr. Kindt, Henry harbors doubts as to the ethical legitimacy of such an enterprise: "It seems like a pretty questionable gimmick . . . I mean, do they have people who actually want to pay to have that done to them?" To which Tulip replies, "It's the times . . It's in the air. Gloom and doom. New York-style. Aris says it falls under the rubric of the *danse macabre*" (127). In other words, the events downtown have produced an unnatural preoccupation with death that may be momentarily relieved by experiencing a version of their own deaths. When Henry confronts Kindt on this subject, the latter recounts an incident when a business deal had gone "terribly wrong" and he "had had to play dead to stay alive." He tells Henry:

> It was so strange . . . to have a pulse when those around me did not, to have hands and feet and toes I could still wiggle when those around me did not, to be able, after those long minutes, to rise and leave when those around me could not. (130)

Such survival surely creates exhilaration, the thrill of being alive when one could be dead, but it also creates survivor's guilt. The act of "playing dead" elicits paradoxical emotions in the participant. It allows one to feel newly and freshly alive (almost reborn), but it also highlights the thin line existing between life and actual death.

The Exquisite takes this a step further, however, strengthening the connections between the mock murder service and the deaths of innocent thousands that September morning:

> Maybe not surprisingly, a considerable number of people were interested in death by falling, or smoke inhalation or sudden impact, and Mr. Kindt was always very interested to hear about how they had been accommodated. (148)

Henry may not be shocked, but choosing to die in the same manner as those unfortunate souls on 9/11 certainly suggests a resorting to radical means to assuage either the uncomfortable revelation of one's own vulnerability, or pangs of guilt. Such solutions either suggest "victim envy" on the part of the survivors, or a desire for empathic connection with the dead, so that *nearly* dying as those people did is an attempt at approximating the latter's experience in those ultimate moments. But we might also conceive of it as an attempt to embrace, or partake of, the ethos of victimization that consumed Manhattan in the aftermath of the attacks, as Rachel Greenwald Smith suggests (164). Durica similarly argues that under these traumatized circumstances "mock murder is a sharp metaphor not only for survivor's guilt but also for our latent desire to experience the veneration accorded to victims of history's outrages" (Durica). Both New York and its populace were victimized and this was brought home by the smoldering hole at the southern tip of Manhattan as well as the missing posters that proliferated throughout the city. This need for experiencing one's near-death as a search for relief is a response to living in a kind of limbo, or state of constant uncertainty, or even one of ever-vigilant alert (as the color-coded system created by the office of Homeland Security more or less ensured). The existence of the service suggests that Henry is not the only one in the city stumbling around, lost. Mock-murder thus acts as a kind of panacea for this extended awareness of the second New York, allowing individuals to meaningfully connect with the victimized "other" with which the city was identified, or more generously with the "darkened shadow" of their "afterselves."

So is the pre-9/11 Manhattan gone forever? Is it irrevocably changed or is this alteration, dramatic though it may be, part of the life cycle of the metropolis? To what extent are the ensuing years part of an adaptation process in which the citizens adjust to their same, but different, city? The acclimation to this shift is, of course, more psychological than physical, as the denizens of Hunt's novel make clear. And the lines between past and present remain blurred, both versions of the city can exist in tandem, and reconciling one's current self with other iterations remains a challenge. As Micaela Morrissette observes, "The effect of this twinning is to make it impossible to choose between realities, or between dreams, or to divide reality from dream" (Morrissette). The novel depicts a desperate search for stability and selfhood in the wake of an event that turned assumptions and beliefs upside down. Hunt relies on the idea of the double for the plot, most of the characters, and the setting of the novel itself. Manhattan, like Henry, possesses two selves, and in the aftermath of trauma, it is not certain which will claim ascendancy.

REPRESENTATION THROUGH INDIRECTION: *CHRONIC CITY*

Jonathan Lethem's *Chronic City*, though not as experimental as *The Exquisite*, also underscores a feeling of doubleness and seeks to understand post-9/11 Manhattan through a series of devices that illuminate thinking about the tragedy without resorting to any of the familiar tropes. After all, the Manhattan represented in the novel is recognizable in many respects. In many respects, but for the snowstorms in August, an apartment building catering exclusively to dogs, a war-free edition of the *New York Times*, a perpetual gray fog that has hovered over Lower Manhattan since the early fall of 2001, a postmodern sculptor who creates gaping chasms in the city that bear a disturbing resemblance to the real Ground Zero, and finally a giant tiger that roams the city periodically destroying (unwanted?) buildings throughout the city. And although Lethem asserts that no given year is provided in the text, a number of clues indicate that the events take place beginning in the fall of 2004 and end in the spring of 2005.

The plot follows the wanderings of Chase Insteadman, a former teen star in a sitcom from the 1980s, now living off his residuals and his brief foray with fame. His current popularity emanates from the fact that he is engaged to Janice Trumbull, an astronaut trapped in a space station along with her colleagues. They are prevented from returning to Earth by a mine field planted in space by the Chinese government. Resources are rapidly diminishing, and Janice has been diagnosed with foot cancer. This information is known to all as she periodically sends missives from space which are then diligently published in the *New York Times*. As such, the whole city religiously follows each episode of the unfolding tragedy, with Chase being the recipient of much communal goodwill and sentiment. In the process, as Patrick Ness notes, Chase "has assumed the role of city hero, a surrogate for everyone's worry" (Ness).

Early in the novel, Chase makes the acquaintance of Perkus Tooth, a cultural critic, who gained notoriety by posting broadsides throughout the city and then writing a column for *Rolling Stone*. The novel essentially tells the story of their complicated and evolving friendship. Over a number of marijuana-aided, if not induced, conversations, Perkus reveals a wide range of paranoid theories to Chase, the most prevalent being that the citizens of Manhattan live in a *Matrix*-like world not of their own making. Chase tells the reader, "Where Perkus took me, in his rantings, in his enthusiasms, in his abrupt, improbable asides, was the world inside the world" (27). Late in the novel, Perkus, now in the throes of a hiccups (hence the gaps in the text), declares:

> Something happened, Chase, there was some rupture in this city. Since then, time's been fragmented. Might have to do with the gray fog, that or some other disaster. Whatever the cause, ever since we've been living in a place that's a replica of itself, a simulacrum, full of gaps and glitches. A *theme park*, really! Meant to halt time's encroachment. Of course such a thing is destined always to fail, time has a way of getting its bills paid. So these disjunctions appear, and we have to explain them away, as tigers or epic sculpture. (389)

Perkus's monologue implies the existence of an original Manhattan, one that was true to itself. In the wake of an event (Perkus even goes so far as to suggest the gray fog is a "disaster"), the city can now only exist as "a replica of itself, a simulacrum." *Chronic City* certainly plays with the notion of simulacra. Everything, including some characters (Oona and Janice), are copies of something or someone else. A recurrent plotline concerns the creation of a virtual computer universe called *Yet Another World*. Even the tiger may be nothing more than a fabrication to hide the existence of a sentient tunnel-drilling robot gone awry, the machinations of the mayor's office.

Fabrications or not, however, *something* has happened, *some* rupture has taken place, bringing about the existence of the artificial New York. As with *The Exquisite*, the text approaches the issue of September 11 tangentially, so that the reader is never told the precise nature of the disaster. Again, the descriptions are sufficiently similar to the reader's own experiences that any exposition is superfluous. We know, for instance, that the existence of this "replica" of the metropolis is the result of some calamity or other, something for which it will be necessary to create monuments. Late in the novel, for instance, the reader is vaguely informed that there will be a "ceremony at the hole downtown" (295). How the hole was created is left entirely to the reader's imagination, but Lethem obviously recognizes that the reader's mind is more than apt to flash to specific images already stored in his or her memory banks. Similarly to *The Exquisite*, then, the novel contains a network of plot devices that allow the reader to connect the text with a post-9/11 Manhattan, and that serve as objective correlatives for the collective emotional response to the terrorist attacks.

The most obvious corollary, that arouses a palpable degree of anxiety on the part of the populace, is the presence of a "gray fog" that has hovered over

Lower Manhattan, with no sign of dissipation, since early fall 2001. Sentences such as the following create an implicit connection between the world of the book and that of the reader: "I know I'm meant to feel we're all in something together, especially after the gray fog stretched out to cover the lower reaches of the island" (65). Again the text shirks explanation, neglecting to elucidate as to why such an occurrence would necessarily create fellow-feeling in the citizenry. Rather, the protagonist's emphasis on a sense of community, brought about by calamity, alludes to the feelings of unity and fellowship (uncharacteristically?) exhibited by New Yorkers in the aftermath of the attacks. The fog also embodies and provides a sense of the free-floating anxiety that has enveloped the city. People are more anxious, and some, such as Chase, are alarmed without realizing it. He (un)consciously avoids visiting Lower Manhattan, until the day he is invited to give an interview at a radio station located somewhere within the fog. His description of the area communicates his level of apprehension:

> You could hear [police sirens] anywhere in the city, but they took on a different cast at the perimeter of the cloud bank that had settled on the island below Chambers. I glimpsed the fog's rim in the crooked canyons from the windows of my cab. It swallowed daylight right up to the bridge's on-ramp, hazy tendrils nestling into the greens around city hall. (234)

Lethem strives to approximate the experience of New Yorkers who seek to get on with their lives, their jobs, their families, all the while conscious of the trauma they have undergone (and could undergo again). The frequent references to the "gray fog" in Chase's narration reveal a similar experience, indicating his own ongoing awareness of its existence. The fog stands in for the wound's ever-presence, and the newly formed fears at the back of everyone's mind as life supposedly returns to normal. The gloom it symbolizes is hammered home when the scheduled radio interview is interrupted by news of a tragedy:

> Those sirens weren't irrelevant, something had happened, close by, and the station was shifting to live coverage, on the street. A man, one of the money people, instead of showing up at the offices of the brokerage house where he worked, had thrown himself into the giant excavation of Noteless' memorial. (234)

The linking of the fog with Noteless's creation (they work together to abet, or even cause, the money man's suicide) signals a narratological strategy on the part of the author.[11] Repeatedly, the uncanny aspects of the plot are linked or mentioned in close proximity to one another, creating an underlying network of subtexts that reveal a level of anxiety existing below the surface of everyday life. Throughout *Chronic City*, then, Lethem's interweaving of allusions and indirect references to 9/11 raise a post-traumatic backdrop against which the novel can be read.

But how are Noteless's creation and the fog intertwined? As with other aspects of the novel, the repeated connections are left unexplained. Later, for instance, the city is subject to a "weird pervasive chocolate smell that floated like a cloud" (173). Chase describes the populace's reactions as follows: "The chocolate cloud tugged Manhattan's mind in two directions, recalling inevitably the gray fog that had descended or some said been unleashed on the lower part of the island, two or three years ago, and that had yet to release its doomy grip on the zone" (173–74). But why should the smell recall the fog, beyond the possibility of its being a naturally occurring phenomenon? Certainly each event is characterized by a randomness, an occurring "out of the blue" that echoes sentiments expressed in the aftermath of 9/11. But it also seems the citizenry has been primed to make these associations, as though these events are working in tandem to create a climate of fear or anxiety. One of the principal characteristics of fear, as Zygmunt Bauman points out, is its capacity to amplify itself:

> The trouble, however, is that those fears do not easily add up. As they descend one by one in a steady, though random succession, they defy our efforts (if efforts we make) to link them together and trace them to their joint roots. They are all the more frightening for being so difficult to comprehend; but even more horrifying for the feeling of impotence they arouse. (20)

Bauman identifies a generalized condition under which most of the world (although primarily the West) now lives. This state of being to which he refers, however, is naturally augmented in the wake of a traumatic event. Inserted within Chase's statement, of course, is the suggestion that someone is, in fact, controlling these phenomena—"some said had been unleashed." We witness again, in the populace's unease, a desperate reaching after explanation. The desire is so strong that a belief in a controlling agent becomes, paradoxically, a comforting thought. Interestingly, the incident in Lethem's novel resembles an actual event—one requiring the intercession of the mayor's office:

> Beginning in fall 2005, bemused residents called the city to complain about a maple syrup smell wafting across sections of Manhattan. Some blamed New Jersey. Others pointed to a candy factory. A few even suspected an unusually fragrant act of terrorism. Earlier this year, Mayor Michael R. Bloomberg officially solved the "Great Maple Syrup Mystery" by linking it to fenugreek seeds from a food additives plant across the Hudson River. (Gottlieb)

But the scenario Lethem presents also recalls, much more tragically and sadly, the unsettling odor of burning corpses and other matter that permeated the air of Lower Manhattan in the weeks following the attacks. Again, we see how the novel's use of the uncanny deepens the reader's experience. Each of these events (fog, smell, tiger, memorial) has a cumulative effect on the populace. These occurrences trouble because they hint at another reality that refuses to be incorporated within the narrative of a metropolis moving constantly and effortlessly forward.

ABYSMAL SPECTACLES

As noted, Lethem's city is also haunted by the works of Laird Noteless, a postmodern sculptor responsible for a number of recent public art installations: ravines, canyons, fjords—gaping and harrowed spaces throughout the city—bearing such names as *Local Chasm* and *Erased Atrocity* (207). These "abysmal spectacles" as Chase calls them, as well as their names, are the text's dark allusions to the wound that festered for years in Lower Manhattan, to that part of the city now turned into a cemetery, and to the inevitably sad and dark memorial that now inhabits the space known as Ground Zero. The connections between trauma, the sculptor's work, and an urge for memorialization, are made abundantly clear throughout the novel. Chase first becomes aware of Noteless's work at a party where he and a couple of the guests examine a drawing: "a crisp architectural-style rendering of a dark pit that plunged between two Manhattan office towers, viewed from above" (30). The drawing is for a project entitled *Expunged Building*. Both the image and the title of the work elicit thoughts of the World Trade Center (an expunged building if ever there was one) and of the crater now existing in its place.

The interplay between the plagues visited on the city and Noteless's work is made apparent when the text later informs the reader that the artist had just "received the commission for the *Memorial to Daylight* popular sentiment had demanded in reply to the gray fog downtown" (96). The reader is sure to wonder as to the reasons one would be asked to create a memorial in response to fog, a seemingly natural occurrence, unless there was some tragedy associated with it. But since no direct mention of any such event is made in the novel, connections are more readily applied to the "real world" September 11. Because, as noted, this fog has hovered over Lower Manhattan since early autumn 2001, making the rupture between the pre- and the post-visible. The name of the memorial itself is likely to cement some of these associations, by emphatically recalling the *Tribute in Light* which commemorates 9/11 by literally illuminating the absence of the Twin Towers. Because in the Manhattan of *Chronic City*, the terrorist attacks have not happened, hence the architectural structures have not been imbued with the significance they now possess in the reader's universe. Indeed, there is only one direct somewhat innocuous reference to the World Trade Center near the end of *Chronic City*. Enumerating the people that Perkus had valued, Chase mentions the exploits of Philippe Petit who "cross[ed] that impossible distance of sky between the towers, now unseen for so many months behind the gray fog" (430). In the world of the novel, then, the towers have not been destroyed, they merely remain "unseen."

This absence, or invisibility—something that continues to haunt the city—is reflected in Noteless's creations. These connections are made evident in the extended description of one of his works, when Chase accompanies his lover, Oona, to view *Urban Fjord* situated on the west bank of the Harlem River: "The chasm seemed to have been hewn out of the earth by unnatural force, the ground's lip curling suddenly downward. . . . The artificial crevasses yawned at least fifty yards across, perhaps a hundred" (my ellipsis, 109). Having approached the work with a degree of skepticism, Chase is taken aback by both its immensity and intense emotional power. The artist's reworking of the terrain has revealed its existential potential, uncovering "an underbelly of roots and stones, and below that, darker stuff, veins of sunless soil, and shadow tapering to total blackness" (109). Chase's descriptions are, of course, evocative, and suggest the sublime: "The longer I stared into the *Fjord*, the more likely it seemed that I'd pitch headfirst into that light-destroying well, so the sky would slam shut and entomb my tiny form inside" (110). As replications of the traumascape in Lower Manhattan, however, these creations demonstrate a greater capacity for re-traumatization than for consolation. As such, both characters are at odds to explain how such a work will provide any kind of relief to the city's residents. "Can you believe they'd put the man who built this in charge of the *Memorial to Daylight*?" Oona asks in disbelief (110). Considering the dark quality that enshrouds most of the artist's oeuvre, Chase is equally perplexed. But he also puts forth the possibility "that in this era of gray fog we'd caught up to Noteless's stark antihumanist vision, even found some flinty comfort there" (97). For is not part of a memorial's function to create access to the pain and suffering experienced on that day? Under such circumstances, there is always the risk of re-traumatizing the viewer. We might thus consider the ways in which these "abysmal spectacles" are truer to that which they seek to memorialize than other such constructions.

At the same time, the names of Noteless's creations evoke the ephemeral quality of such enterprises (what exactly would a monument to daylight memorialize?) and the titles used to convey a sense of emptiness at the core of the city. The reader is unlikely to miss the intentional reference to *Reflecting Absence*—the name of the 9/11 memorial by Michael Arad and Peter Walker, pools of water that now fill the footprints of the Twin Towers. The presence of Noteless's work in Lethem's novel raises questions about our ability to truly memorialize absence and loss. The stark and uncompromising quality of the sculptor's work highlights the degree to which most monuments efface what they claim to memorialize. As David Simpson observes, "all monuments are implicated in violence, whether in what they represent . . . in what they image iconographically . . . or in what they stimulate in the afterlife of public conflict and debate" (76). Rather than sanitizing the atrocity, Noteless's creations preserve that which is most horrific, but also most sublime about the traumascape of Ground Zero. It is as though his works are brought into existence by the recovery and reconstruction efforts that seem more intent on erasing or glossing over the trauma. In this way, Noteless's creations reflect the dark side of memorialization, and embody an ingrained fear that Manhattan will forever be connected to the horrors of September 11, in much the same way that Hiroshima—no matter the passing of time—remains indelibly associated with the atrocities of nuclear warfare.

Perhaps the most fantastical element of the novel and one that appears to have little to do with 9/11, at least on the surface, comes in the form of a giant tiger roaming the streets of Manhattan. When the reader first learns of the tiger, it is merely causing traffic jams and subway delays, and much speculation is given over to the fact that its existence may be nothing more than a rumor. As the novel progresses, however, the creature is increasingly linked with destruction, and the annihilation of buildings in particular (something to which readers are likely to be overly attentive and sensitive in the aftermath of September 11). Still the novel deals with the tiger's presence matter-of-factly, not really questioning its provenance, or the likelihood that such a creature could remain out of sight on the bustling streets of the metropolis. Someone suggests at one point that the carnivore is simply a fabrication of the mayor's office seeking to explain the destruction actually committed by a tunnel-drilling robot that has run amok somewhere beneath Second Avenue (in the process of creating the much-anticipated subway line). Chase's friend, Richard Abneg, a left-leaning social justice advocate now on the mayor's payroll, tells the story of two robots used to dig the Chunnel, each starting at opposite ends. When they met in the middle, their job complete, they were "retired" and, in a consoling gesture, buried together at sea. There is an anthropomorphic quality to Abneg's tale, particularly when he turns to the situation in New York: "We made a mistake, though. We cut corners when we commissioned our own project. We only had to build a single machine, just digging in one direction, with nothing coming from the other side. I guess the thing got lonely. . . . At night sometimes it comes up from underneath and sort of, you know, ravages around" (163). Interestingly, the idea of robots experiencing loneliness is accepted just as readily as that of giant tigers roaming the streets of Manhattan.

When asked why the beast has not been stopped, Abneg contends that the people of the city are desperate for the subway line and that the damage caused is "really exaggerated." He even admits that "a certain amount of the buildings it's taken out were pretty much dead wood in the first place" (164). To which Perkus replies, "That's how urban renewal works" (164). Abneg's comment suggests the rampaging robot/tiger actually serves the administration's purpose, while Perkus's observation affirms that structural liquidation of this kind is actually an integral part of a city's cyclical existence. The destruction caused by the tiger reflects the ongoing life of a thriving city wherein a long-standing building is destroyed one day and replaced by a new one the next. Because, inevitably, the city is always in some state of deterioration—the tiger is merely accelerating improvements to the city's infrastructure. Whether tiger or robot, what is significant is that such a thing can be imaginatively brought into existence, and made to embody various anxieties percolating within the city. In fact, Abneg admits that the tiger story was not originally of their making. A woman had spotted a coyote in Central Park, but reported sighting a tiger. The media ran with the story and, in Abneg's words, "the image just colonized the public imagination" (164). This plays on the notion that people actively need something to fear, and bears a comical resemblance, of course, to the conspiracy theories which contend that it was not al-Qaeda, but the American government that worked to bring down the Twin Towers. In Lethem's version of things, the tiger, like al-Qaeda, is nothing more than a convenient smokescreen for the machinations of the local administration. As we shall see, however, the explanation of the existence of the tiger as part of the mayor's office's manipulations of its populace, does not go uncontested. For though the mayor's chief aide herself tells Chase that the escaped tiger is nothing more than "a distraction" (447), the sighting of the beast by both Chase and Richard near the end of the novel contradicts, or at least undermines, the conspiratorial narrative constructed throughout the text. At the same time, the deeds of the tiger do resemble those carried out by al-Qaeda against the United States in significant ways. Its actions are entirely unpredictable; the beast does not seem to follow any logic, and often takes the city by surprise. And despite knowing the culprit causing the destruction (as with bin Laden), the officials are unable to track it down. In fact, Abneg becomes something of a scapegoat for the "spiraling fiasco of the giant escaped tiger's non-capture" (397). Thus an air of mystery surrounds the existence of the tiger, in much the same way that al-Qaeda was an unknown entity to many on the morning of September 11. This feeling is compounded by a sense of incredulity as to the inability of the authorities to capture the tiger, recalling the frustration exhibited by many that the greatest power in the world proved incapable of tracking down one man.[12]

The air of mystery that often surrounds a terrorist attack—the inability to determine how and why such an event has occurred—compels people to search for answers wherever they might find them. As such, one of the principal effects of terrorism is the creation (and possible escalation) of anticipatory fear—waiting for the next strike, but not really knowing from whence it will come. The greatest impact of a terrorist act is its capacity to accentuate the degree of *not knowing* on the part of the terrorized. As Zygmunt Bauman observes, "Fear is at its most fearsome when it is diffuse, scattered, unclear, unattached, unanchored, free floating, with no clear address or cause; when it haunts us with no visible rhyme or reason, when the menace we should be afraid of can be glimpsed everywhere but is nowhere to be seen" (2). People thus seek to reduce their levels of fear by attaching or anchoring them to something concrete (al-Qaeda, an untrustworthy government, a tiger). In the anxious days and weeks after September 11, people desperately sought signs or forewarnings of future attacks. But since it was impossible to identify where and when the next attack might occur, anything could be a sign. Unattended backpacks, too many turbans congregating in one place, almost *any* kind of suspicious activity, became a potential harbinger of future calamity. Anything that recaptured or rekindled, if only briefly, the emotions felt that day, was evaluated for its "terroristic" potential. Greater suspicion was cast, of course, on unexplainable incidents that were both violent and shocking. Two such instances were the anthrax attacks begun on September 18, 2001 (in which five people were killed, and another seventeen infected), and the crash of America Airlines Flight 587 in Queens on November 12, 2001. Following closely on the heels of the attacks carried out by al-Qaeda, these events were immediately interpreted as possible new acts of terrorism.[13] And though the connections were not readily apparent, this did not prevent people from reaching conclusions as to the ultimate significance of these occurrences.

Chronic City illuminates this desperate hankering for connections, a need to understand how the disparate pieces in the puzzle fit together. For instance, there is no rational reason for associating tiger and fog, aside for their existence as sources of fear, and yet for Chase these links are clear. After all, these "spectacles" cannot simply be random occurrences, surely they must mean *something*. At the same time, much like Chase, people were unsure as to their own personal abilities to read the signs of impending catastrophe. They turned to the government, relying on its capacity to tell them whether they were safe or not. A further connection between the terrorist attacks and the tiger is thus made explicit when the city installs a website allowing citizens to track "the tiger's movements and recommended it to those seeking forewarning of traffic tie-ups and subway cancellations" (200). This may seem innocuous enough; a later mention, however, refers to the possibility of "casualties or damage" (226). And the city, much like Homeland Security after the attacks, institutes an alert system: "the site ranked risk of an attack tonight as Yellow, or Low-to-Moderate" (226–27). Though this is utilized primarily for satirical purposes, the existence of the tiger (like the fog, like Noteless's creations) reveals an uneasiness—a kind of free-floating anxiety—that still lies in the heart of Manhattan.

Chase, as "the surrogate for everyone's worry," becomes the conduit through which the reader is made to feel a sense of disquiet or unsettlement, similar to that which pervaded Manhattan in the weeks after the event. Returning from his apprehensive visit to Lower Manhattan, Chase reveals a degree of ignorance, and a scrambling to read the signs, if signs there are, of looming danger. This section of the novel is thus likely to fill the reader with foreboding, for the narrative skips from one anxious moment to the next, creating a web of potential connections between the various forces plaguing the city. That evening, as they head out the door on their way to their favorite burger joint, Chase describes Perkus's ensemble as giving him the appearance of "an Irish folksinger or terrorist" (236–37). The very next moment the ground begins to "shudder beneath our feet, a wrenching seizure in the earth below" (237). Chase even posits that he may have heard something resembling a roar. Having planted the seed in the reader's mind in the previous sentence, the text makes the link between terror and the tiger explicit. The real danger the tiger (if tiger it is) poses is also revealed when, in destroying the restaurant, it kills a waitress and two others in the process. Chase further reinforces the connection between the uncanny spectacles when he associates the police response to the tiger's attack with his experiences earlier in the day: "Then the sirens came, as if replying to those in the morning's fog, and converged on us where we swayed stupefied in the blossoming dust" (237–38). The tiger's attack is thus directly linked with the fog in Lower Manhattan, and the unnamed disaster that occurred downtown. At the same time, Chase's choice of words—"blossoming dust"—are sure to evoke additional associations for the reader, recalling the ash that rained down on the city after the collapse of the Twin Towers. And the damage caused by the tiger—what is described as the "site" in the novel—is sure to summon other familiar images in the mind of the reader:

> the crater and the surrounding street blazed white, lit by emergency spotlights that had been cranked into position to facilitate specialists crawling over rubble, perhaps sounding within it with stethoscopes for Morse tapping or cries. (243)

The similarity with the 9/11 attacks is further strengthened by the fact that there are no survivors. Chase notes that "the ambulances didn't bother leaving the scene" (245), evoking those desperate hours when medical personnel waited in vain for the injured to arrive after the collapse of the Twin Towers. Finally, the crater left in the wake of the tiger's path subsequently becomes a "quarantined block" (297), an image that can do nothing but awaken memories of the area cordoned off around Ground Zero in the aftermath.

The tiger (like al-Qaeda) thus becomes the object of fear, the focus of the public's scrutiny. In this way, the animal acts as the perfect vehicle for the local administration, or so one strain of the narrative goes. The tiger's appearance is undeniably serendipitous (for some), just as it can be argued that the events of September 11 played right into the hands of those looking for a reason to invade Iraq. The conclusion of the novel certainly seems to support the idea that those in power will use whatever means at their disposal to distract the populace from the reality of the situation (whatever it might be). At the same time, this network of meanings is put into question at the end of the novel when, in the midst of yet another snowstorm, the tiger is sighted by Chase and Richard. Instead of an aggressive creature bent on destruction, we witness a large animal ("a second story tiger") moving languidly and serenely down Lexington Avenue in the snow. As a result, Chase is not fearful. Instead, he feels an attraction to, or kinship with, the beast: "I found myself wishing I could rush to it and grip its striped, smooth-ridged fur with both hands and also bury my face there, then climb into its fur and be borne away elsewhere, out of Perkus's city, out of my own" (433). This description refutes Abneg's narrative of a sentient, but distraught, robot taking its frustrations out on the city. As Chase observes, the tiger "had no remotely mechanical aspect to it, nor appeared in any sense to have emerged from underground or be about to return to fugitive excavations, seemed instead to be wholly of flesh and fur" (433). This fact, then raises the question, why would Richard Abneg bother to construct an elaborate tale? That the mayor's office uses the presence of the tiger to its advantage remains probable. In fact, they may very well have framed the tiger for the destruction of unwanted buildings, and used its alleged actions as a means of forcing residents (such as Perkus) to vacate more cherished real estate. What is also clear, however, is that there are elements within the world that exist beyond the reach and control of the manipulators. The tiger's origins remain clouded in mystery, and the benign creature sighted by Chase and Richard does not conform to the picture painted by the media or city officials.

The disconnect between what Chase has previously thought or been led to believe about the tiger and his seeing the beast for himself causes him to reach for an explanation—the tiger must have a twin. Thus, in the spirit of the novel's emphasis on doubleness, he conceives of the possibility that there may be two tigers, one good and one evil, roaming the city:

> Fearless and splendid, the tiger seemed quite outside the scope of Tiger-Watch or of the tracking throngs that massed to rubberneck at its destroyings. Possibly there were two tigers, the famous and chaotic one that lit the tabloid frenzy, and this more dignified one, who showed itself to us alone. (434)

The revelation of the tiger's actual existence comes hot on the heels of Chase's realization that his engagement to Janice Trumbull is literally nothing more than a fiction (perhaps perpetuated with the complicity of the *New*

York Times). The existence of both narratives reveal, if nothing else, the conviction held by those in the upper echelons that the masses can be tamed and mesmerized if they are entertained and kept busy by the latest "spectacle." When the mayor's aide tells Chase that the tiger is nothing more than a "distraction," the latter recognizes that his engagement with Janice, much like the tale of the destructive tiger, is just another way of keeping the populace engrossed and its focus elsewhere (447). The word "distraction" can simply indicate a form of entertainment, something to take one's mind off one's worries. However, the more sinister interpretation indicates a conscious attempt to divert attention away from one object onto another. While both Chases's relationship and the tiger's actions serve as distractions, the difference is that the former is entirely fabricated, while the tiger actually exists. It is significant, of course, that the animal is seen by both Chase and Richard, lest the reader infer that this is little more than a hallucination. The tiger, in a sense, represents a strand of reality not easily subsumed within the (social) order of things. Indeed, the conclusion of the novel suggests that the greatest difficulty lies in now living in this double world, where giant tigers may be both destructive and benign.

CONCLUSION

A disaster, or the *something* that happened in Lethem's text, has awoken a consciousness of two irreconcilable realities at the heart of the city, or that the city itself now exists as two irreconcilable realities. As his tale comes to an end, Chase points to the impossibility of distinguishing one from the other: "Our sphere of the real (call it Manhattan) was riddled with simulations, yet was the world at hand. Or the simulation was riddled through with the real" (448–49). Like Henry from *The Exquisite*, we may catch glimpses when one world briefly comes into focus. But these worlds bleed into each other so that real and unreal, past and present, graveyard and carnival are often indistinguishable. Or, at least, it is difficult to identify where one ends and the other begins. In this environment, the citizens have also become "other" to themselves. They can no longer be sure whether they are living genuine lives, or ones constructed for them. These novels give form to a sense of doubleness created by life continuing on in the aftermath of September 11—a life lived as though nothing has changed, but where everyone continues to harbor the nagging suspicion that it just may have. These texts reveal characters unable to reconcile the existence of discordant "realities" summoned in the wake of the terrorist attacks. And they are part of a populace who are more fretful and anxious, revealing their emotional states through the hiring of a mock-murder service or believing in the existence of a giant tiger.

It is worth recalling Jill Bennett's notion of sense memory and the ways in which the trauma continues to make itself felt in the present. To borrow Bennett's phrasing we might consider the possibility of a 9/11 self that "retains a capacity to affect, to trigger emotion in the present" (26). New York's 9/11 self continues to assert itself, remaining present and troubling its current self. Through the experiences of Henry and Chase, the reader is made to feel the lingering effects of trauma—an unsettledness revealed in the ways the community works through, not always successfully, its relationship with the "horror downtown." We might say that 9/11 has created an overabundance of otherness, not so easily subsumed within narratives of recovery and resilience.

NOTES

1. Tanner further contends that arguments made by others neglect "to explore how the public's reaction to 9/11 has been shaped by a screen culture that renders the very opposition of distance and intimacy a false distinction" (61).

2. See Huyssen, 161–63.

3. Indeed, one might go further and construct parallels between the contours that now signal where the Buddhas once stood in the Bamiyan Valley, and the preserved footprints of the Twin Towers. Each memorializes the loss by framing the absence.

4. See both Turner and Zeitlin.

5. In an essay noting the number of twinned structures existing in New York City, David Dunlap observes that "Anthropomorphism is irresistible when contemplating twin towers, as the term itself suggests. They may be discerned as legs, like the Colossus of Rhodes. They may be imagined as arms raised to the heavens. They may be thought of as siblings or partners or husband and wife" (Dunlap). Such conceptualizations meant that a number of people remarked on the impossibility of conceiving of one Tower left standing in the absence of the other, as though this would be an intolerable state for the remaining other. Just such an alternate universe scenario is offered in the graphic comic *Ex Machina*, in which the hero arrives only in time to divert the second plane from striking the South Tower. On a full-page spread, we see a lone tower standing while a beam of light emerges from the ruins of the other. It is a powerful image of what might have been, but it also serves as another means of representing the Towers' simultaneous absence/presence.

6. In *Contentious City*, a book on the impact of the attacks on local politics, John Mollenkopf entitles his introduction, "Repairing the Hole in the Heart of the City." Again, the personification of the metropolis is explicit.

7. The same impulse is evident in Beigbeder's *Windows on the World*. The novel offers a minute-by-minute narrative leading to the moment of the North Tower's implosion. In describing that fateful moment, the author arranges the words in such a manner as to visually recreate the semblance of the buildings on the page.

8. So prevalent was this feeling that two different writers, Richard Bernstein and Kristiaan Versluys, chose to use the phrase as the title for their respective books on 9/11.

9. A New York acquaintance of mine told me that many people living in Midtown and higher went about living their lives as though there were not smoking ruins at the southern tip of the island; that the impact on their daily lives was in fact minimal. These comments reveal the experience of simultaneously living in changed and unchanged worlds.

10. In his acknowledgments, Hunt makes reference to writers of New York novels who came before him, and observes: "All of our New Yorks, after all, are partially dreamt. Many, like Henry's, are shaped by the brilliant dreamers who have been there before us" (246).

11. Connections are also made between the fog and the "money men" who work on the southern part of the island (31, 341). With a degree of prescience, Lethem anticipates the pall that will settle over the financial district in the wake of crash of the housing market in 2008. At one point Chase admits, "I ought to feel sympathy for the moneymen, ashen and dim in aspect, forgetful, sleepy, never quite themselves anymore" (65). When asked in an interview whether his novel, in light of the economic downturn, "reflect[ed] a time that has passed," Lethem replies: "I hope the book floats in time a little bit. It was certainly meant to. It doesn't even mention a year. But the money never goes away. I mean, the restaurants and bars are full in Manhattan. It can sometimes seem almost like zombie money—it just goes on doing what it did even though it's not alive anymore" (Cruz, *Time*).

12. The Navy Seals eventually did track the al-Qaeda leader down, of course, on the evening of May 2, 2011—nearly a decade after the attacks on the World Trade Center.

13. In retrospect, the anthrax attacks were acts of terror also, but not in the ways people initially assumed.

Epilogue

The re-calibration of global dynamics after 9/11 was cause for measured optimism on the part of a number of writers and thinkers. Like others, David Simpson wonders whether the event might not be framed as a potential global turning point: "to a remarkable degree the sight of those falling towers, the fates of those who died, and the grief of those who survived elicited a worldwide outpouring of sympathy and response that was clearly announced and reported. Could this have been a utopian moment, an opening?" (166). And while there is a silver lining aspect here, the phrasing of the question implies that the moment has already passed. If there was such a window of opportunity, its existence was brief. The reification of the notion of American innocence, combined with an ever more fervent call for revenge, meant that the divide between "us and them" was soon firmly re-established. Simpson suspects as much when he asks, "if there was on September 12, 2001, and for some time thereafter such a potential for the making of common cause, has it been lost forever by the invasion of Iraq and the ongoing brutality it has perpetrated on both the enemy and the homeland?" (167). And yet, there are some observable vacillations within Simpson's arguments. He does not give up on the idea of the "making of a common cause" so easily. For instance, he argues that the incidents at Abu Ghraib, as horrible as they were, may have actually "set in motion a process of interference and interrogation of the self-other, homeland-foreigner binary" (167). In other words, the categories of victim and perpetrator cannot be so rigidly maintained in the face of these shocking discoveries. Because the attribution of American innocence is seriously undermined by these revelations, Simpson identifies these moments as opportunities for breaking down barriers between peoples.

In an appended introduction to a collection of essays entitled *For Love of Country?*, Martha Nussbaum similarly wrestles with the two opposing impulses elicited by 9/11: an inclusive looking outward and an exclusive turning inward. Clearly addressing an American readership, she begins by contending that "the crisis has expanded our imaginations." As a result, she notes, "We find ourselves feeling sympathy for many people who did not even cross our minds before" (ix). Nussbaum's list begins by including heroes such as New York firefighters and the brave individuals aboard United 93, but then grows to comprise Arab Americans, a Sikh taxi driver, and even people living beyond American borders, such as Afghani women and girls. In a positive twist, then, the event has extended empathetic horizons. Nussbaum is aware, of course, that one tends to be more typically concerned with people closer at hand. She warns that more often "our imaginations remain oriented to the local" (x). In other words, our gaze turns inward, remaining firmly fixed on ourselves. The distant "other" is too far removed to elicit any compassion on our parts. This inability to care for the other is exacerbated in those circumstances when we believe that the situation calls for deciding between "us" and "them." In those situations, fear and anxiety contribute to a hardening of divisions and a seeking-after that which sets us apart from the other. This prioritizing of "us," Nussbaum observes, "can easily flip over into a demonizing of an imagined 'them,' a group of outsiders who are imagined as enemies of the invulnerability and the pride of the all-important 'us'" (x). Despite these recognitions, Nussbaum still believes that people have the capacity to teach themselves to be otherwise. If we are to find ways of connecting with others, she argues, we must willfully seek to counteract these inclinations. In order for "our moral natures and our emotional natures . . . to live in any sort of harmony," she maintains, "we must find devices through which to extend our strong emotions and our ability to imagine the situation of others to the world of human life as a whole" (xiii). The events of September 11 and their aftermath have raised our awareness of others. We must now build upon that awareness. Nussbaum thus gives voice to the dream that out of the ashes of the World Trade Center would arise a greater mindfulness of the common humanity that binds us all:

> We can take this disaster as an occasion for narrowing our focus, distrusting the rest of the world, and feeling solidarity with Americans alone. Or we can take it as an occasion for expansion of our ethical horizons. Seeing how vulnerable our great country is, we can learn something about the vulnerability all human beings share. (xiii–xiv)

Again, Nussbaum appears to be arguing for a resistance to one's own natural impulses (indeed, she calls upon biology) and for a conscious striving to engage with difference and educate oneself about the other. She does not specifically identify the "devices" she calls upon, but education plays a fundamental role, as her allusions to children make clear.

There is a slight hint of wishful-thinking in the strategies employed by Simpson and Nussbaum. In both cases, the writers identify actions or events that were clearly utilized to emphasize difference—the "us-them" binary—in both directions. The events of 9/11 and the actions committed at Abu Ghraib reveal a distinct lack of empathy on the part of the actors, and a willful emphasis on establishing and reifying the otherness of those upon whom the violence is perpetrated. And yet, both Simpson and Nussbaum identify these events as plausible starting points for disassembling those very binaries. Both hold out some hope for a greater interconnectedness among peoples and an increased global appreciation of the humanity of each and every living person. Simpson, more so than Nussbaum, however, remains painfully aware of the direction events are more likely to take. This does not stop him from wishing for positive change, but his feet remain firmly rooted to the ground. In what reads like a response to Butler's injunction that, in the light of the tragedy, we must acquire a "keener sense of the value of life, all life," Simpson asserts, "The history happening now has put radical pressure on the domestic humanist project of encouraging sympathy for others by way of shared feelings. The pursuit of a war against innocent people and the apparent tolerance of avoidable deaths (our own and those of others) suggest that we have *not* after all learned to suffer with others by way of a common sensing of a vulnerable body. Not yet" (8).

Much was made of the world having changed after 9/11. I would suggest instead that the events signaled a change of direction, demanding a shift in priorities. The presence of others asserted itself into the collective psyche of the American people in a way it had never done before. And the disorientation caused by the attacks, the apparent disjunction between how Americans thought about themselves and how others apparently did, inevitably led to a search for meaning, and attempts to bridge the gap between those two poles. If we conceptualize these post-9/11 fictions as a reflection of current conditions, it is safe to say that Simpson's "Not yet" still applies. As such, what we encounter in these novels are individuals who seek to make sense of this world in the aftermath of the attacks and who recognize that such attempts will be largely contingent on their limited abilities to negotiate the presence of others within their specific circumstances. Reading these novels as encounters with otherness, however, reveals the degree to which the exercising of empathy is a challenging, frustrating, sometimes painful, but ultimately essential activity. Some of the chapters analyze texts that we might consider assertions of otherness in the face of an all-encompassing sameness. So the individuals in the graphic novels react to the formation of the national narratives of resilience and recovery that would subsume their individual experiences. The French novels examined react to American narratives of innocence and exceptionalism, and the presumption that the rest of the world should endorse these as well. The novels in which the terrorist plays a central role seek to provide a perspective that allows us to see how we are viewed by others. In the process, we gain a better understanding of ourselves but also a deeper appreciation of the obstacles preventing stronger connection. We might thus think of these texts as pleas for the recognition of otherness. The protagonists in the novels by Lethem and Hunt have otherness thrust upon them by the radical alteration to the city after an unnamed event in Lower Manhattan. The texts also postulate the city itself as a character, transformed into an "other," with which the protagonists will now need to incorporate into their own altered sense of selves. Their efforts at greater understanding, however, prove largely unsuccessful. Finally, the texts by DeLillo, McEwan, and Waldman all present characters who genuinely seek to understand the other. As a result of her exposure to the performance artist, Falling Man, Lianne seeks to more fully connect with the plight of the victims, but also with the artist himself whose performance might be termed a radical expression of empathy. The well-intended neurosurgeon of McEwan's novel seeks to connect with a more vulnerable (albeit violent) other, but social positioning and his use of empathy to maintain a dominant position obviously prevent him from ever truly connecting with the other. Finally, Waldman's novel demonstrates the ways in which the attacks caused a retrenchment in the American landscape, with Arab and Muslim-Americans seemingly transformed into "others" overnight. The plight of Mohammad Khan reveals the very real limitations of empathy, particularly in the face of limited knowledge, entrenched stereotypes, and collective anxiety in the wake of the attacks. As we can see, textual responses to this disorientation vary in character, ranging from hopefulness to resignation. And empathy is accorded varying degrees of prominence, though often it is shown to fail or come up short.

Perhaps a collective reading of these texts paints too negative a portrait, suggesting the ultimate inaccessibility of the other, and the irresolvable quality of the problem of otherness. This may be the result, in part, of the ambitions of serious literature which is often more interested in conflict than in resolution. And it may well be that the problem of otherness is in fact irresolvable and perpetual, even with the greater interconnectedness that globalization ostensibly brings. But perhaps the role of fiction is not to solve the problem of otherness. Elaine Scarry argues as much, noting that literature "is most helpful not *insofar* as it takes away the problem of the Other . . . but instead takes as its own subject the problem of Imagining Others" (48). We might thus think of these fictions as determined efforts to investigate the potential for, and of, empathetic thinking. Perhaps we should think of empathy as promoting a type of irresolution, since it is an inherently inconclusive and uncertain activity. We can never be sure that we have truly felt what the other feels, nor can we ever affirm that our knowledge of the other is anything more than incomplete. We can only hope that one's openness to otherness has afforded worthwhile glimpses with which to build better relations with that other. These novels offer the reader opportunities to witness empathy in action, in both their attempts to present the inner life of its characters, and in their depictions of the efforts made by the characters themselves to engage in empathy. And, indeed, the text may position the reader in such a way as to allow her to examine her own efforts at connecting, or not, with the characters presented in the novels. This understanding is effected first through a genuine willingness to know the other, to accept his story, no matter how troubling or radically different it may be from one's own. Opening oneself up to the other's story allows for the exercising of empathy and a potential recognition (and appreciation) of that which makes him same but also, and more important, that which makes him different. In the process, a growing recognition of the other's unknowability should give the reader pause, putting into question any stable sense of self. This discomfort may cause the reader to examine the contingency of his own positions, thus opening up an ethical consideration of his very relations with the other.

Bibliography

Abel, Marco. "Don DeLillo's 'In the Ruins of the Future': Literature, Images, and the Rhetoric of *Seeing* 9/11." *PMLA*, 118.5 (October 2003): 1236–50.
Abderrahmane, Semmar. "Salim Bachi: Le périple d'un Kamikaze." *Limag* http://www.limag.refer.org/Textes/Semmar/Bachi.htm. October 24, 2010.
Adrian, Chris. *A Better Angel: Stories*. New York: Farrar, Straus and Giroux: 2008.
Agamben, Giorgio. *Homo Sacer: Sovereign Power and Bare Life*. Trans. by Danielle Heller-Roazen. Stanford, CA: Stanford University Press, 1998.
Amis, Martin. *The Second Plane: September 11, Terror and Boredom*. New York: Alfred A. Knopf, 2008.
Andrieux, Jean-Yves and Frédéric Seitz. *Le World Trade Center: Une Cible Monumentale*. Belin-Herscher; Paris, 2002.
Anker, Elizabeth S. "Allegories of Falling and the 9/11 Novel." *American Literary History* 23.3 (Fall 2011): 463–82.
Appadurai, Arjun. *Fear of Small Numbers: An Essay on the Geography of Anger*. Durham, NC and London: Duke University Press, 2006.
Arizti, Barbara. "'Welcome to contemporary trauma culture': Foreshadowing, Sideshowing, and Trauma in Ian McEwan's *Saturday*." In *Trauma in Contemporary Literature: Narrative and Representation*. (Eds. Marita Nadal and Monica Calvo). New York, Routledge, 2014: 237–48.
Bachi, Salim. *Tuez-les tous*. Paris: Gallimard, 2006.
Baelo-Allué, Sonia. "The Depiction of 9/11 in Literature: The Role of Images and Intermedial References." *Radical History Review* 111 (Fall 2011): 184–93.
Bald, Sunil. "Memories, Ghosts, and Scars: Architecture and Trauma in New York and Hiroshima." *Journal of Transnational American Studies* 3.1 (2011): 1–9.
Ballen, Ken. *Terrorists in Love: The Real Lives of Islamic Radicals*. New York: Free Press, 2011.
Banita, Georgiana. "Middle Hours: Terrorism and Narrative Emplotment in Andre Dubus III's *The Garden of Last Days*" in *Literature and Terrorism: Comparative Perspectives*. (Ed. Michael C. Frank and Eva Gruber). Amsterdam and New York: Rodopi, 2012: 213–32.
———. *Plotting Justice: Narrative Ethics and Literary Culture After 9/11*. Lincoln and London: University of Nebraska Press, 2012.
Barbaro, Michael. "Debate Heats Up About Mosque Near Ground Zero." *New York Times*. http://www.nytimes.com/2010/07/31/nyregion/31mosque.html?pagewanted=all&_r=. July 30, 2010.
Bauman, Zygmunt. *Liquid Fear*. Malden, MA: Polity, 2006.

Baudrillard, Jean. *The Spirit of Terrorism* and *Requiem for the Twin Towers*. Trans. by Chris Turner. London and New York: Verso, 2002.
Beck, Ulrich. *The Cosmopolitan Vision*. Trans. by Ciaran Cronin. Cambridge, UK: Polity, 2006.
Beigbeder, Frédéric. *Windows on the World*. Paris: Gallimard, 2003.
———. *Windows on the World*. Trans. by Frank Wynne. New York: Hyperion, 2004.
Benaïssa, Slimane. *The Last Night of a Damned Soul*. Trans. by Janice and Daniel Cross. New York: Grove Press, 2003.
Bennett, Jill. *Empathic Vision: Affect, Trauma, and Contemporary Art*. Stanford: Stanford University Press, 2005.
———. "The Limits of Empathy and the Global Politics of Belonging." In *Trauma at Home: After 9/11*. (Ed. Judith Greenberg). Lincoln: University of Nebraska Press, 2003: 132–38.
Bernstein, Richard. *Out of the Blue: The Story of September 11, 2001, From Jihad to Ground Zero*. New York: Henry Holt and Company, 2002.
Bertrand, Donald. "WTC Display Tanked After Uproar." *Daily News* September 25, 2002: 5.
Bhabha, Homi K. "Terror and after..." *parallax* 8.1 (2002): 3–4.
Bird, Benjamin. "History, Emotion, and the Body: Mourning in Post-9/11 Fiction." *Literature Compass* 4.3 (2007): 561–75.
Bird, Jon. "The Mote in God's Eye: 9/11, Then and Now." *Journal of Visual Culture* 2.1 (2003): 83–97.
Birnbaum, Robert. July 20, 2005. Interview with Ian McEwan. *The Morning News*. www.themorningnews.org/archives/birnbaum_v/ian_mcewan.php. April 2, 2009.
Bleiker, Ronald. "Art After 9/11." *Alternatives* 31 (2006): 77–99.
Blessington, Francis. "Politics and the Terrorist Novel." *Sewanee Review*, 116:1 (Winter 2008): 116–24.
Blocker, Jane. *Seeing Witness: Visuality and the Ethics of Testimony*. Minneapolis: University of Minnesota Press, 2009.
Boler, Megan. "The Risks of Empathy: Interrogating Multiculturalism's Gaze." *Cultural Studies* 11.2 (1997): 253–73.
Borradori, Giovanna. *Philosophy in a Time of Terror: Dialogues with Jurgen Habermas and Jacques Derrida*. Chicago and London: The University of Chicago Press, 2003.
Bourget, Carine. *The Star, the Cross, and the Crescent: Religions and Conflicts in Francophone Literature from the Arab World*. Lanham, MD: Lexington Books, 2010.
Boylan, Roger. Jan./Feb. 2006. "Ian McEwan's Family Values." *Boston Review*. http://bostonreview.net/br31.1/boylan.html. March 20, 2009.
Bradley, Arthur. 2009. "The New Atheist Novel: Literature, Religion, and Terror in Amis and McEwan." *The Yearbook of English Studies* 39.1–2: 20–38.
Bragard, Véronique, Christophe Dony, and Warren Rosenberg (eds.). *Portraying 9/11: Essays on Representations in Comics, Literature, Film and Theatre*. Jefferson, NC: McFarland & Company, 2011.
Brassett, James. "Cosmopolitan Sentiments After 9-11? Trauma and the Politics of Vulnerability." *Journal of Critical Globalisation Studies* 2 (2010): 12–29.
———. "Cosmopolitanism vs. Terrorism? Discourses of Ethical Possibility Before and After 7/7." *Millenium: Journal of International Studies* 36.2 (2008): 311–38.
Breithaupt, Fritz. "How is it Possible to have Empathy? Four Models." In *Theory of Mind and Literature*. (Eds. Paula Leverage, Howard Mancing, Richard Schweickert, and Jennifer Marston William). West Lafayette, IN: Purdue University Press, 2011: 273–86.
Brown, Richard. 2008. "Politics, the Domestic and the Uncanny Effects of the Everyday in Ian McEwan's *Saturday*." *Critical Survey* 20.1: 80–93.
Butler, Heidi. 2011. "The Master's Narrative: Resisting the Essentializing Gaze in Ian McEwan's *Saturday*." *Critique* 52.1: 101–13.
Butler, Judith. *Precarious Life: The Powers of Mourning and Violence*. New York: Verso, 2004.
Button, Gregory V. "Popular Media Reframing of Man-Made Disasters: A Cautionary Tale" in *Catastrophe and Culture: The Anthropology of Disaster* (Eds. Susanna M. Hoffman and Anthony Oliver-Smith). School of American Research Press: Santa Fe, 2002: 143–58.

Cainkar, Louise A. *Homeland Insecurity: The Arab American and Muslim American Experience After 9/11*. New York: Russell Sage Foundation, 2009.
Caminada, Carlos. July 16, 2004. "Ian McEwan, Finishing New Novel, Ponders World After Sept. 11." Bloomberg. www.bloomberg.com. September 1, 2005.
Carroll, Hamilton. "'Like Nothing in this Life': September 11 and the Limits of Representation in Don DeLillo's *Falling Man*." *Studies in American Fiction* 40.1 (2013): 107–27.
Caruth, Cathy. *Unclaimed Experience: Trauma, Narrative, and History*. Baltimore: Johns Hopkins University Press, 1996.
Chermak, Steven, Frankie Y. Bailey and Michelle Brown (eds.). *Media Representations of September 11*. Westport, CT: Praeger, 2003.
Chiozza, Giacomo. *Anti-Americanism and the American World Order*. Baltimore: The Johns Hopkins University Press, 2009.
Chomsky, Noam. *9/11*. New York: Seven Stories Press, 2002.
Chouliaraki, Lilie. *The Spectatorship of Suffering*. London: Sage Publications, 2006.
Cilano, Cara N. *Post-9/11 Espionage Fiction in the U.S. and Pakistan*. New York: Routledge, 2014.
———. (ed.). *From Solidarity to Schisms: 9/11 and After in Fiction and Film from Outside the US*. Amsterdam and New York: Rodopi, 2009.
Cole, Teju. *Open City*. New York: Random House, 2011.
Colin, Fabrice and Laurent Cilluffo. *World Trade Angels*. Paris: Denoel, 2006.
Colombani, Jean-Marie. *Tous Américains? Le monde après le 11 septembre 2001*. Paris: Fayard, 2002.
Conte, Joseph M. "Don DeLillo's *Falling Man* and the Age of Terror." *Modern Fiction Studies* 57.3 (Fall 2011): 559–83.
Coplan, Amy. "Empathic Engagement with Narrative Fictions." *The Journal of Aesthetics and Art Criticism* 66.2 (Spring 2004): 141–52.
Coulter-Smith, Graham and Maurice Owen (eds.) *Art in the Age of Terrorism*. London: Paul Holberton, 2005.
Cvek, Sven. *Towering Figures: Reading the 9/11 Archive*. Amsterdam and New York: Rodopi, 2011.
Däwes, Birgit. *Ground Zero Fiction: History, Memory, and Representation in the American 9/11 Novel*. Heidelberg: Winter, 2012.
Dean, Carolyn J. *The Fragility of Empathy After the Holocaust*. Ithaca: Cornell University Press, 2004.
DeLillo, Don. *Falling Man*. Scribner: New York, 2007.
———. "In the Ruins of the Future: Reflections on Terror and Loss in the Shadow of September." *Harper's*, (December 2001): 33–40.
DeRosa, Aaron. "The End of Futurity: Proleptic Nostalgia and the War on Terror." *LIT: Literature Interpretation Theory* 25.2 (2014): 88–107.
———. "Alterity and the Radical Other in Post-9/11 Fiction: DeLillo's *Falling Man* and Walter's *The Zero*." *Arizona Quarterly* 69.3 (Autumn 2013): 157–83.
———. "Analyzing Literature after 9/11." *Modern Fiction Studies* 57.3 (Fall 2011): 607–18.
Didion, Joan. *Fixed Ideas: America Since 9/11*. New York: New York Review Books, 2003.
Diprose, Rosalyn. "Responsibility in a Place and Time of Terror." *borderlands* 3:1 (2004). http://www.borderlands.net.au/vol3no1_2004/diprose_terror.htm. May 19, 2011.
Dirda, Michael. March 20, 2005. "Shattered." Rev. of *Saturday*, by Ian McEwan. *Washington Post*: T1.
Dobson, Andrew. "Thick Cosmopolitanism." *Political Studies* 54 (2006): 165–84.
Dodge, Jason J. "September 11 and Public Grief: Grieving Otherwise in Jess Walter's *The Zero*." *Critique: Studies in Contemporary Fiction* 55.2 (2014): 152–65.
Donadio, Rachel. "Under Western Eyes." *New York Times*, June 11, 2006. http://www.nytimes.com/2006/06/11/books/review/11donadio.html. October 4, 2010.
Dony, Christophe and Caroline van Linthout. "Comics, Trauma and Cultural Memory(ies) of 9/11." *The Rise and Reason of Comics and Graphic Literature: Critical Essays on the Form*. ed. Joyce Goggin and Dan Hassler-Forest. Jefferson, NC: McFarland & Company, 2010: 179–87.

Drew, Richard. "The Horror of 9/11 That's All Too Familiar." *Los Angeles Times* September 10, 2003. http://articles.latimes.com/print/2003/sep/10/opinion/oe-drew10. May 16, 2008.
Dubus, Andre III. *The Garden of Last Days.* New York: W. W. Norton & Company, 2008.
Dudziak, Mary L (ed.). *September 11 in History: A Watershed Moment?* Durham and London: Duke University Press, 2003.
Dunlap, David. "Even Now, A Skyline of Twins." *New York Times*, November 2, 2001. http://www.nytimes.com/2001/11/02/arts/even-now-a-skyline-of-twins.html?pagewanted=all. Accessed March 2, 2012.
Dupuy, Jean Pierre. "Anatomy of 9/11: Evil, Rationalism, and the Sacred." *SubStance* 37.1 (2008): 33–51.
Durand, Alain-Philippe. "Beyond the Extreme: Beigbeder's *Windows on the World.*" In *Novels of the Contemporary Extreme* (eds. Alain-Philippe Durand and Naomi Mandel). London and New York: Continuum, 2006: 109–20.
Durham, Carolyn A. "Daring to Imagine: Frédéric Beigbeder's *Windows on the World* and Slimane Benaïssa's *La Dernière Nuit d'un Damné.*" *From Solidarity to Schisms: 9/11 and After in Fiction and Film from Outside the U.S..* (Ed. Cara Cilano). Amsterdam: Rodopi, 2009: 165–82.
Durica, G.P. Rev. of *The Exquisite*, by Laird Hunt. *Chicago Review* 53.2–3 (2007).
Duvall, John N. "Witnessing Trauma: Falling Man and Performance Art." In *Don DeLillo: Mao II, Underworld, Falling Man.* (Ed. Stacey Olster). New York: Continuum, 2011: 152–68.
Duvall, John N. and Robert P. Marzec. "Narrating 9/11." *Modern Fiction Studies* 57.3 (Fall 2011): 381–400.
Dwyer, Jim and Kevin Flynn. *102 Minutes: The Untold Story of the Fight to Survive Inside the Twin Towers.* New York: Times Books, 2005.
Eagleton, Terry. *Trouble with Strangers: A Study of Ethics.* Malden, MA: Wiley-Blackwell, 2009.
Edkins, Jenny. *Trauma and the Memory of Politics.* Cambridge: Cambridge University Press, 2003.
Eisinger, Peter. "The American City in the Age of Terror: A Preliminary Assessment of the Effects of September 11." *Urban Affairs Review* 40 (2004): 115–30.
Engle, Karen. *Seeing Ghosts: 9/11 and the Visual Imagination.* Montreal and Kingston: McGill-Queen's University Press, 2009.
Erikson, Kai. "Epilogue: The Geography of Disaster" in *Wounded City: The Social Impact of 9/11.* (Ed. Nancy Foner). New York: Russell Sage Foundation, 2005: 351–61.
Espiritu, Karen. "'Putting Grief into Boxes': Trauma and the Crisis of Democracy in Art Spiegelman's *In The Shadow of No Towers.*" *The Review of Education, Pedagogy, and Cultural Studies* 28 (2006): 179–201.
Faludi, Susan. *The Terror Dream: Fear and Fantasy in Post-9/11 America.* New York: Metropolitan Books, 2007.
Faulkner, Joanne. "The Innocence of Victimhood Versus the 'Innocence of Becoming': Nietzsche, 9/11 and the 'Falling Man.'" *Journal of Nietzsche Studies* 35-36 (2008): 67–85.
Felman, Shoshana, and Dori Laub. *Testimony: Crises in Literature, Psychoanalysis, and History.* New York: Routledge, 1992.
Fishko, Robert. "Art in Troubled Times ." 2003. http://art-for-a-change.com/blog/2006/04/eric-fischl-and-death-of-painting.html. May 11, 2008.
Fitzpatrick, Andrea D. "The Movement of Vulnerability: Images of Falling and September 11." *Art Journal* 66.4 (Winter 2007): 85–102.
Foer, Jonathan Safran. *Extremely Loud and Incredibly Close.* New York: Houghton Mifflin, 2005.
Foner, Nancy (ed.) *Wounded City: The Social Impact of 9/11.* New York: Russell Sage Foundation, 2005.
Forde, Pat. "In Spirit." *Analog: Science Fiction and Fact*, 122:9 (September 2002): 10–51.
Freedberg, David and Vittorio Gallese. "Motion, Emotion, and Empathy in Esthetic Experience." *Trends in Cognitive Science* 11.5 (2007): 197–203.

Bibliography 261

Freund, Charles Paul. "Rebuild the Buddhas of Bamiyan?" *Slate* January 18, 2002. http://www.slate.com/articles/arts/culturebox/2002/01/wonders_never_cease.html. Accessed October 5, 2011.

Friend, David. *Watching the World Change: The Stories Behind the Images of 9/11*. New York: Farrar, Straus and Giroux, 2006.

Frost, Laura. "Still Life: 9/11's Falling Bodies." In *Literature after 9/11*. (Eds. Ann Keniston and Jeanne Follansbee Quinn). Routledge: New York, 2008: 180–206.

———. "*Falling Man*'s Precarious Balance." *The American Prospect*. Rev. of *Falling Man*, by Don DeLillo. May 9, 2007. http://prospect.org/article/falling-mans-precarious-balance. May 4, 2008.

Gamal, Ahmed. "'Encounters with Strangeness' in the Post-9/11 Novel." *Interdisciplinary Literary Studies* 14.1 (2012): 95–116.

Gambetta, Diego (ed.) *Making Sense of Suicide Missions*. Updated Edition. New York and Oxford: Oxford University Press, 2006.

Ganguly, Debjani. "The World Novel, Mediated Wars, and Exorbitant Witnessing." *The Cambridge Journal of Postcolonial Literary Inquiry* 1.1 (2014): 11–31.

Garcin, Christian. *La jubilation des hasards*. Paris: Gallimard, 2005.

Géniès, Bernard. "Sept. 11, the Novel: Possible or Not?" November 2003. www.worldpress.org/print_article.cfm?article_id=1698&dont=yes. Accessed October 13, 2008.

Gilmore, Leigh. *The Limits of Autobiography: Trauma and Testimony*. Ithaca and London: Cornell University Press, 2001.

Gleich, Lewis S. "Ethics in the Wake of the Image: The Post-9/11 Fiction of DeLillo, Auster, and Foer." *Journal of Modern Literature* 37.3 (Spring 2014): 161–76.

Goldman, Russell and Jake Tapper. "Islamic Center 'Ground Zero Mosque' Controversy Heats Up." ABC News. http://abcnews.go.com/Politics/islamic-center-ground-mosque-controversy-heats/story?id=11435030. August 19, 2010.

Goupil, Didier. *Le jour de mon retour sur terre*. Monaco: Le Serpent à Plumes, 2003.

Gray, Richard. *After the Fall: American Literature Since 9/11*. Malden, MA: Wiley-Blackwell, 2011.

———. "Open Doors, Closed Minds: American Prose Writing at a Time of Crisis." *American Literary History* 21.1 (Spring 2009): 128–51.

Greenberg, Judith (ed.) *Trauma at Home: After 9/11*. Lincoln and London: University of Nebraska Press, 2003.

———. "Wounded New York" in *Trauma at Home: After 9/11* (Ed. Judith Greenberg). Lincoln and London: University of Nebraska Press, 2003: 21–35.

Guisan, Catherine. "Of September 11, Mourning and Cosmopolitan Politics." *Constellations* 16.4 (2009): 563–78.

Gulddal, Jesper. "'The one great Hyperpower in the Sky': anti-Americanism in contemporary European literature." *Cambridge Review of International Affairs* 20:4 (December 2007): 677–92.

Hadley, Elaine. "On a Darkling Plain: Victorian Liberalism and the Fantasy of Agency." *Victorian Studies* 48.1 (2008): 92–102.

Hage, Ghassan. "'Comes a Time We Are All Enthusiasm': Understanding Palestinian Suicide Bombers in Times of Exighophobia." *Public Culture* 15.1 (2003): 65–89.

Hale, Dorothy J. "Fiction as Restriction: Self-Binding in New Ethical Theories of the Novel." *Narrative* 15.2 (2007): 187–206.

Halpern, Jodi, and Harvey M. Weinstein. "Rehumanizing the Other: Empathy and Reconciliation." *Human Rights Quarterly* 26 (2004): 561–83.

Harold, James. "Empathy with Fictions." *British Journal of Aesthetics* 40:3 (2000): 340–55.

Harris, Sam. *The End of Faith: Religion, Terror, and the Future of Reason*. New York and London: W.W. Norton & Company, 2004.

Harvey, David. "The City as Body Politic" in *Wounded Cities: Destruction and Reconstruction in a Globalized World*. (Eds. Jane Schneider and Ida Susser). Oxford and New York: Berg, 2003: 25–44.

Hatfield, Charles. *Alternative Comics: An Emerging Literature*. Jackson: University Press of Mississippi, 2005.
Held, David. *Cosmopolitanism: Ideals and Realities*. Cambridge, UK: Polity, 2010.
———. "Cosmopolitanism after 9/11." *International Politics* 47.1 (2010): 52–61.
Heller, Dana (ed.) *The Selling of 9/11: How a National Tragedy Became a Commodity*. New York: Palgrave, 2005.
Hénaff, Marcel. "Global Terror, Global Vengeance?" *SubStance* 37:1 (2008): 72–97.
Hesford, Wendy S. "Documenting Violations: Rhetorical Witnessing and the Spectacle of Distant Suffering." *Biography* 27.1 (Winter 2004): 104–44.
Hillard, Molly Clark. "'When Desert Armies Stand Ready to Fight': Re-Reading McEwan's *Saturday* and Arnold's 'Dover Beach.'" *Partial Answers* 6.1 (2008): 181–206.
Holloway, David. *Cultures of the War on Terror: Empire, Ideology, and the Remaking of 9/11*. Montreal and Kingston: McGill-Queen's University Press, 2008.
Holmes, Stephen. "Al-Qaeda, September 11, 2001." *Making Sense of Suicide Missions*. (Ed. Diego Gambetta). Updated Edition. New York and Oxford: Oxford University Press, 2006: 131–72.
Houen, Alex. *Terrorism and Modern Literature, from Joseph Conrad to Ciaran Carson*. Oxford: Oxford University Press, 2002.
Hunt, Laird. *The Exquisite*. Minneapolis: The Coffee House Press, 2006.
Hutton, Margaret-Anne. "Constructions of Europe and America in French '9/11' Prose Texts." *Contemporary French Civilization* 36.3 (2011): 249–67.
Huyssen, Andreas. *Presents Past: Urban Palimpsests and the Politics of Memory*. Stanford: Stanford University Press, 2003.
Irom, Bimbisar. "Alterities in a Time of Terror: Notes on the Subgenre of the American 9/11 Novel." *Contemporary Literature* 53.3 (Fall 2012): 517–47.
Jamal, Amaney and Nadine Naber (eds.). *Race and Arab Americans Before and After 9/11: From Invisible Citizens to Visible Subjects*. Syracuse, NY: Syracuse University Press, 2008.
Jamal, Amaney. "Civil Liberties and the Otherization of Arab and Muslim Americans" in *Race and Arab Americans Before and After 9/11: From Invisible Citizens to Visible Subjects* (Eds. Amaney Jamal and Nadine Naber). Syracuse, NY: Syracuse University Press, 2008: 114–30.
Jamison, Leslie. *The Empathy Exams: Essays*. Minneapolis, MN: Graywolf Press, 2014.
Jewell, Jim. Rev. of *The Exquisite*, by Laird Hunt. http://fivecreviews.blogspot.com/2007/01/book-exquisite-by-laird-hunt.html. June 10, 2013.
Judt, Tony and Denis Lacorne (eds.) *With Us or Against Us: Studies in Global Anti-Americanism*. Gordonsville, VA: Palgrave Macmillan, 2005.
Junod, Tom. "The Falling Man." *Esquire*, September 2003. www.esquire.com/print-this/features/ESQ0903-SEP_Falling Man. February 2, 2008.
Just, Ward. *Forgetfulness*. Boston and New York: Houghton Mifflin Co., 2006.
Kahane, Claire. "Uncanny Sights: The Anticipation of the Abomination" in *Trauma at Home: After 9/11* (Ed. Judith Greenberg). Lincoln and London: University of Nebraska Press, 2003: 107–16.
Kakutani, Michiko. "Portraying 9/11 as a Katzenjammer Catastrophe." Rev. of *In the Shadow of No Towers* by Art Spiegelman. *New York Times*, August 31, 2004. nytimes.com/2004/08/31/books/books-of-the-times-portraying-9-11-as-a-katzenjammer-catastrophe.html. February 11, 2008.
Kalfus, Ken. *A Disorder Peculiar to the Country*. New York: HarperCollins, 2006.
Kaplan, E. Ann. *Trauma Culture: The Politics of Terror and Loss in Media and Literature*. New Brunswick, NJ: Rutgers University Press, 2005.
Kaplan, Peter W. "New York." The Encyclopedia of 9/11. *New York Magazine*. September 8–12, 2011: 96–98.
Keeble, Arin. *The 9/11 Novel: Trauma, Politics, Identity*. Jefferson, NC: McFarland & Company, 2014.
Kearney, Richard. *Strangers, Gods and Monsters: Interpreting Otherness*. New York: Routledge, 2003.
Keen, Suzanne. *Empathy and the Novel*. Oxford: Oxford University Press, 2007.

Keniston, Ann and Jeanne Follansbee Quinn (eds.) *Literature After 9/11*. New York and London: Routledge, 2008.
Kilde, Jeanne Halgren. "The Park 51/Ground Zero Controversy and Sacred Sites as Contested Space." *Religions* 2 (2011): 297–311.
Kirsch, Adam. "In the Shadow of the Twin Towers." *Prospect*. May 25, 2011. http://www.prospectmagazine.co.uk/magazine/9-11-american-fiction-literature-terrorism/#.UrS03fRDt8E. November 18, 2011.
Knapp, Kathy. *American Unexceptionalism: The Everyman and the Suburban Novel after 9/11*. Iowa City, IA: University of Iowa Press, 2014.
Kobek, Jarett. *ATTA*. Los Angeles: semiotext(e), 2011.
Koopman, Emy. "Reading the Suffering of Others: The Ethical Possibilities of 'Empathic Unsettlement.'" *Journal of Literary Theory* 4.2 (2010): 235–52.
Koss, Juliet. "On the Limits of Empathy." *The Art Bulletin* 88.1 (2006): 139–57.
Kotzin, Miriam N. "Eric Fischl: The *Per Contra* Interview." *Per Contra* (Fall 2006). http://www.percontra.net/archive/4fischl2.htm. October 11, 2008.
Kristeva, Julia. *Hatred and Forgiveness*. Trans. by Jeanine Herman. New York: Columbia University Press, 2010.
Kusiel, Richard F. *The French Way: How France Embraced and Rejected American Values and Power*. Princeton: Princeton University Press, 2012.
LaCapra, Dominick. *Writing History, Writing Trauma*. Baltimore: Johns Hopkins University Press, 2000.
Landsberg, Alison. "America, the Holocaust, and the Mass Culture of Memory: Toward a Radical Politics of Empathy." *New German Critique* 71 (1997): 63–86.
Lang, Luc. *11 septembre, mon amour*. Paris: Stock, 2003.
Lather, Patti. "Against Empathy, Voice and Authenticity." *Voice in Qualitative Inquiry: Challenging Conventional, Interpretive, and Critical Conceptions in Qualitative Research*. (Eds. Alicia Y. Jackson and Lisa A. Mazzei). New York and London: Routledge, 2009: 17–26.
Laub, Dori. "September 11, 2001—An Event without a Voice." In *Trauma at Home: After 9/11*. (Ed. Judith Greenberg). Lincoln and London: University of Nebraska Press, 2003: 204–15.
Lawless, Andrew. "Literature as an Anti-Memorial – Amy Waldman in Interview." http://www.threemonkeysonline.com/literature-as-an-anti-memorial-amy-waldman-in-interview/. No Date. Retrieved January 31, 2014.
Leach, Neil. "9/11" in *Urban Memory: History and Amnesia in the Modern City*. (Ed. Mark Crinson). New York: Routledge, 2005: 169–91.
Lentricchia, Frank and Jody McAuliffe. *Crimes of Art + Terror*. Chicago and London: The University of Chicago Press, 2003.
Lethem, Jonathan. *Chronic City*. New York: Doubleday, 2009.
Leverage, Paula, Howard Mancing, Richard Schweickert, and Jennifer Marston William (Eds.). *Theory of Mind and Literature*. West Lafayette, IN: Purdue University Press, 2011.
Liao, Pei-Chen. *Post-9/11 South Asian Diasporic Fiction: Uncanny Terror*. New York: Palgrave MacMillan, 2013.
Lowenstein, Adam. "Cinema, Benjamin, and the Allegorical Representation of September 11." *Critical Quarterly* 45.1–2 (2003): 73–84.
Lundeen, Kathleen. "Who Has the Right to Feel? The Ethics of Literary Empathy." In *Mapping the Ethical Turn: A Reader in Ethics, Culture, and Literary Theory*. (Eds. Todd F. Davis and Kenneth Womack). Charlottesville, VA: University Press of Virginia, 2001: 83–92.
Lurie, Susan. "Spectacular Bodies and Political Knowledge: 9/11 Cultures and the Problem of Dissent." *American Literary History* 25.1 (Spring 2013): 176–89.
———. "Falling Persons and National Embodiment: The Reconstruction of Safe Spectatorship in the Photographic Record of 9/11." *Terror, Culture, Politics: Rethinking 9/11*. Eds. Daniel J. Sherman, and Terry Nardin. Bloomington and Indianapolis: Indiana University Press, 2006: 44–68.
Margalit, Avishai. "The Suicide Bombers." *New York Review of Books*. January 16, 2003.
Margolis, Joseph. *Moral Philosophy After 9/11*. University Park, PA: The Pennsylvania State University Press, 2004.

Mars-Jones, Adam. "As His World Came Tumbling Down." Rev. of *Falling Man*, by Don DeLillo. *The Observer* May 12, 2007. http://www.theguardian.com/books/2007/may/13/fiction.dondelillo. May 4, 2008.

Mauro, Aaron. "The Languishing of the Falling Man: Don DeLillo and Jonathan Safran Foer's Photographic History of 9/11." *Modern Fiction Studies* 57.3 (Fall 2011): 584–606.

McDermott, Terry. *Perfect Soldiers: Who They Were, Why They Did It.* New York: Harper, 2005.

McEwan, Ian. *Saturday.* London: Jonathan Cape, 2005.

———. *Atonement.* London: Jonathan Cape, 2001.

———. "Beyond Belief." *The Guardian.* September 12, 2001. www.guardian.co.uk/world2001/sep/12/september11.politicsphilosophyand society. July 25, 2008.

———. "Only love and then oblivion." *The Guardian.* September 15, 2001. www.guardian.co.uk/world2001/sep/15/september11.politicsphilosophyandsociety2. July 25, 2008.

McInerney, Jay. "The Devil Wears Nada." Rev. of *The Garden of Last Days*, by Andre Dubus III. *New York Times*, June 22, 2008. http://www.nytimes.com/2008/06/22/books/review/McInerneyt.html?pagewanted=all&_r=0. May 16, 2010.

———. *The Good Life.* New York: Vintage, 2007.

Melnick, Jeffrey. *9/11 Culture: America Under Construction.* West Sussex, UK: Wiley-Blackwell, 2009.

Metcalf, Stephen. "French Twist." Review of *Windows on the World* by Frédéric Beigbeder. *New York Review of Books*, April 17, 2005. http://www.nytimes.com/2005/04/17/books/review/17METCALF.html October 10, 2008.

Meunier, Sophie. "The Distinctiveness of French Anti-Americanism." In *Anti-Americanisms in World Politics* (ed. By Peter J. Katzenstein and Robert O. Keohane). Ithaca and London: Cornell University Press, 2007: 129–56.

Meyers, Diana Tietjens. *Subjection and Subjectivity; Psychoanalytic Feminism and Moral Philosophy.* New York and London; Routledge, 1994.

Michael, Magali Cornier. "Writing Fiction in the Post-9/11 World: Ian McEwan's *Saturday*." In *From Solidarity to Schisms: 9/11 and After in Fiction and Film from Outside the US,* (Ed. Cara Cilano,) Amsterdam and New York: Rodopi, 2009: 25–51.

Miller, Nancy. "Reporting the Disaster." *Trauma at Home: After 9/11.* Ed. Judith Greenberg. Lincoln and London: University of Nebraska Press, 2003: 39–47.

Minzesheimer, Bob. "*American Widow* pours out 9/11 grief in graphic images." *USA Today.* September 8, 2008. www.usatoday.com/life/books/news/2008-09-08-american-widow_N.htm. October 2, 2009.

Mitchell, W. J. T. *What do Pictures Want?: The Lives and Loves of Images.* Chicago and London: The University of Chicago Press, 2005.

Moghaddam, Fathali M. *From the Terrorists' Point of View: What They Experience and Why They Come to Destroy.* Westport, CT: Praeger Security International, 2006.

Mohamed, Besheer and John O'Brien. "Ground Zero of Misunderstanding." *Contexts* 10 (2011): 62–64.

Mollenkopf, John (ed.) *Contentious City: The Politics of Recovery in New York City.* New York: Russell Sage Foundation, 2005.

Moraru, Christian. *Cosmodernism; American Narrative, Late Globalization, and the New Cultural Imaginary.* Ann Arbor: The University of Michigan Press, 2011.

Morrissette, Micaela. "The Company of Phantoms." Rev. of *The Exquisite*, by Laird Hunt. *Jacket Magazine* 34 (October 2007). http://jacketmagazine.com/34/morrissette-hunt.shtml. January 21, 2013.

Morton, Patricia A. "'Document of Civilization and Document of Barbarism': The World Trade Center Near and Far" in *Terror, Culture, Politics: Rethinking 9/11* (Eds. Daniel J. Sherman and Terry Nardin). Bloomington and Indianapolis: Indiana University Press, 2006: 15–32.

Muller, Christine. "Witnessing the Fall: September 11 and the Crisis of the Permeable Self" in *The War on Terror and American Popular Culture: September 11 and Beyond* (Eds. Andrew Schopp and Matthew B. Hill). Rutherford, NJ: Farleigh Dickinson University Press, 2009: 45–64.

Murphy, Dean E. *September 11: An Oral History.* New York: Doubleday, 2002.

Newman, Judie. *Utopia and Terror in Contemporary American Fiction.* New York: Routledge, 2013.

Nissenson, Hugh. *The Days of Awe.* Naperville, IL: Sourcebooks, 2005.

Nussbaum, Martha C. *For Love of Country?* Second Ed. (with new introduction). Boston: Beacon Press, 2002.

———. *Cultivating Humanity: A Classical Defense of Reform in Liberal Education.* Harvard: Harvard University Press, 1998.

Obajtek-Kirkwood, Anne-Marie. "Voix diverses sur le 11 septembre: Celles de Michel Vinaver et Luc Lang." *Romance Studies* 28:3 (July 2010): 206–16.

Oliver, Kelly. "Technologies of Violence and Vulnerability." In *Democracy in Crisis: Violence, Alterity, Community,* edited by Stella Gaon, 90-109. Manchester : Manchester University Press, 2009.

Oliver, Sophie Anne. "Trauma, Bodies, and Performance Art: Towards an Embodied Ethics of Seeing." *Continuum: Journal of Media & Cultural Studies* 24.1 (2010): 119–29.

O'Neill, Joseph. *Netherland.* New York: Pantheon Books, 2008.

Orr, David. "Who Needs Mace? Whip Out that Sonnet." *New York Times.* June 26, 2005. www.nytimes.com. March 17, 2009.

Otto, Stacy. "A Garden from Ashes: The Post-9/11 Manhattan City-Shrine, the Triangle Fire Memorial March, and the Educative Value of Mourning." *Journal of Social History* 47.3 (2014): 573–92.

Ouroussoff, Nicolai. "Towers' Symbolic Image." *Los Angeles Times,* September 13, 2001. http://articles.latimes.com/2001/sep/13/news/mn-45326. February 20, 2012.

Oxley, Julinna C. *The Moral Dimensions of Empathy: Limits and Applications in Ethical Theory and Practice.* Hampshire, UK: Palgrave Macmillan, 2011.

Page, Max. *The City's End: Two Centuries of Fantasies, Fears, and Premonitions of New York's Destruction.* New Haven and London: Yale University Press, 2008.

Palumbo-Liu, David. *The Deliverance of Others: Reading Literature in a Global Age.* Durham and London: Duke University Press, 2012.

———. "Preemption, Perpetual War, and the Future of the Imagination." *boundary 2* 33.1 (2006): 151–69.

———. "Multiculturalism Now: Civilization, National Identity, and Difference Before and After September 11th." *boundary 2* 29.2 (2002): 109–27.

Pape, Robert A. *Dying to Win: The Strategic Logic of Suicide Terrorism.* New York; Random House, 2005.

Paz, Sharon. "Press Statement." September, 2002. www.sharonpaz.com/falling/index.html. February 2, 2008.

Peters, John Durham. "Witnessing." Media Witnessing: Testimony in the Age of Mass Communication . Eds. Paul Frosh and Amit Pinchevski. Houndmills, UK: Palgrave, 2009. 23–41

Peyser, Andrea. "Shameful Art Attack." *New York Post.* September 18, 2002. http://nypost.com/commentary/57305.htm. June 3, 2008.

Poland, Warren S. "The Limits of Empathy." *Imago* 64.1 (Spring 2007): 87–93.

Post, Jerrold M. *The Mind of the Terrorist: The Psychology of Terrorism from the IRA to al-Qaeda.* New York: Palgrave MacMillan, 2007.

Qureshi, Emran and Michael A. Sells (eds.) *The New Crusades: Constructing the Muslim Enemy.* New York: Columbia University Press, 2003.

Rakoff, David. "The Way We Live Now." *New York Times.* October 27, 2002.

Ramazani, Vaheed. "September 11: Masculinity, Justice, and the Politics of Empathy." *Comparative Studies of South Asia, Africa and the Middle East* 21.1–2 (2001): 118–24.

Randall, Martin. *9/11 and the Literature of Terror.* Edinburgh: Edinburgh University Press, 2011.

Redfield, Marc. *The Rhetoric of Terror: Reflections on 9/11 and the War on Terror.* New York: Fordham University Press, 2009.

Rehr, Henrik. *Tribeca Sunset: A Story of 9/11.* New York: iBooks, 2005.

———. *September 12.* www.webcomicsnation.com/henrikrehr/sep/series.php. August 4, 2009.
Revel, Sandrine. *Le 11ᵉ jour.* Paris: Delcourt, 2002.
Richardson, Louise. *What Terrorists Want: Understanding the Enemy, Containing the Threat.* New York: Random House, 2006.
Riding, Alan. "French Feel the Anguish in Books Inspired by 9/11." *New York Times* September 3, 2003. http://www.nytimes.com/2003/09/03/books/french-feel-the-anguish-in-books-inspired-by-9-11.html. October 16, 2008.
Rifkin, Jeremy. *The Empathic Civilization: The Race to Global Consciousness in a World in Crisis.* New York: Jeremy P. Tarcher/Penguin, 2009.
Rinaldi, Nicholas. *Between Two Rivers.* HarperCollins, 2004.
Rosan, Peter J. "The Poetics of Intersubjective Life: Empathy and the Other." *The Humanistic Psychologist* 40.2 (2012): 115–35.
Rosanvallon, Pierre. "Europe-Etats-Unis: les deux universalismes." Le Monde Feb. 2, 2005. Web. April 4, 2012. http://www.lemonde.fr/international/article/2005/02/21/europe-etats-unis-les-deux-universalismes_398914_3210.html.
Rose, Charlie. March 30, 2005. Interview with Ian McEwan. *Charlie Rose.* www.charlierose.com. March 22, 2009.
Rothberg, Michael. "A Failure of the Imagination: Diagnosing the Post-9/11 Novel: A Response to Richard Gray." *American Literary History* 21.1 (Spring 2009): 152–158.
Rothstein, Edward. "Recapturing the Spirit of a City as It Reeled From Its Wounds." *New York Times*, September 7, 2011. www.nytimes.com/2011/09/08/arts/design/911-exhibition-at-new-york-historical-society-review.html?pagewanted=all. Accessed September 11, 2011.
Royle, Nicholas. *The Uncanny.* New York: Routledge, 2003.
Saal, Ilka. "Regarding the Pain of Self and Other: Trauma Transfer and Narrative Framing in Jonathan Safran Foer's *Extremely Loud and Incredibly Close*." *Modern Fiction Studies* 57.3 (Fall 2011): 453–76.
Salaita, Steven. "Ethnic Identity and Imperative Patriotism: Arab Americans Before and After 9/11." *College Literature* 32.2 (Spring 2005): 146–68.
Sardar, Ziauddin. "Welcome to Planet Blitcon." *New Statesman.* December 11, 2006. http://www.newstatesman.com/print/200612110045. October 4, 2010.
Scarry, Elaine. "The Difficulty of Imagining Other Persons" In *The Handbook of Interethnic Coexistence* (Ed. Eugene Wiener). New York, Continuum, 1998: 40–62.
Schaefer, Annette. "Inside the Terrorist Mind." *Scientific American Mind*, 18:6 (December 2007–January 2008): 72–79.
Schehr, Lawrence. "Éffondrements: Frédéric Beigbeder's *Windows on the World*." *French Cultural Studies* 21:2 (2010): 131–141.
Schneemann, Carolee. *Terminal Velocity.* October 2001. http://www.pores.bbk.ac.uk/2/schneeman.htm. September 26, 2012.
Schopp, Andrew and Matthew B. Hill (eds.) *The War on Terror and American Popular Culture: September 11 and Beyond.* Madison: Farleigh Dickinson University Press, 2009.
Schuerewegen, Franc. "Tours et Détours (Vu de France)." *Contemporary French Civilization* 29:2 (Summer/Fall 2005): 137–53.
Schulman, Helen. *A Day at the Beach.* New York: Houghton Mifflin, 2007.
Schulz, David P. and G. Mitchell Reyes. "Ward Churchill and the Politics of Public Memory." *Rhetoric and Public Affairs* 11.4 (2008): 631–58.
Schwartz, Lynne Sharon. *The Writing on the Wall.* New York: Counterpoint, 2005.
Scott, A. O. "A Splintering Psyche or Omens of Disaster?" Review of *Take Shelter. New York Times*, September 29, 2011. http://movies.nytimes.com/2011/09/30/movies/take-shelter-with-michael-shannon-and-jessica-chastain.html. Accessed October 3, 2011.
Scott, Jill. *A Poetics of Forgiveness: Cultural Responses to Loss and Wrongdoing.* New York: Palgrave Macmillan, 2010.
Seeley, Karen. "The Psychological Treatment of Trauma and the Trauma of Psychological Treatment: Talking to Psychotherapists about 9/11" in *Wounded City: The Social Impact of 9/11.* (Ed. Nancy Foner). New York: Russell Sage Foundation, 2005: 263–89.
Sherman, Daniel J. and Terry Nardin (eds). *Terror, Culture, Politics: Rethinking 9/11.* Bloomington and Indianapolis: Indiana University Press, 2006.

Shore, Zachary. *Breeding Bin Ladens: America, Islam, and the Future of Europe*. Baltimore: The Johns Hopkins University Press, 2006.
Shuman, Amy. *Other People's Stories: Entitlement Claims and the Critique of Empathy*. Urbana and Chicago: University of Illinois Press, 2005.
Sicher, Efraim and Natalia Skradol. "A World Neither Brave Nor New: Reading Dystopian Fiction after 9/11." *Partial Answers* 4:1 (January 2006): 151–79.
Simpson, David. "Telling It Like It Isn't." In *Literature after 9/11*. (ed. by Keniston and Quinn). New York: Routledge, 2008: 209–223.
———. *9/11: The Culture of Commemoration*. Chicago: The University of Chicago Press, 2006.
Singer, Henry (dir.). *The Falling Man*. The Passionate Eye. Canadian Broadcasting Corporation, 2003.
Smelser, Neil J. "Epilogue: September 11, 2001, as Cultural Trauma" in *Cultural Trauma and Collective Identity* (Eds. Alexander et al.). Berkeley: University of California Press, 2004: 264–82.
Smith, Rachel Greenwald. "Organic Shrapnel: Affect and Aesthetics in September 11 Fiction." *American Literature* 83:1 (March 2011): 153–74.
Smith, Terry. *The Architecture of Aftermath*. Chicago and London: University of Chicago Press, 2006.
Smith, Zadie. Interview with Ian McEwan. *The Believer* 3.6 (August 2005): 47–63.
Solnit, Rebecca. *The Faraway Nearby*. New York: Viking, 2013.
Sontag, Susan. *At the Same Time: Essays and Speeches*. New York: Farrar, Straus and Giroux, 2007.
———. *Regarding the Pain of Others*. New York: Picador, 2003.
Sorkin, Michael and Sharon Zukin (eds.) *After the World Trade Center: Rethinking New York City*. New York and London: Routledge, 2002.
Spiegelman, Art. *In the Shadow of No Towers*. New York: Pantheon Books, 2004.
Spivack, Carla. "Disappearing Civil Liberties: The Case of Post-9/11 Fiction." *New England Law Review* 44.4 (Summer 2010): 869–83.
Spivak, Gayatri Chakravorty. "Terror: A Speech After 9-11." *boundary 2* 31.2 (2004): 81–111.
Stueber, Karsten R. *Rediscovering Empathy: Agency, Folk Psychology, and the Human Sciences*. Cambridge, MA: MIT Press, 2006.
Sturken, Marita. *Tourists of History: Memory, Kitsch, and Consumerism from Oklahoma City to Ground Zero*. Durham and London: Duke University Press, 2007.
———. "The Aesthetics of Absence: Rebuilding Ground Zero." *American Ethnologist* 31.3 (2004): 311–25.
Sumner, Christopher. "Don DeLillo's *Falling Man* and the Protective Shield against Stimuli." *American Imago* 71.1 (Spring 2014): 1–27.
Swartz, Anne K. "American Art After September 11: A Consideration of the Twin Towers." *Symploke* 14.1–2 (2006): 81–97.
Szalai, Jennifer. "Day-Tripper: The Mundane Raptures of Ian McEwan." *Harper's Magazine*, December 3, 2008: 87–92.
Taylor, Charles. "A Grief Observed." Rev. of *American Widow* by Alissa Torres. *New York Times*, September 7, 2008. nytimes.com/2008/09/07/books/review/Taylor-t.html. March 14, 2009.
Temlali, Yassin. "Interview with Salim Bachi." *BabelMed*. June 20, 2007. http://www.babelmed.net/Pais/Mediterranee/Litterature/salim_bachi.php?c=2462&m=319&l=fr.October 23, 2010.
Thomas, Samuel. "Outtakes and Outrage: The Means and Ends of Suicide Terror." *Modern Fiction Studies* 57:3 (2011): 425–49.
Thurschwell, Adam. "Writing and Terror: Don DeLillo on the Task of Literature after 9/11." *Law & Literature* 19.2 (2007): 277–302.
Tiffany, Matthew. Rev. of *The Exquisite*, by Laird Hunt. *PopMatters* http://www.popmatters.com/pm/tools/print/8172/. Accessed June 11, 2013.
Torres, Alissa, and Sungyoon Choi. *American Widow*. New York: Villard, 2008.

Torres, Alissa. "The Reluctant Icon." www.salon.com. January 25, 2002. http://dir.salon.com/story/mwt/feature/2002/01/25/widow_speaks.html. March 8, 2009.
Travis, Molly Abel. "Beyond Empathy: Narrative Distancing and Ethics in Toni Morrison's *Beloved* and J. M. Coetzee's *Disgrace*." *Journal of Narrative Theory* 40.2 (Summer 2010): 231–50.
Trigg, Dylan. *The Aesthetics of Decay: Nothingness, Nostalgia, and the Absence of Reason*. New York: Peter Lang, 2006.
Trimarco, James and Molly Hurley Depret. "Wounded Nation, Broken Time" in *The Selling of 9/11: How a National Tragedy Became a Commodity*. (Ed. Dana Heller). New York: Palgrave Macmillan, 2005: 27–53.
Tumarkin, Maria. *Traumascapes: The Power and Fate of Places Transformed by Tragedy*. Melbourne: Melbourne University Press, 2005.
Updegraff, John A., Roxane Cohen Silver, and E. Alison Holman. "Searching for and Finding Meaning in Collective Trauma: Results from a National Longitudinal Study of the 9/11 Terrorist Attacks." *Journal of Personality and Social Psychology* 95: 3 (2008): 709–22.
Updike, John. *Terrorist*. New York: Knopf, 2006.
Vale, Lawrence J., and Thomas J. Campanella (eds.) *The Resilient City: How Modern Cities Recover from Disaster*. Oxford: Oxford University Press, 2005.
Van Schepen, Randall. "Falling/Failing 9/11: Erich Fischl's *Tumbling Woman* Debacle." *Aurora: The Journal of the History of Art* 9 (2008): 116–43.
Versluys, Kristiaan. *Out of the Blue: September 11 and the Novel*. New York: Columbia University Press, 2009.
———. "Art Spiegelman's *In The Shadow of No Towers*: 9/11 and the Representation of Trauma." *Modern Fiction Studies* 52.4 (Winter 2006): 980–1003.
Victoroff, Jeff. "The Mind of the Terrorist: A Review and Critique of Psychological Approaches." *Journal of Conflict Resolution*, 49:1 (February 2005): 3–42.
Virilio, Paul. *Ground Zero*. London and New York: Verso, 2002.
Waldman, Amy. *The Submission*. New York: Farrar, Straus and Giroux, 2011.
Wall, Katherine. "Ethics, Knowledge, and the Need for Beauty: Zadie Smith's *On Beauty* and Ian McEwan's *Saturday*." *University of Toronto Quarterly* 77.2 (2008): 757–88.
Wallace, Elizabeth Kowaleski. "Postcolonial Melancholia in Ian McEwan's *Saturday*." *Studies in the Novel* 39.4 (2007): 465–80.
Walter, Jess. *The Zero*. New York: ReganBooks, 2006.
Walter, Natasha. "The Leap Into the Terrorist Mind Appears Too Great for Most Authors." *The Guardian*, July 24, 2006. http://guardian.co.uk/commentisfree/2006/jul/24/comment.books. October 27, 2010.
Ward, Frazer. *No Innocent Bystanders: Performance Art and Audience*. Hanover, NH: Dartmouth College Press, 2012.
Wedell, Noura. "Jarett Kobek's Portrait of a Hijacker." *Bomblog*. March 8, 2012. Rev. of Jarett Kobek's *ATTA*. http://bombsite.com/articles/6362. August 17, 2012.
West, Paul. *The Immensity of the Here and Now: A Novel of 9/11*. Rutherford NJ: Voyant Publishing, 2003.
Wing, Jennifer. "Carolee Schneemann Still Pushing the Edges of Decorum." October 23, 2011. http://www.kplu.org/post/carolee-schneemann-still-pushing-edges-decorum. September 26, 2012.
Whitehead, Colson. *The Colossus of New York: A City in Thirteen Parts*. New York: Random House, 2003.
Whitlock, Gillian. "Autographics: The Seeing 'I' of the Comics." *Modern Fiction Studies* 52.4 (Winter 2006): 965–79.
Wood, James. "On a Darkling Plain." Rev. of *Saturday*, by Ian McEwan. *The New Republic*. April 18, 2005. www.tnr.com/article/darkling-plain#. March 30, 2009.
Wright, Lawrence. *The Looming Tower: Al-Qaeda and the Road to 9/11*. New York: Vintage Books, 2007.
Zahavi, Dan. "Beyond Empathy: Phenomenological Approaches to Intersubjectivity." *Journal of Consciousness Studies* 8.5-7 (2001): 151–67.

Zalewski, Daniel. "The Background Hum: Ian McEwan's Art of Unease." *New Yorker*, February 23, 2009: 47–61.
Zehfuss, Maja. "Forget September 11." *Third World Quarterly* 24.3 (2003): 513–28.
Žižek, Slavoj. *Welcome to the Desert of the Real!: Five Essays on September 11 and Related Dates*. London and New York: Verso, 2002.

Index

al-Qaeda, 42, 85, 126n17, 145, 174, 196, 199, 242, 243, 245, 249n12. *See also* terrorism; bin Laden, Osama
Amis, Martin: "The Last Days of Muhammad Atta", 14, 22, 135–138, 145
Anker, Elizabeth, 47, 69, 70, 77n2

Bachi, Salim: *Tuez-les tous*, 129, 144, 152–161
Ballen, Ken, 128, 129
Banita, Georgiana, 16, 19, 23–28, 63–64, 75, 139
Baudrillard, Jean, 111, 121, 125n8, 125n9, 126n17
Bauman, Zygmunt, 239, 243
Beck, Ulrich, 1, 123–124
Beigbeder, Frédéric: *Windows on the World*, 12, 14, 38, 40, 55, 58–59, 71, 102, 118–122, 124, 126n16, 248n7
Bennett, Jill, 30, 32–33, 35, 44, 60, 73, 248
Bhabha, Homi, 3–4, 17
bin Laden, Osama, 85, 153, 159, 174, 189n1, 242. *See also* al-Qaeda; terrorism
Blocker, Jane, 80, 85, 91
Brassett, James, 1, 8–10, 105, 106, 107, 125n5
Bush Administration, 6, 7
Butler, Heidi, 189n8

Butler, Judith, 4, 5–8, 25, 44, 151, 163, 167, 168, 176, 177, 182–183, 187–188, 191, 192, 214, 253

Caruth, Cathy, 67
Cilano, Cara, 27, 40, 101–102, 104, 108, 124
clash of civilizations, 1, 4, 105, 132
Colombani, Jean-Marie, 105, 108, 117, 122, 123
Conte, Joseph, 76, 78n8
Coplan, Amy, 62
cosmopolitanism, 1–2, 4, 7, 8, 9

Däwes, Birgit, 17, 19–23, 27, 28, 129, 134, 137, 142, 165
DeLillo, Don, 78n6, 79; *Falling Man*, 12, 13, 16, 22, 38, 65, 66–77, 149; "In the Ruins of the Future", 66, 79, 80–81, 97
Derrida, Jacques, 111, 125n7, 126n17, 132, 163, 168
Drew, Richard, 38, 47–48, 49
Dubus III, Andre: *The Garden of Last Days*, 129, 139–144, 147, 148, 149, 154, 161, 162
Duvall, John N., 69

empathy, 1, 3, 5–6, 9–10, 22–23, 25–26, 28–30, 38, 39, 40, 41, 44, 52, 53, 55, 56, 57, 58, 62, 65, 74, 75, 96, 102, 105, 106–108, 113, 114, 115, 117, 119, 120,

122, 123–124, 128, 129, 131, 133–134, 137, 138, 139, 140, 141, 146, 163, 167, 168–169, 177–178, 181, 184–185, 186, 188, 189n1, 191–192, 201, 215, 220, 221, 224, 253–254; and fiction, 32–37, 161–165; and reader, 38, 40, 44, 57, 58, 65, 96, 146, 159, 254; and artist/novelist, 40, 52–53, 75, 102, 111, 119, 129; modeling, 58–60; directional quality of, 5, 9, 30, 108, 134, 169; limitations, 30, 111, 124; and sympathy and/or compassion, 1, 10, 25, 106, 181
Engle, Karen, 48–49, 72, 77n1
Erikson, Kai, 218

falling people, 21, 38, 47–51, 53, 55, 60, 61–62, 63–65, 66, 67, 68, 69, 71, 72, 74, 75, 77n3, 79, 81, 87, 122, 251
Faludi, Susan, 79, 87, 99n7
Felman, Shoshana, 60
Fischl, Eric, 38, 49, 51–53
Fitzpatrick, Andrea, 49
Freedberg, David (and Vittorio Gallese), 60
Friend, David, 82
Frost, Laura, 55, 72, 78n7

Garcin, Christian: *La jubilation des hasards*, 109–111, 112, 120
Goupil, Didier: *Le jour de mon retour sur terre*, 113–114, 115, 120, 121, 125n12
Gray, Richard, 16–19, 27, 28, 140, 225, 228
grief, 2, 6, 13, 84, 85, 86, 87–90, 93, 97, 116, 182, 191, 193, 223, 251
Ground Zero, 42, 78n5, 85, 95, 113, 121, 193–195, 197, 199–200, 207, 215, 216n5, 218, 222, 224, 227, 232, 233, 236, 240, 241, 245

Hadley, Elaine, 189n6, 190n10
Hage, Ghassan, 151, 159–160
Hale, Dorothy, 25, 32
Halpern, Jodi (and Harvey Weinstein), 131, 134
Harvey, David, 222
Hillard, Molly, 178, 190n10
Holmes, Stephen, 145, 150, 160
Hunt, Laird : *The Exquisite*, 229–235

Huyssen, Andreas, 232

Judt, Tony, 105, 108, 125n2
Junod, Tom, 48, 53

Kahane, Claire, 224
Kalfus, Ken: *A Disorder Peculiar to the Country*, 78n5
Kaplan, E. Ann, 82, 83, 84, 90, 191, 226
Kearney, Richard, 131, 163
Keen, Suzanne, 9, 28, 30, 96, 141, 188
Kilde, Jeanne, 194–195
Kobek, Jarrett: *ATTA*, 145–149
Koopman, Emy, 38, 57–58, 63, 65

Landsberg, Alison, 59, 73
Lang, Luc, 118, 119; *11 septembre mon amour*, 115–118
Lather, Patti, 133, 134, 178
Lethem, Jonathan : *Chronic City*, 20, 43, 226, 228, 236–247, 249n11
Lurie, Susan, 48, 77n1

McDermott, Terry, 127–128, 129, 138, 148, 165n1
McEwan, Ian, 190n9; *Saturday*, 7, 12, 41, 167–189, 189n2, 189n3, 189n4, 253
Melnick, Jeffrey, 95
memorialization, 23, 89, 97, 121, 193, 214, 222, 241, 248n3
Meunier, Sophie, 126n16
Michael, Magali Cornier, 173, 186
Miller, Nancy, 89–90
Moraru, Christian, 5, 34, 36, 37
Morrissette, Micaela, 235

New York City, 3, 20, 43, 50, 82, 95, 97, 118, 120, 156, 191, 193, 194, 220, 222, 224, 226, 227, 229, 230, 231–233, 235, 236, 237, 240, 241, 248
9/11 Memorial, 42, 193–194, 197, 216n5, 222–224, 227, 240, 241. *See also* memorialization
Nussbaum, Martha, 25, 32, 106, 251–253

Oliver, Kelly, 183–185, 186
Oliver, Sophie, 73–74
otherness, 1, 2, 10, 11, 13, 14, 18, 23, 25–28, 32, 33, 34–37, 39, 40, 44, 57,

65, 71, 77, 80, 81, 131, 133, 134, 139,
140, 152, 193, 197, 200, 209, 213, 253
Ouroussoff, Nick, 3
Oxley, Julinna, 29, 30, 107, 181

Palumbo-Liu, David, 1, 34, 35, 36, 37, 39,
44, 57, 80, 81, 131
Paz, Sharon, 53–54

Rehr, Henrik, 99n9; *Tribeca Sunset*, 80,
84, 86–87, 91, 95, 97, 99n6
Rosan, Peter, 10, 184
Rosanvallon, Pierre, 103

Salaita, Steven, 216n2
sameness, 1–2, 4, 5, 9, 14, 18, 22, 28, 33,
34, 36–37, 39, 44, 48, 49, 53, 57, 58,
62, 63, 65, 71, 77, 80, 81, 105, 106,
107, 123, 124, 129, 131, 132–134, 139,
141, 152, 178, 197, 201, 204, 221, 253
Schehr, Lawrence, 113
Schulman, Helen: *A Day at the Beach*, 38,
60, 61–65, 78n4
Seeley, Karen, 218–219
Simpson, David, 192, 193, 202, 216n5,
227, 241, 251, 253
Skarbakka, Kerry, 49, 50–51
Smith, Rachel Greenwald, 235
Smith, Terry, 221
Spiegelman, Art, 223; *In the Shadow of No
Towers*, 12, 13, 39, 80, 84–86, 88, 91,
94, 96, 97, 98n3, 99n6, 223
Spivak, Gayatri, 40, 129, 167–168, 169
Stueber, Karsten, 30, 106
Sturken, Marita, 192, 193, 223–224

terrorism, 1–3, 6, 14, 19, 22, 28, 40, 80,
110, 111, 114, 125n7, 127–165, 165n1,
168, 174, 186, 190n9, 196, 199,
204–205, 207, 214, 215, 217, 234, 243,
253; and art, 52, 68, 69, 78n5, 78n7;
and the novel, 78n6, 161–165
Torres, Alissa: *American Widow*, 39, 80,
84, 87–88, 90, 91–93, 95, 97, 98n2,
99n6, 99n8
trauma, 2, 9–10, 12–13, 20, 38, 39, 42, 43,
48, 49, 51, 52, 55–58, 62, 65, 66–67,
68, 72–74, 75, 76, 77n2, 83, 84–85, 86,
90, 91, 94, 96, 97, 99n6, 133, 168, 182,
197, 217–220, 225, 228, 232, 238, 239,
248. *See also* falling people
Tumarkin, Maria, 224, 241

Versluys, Kristiaan, 12–14, 16, 22, 27, 28,
119, 125n10, 129, 248n8
vulnerability, 2, 4, 6–10, 18, 42, 43, 48, 49,
55, 69, 72, 75, 93, 97, 101, 104,
105–106, 108, 112, 122, 123, 124, 163,
167–168, 169, 171, 176, 180, 181, 182,
183–186, 187, 191, 192, 195, 196, 197,
217, 218, 219, 227, 231, 233, 235, 252

Waldman, Amy, 253; *The Submission*, 42,
191–215
Wall, Katherine, 178
witnessing, 13, 38, 39, 48, 61, 62, 63,
64–65, 69, 72, 76, 79, 80, 82, 84, 85,
87, 94, 96, 98n3, 217, 218, 224, 228
World Trade Center, 3, 55, 58, 61, 63, 66,
67, 77n3, 87, 90, 91, 96, 111–112, 119,
120–121, 124, 125n10, 125n11, 139,
142, 146, 149, 156, 170, 173, 192, 194,
213, 218, 220, 222, 226, 227, 230, 240,
241, 242, 245, 248n3, 248n5, 251
Žižek, Slavoj, 132

About the Author

Tim Gauthier is director of the Interdisciplinary Degree Programs at the University of Nevada, Las Vegas (UNLV). His research focuses on contemporary fiction and spans post-colonial concerns and artistic reactions to social and personal trauma experiences. In addition to peer-reviewed publications, he is the author of *Narrative Desire and Historical Reparations*—a study of A. S. Byatt, Ian McEwan, and Salman Rushdie, published by Routledge in 2006.